Advanced Capital

This book is a companion volume to the author's classic *The Capital Budgeting Decision* and explores the complexities of capital budgeting as well as the opportunities to improve the decision process where risk and time are important elements.

There is a long list of contenders for the next breakthrough for making capital budgeting decisions and this book gives in-depth coverage to:

- **Real options.** The value of a project must take into consideration the flexibility that it provides management, acknowledging the option of making decisions in the future when more information is available. This book emphasizes the need to assign a value to this flexibility, and how option-pricing theory (also known as contingent claims analysis) sometimes provides a method for valuing flexibility.
- **Decomposing cash flows.** A project consists of many series of cash flows and each series deserves its own specific risk-adjusted discount rate. Decomposing the cash flows of an investment highlights the fact that while managers are generally aware that divisions and projects have different risks, too often they neglect the fact that the cash flow components may also have different risks, with severe consequences on the quality of the decision-making.

Designed to assist business decisions at all levels, the emphasis is on the applications of capital budgeting techniques to a variety of issues. These include the hugely significant **buy versus lease** decision which costs corporations billions each year. Current business decisions also need to be made considering the cross-border implications, and **global business aspects**, identifying the specific aspects of international investment decisions, which appear throughout the book.

Harold Bierman, Jr. is the Nicholas H. Noyes Professor of Business Administration at the Johnson Graduate School of Management, Cornell University.

Seymour Smidt is Professor Emeritus at the Johnson Graduate School of Management, Cornell University.

Advanced Capital Budgeting

Refinements in the economic analysis of investment projects

Harold Bierman, Jr. and Seymour Smidt

Routledge
Taylor & Francis Group

NEW YORK AND LONDON

First published 2007 by Routledge
711 Third Ave, New York, NY 10017

Simultaneously published in Great Britain
by Routledge
2 Park Square, Milton Park, Abingdon, Oxon OX14 4RN

Routledge is an imprint of the Taylor & Francis Group, an informa business

© 2007 Harold Bierman, Jr. and Seymour Smidt

Typeset in Perpetua and Bell Gothic by Newgen Imaging Systems (P) Ltd, Chennai, India

Library of Congress Cataloging in Publication Data
Bierman, Harold.
Advanced capital budgeting: refinements in the economic analysis of investment projects /
Harold Bierman, Jr. and Seymour Smidt.
    p. cm.
    Includes bibliographical references and index.
    1. Capital budget. 2. Capital investments – Evaluation. I. Smidt, Seymour. II. Title.
HG4028.C4B537 2006
658.15′4 – dc22   2006019474

British Library Cataloguing in Publication Data
A catalogue record for this book is available from the British Library

ISBN10: 0–415–77205–2 (hbk)   ISBN13: 978–0–415–77205–1 (hbk)
ISBN10: 0–415–77206–0 (pbk)   ISBN13: 978–0–415–77206–8 (pbk)

Contents

List of illustrations   xiii
Preface   xvii

PART I
CAPITAL BUDGETING AND VALUATION UNDER CERTAINTY   1

1   THE STATE OF THE ART OF CAPITAL BUDGETING   3
    Decision-making and corporate objectives   3
    The evolution of capital budgeting practice   5
    Surveys of practice   5
    The discount rate   7
    Cash flow components   8
    The calculation of the discount rate   8
    The time risk interaction   8
    Real options   9
    Three problems   10
    Time discounting   10
    Present value addition rule   11
    Present value multiplication rule   11
    The term structure of interest rates   11
    Risk and diversification   13
    Strategic considerations   14
    Three basic generalizations   16
    The capital market   16
    Global business aspects   17
    Conclusions   17
    Problems   18
    Discussion question   19
    Bibliography   19

2   AMOUNTS DISCOUNTED AND DISCOUNT RATES   21
    The FCF method   23
    The CCF method   24
    The adjusted present value method   25

Equivalence of the methods   26
The FCF method   27
The CCF calculation: the value to investors   27
Adjusted present value   28
Costs of financial distress   29
The costs of capital   29
The WACC with debt   31
Valuation: a summary   32
With no debt   33
With $600 of debt substituted for stock   33
With debt (use of APV)   34
The use of r^* (the CCF method)   34
Calculation of discount rates   35
Finite-lived assets   36
Global business aspects   36
Conclusions   37
Problems   38
Discussion question   39
Bibliography   39
Appendix derivations   39

PART II
CAPITAL BUDGETING AND VALUATION UNDER UNCERTAINTY   **41**

3   CAPITAL BUDGETING WITH UNCERTAINTY   43
Tree diagrams   43
Period-by-period summaries   46
Sensitivity analysis   46
Simulation   48
Risk preferences   50
Certainty equivalents   52
Time and risk   53
Risk adjusted discount rates   54
The required return   55
Default-free rate of discount   55
The borrowing rate   57
Changing the uncertainty   57
Global business aspects   58
Conclusions   58
Problems   59
Discussion question   60
Bibliography   60

4   ELEMENTS OF TIME AND UNCERTAINTY   62
The investment process   63
The discount rate   66
Converting expected cash flows   68
The discount rate assumption   69
Capital budgeting with constant risk aversion   69

Capital budgeting with a constant risk adjusted rate 71
A capital market perspective 73
A qualification of the CAPM decision rule 74
Global business aspects 74
Conclusions 74
Quiz 75
Problems 75
Discussion question 76
Solution to quiz 76
Bibliography 77

5   THE STATE PREFERENCE APPROACH   79
Prices with certainty 79
Prices with uncertainty 80
The three factors 82
The expected risk-adjustment 84
Countercyclical assets 84
Required rates of return 85
Application of the risk-adjusted present value approach 86
Multiperiod investments 86
Applying the risk-adjusted present value factors 88
Global business aspects 90
Conclusions 90
Problems 91
Discussion question 93
Bibliography 94

6   RESOLUTION OF UNCERTAINTY   95
Risks, returns and the resolution of uncertainty 95
Introducing the three assets 97
Asset values by node 101
Expected rates of return by asset and node 102
Conclusions about the three assets 104
An alternative calculation 106
Introducing the two projects 107
Global business aspects 108
Generalizations 108
Problems 109
Discussion question 111
Bibliography 111

7   DIVERSIFICATION AND RISK REDUCTION   112
Systematic and unsystematic risk 113
Diversification 114
Introduction to portfolio analysis 115
The portfolio problem in perspective 116
The co-variance 117
The efficient frontier of investment alternatives 120
Perfect positive correlation 120

Perfect negative correlation 121
Imperfect correlation 122
The power of diversification: independent investments 122
Positively correlated investments 124
Observations regarding diversification 126
The risk-free asset 127
The assumptions 127
Portfolio analysis with a riskless security: the capital asset pricing model 128
The expected return 130
Use of the CAPM 131
Systematic and unsystematic risk 131
Implications for corporate investment policy 133
Unsystematic risk 134
Global business aspects 134
Conclusions 135
Review problem 1 136
Review problem 2 136
Review problem 3 136
Problems 137
Discussion question 140
Solution to review problem 1 140
Solution to review problem 2 141
Solution to review problem 3 141
Bibliography 142
Appendix: Statistical background 143

8   **PROJECTS WITH COMPONENTS HAVING DIFFERENT RISKS**   **145**
A new product project with two different cash flow components 146
Calculating the value of an asset by discounting its net cash flow 147
Increasing the proceeds 150
A new market for an old product 150
Disadvantages of using a single discount rate 152
Finding the composite discount rate for projects with a finite life 152
Buy versus lease 154
Discount rates and corporate income taxes 156
The present value calculation technique used 157
Global business aspects 157
Conclusions 158
Problems 158
Discussion question 160
Bibliography 160
Appendix: Derivation of the formula for the after-tax discount rate for
a cash flow component 160

9   **PRACTICAL SOLUTIONS TO CAPITAL BUDGETING**
    WITH UNCERTAINTY   **162**
The two basic approaches 162
Approach 1: Using payback, present value profile, and sensitivity analysis 163
Approach 2: Calculate the net present value of the expected cash flows 164

WACC: The weighted average cost of capital 165
The cost of retained earnings 167
Costs of retained earnings and of equity with investor taxes 168
Costs of retained earnings with investor taxes 168
Cost of new equity capital with investor taxes 169
Debt and income taxes 171
The relevant source of funds 171
Global business aspects 172
Computing the firm's weighted average cost of capital 172
Capital structure and the effect on the WACC 173
The optimum capital structure 174
The firm's WACC and investments 175
The project's WACC 177
The pure play 177
Default-free rate of discount 178
Discounting stock equity flows 179
Simulation and the Monte Carlo method 181
Value-at-risk 183
Conclusions 183
Problems 184
Discussion question 185
Bibliography 186

PART III
OPTION THEORY AS A CAPITAL BUDGETING TOOL 187

10 REAL OPTIONS AND CAPITAL BUDGETING 189
Two types of stock options 192
Valuing call options on common stock 193
The value of a call option on common stock: a numerical example 193
Formulas for call option valuation 195
Formulas for composition of the replicating portfolio 196
Certainty equivalent formulas for the value of an option 198
A multi-period call option 199
The replicating portfolio method for a two-period option 199
The certainty equivalent method for a two-period option 201
Number of periods 202
Valuing real options 202
Description and valuation of the underlying asset without flexibility 203
An option to abandon 206
An option to expand 209
Multiple options on the same asset 210
Conclusions 210
Problems 211
Discussion question 211
Bibliography 212
Appendix A: Increasing accuracy by using a large number of short periods 213
Appendix B: Valuation with multiple options on an asset 215

ix

PART IV
APPLICATIONS OF CAPITAL BUDGETING   219

11 GROWTH CONSTRAINTS   221
    External capital rationing   221
    Internal capital rationing   222
    Scarce factors of production   223
    Ranking of investments   223
    Programming solutions   224
    Global business aspects   224
    Conclusions   224
    Problems   225
    Discussion question   227
    Bibliography   227

12 THE VALUATION OF A FIRM   228
    Present value of dividends   229
    Present value of earnings minus new investment   230
    Present value of growth opportunities   230
    A terminal value model   231
    Multipliers   231
    Free cash flow   232
    Book value   233
    Value with zero debt   233
    Market capitalization   236
    Substitution of debt for equity   236
    Option theory   237
    Present value of economic income   237
    Valuation for acquisition   238
    DCF versus comparables   238
    Mergers and acquisitions   238
    Forecasting the post-acquisition price   239
    Global business aspects   241
    Conclusions   241
    Problems   241
    Discussion question   242
    Bibliography   242

13 USING ECONOMIC INCOME (RESIDUAL INCOME)
    FOR VALUATION   243
    The discounted cash flow model accepted by finance theorists 244
    The economic income model   244
    Valuation using economic income   246
    Other methods of valuation   248
    Comparing ROI and economic income   249
    Global business aspects   250
    Conclusions   250
    Problems   250
    Discussion question   254
    Bibliography   254

14 PRESENT VALUE ACCOUNTING   255
    A management seminar   255
    Basic concepts   256
    Economic depreciation, income, and return on investment   256
    Application to assets with zero present value   257
    An investment with a positive net present value   258
    Combining investments   259
    Two investments with different risks   260
    Better income measures   262
    Internal rate of return and taxes   263
    Global business aspects   265
    Conclusions   265
    Problems   266
    Discussion question   270
    Bibliography   270

15 PERFORMANCE MEASUREMENT AND MANAGERIAL
    COMPENSATION   272
    Problems of agency   273
    Performance measurement and managerial compensation   274
    Accounting measures   274
    Income   275
    Return on investment (ROI)   275
    ROI and investment decision-making   277
    The case of the resource benefiting the future   277
    The computation of income and ROI   278
    Comparing ROI and economic income   280
    Summary of complexities   280
    Summary of economic income advantages   282
    Time adjusted revenues   282
    A non-zero net present value   283
    Incentive consideration   284
    PVA   286
    Cash flow return on investment   286
    Planning implications   287
    In conclusion: To measure performance   288
    Some generalizations regarding compensation   290
    Rewarding bad performance   290
    Global business aspects   290
    Conclusions   290
    Problems   291
    Discussion question   295
    Bibliography   296

16 FLUCTUATING RATES OF OUTPUT   297
    A plant limited to one type of equipment and two alternatives 298
    Optimum equipment mix   301
    More periods or more equipment types   304
    Conclusions   305
    Problems   305
    Bibliography   310

CONTENTS

17 INVESTMENT DECISIONS WITH ADDITIONAL INFORMATION   311
   The opportunity to replicate   312
   The basic model   312
   Delaying other investments   315
   The winner's curse   316
   Conclusions   317
   Problems   317
   Discussion question   318
   Bibliography   318

18 INVESTMENT TIMING   320
   Basic principles of when to start and stop a process 321
   Growth-type investments   322
   Example: The tree farm   325
   Equipment replacement   328
   The strategy of capacity decisions   329
   The basic decision   329
   Performance measurement and the timing decision   330
   Competitors: Preempting the market   331
   Perfect predictions of interest rates   333
   Conclusions   334
   Problems   334
   Discussion question   338
   Bibliography   338

19 BUY VERSUS LEASE   339
   Borrow or lease: The financing decision   340
   A lease is debt   341
   Buy or lease with taxes : using the after-tax borrowing rate (method 1) 342
   Using a risk-adjusted discount rate (method 2)   345
   Computing the implied interest rate on the lease (method 3) 346
   Risk considerations in lease-versus-borrow decisions 347
   The rate of discount   347
   Recommendations   349
   Leases and purchase options   349
   Importance of terminal value   350
   Leveraged leases   352
   Cancelable leases   354
   The alternative minimum tax   355
   Global business aspects   355
   Conclusions   355
   Problems   356
   Discussion question   359
   Bibliography   360

   Name index   361
   Subject index   363

Illustrations

FIGURES

3.1	Tree diagrams	45
3.2	Two choices and two outcomes	51
3.3	Risk-adjusted required rate of return	54
5.1	Tree diagram of cash flow	80
5.2	Cash-flow pattern of countercyclical asset	85
5.3	Probabilities for a two-period investment (tree diagram)	87
5.4	Cash flows of an investment that costs $300 (tree diagram)	88
5.5	Investment cash flows (tree diagram)	89
5.6	Value of the asset one period from now (tree diagram)	89
5.7	Tree diagram of investment	92
5.8	Tree diagram of single-period RAPVFs	93
6.1	Assets A, B and C and their cash flows	98
6.2	Asset values by asset and node	103
6.3	Expected rates of return by asset and node	105
7.1	Available investments	115
7.2	Examples of co-variation	117
7.3	Choosing portfolios	120
7.4	Perfect linear dependence	121
7.5	Perfect negative correlation	121
7.6	Two securities and different values of ρ	122
7.7	One investment: investment E	123
7.8	Two independent investments (half of E and half of F)	123
7.9	Risk and number of securities	124
7.10	The capital market line	128
7.11	Risk reduction by diversification	132
7.12	Expected return and risks for different portfolios	138
9.1	Relationship between amount of risk, the required return, and the weighted average cost of capital (WACC)	177
10.1	The underlying stock prices over two periods	200
10.2	Underlying asset	204
10.3	Decision tree for the option to abandon	206
16.1	Total costs for the two alternatives	301

17.1	The basic decision model	313
17.2	Investment decision tree	314
18.1	Contribution to overhead at time t	321
18.2	Determination of optimum time to harvest trees	323

TABLES

1.1	What firms do: a survey in 1976 of capital budgeting techniques in use	6
1.2	Percentage of firms using method	6
1.3	Use of DCF (IRR or NPV) as primary or secondary methods	7
1 4	Distribution of responses: the five investment evaluation methods used as primary or secondary methods	7
3.1	An investment with uncertainty	44
3.2	Period-by-period summary of the cash flow of an uncertain investment	47
3.3	Summary measures of the worth of an uncertain investment, based on best estimate of cash flows	47
3.4	Sensitivity analysis	47
3.5	Frequency distribution of net present value of an uncertain investment	49
3.6	Risk analyses of an uncertain investment based on net present value using a 10% discount rate	49
4.1	Values of r_n given constant values of j; values of r_n if $j = 1.10$, $r_f = 0.04$	71
4.2	With implied values of the risk conversion factors (j_n); constant discount rate ($r_n = 0.144$) and $r_f = 0.04$	71
6.1	Common economic environment for assets A, B and C	99
6.2	Asset values by asset and node ($)	101
6.3	Expected rates of return by asset and node (%)	103
6.4	Uncertainty resolution and expected rate of return for assets A, B and C	106
6.5	Project values by project and node ($)	107
6.6	Expected rates of return by project and node (%)	107
6.7	Uncertainty resolution and expected rate of return for projects 1 and 2	108
7.1	Portfolio variance as fraction of individual security variance where $var(R) = 1$ and the number of securities is changed	125
8.1	Project A: cash flow	146
8.2	Project A: present value using the component cash flow procedure	147
8.3	Present value of project A using the project cash flow procedure with a 10% hurdle rate	148
8.4	Comparison of the project A NPVs that result from using the project cash flow procedure (PCFP) and the component cash flow procedure (CCFP) ($)	148
8.5	Project A present value using the project cash flow procedure with a 13.88% hurdle rate	149
8.6	Project B cash flows	151
8.7	Project B present value using the component cash flow procedure mutually exclusive alternative to project B	151

8.8	Project B-1 present value using the component cash flow procedure. Project B-1 is a mutually exclusive alternative to Project B	151
8.9	Project C present value using the component cash flow procedure	153
8.10	Buy versus lease: summary of recommended analysis	156
9.1	Estimate of weighted average cost of capital	173
9.2	Frequency distribution of net present value of an uncertain investment	182
10.1	Variables for stock option valuation example	196
10.2	Calculation of the certainty equivalent at time 2	202
10.3	Variables for real option valuation example	205
10.4	Valuing the investment with the abandonment option	208
10.5	Calculating factory values at the expiration with an expansion option	209
10.6	Calculating factor values prior to expiration with an expansion option	209
14.1	Calculation of the net present value of asset A at times 0 and 1 $(r = 10\%)$	257
14.2	Computation of net present value for asset B at 10%	258
14.3	Computation of internal rate of return for investment B $(r = 20\%)$	258
14.4	Calculation of the net present value of asset E at times 1 and 2 $(r = 10\%)$	260
14.5	Cash flows of asset F	261
14.6	Calculation of NPV of asset D at times 0 and 1 $(r = 0.20)$	261
15.1	Income and investments for each of the three years in use	279
15.2	Present value of the investment at three moments in time	279
16.1	Basic data on equipment types	298
16.2	Seasonal production pattern	300
16.3	Seasonal production schedule form for multiple equipment plant – analysis for first increment (thousands)	302
16.4	Step 2: seasonal production schedule for multiple equipment plant – analysis for first two increments (thousands)	303
16.5	Final version seasonal production schedule for multiple equipment plant – analysis for all three increments (thousands)	304
16.6	Final version seasonal combining quarters with equal production – seasonal production schedule for multiple equipment plant (thousands)	305
16.7	Cost characteristics of alternative types of widget production facilities	306
16.8	Estimated demand for widgets	306
16.9	Cost data	308
16.10	Two alternative sizes	308
16.11	Predicted demand for automobiles	309
16.12	Types of generating equipment and costs	309
16.13	Generating units and characteristics	309
18.1	Net realizable value from one growth cycle	326
18.2	Calculations when land value is $500	327
18.3	Value of land when crops are harvested at various ages	327
18.4	Return earned	328
18.5	Data for years 1 and 2 of the two investments	330
18.6	Values and depreciation expenses	331
18.7	Incomes and returns on investment B	331
18.8	Firm A's net present value conditional on B's actions	332

18.9	Firm B's net present value conditional on A's actions	332
18.10	York State Electric refunding calculations	337
18.11	Analysis of Bi-State Electric position	337
19.1	Cash flows	347
19.2	Balloon payment debt and after-tax cash flows	351
19.3	Cash flows	353
19.4	Debt amortization	353
19.5	Lease analysis (1)	358
19.6	Lease analysis (2)	359

Preface

The history of capital budgeting is a series of time periods where managers thought they had found exact solutions to making investment decisions only to find that new improved methods of thinking of the issues introduced complexities and solutions. Thus until early in the 1950s the payback and accounting return on investment were the primary methods used by business. The internal rate of return (called by different names) then reigned for a brief time in the mid fifties only to be replaced by the net present value method. Both of these discounted cash flow methods initially used the firm's weighted average cost of capital either as the rate of discount for computing present values or as the required return. It was then recognized that not only did a corporation have a risk measure, but so did divisions, and individual projects. We argue in this book that investments have cash flow components that might require different discount rates.

Now there is a long list of contenders for the next break-through for making capital budgeting decisions. Leading the list are real options. The value of a project must take into consideration the flexibility that it provides management. One project may commit management to a definite course of action; another may provide flexibility by giving managers the alternative of making decisions in the future when more information is available. We emphasize the need to assign a value to this flexibility. We point out that option-pricing theory (also known as contingent claims analysis) sometimes provides a method for valuing flexibility. But even though many knowledgeable managers already incorporate the basic concepts, it is useful to acknowledge formally the necessity of considering all decision alternatives and of using option theory where appropriate and feasible.

Close behind options in importance is the thought that a project consists of many series of cash flows and that each series deserves its own specific risk adjusted discount rate. Decomposing the cash flows of an investment may lead to significantly different results than the calculation of the net present value of an investment's net cash flow. We expand on this conjecture in this book.

Even the use of one risk adjusted rate for a series of cash flows must be questioned. Under what conditions is it correct to use $(1 + r)^{-n}$ with the same r for all values of n to compute the present value of a cash flow?

This book explores the complexities of capital budgeting as well as the opportunities to improve the decision process where risk and time are important elements.

We assume that the reader of this book has read and understood the core chapters of *The Capital Budgeting Decision* or the equivalent material in a basic corporate finance text. In this book, we have not gone over the basic concepts of time value, NPV, or IRR. If you are not familiar with these concepts, we strongly recommend that you do some reading to establish a necessary foundation before starting this book.

This book assumes the reader has an appreciation for the usefulness of net present value (NPV) and the cases where NPV is superior to alternative measures of investment worth. Part I of this book summarizes the basic elements of time discounting but the two chapters do not attempt to replicate the essentials of capital budgeting.

Part II expands on Capital Budgeting under conditions of uncertainty. Chapter 8, "Projects with Components Having Different Risk," highlights the fact that while management is generally aware that divisions and projects have different risks, too often they neglect the fact that the cash flow components may also have different risks. Chapter 6 contains complex examples that can be omitted on first reading.

Part III deals with the application of option theory to capital budgeting. The topic is set aside in its own section to highlight the importance of option theory.

Part IV consists of applications of capital budgeting techniques to a variety of decisions. While present value accounting is not likely to be accepted by the FASB in the near future, the basic concepts are important to a wide range of managerial decisions. One of the more important chapters to a business manager is "Buy versus Lease." The leases of corporations amount in the trillions. Unfortunately, a widely used calculation of the cost of leasing is wrong and understates the cost of leasing. This calculation is exploited by lessors to sell leasing to managements.

Current business decisions should be made considering the international implications of the decisions. Throughout the book we have scattered sections titled "Global Business Aspects." The objective of these sections is to identify the specific aspects of international investment decisions that expand the domestic decisions. We decided to avoid limiting our discussion of international aspects to one chapter since we believe that decisions involving cross border factors is of a general nature and the reader should be reminded of this throughout the book.

Lauren McEnery read an early version of *The Capital Budgeting Decision* and the first chapter of this book and offered many useful suggestions. We thank her.

The tree diagrams in this text were drawn with the help of PrecisionTree, a software product of Palisade Corporation, Ithaca, NY. For more information visit their website at www.palisade.com, or call 800-432-RISK (7475).

Harold Bierman, Jr.

Ithaca, New York

Seymour Smidt

Part I

Capital budgeting and valuation under certainty

Well, I come down in the morning and I take up a pencil and I try to think.
(Hans Bethe, quoted by Bob Herbert, *New York Times*, February 14, 2005, quoting from *Timebends* by Arthur Miller)

It is useful first to consider capital budgeting with the most simple of assumptions. While the assumption of certainty is not realistic, it does enable us to establish some easily understood and theoretically correct decision rules. Even in these two chapters the presence of uncertainty is implicit in the calculations.

Part I offers very specific and exact solutions to the capital budgeting decision. The basic conclusion is that with independent investments accept all prospects with a positive NPV. With mutually exclusive investments accept the alternative with the largest NPV.

Chapter 1

The state of the art of capital budgeting

Considering the accidents to which all human Affairs and Projects are subject in such a length of Time, I have perhaps too much flattered myself with a vain Fancy that these Dispositions will be continued without interruption and have the Effects proposed.

(B. Franklin's Will)

In 1790, Franklin made a £2,000 gift to Boston and Philadelphia. £1,000 of the funds were to be spent after 1990. In 1990 the bequest was worth $6.5 million.

(*New York Times*, April 21, 1990. Author's note: Assuming the £1,000 was worth $4,000, the investment earned 0.03766 per year)

Capital budgeting theory keeps evolving. At one point, some felt that net present value (NPV) was so conceptually sound and practically useful that no further improvements were feasible. The basic NPV examples are beautiful (at least to some eyes) in their consistent and easily understood logic.

But we now know that there are important ways of improving the NPV calculation and this book focuses on these techniques.

DECISION-MAKING AND CORPORATE OBJECTIVES

The primary motivation for investing in a corporation is the expectation of making a larger risk-adjusted return than can be earned elsewhere. The managers of a corporation have the responsibility of administering the affairs of the firm in a manner consistent with the expectation of returning the investor's original capital plus the required return on their capital. The common stockholders are the residual owners, and they earn a return only after the investors in the more senior securities (debt and preferred stock) have received their contractual claims. We will assume that the objective of the firm is to maximize its common stockholders' wealth position. But even this narrow, relatively well-defined definition is apt to give rise to misunderstanding and conflict. It is possible that situations will arise in which one group of stockholders will prefer one financial decision while another group of stockholders will prefer another decision.

For example, imagine a situation in which a business undertakes an investment that its management believes to be desirable, but the immediate effect of the investment will be to depress earnings and lower the common stock price today because the market does not have the same information that the management has. In the future, it is expected that the market will realize that the investment is desirable, and at that time the stock price will reflect the enhanced value. But a stockholder expecting to sell the stock in the near future would prefer that the investment had been rejected, whereas a stockholder holding for the long run might be pleased that the investment was undertaken. Theoretically, the problem can be solved by improving the information available to the market. Then the market price would completely reflect the actions and plans of management. However, in practice, the market does not have access to the same information set as management does.

A corporate objective such as "profit maximization" does not adequately or accurately describe the primary objective of the firm, since profits as conventionally computed do not effectively reflect the cost of the stockholders' capital that is tied up in the investment, nor do they reflect the long-run effect of a decision on the shareholder's wealth. Total sales or share of product market objectives are also inadequate normative descriptions of corporate goals, although achieving these goals may also lead to maximization of the shareholders' wealth position by their positive effect on profits.

It is recognized that a complete statement of the organizational goals of a business enterprise embraces a much wider range of considerations, including such things as the prestige, income, security, and power of management, and the contribution of the corporation to the economic and social environment in which it exists and to the welfare of the labor force it employs. Since the managers of a corporation are acting on behalf of the common stockholders, there is a fiduciary relationship between the managers (and the board of directors) and the stockholders. The common stockholders, the suppliers of the risk capital, have entrusted a part of their wealth position to the firm's management. Thus the success of the firm and the appropriateness of management's decisions must be evaluated in terms of how well this fiduciary responsibility has been met. We define the primary objective of the firm to be the maximization of the value of the common stockholder's ownership rights in the firm but recognize that there are other objectives.

Business organizations are continually faced with the problem of deciding whether the commitments of resources – time or money – are worthwhile in terms of the expected benefits. If the benefits are likely to accrue reasonably soon after the expenditure is made, and if both the expenditure and the benefits can be measured in dollars, the solution to such a problem is relatively simple. If the expected benefits are likely to accrue over several years, the solution is more complex.

We shall use the term *investment* to refer to commitments of resources made in the hope of realizing benefits that are expected to occur over a reasonably long period of time in the future. Capital budgeting is a many-sided activity that includes searching for new and more profitable investment proposals, investigating engineering and marketing considerations to predict the consequences of accepting the investment, and making economic analyses to determine the profit potential of each investment proposal. While the specific calculations use the investment's expected cash flows to compute the net present value, the implicit assumption is that a positive net present value will add the same amount to the firm's value.

THE EVOLUTION OF CAPITAL BUDGETING PRACTICE

Capital budgeting theory and practice received a major thrust in 1951. In that year, two books were published that opened the door to new managerial techniques for making capital budgeting decisions using discounted cash flow methods of evaluating investments. *Capital Budgeting* was written by Joel Dean and *The Theory of Investment of the Firm* by Vera and Friedrich Lutz.

Dean, a respected academician who did a large amount of business consulting, wrote his book for business teachers and managers. The Lutzes were economists interested in capital theory, and wrote their book for the economic academic community. Both books were extremely well written and are understandable. They initially caused academics and subsequently business managers to rethink how investments should be reevaluated. Up to the late 1950s payback and accounting return on investment were the two primary capital budgeting methods used by large firms, with less than 5 percent of the largest firms using a DCF method. Today, almost all large corporations use at least one DCF method.

The two books were followed by a series of articles on capital budgeting in 1955 in *The Journal of Business* (University of Chicago). In 1960, *The Capital Budgeting Decision* by Bierman and Smidt was published by Macmillan. This book established the clear superiority of net present value (NPV) but also described how internal rate of return (IRR) could be used correctly. The limitations of alternative methods were also defined.

SURVEYS OF PRACTICE

Prior to 1960, very few corporations used discounted cash flow methods for evaluating investments. Surveys indicate that the situation has changed. Gitman and Forrester showed in a 1976 study that 67.6 percent of the major US firms

5

responding used internal rate of return as either the primary or secondary method and that 35.7 percent used net present value (see Table 1.1).

In a second study (see Table 1.2), Scholl, Sundem, and Gaijsbeck found that 86 percent of the major firms responding used internal rate of return or present value, thus confirming the magnitudes of the Gitman–Forrester study.

In 1992, Bierman made a survey of the capital budgeting practices of the 100 largest of the Fortune 500 Industrial firms. Sixty-eight firms supplied usable information (see Tables 1.3 and 1.4). The survey results indicate that all the firms used time discounting, and sixty-seven of the firms used either NPV or IRR. However, despite the academic literature conclusions that ROI is not useful, close to 50 percent still used ROI to evaluate investments. WACC was the most popular discount rate, but the risk adjusted rate for the project, was also extensively used.

Graham and Harvey (2001 and 2002) sought responses from approximately 4,440 companies and received 392 completed surveys. They found that 74.9 percent of the

Table 1.1 What firms do: a survey in 1976 of capital budgeting techniques in use

Method	Primary number of firms	%	Secondary number of firms	%
Internal rate of return	60	53.6	13	14.0
Rate of return (average)	28	25.0	13	14.0
Net present value	11	9.8	24	25.8
Payback period	10	8.9	41	44.0
Benefit/cost ratio	3	2.7	2	2.2
Total responses	112	100.0	93	100.0

Source: L. J. Gitman and J. R. Forrester, Jr., "A Survey of Capital Budgeting Techniques Used by Major Firms," Financial Management, fall 1977, pp. 66–71.

Table 1.2 Percentage of firms using method

Method	% of firms
Payback	74
Accounting return on investment	58
Internal rate of return	65
Net present value	56
Internal rate of return or present value	86
Use only one method (of which 8% is a DCF method)	14

Source: L. D. Scholl, G. L. Sundem, and W. R. Gaijsbeck, "Survey and Analysis of Capital Budgeting Methods," Journal of Finance, March 1978, pp. 281–7. There were 429 firms selected and 189 responses. The firms were large and stable. Major financial officers were sent the survey.

Table 1.3 *Use of DCF (IRR or NPV)[a] as primary or secondary methods*

	Number of firms	%
Primary	65	96
Secondary	2	3
Not used	1	1
	68	100

Note:
a Results of survey conducted by
   H. Bierman, Jr. in 1992. Not published.

Table 1.4 *Distribution of responses:* [a] *the five investment evaluation methods used as primary or secondary methods*

The investment evaluation methods used are:	Number of firms			
	A primary method	A secondary method	Not used	Total
Payback	17	40	11	68
Accounting return on investment (income divided by investment)	6	29	33	68
Internal rate of return (discounted cash flow percentage)	59	7	2	68
Net present value (a discounted dollar measure)	41	17	10	68
Present value of benefits/present value of outlays	10	14	44	68

Note:
a Results of survey conducted by H. Bierman, Jr. in 1992. Not published.

CFOs used NPV and 75.7 percent used IRR. They did not reveal what percentage of the respondents used either NPV or IRR (or APV or Profitability Index). The survey included both large and small corporations.

THE DISCOUNT RATE

For many years the discounted cash flow methods were implemented using the firm's weighted average cost of capital (WACC) as the required return. If the firm's investors required a return of 0.10, then it seemed reasonable to require that incremental investments yield at least 0.10. But then managers realized that the new investments being considered frequently had different risks from the assets currently owned by the firm. With different risks the new investments required a different discount rate than the firm's WACC.

CASH FLOW COMPONENTS

Any investment project being considered will have several series of cash flow components. Each of these series is likely to have a different risk and require a different discount rate. It will normally not be valid to discount the investment's net cash flows of a period using one discount rate if the components of these net cash flows have different risks.

THE CALCULATION OF THE DISCOUNT RATE

Assume that the risk of a cash flow stream has been identified as being consistent with β (beta). One conventional calculation of the project's required expected return ($\bar{r}_i$) is to use the capital asset pricing model formulation:

$$\bar{r}_i = r_f + (\bar{r}_m - r_f)\beta_i$$

where

r_f is the default free return
$\bar{r}_i$ is the market's expected return
β_i is the measure of the project's systematic risk.

The project's non-systematic risk is not included in the calculation of the discount rate. Non-systematic risk can jeopardize a firm's ability to execute its strategy; this can affect the firm's value even if the well-diversified investor can eliminate non-systematic risk. The value of the firm may be harmed by undertaking high risk projects even if the risks are non-systematic.

THE TIME RISK INTERACTION

Under what circumstances is the use of $(1 + r)^{-n}$ correct for any value of n if r is correct for n equal to one? Normally we assume that risk compounds through time, but that is not always the situation.

For example, consider a situation where all the risk is at time zero. A firm is drilling an oil well and there is 0.7 probability of a productive well. If oil is found then the oil can be sold through time to a large oil company. The risk is mostly at time zero, even if there is some future price risk. But increasing the discount rate is not an effective way of reflecting the dry well risk.

It is not likely to be correct to apply the formula $(1 + r)^{-n}$ using one value of r to transform all cash flows of all time periods back to the present, if r includes both a pure time value and a risk factor. Thus we need better methods of taking into consideration risk and time value than using a risk-adjusted discount rate (r) in the formula $(1 + r)^{-n}$.

Consider a situation where a $1,000 contractual cash flow to be received at time 1 has 0.9 probability of being received (the expected value is $900) and risk aversion reduces the expected value to a certainty equivalent of $0.8(900) = \$720$. With a 0.10 risk-free discount rate, the present value of the certainty equivalent is:

$$PV = \frac{720}{1.10} = \$654.55$$

This is equivalent to discounting the time 1 $900 expected value by 0.375.

$$PV = \frac{900}{1.375} = \$654.54$$

Now assume the same payoff takes place at time 10 so that the present value of the certainty equivalent is now:

$$PV = \frac{720}{(1.10)^{10}} = \$277.59$$

This is equivalent to discounting the $900 expected value by 0.12482.

$$PV = \frac{900}{(1.12482)^{10}} = \$277.59$$

When the cash flow occurred at time 1, 0.375 was the equivalent risk-adjusted rate. When the cash flow occurred at time 10, 0.12482 was the equivalent risk-adjusted rate. The risk-adjusted discount rate is different for each cash flow received in a different time period. For many long-lived investments, a lower discount rate should be used for cash flows that are more distant in time.

REAL OPTIONS

The real options literature has opened up an extensive new path for capital budget-ing. Considering directly the existence of a project's real options adds value to the conventionally computed NPV calculations. Projects that previously would have been rejected now can become eligible for acceptance by considering the value of options available to the firm. The value of an option cannot be negative so including the value of real options adds to the project's value.

Two of the more important types of options are the "waiting option" and the "option to change or extend use." With the waiting option the right to delay the investment has value. The option to change the use of an asset (flexibility) has value as does the fact that an investment today may enable the firm to reap value in the future (extend the use of the investment).

THREE PROBLEMS

There are three problems in determining the present value of a future amount (after the future amount has been determined) for a given event.

First, the time value of money must be considered. One of the basic concepts of business economics and managerial decision-making is that the present value of an amount of money is a function of the time of receipt or disbursement of the cash. A dollar received today is more valuable than a dollar to be received in some future time period. The only requirement for this concept to be valid is that there be a positive rate of interest at which funds can be invested.

Secondly, the probability of the event (the dollar outcome) must be determined so that an expected value can be computed.

Third, the dollar amount must be translated to a value amount or alternatively the future uncertain dollar amounts must be translated into a certainty equivalent or the discount rate must be adjusted to take risk into consideration. One way or another, the riskiness of the project must be considered beyond merely considering the probabilities of the outcomes.

Each of the above three problems has additional complexities and insights. We will start with time discounting.

TIME DISCOUNTING

The time value of money affects a wide range of business decisions, and a knowledge of how to incorporate time value considerations systematically into a decision is essential to an understanding of finance. The basic building block for computing the present value of a future cash flow of $1 is:

$$PV = (1 + r)^{-n}$$

where PV is the present value of a dollar to be received at the end of the period n using a rate of r per period. The PV equals one divided by $(1 + r)$ to the n-th power.

The quantity $(1 + r)^{-n}$ is called the *present value factor*. The present value factor gives the present value of a future $1. The specific numerical value of the present value factor is a function of the values of n and r. To find the present value of X dollars, multiply X by the appropriate present value factor. For example, if the future amount to be received at time 2 is $100, and the discount rate is 0.10, then the present value factor is $(1.1)^{-2} = 0.8264$, and the present value of the $100 is $82.64.

PRESENT VALUE ADDITION RULE

The present value of any set of cash flows is the sum of the present values of each of the cash flows in the set.

An amount of $100 is to be received at the end of period one and an amount of $200 is to be received at the end of period two. The time value of money is 0.10. What is the total present value of two cash flows? Using the present value addition rule we can calculate the present value of each cash flow, and add the present values. The calculations are shown in the following table:

Period t	Cash flows X_t	Present value factors PVF$(t, 0.10)$	Present value PV
1	$100	0.9091	$90.91
2	$200	0.8264	165.28
		Total present value using 0.10 =	$256.19

By using the formula for the present value of a future cash flow and the present value additional rule, one could calculate the present value of any possible set of discrete cash flows.

PRESENT VALUE MULTIPLICATION RULE

The present value factors of two consecutive time periods can be multiplied to obtain the present value for the entire time period. For example, if with an 8 percent discount rate, the present value factor for a dollar to be received in 3 years is 0.7938, and the present value factor for a dollar in 9 years is 0.5002, the present value of a dollar in 12 years is $0.7938 \times 0.5002 = 0.3971$ or $(1.08)^{-12} = 0.3971$.

It is not necessary that the interest rates for the successive time periods be the same.

THE TERM STRUCTURE OF INTEREST RATES

Bonds maturing in different years offer different yields. This implies that to be exact one should not use the same interest rate to discount the cash flows of different time periods. This set of interest rates for different time periods is called a yield curve. Usually the yield curve is upward sloping and reflects the yield or cost of US Treasury zero coupon bonds maturing in different years. These rates are spot rates and we will use R_i for the spot rate for a dollar to be received in i years. For example, assume:

$$R_1 = 0.05000$$
$$R_2 = 0.05499$$
$$R_3 = 0.06326$$

If $100 is to be received at the end of each of three years we have for the present values

Time	Spot rate PV factors	PV of $100
1	$(1.05)^{-1} = 0.9524$	95.24
2	$(1.05499)^{-2} = 0.8985$	89.95
3	$(1.06326)^{-3} = 0.8319$	83.19

The spot rates imply a series of one period forward rates (r_i). For example:

$$(1.05)(1 + r_2) = (1.05499)^2$$
$$r_2 = 0.06$$

and

$$(1.05)(1.06)(1 + r_3) = (1.06326)^3$$
$$r_3 = 0.08$$

The yield curve can be described in terms of spot rates. In addition, present values can be computed using either spot rates (as above) or forward rates.

The forward rate for year 1 is identical to the spot rate for year 1. The forward rate for period t can be interpreted as the interest rate applicable for a one period loan during period t. Thus the forward rates corresponding to the term structure of spot rates in this example are $r_1 = 0.05$, $r_2 = 0.06$, and $r_3 = 0.08$.

Now assume a 0.10 three-year bond that pays $100 interest per year and $1,000 at maturity. The present value of this bond using the above term structure is:

Time	Cash flow	PV factor	PV of flows
1	100	0.9524	95.24
2	100	0.8985	89.85
3	1,100	0.8319	915.09
			PV = $1,100.18

If the above term structure applies, the bond has a present value of $1,100.18. With this present value (or cost) the bond selling at $1,100.18 would have a yield to maturity of 0.06236.

Time	Cash flow	PV factors	PV
1	100	$(1.06236)^{-1}$	94.13
2	100	$(1.06236)^{-2}$	88.61
3	1,100	$(1.06236)^{-3}$	917.44
			1,100.18

If desired, and if the above term structure applies, the first year's interest payment can be "stripped" and sold for $95.24 at time zero. The second year's interest can be sold for $89.85 and the third year's interest and principal sold for $915.09 both at time zero.

The 0.06236 yield to maturity is a weighted average of the three spot rates or the three forward rates.

RISK AND DIVERSIFICATION

The risk of a project consists of two elements, the probability of the outcome and the risk preference of the investor given the outcome and the probability of its occurrence. There is normally a desire on the part of the investor to diversify and reduce the amount of risk.

Diversification of risk is based on an assumption that all outcomes are not perfectly correlated. Assume a situation where an outlay of $800 leads to:

0.5 probability of $1,800
0.5 probability of $0

There is 0.5 probability of losing the outlay of $800. But assume there is an opportunity to buy two $400 independent investments each with 0.5 probability of obtaining $900 and 0.5 probability of $0.

Now the outcomes for two $400 independent investments are:

0.25 probability of $1,800
0.50 probability of $900
0.25 probability of $0

The expected value of investing in one investment costing $800 leads to an expected value of:

$$0.50\ (1,800 - 800) = \ \ \$500$$
$$0.50\ (-800) = \ -400$$
$$\text{Expected Value}\ \ \underline{\ \$100\ }$$

The expected value buying two $400 independent investments is:

$$0.25\ (1,800 - 800) = \ \ \$250$$
$$0.50\ (900 - 800) = \ \ \ \ \ \ 50$$
$$0.25\ (-800) = \ -200$$
$$\text{Expected Value}\ \ \underline{\ \$100\ }$$

The expected value of the two strategies are identical. However, the spreads of the outcomes (the variances) change. Instead of 0.5 probability for the two extreme outcomes the probability of these outcomes is 0.25 and some of the probability is shifted to the less extreme results of $900 proceeds and $100 gain. The variance of outcomes is reduced by 50 percent. If the number of identical independent investments were increased further, and the total investment remained unchanged, the expected value would remain $100 and the variance of outcomes would be reduced. If the number of investments were infinite the variance of outcomes would be equal to zero.

As long as the investments were not perfectly correlated it is possible to find a mix of investments that will reduce risk. If the expected values of the investments differ, the expected value of the portfolio of investments will be less than the expected value of the investment with the highest expected value, keeping the total investment constant.

The two primary factors that make finance an interesting and complex subject are the elements of *time* and *risk*. Because decisions today often affect cash flow for many future time periods and we are not certain as to the outcomes of our actions, we have to formulate decision rules that take risk and time value into consideration in a systematic fashion. These two problems are as intellectually challenging as any problems that one is likely to encounter in the world of economic activity.

Frequently, the existence of uncertainty means that the decision-maker faces alternatives that involve trade-offs of less return and less risk or more return and more risk. A large part of the study of finance has to do with learning how to approach this type of risk-return trade-off choice.

STRATEGIC CONSIDERATIONS

Strategic considerations might overwhelm the numerical calculations of value as a factor in decision-making. An investment might be desirable for the firm's strategic objectives independent of the NPV measure. Of course, if the NPV were calculated correctly it would include the other indirect values that we are labeling as strategic considerations.

Investment decisions may be tactical or strategic. A tactical investment decision generally involves a relatively small amount of funds and does not constitute a major departure from what the firm has been doing in the past. The consideration of a new machine tool by Ford Motor Company is a tactical decision, as is a buy or lease decision made by Exxon Mobil Oil Company.

Strategic investment decisions involve large sums of money and may also result in a major departure from what the company has been doing in the past. Strategic decisions directly affect the basic course of the company. Acceptance of a strategic investment will involve a significant change in the company's expected profits and in the risks to which these profits will be subject. These changes are likely to lead stockholders and creditors to revise their evaluation of the company. If a private corporation undertook the development of a supersonic commercial transport (costing over $9 billion), this would be a strategic decision. If the company failed in its attempt to develop the commercial plane, the very existence of the company would be jeopardized. Frequently, strategic decisions are based on intuition rather than on detailed quantitative analysis.

The investment strategy of a firm is a statement of the formal criteria it applies in searching for and evaluating investment opportunities. Strategic planning guides the search for projects by identifying promising product lines or geographic areas in which to search for good investment projects. One firm may seek opportunities for rapid growth in emerging high-technology businesses, another may seek opportunities to become the low-cost producer of commodities with well-established technologies and no unusual market problems; a third firm may look for opportunities to exploit its special knowledge of a particular family of chemicals. A strategy should reflect both the special skill and abilities of the firm (its comparative advantage) and the opportunities that are available as a result of dynamic changes in the world economy.

Strategic planning leads to the choice of the forest; project analysis studies chooses between the individual trees. The two activities should complement and reinforce each other. Project analysis may provide a feedback loop to verify the accuracy of the strategic plan. If there are good opportunities where the strategic plan says they should be found, and few promising opportunities in lines of business that the strategy identifies as unattractive, confidence in the strategic plan increases. Alternatively, if attractive projects are not found where the plan had expected them, or if desirable projects appear in lines of business that the strategic plan had identified as unattractive, a reassessment of both the project studies and the strategic plan may be in order.

THREE BASIC GENERALIZATIONS

We offer three generalizations that are useful in the types of financial decisions that are to be discussed. The first generalization is that investors prefer more return (cash) to less, all other things being equal. Investors who thought that the returns were excessively high could distribute the excess in such a manner that the results would meet their criterion of fairness.

The second generalization is that investors prefer less risk (a possibility of loss) to more risk and have to be paid to undertake risky endeavors. This generalization is contrary to common observations such as the existence of race tracks and gambling casinos (the customers of such establishments are willing to pay for the privilege of undertaking risky investments), but the generalization is useful even if it does not apply to everyone all the time.

The third generalization is that everyone prefers cash to be received today rather than for the same amount to be received in the future. This only requires the reasonable assumption that the funds received today can be invested to earn some positive return. Since this is the situation in the real world, the generalization is reasonable.

These three generalizations are used implicitly and explicitly throughout the book.

THE CAPITAL MARKET

Corporations at some stage in their life go to the capital market to obtain funds. The market that supplies financial resources is called the capital market and it consists of all savers (banks, insurance companies pension funds, people, etc.). The capital market gathers resources from the savers of society (people who consume less than they earn) and rations these savings out to the organizations that have a need for new capital and that can pay the price that the capital market defines for capital.

The availability of funds (the supply) and the demand for funds determine the cost of funds to the organizations obtaining new capital and the return to be earned by the suppliers of capital. The measure of the cost of new capital becomes very important to a business firm in the process of making decisions involving the use of capital. We shall have occasion to use the market cost of funds (the interest rate) frequently in our analyses, and you should be aware of the relevance of capital market considerations to the decisions of the firm.

Actually there is not one market cost of funds; rather, there is a series of different but related costs depending on the specific terms on which the capital is obtained and the amount of risk associated with the security. One of the important objectives of this book is to develop an awareness of the cost of the different forms of capital (common stock, preferred stock, debt, retained earnings, etc.) and of the factors that determine these costs. This is a complex matter, since the cost of a specific form of capital for one firm will depend on the returns investors can obtain from other firms, on the characteristics of the assets of the firm that is attempting to raise additional capital, and on the capital structure of the firm. We can expect that the larger the risk, the higher the expected return that will be needed to attract investors.

GLOBAL BUSINESS ASPECTS

When an investment decision is being made that involves investment of resources in one or more other countries, the following factors must be considered:

1   The tax implications (e.g., foreign tax credit laws and ability to defer domestic income taxes). This can affect the type of capital to be used.
2   The choice of the discount rate to evaluate the investment (the inflation rate of the investment location is relevant).
3   The political risks of the location.
4   How the risk of this specific investment affects the firm's risk.
5   The use of a different currency for the evaluation.
6   Determine the accounting effects that will occur through time.

Obviously a large amount of specialized knowledge will be required to incorporate the above factors in an intelligent useful manner in the investment decision.

CONCLUSIONS

The decision-makers must not rely on any one quantitative measure as the sole guide for making decisions. Just because the quantitative measure used indicates the direction of a decision does not mean that this is the decision that should be made. On the other hand, there tend to be useful quantitative measures that can be obtained.

Most capital budgeting decision-making can be reduced to evaluating incremental cash flows. There are four steps in the analysis. First, the relevant incremental cash flows must be estimated for different states of nature. Second, there must be some way to take into consideration the basic time value of money. Third, there must be some means of dealing with uncertainty if the cash flows are not known with certainty. Fourth, the investor's risk preferences must be incorporated into the decision process.

These four steps are necessary to determine the present value of sums of money to be received or paid at various times in the future.

As long as certainty is assumed we can arrive at an exact solution to a capital budgeting decision problem. Once uncertainty is introduced it is much less definite that an exact reliable quantitatively based decision can be obtained. There is likely to be a qualitative element of the decision that allows for the possibility that an alternative decision alternative is more desirable than the one dictated by the quantitative calculations.

The basic building blocks of this book are three generalizations:

1   Investors prefer more expected return to less.
2   Investors prefer less risk to more risk.
3   Investors prefer an amount of cash to be received earlier than the same amount to be received later.

All modern finance is built on these generalizations. Some investors accept or seek risk, but they normally do so with the hope of some monetary gain. They expect to be compensated for the risk they undertake.

Corporations, or more exactly, the managers running the corporations, have many different goals. We have simplified the complex set of objectives that exist to one basic objective, the maximization of the value of the stockholders' ownership rights in the firm. While a simplification, it enables us to make specific recommendations as to how corporate financial decisions should be made.

We shall find that while some financial decisions may be solved exactly, more frequently we shall only be able to define and analyze the problem. We may not always be able to identify the optimum decision with certainty, but we shall generally be able to describe some errors in analysis to avoid. In just about all cases in corporate finance, useful insights for improved decision-making can be obtained by applying modern finance theory.

PROBLEMS

1   Assume a firm has a beta of one.
     The value of $\bar{r}_m$ is 0.09 and $r_f = 0.03$.
     a.   Determine the firm's required expected return.
     b.   If r_f increases to 0.06, what is the new value of the firm's required expected return?
     c.   What would you expect to happen to $\bar{r}_m$ if r_f increases from 0.03 to 0.06?
2   The annual interest rate for time 0 to time 10 is 0.06. The annual interest rate for time 10 to time 15 is 0.20
     a.   What is time zero present value of $100 to be received at time 10?
     b.   What is the time zero present value of $100 to be received at time 15?

3   The following forward rates apply:

$r_1 = 0.10$

$r_2 = 0.08$

$r_3 = 0.05$

Determine the spot rates for each of the three years to the nearest basis point.

4   (*Continue 3*)

a.   Compute the time zero present value of $100 to be received at time 3.

b.   Compute the time zero present value of $100 to be received at time 3 if 0.10 is the forward rate for all three years.

DISCUSSION QUESTION

Do you agree with the conclusion that investors prefer less risk and higher expected return?

BIBLIOGRAPHY

Classic articles

Dean, J., "Measuring the Productivity of Capital," *Harvard Business Review*, January–February 1954, pp. 120–30.

Dorfman, Robert, "The Meaning of the Internal Rate of Return," *Journal of Finance*, December 1981, pp. 1010–23.

Gitman, Lawrence J. and John R. Forrester, Jr., "Forecasting and Evaluation Practices and Performance: A Survey of Capital Budgeting Techniques Used by Major US Firms," *Financial Management*, fall 1977, pp. 66–71.

Graham, J. and C. Harvey, "The Theory and Practice of Corporate Finance: Evidence from the Field," *Journal of Financial Economics*, 60, 2001, pp. 187–243.

Graham, J. and C. Harvey, "How Do CFOs Make Capital Budgeting and Capital Structure Decisions?" *Journal of Applied Corporate Finance*, spring 2002, pp. 8–23.

Hirschleifer, J., "On the Theory of Optimal Investment Decisions," *Journal of Political Economy*, August 1958, pp. 329–52.

Lorie, J. H. and L. J. Savage, "Three Problems in Rationing Capital," *Journal of Business*, October 1955, pp. 229–39.

Schall, L. and G. Sundem, "Capital Budgeting Methods and Risk: A Further Analysis," *Financial Management*, spring 1980, pp. 7–10.

Solomon, E., "The Arithmetic of Capital Budgeting Decisions," *Journal of Business*, April 1956, pp. 124–9.

Classic books

Bierman, H. and S. Smidt, *The Capital Budgeting Decision*, New York: Macmillan Publishing Company, 1960.

Boness, A. J., *Capital Budgeting*, New York: Praeger Publishers, 1972.

Dean, J., *Capital Budgeting*, New York: Columbia University Press, 1951.

Fisher, I., *The Theory of Interest*, New York: Macmillan Publishing Company, 1930.

Grant, E. L., W. G. Ireson, and R. S. Leavenworth, *Principles of Engineering Economy*, 8th edn, New York: Ronald Press, 1990.

Levy, H. and M. Sarnat, *Capital Investment and Financial Decisions*, 4th edn, Englewood Cliffs, NJ: Prentice-Hall, 1990.

Lutz, F. and V. Lutz, *The Theory of Investment of the Firm*, Princeton, NJ: Princeton University Press, 1951.

Masse, P., *Optimal Investment Decisions: Rules for Action and Criteria for Choices*, Englewood Cliffs, NJ: Prentice-Hall, 1962.

Merrett, A. J. and A. Sykes, *Capital Budgeting & Company Finance*, New York: Longman, 1966.

Solomon, E., *The Management of Corporate Capital*, New York: Free Press, 1959.

Stern, J. M. and D. H. Chew, Jr., *The Revolution in Corporate Finance*, 4th edn, Malden, MA: Blackwell Publishing, 2003.

Chapter 2

Amounts discounted and discount rates

Knowing what was wrong has been relatively easy. Knowing what is right has proved to be extremely difficult.

(Mikhail Gorbachev, quoted by Henry A. Kissinger, *Newsweek*, September 2, 1991, p. 60)

A common procedure in capital budgeting is to estimate the value of an asset by discounting its expected future cash flows by an appropriate discount rate representing the project's cost of capital. Under the US tax laws, corporations are permitted to deduct interest on debt in computing taxable income. With debt interest deductible for taxes, how assets are financed will affect the amount of corporate taxes paid. Therefore, the value of assets may depend on how they are financed.

Several different definitions of cash flows are used reflecting different methods of taking the debt interest tax benefits into account. In the most popular approach, the cash flows, referred to as free cash flows, do not include the tax savings from debt. The tax savings are incorporated into the discount rate. Other approaches include the tax savings in the cash flows and require different discount rate concepts.

If the same assumptions are made about the characteristics of the asset and how it is to be financed, all of the cash flow concepts should lead to the same asset value. It is necessary that each cash flow definition be paired with the appropriate discount rate to achieve the same asset value. For simplicity of presentation, we will assume in this chapter cash flow perpetuities and a constant amount of debt leverage.

Whenever the term "cash flow" is used, assume that it is equivalent to "free cash flow" and that any necessary capital expenditure is subtracted.

In this chapter, we will focus on three methods of calculating value:

1. free cash flow (FCF);
2. capital cash flow (CCF);
3. adjusted present value (APV).

The terminology used in this chapter is consistent with Ruback (2002), but the definition of APV differs somewhat. If the three methods are applied as recommended in this chapter, they will result in the same net present values.

All three methods require estimates of cash flows and discount rates. The following table defines some of the differences in the mechanics of calculation. The financing tax shields are the reduction in corporate income taxes that occurs when interest expense is deducted in computing the corporation's taxable income. Because interest expense is deductible in computing corporate taxes, the after-tax cost of debt to the corporation is less than the return received by the corporate debtholders. By contrast, with equity, the after-tax cost to the corporation is the same as the before-tax return received by investors.

	FCF	CCF and APV
After-tax cash flows	Financing tax shields are not included in the amounts discounted	Financing tax shields are explicitly included in the amounts discounted
Discount rate	The discount rates used reflect the after-tax cost to the corporation of the payments made to investors. The after-tax costs reflect the tax benefits of deducting interest expense from taxable income	The discount rates used reflect the returns received by investors. They do not include the tax benefits received by corporations as a result of being able to deduct interest expense from taxable income

Assume a project has the same risk characteristics as the overall corporation. The FCF calculation requires a discount rate that measures the cost to the corporation of paying its capital suppliers their required returns. The measure used is the firm's weighted average cost of capital (WACC). The costs used in computing the WACC are measured after-tax to the corporation. The WACC depends on the firm's capital structure, the ratio of the market value of its debt to the market value of its equity. If this ratio changes, the WACC will also change. Therefore, using a constant WACC through time implies a constant capital structure. The CCF and APV calculations can more readily cope with the situation where the percentage of debt in the capital structure is changing. The FCF method can be used when the capital structure changes over time, but changes in the capital structure would require changes in the discount rate. By contrast, with the CCF and APV methods, it is usually assumed that changes in capital structure do not affect the discount rate but do effect the magnitude of the cash flows that are discounted. In principle, all three methods, if used properly, should give the same result. But when changes in the capital structure are expected, the CCF and APV methods may be easier to implement than the FCF method.

THE FCF METHOD

The FCF method uses the forecasts of free cash flow and discounts the forecasted cash flow at the project's WACC which we denote as k_0. Assume that X is the expected value of earnings before interest and taxes (EBIT) but the capital expenditures are equal to the depreciation expense and there is no change in required working capital so that $X(1 - t_c)$ also equals the expected free cash flow for the unlevered firm. Assume also that the actual realizations of EBIT from year to year are equal to X plus a random amount with an expected value of zero and which is uncorrelated from year to year. Thus year-to-year changes in the actual value of X do not lead to changes in the value of the stock because they do not lead to changes in the expected future X. Then using FCF, the value of the levered firm (V_L) is defined to be:

$$V_L = \frac{(1 - t_c)X}{k_0} \tag{2.1}$$

The $(1 - t_c)X$ term does not reflect the use of debt leverage, but the value of the weighted average cost of capital (k_0) does reflect the interest tax shield. The WACC is defined to be:

$$k_0 = (1 - t_c)k_i\frac{B}{V_L} + k_e\frac{S}{V_L} \tag{2.2}$$

where

t_c is the corporate tax rate
k_i is the cost of debt (contractual interest rate equal to market yield)
B is the market value of debt
V_L is the value of the levered firm and equal to $B + S$
k_e is the cost of equity capital (depends on the amount of debt)
S is the market value of stock equity
k_0 is equal to WACC.

By definition

$$V_L = S + B \tag{2.2a}$$

The capital structure is said to be constant if the ratio B/V_L is constant through time. If the capital structure is constant and the expected values of X and t_c do not change, then equation (2.1) measures correctly the value of the levered firm.

23

THE CCF METHOD

The capital cash flow method uses the cash flows (benefits) flowing to all capital contributors. The total benefits are:

$$\text{CCF (total benefits)} = (X - I)(1 - t_c) + I \tag{2.3}$$

where the term $(X - I)(1 - t_c)$ is the after-corporate tax benefits of the stock-holders and I is the interest paid to debtholders.

Equation (2.3) simplifies to

$$\text{CCF (total benefits)} = X(1 - t_c) + t_c I \tag{2.4}$$

In this expression, the first term is the FCF and the second term is the value of the interest tax shield.

The present value of the total benefits is computed using a discount rate $r*$ that does not reflect the interest tax shield. The discount rate $r*$ is defined to be:

$$r* = k_i \frac{B}{V_L} + k_e \frac{S}{V_L} \tag{2.5}$$

The discount rate $r*$ is the average return required by investors in the levered investment. An investor who buys all the debt and all the stock (or the same proportion of each) will earn an expected return of $r*$ (before investor tax).

Assuming X is a perpetuity and the amounts of B and S do not change:

$$V_L = \frac{(X - I)(1 - t_c) + I}{r*} \tag{2.6}$$

Alternatively, using equation (2.4) as the expression for the CCF, this can be written as:

$$V_L = \frac{X(1 - t_c) + t_c I}{r*} \tag{2.6a}$$

The interest tax shield is in the numerator of (6a) but it does not affect the discount rate $r*$ (see equation (2.5)).

A classic financial relationship for determining the effect on the value (V_u) of a firm with zero debt of substituting B of debt for B equity is:

$$V_L = V_u + t_c B \tag{2.7}$$

where there are zero investor taxes and no costs of financial distress and:

- V_L is the value of a levered firm or project
- V_u is the value of an unlevered firm or project (using the cost of equity with zero debt)
- t_c is the corporate tax rate
- t_cB is the value added by substituting B of debt for B of equity.

Since the free cash flows are assumed to be a level annuity, the value of the unlevered firm is given by

$$V_u = \frac{X(1 - t_c)}{k_e(0)} \qquad (2.8)$$

where $k_e(0)$ is the cost of equity capital with zero debt. The tax shield of interest has a value of $t_cI = t_ck_iB$ with a present value of t_cB using k_i as the discount rate. Adding t_cB to V_u we obtain equation (2.7). Equation (2.8) is equivalent to equation (2.1).

THE ADJUSTED PRESENT VALUE METHOD

The adjusted present value method starts by computing the investment's net present value, assuming the investment is financed completely with stock equity capital, using a stock equity cost of capital. Then, there is added to the present value of the after-tax benefits without considering debt financing, the present value of the tax savings resulting from the debt interest associated with the debt used to finance the investment. The tax savings are discounted using the before-tax borrowing rate (the tax savings are assumed to have the same risk as the debt flows). We will assume there are zero debt issue costs and that all the cash flows are perpetuities.

$$\text{Adjusted present value} = \frac{FCF}{k_e(0)} + \frac{t_cI}{k_i} \qquad (2.9)$$

Note the use of two discount rates. This is particularly important where the asset has a finite life. Also note that the first term is actually V_u and the second term simplifies to

$$\frac{t_cI}{k_i} = \frac{t_c(Bk_i)}{k_i} = t_cB.$$

There are alternative interpretations of APV with different methods of calculation. We prefer a process where the asset's value is not affected by the method of calculation, and the calculations can be explained logically.

25

EQUIVALENCE OF THE METHODS

If there is no debt, all three methods are identical and produce the same value. If there is debt, the three methods (as defined) will give identical values if the cash flows and discount rates are correctly computed (as described above). The discount rates must be carefully defined.

We will illustrate the equivalence of the three methods using a perpetuity of cash flow benefits.

EXAMPLE 2.1

Assuming a perpetual set of constant cash flows is the easiest situation with which to illustrate the equivalence of the three methods. We will first establish an example using FCF and then use a procedure that computes the present value of the stock equity flows. Then we will use the same example to illustrate the CCF and APV.

To describe a project, we need to know, at a minimum, the project's expected cash flows, X, the tax rate t_c and the risk characteristics of the project. With this information we can compute the value of the unlevered project. For our example we assume the following:

X = expected earnings before interest and taxes (EBIT) assuming required capital expenditures equal depreciation and no change in working capital, $153,846.15.

$k_e(0)$ = cost of equity with zero debt = 0.125

t_c = tax rate = 0.35

With this information and using equation (2.8) the value of the unlevered project can be computed.

$$V_u = \frac{\$153,846.15(1 - 0.35)}{0.125} = \frac{\$100,000}{0.125} = \$800,000$$

Assuming the project costs $700,000, the NPV of the project would be $100,000. However, the value of project might be increased by including some financial leverage. To take this into account we need to know, the amount of debt, the required interest rate on the debt and the required return on the levered equity. Both the interest rate on the debt and required return on the leveraged equity will depend on the amount of debt. Assume the following values:

B = value of debt, $500,000

k_i = borrowing rate for the debt (coupon and market yield) = 0.10

k_e = cost of equity with $500,000 debt, 0.1421053

The values of the following variables will be calculated from the above assumptions:

V_L = the value of the levered firm

S = value of stock

k_0 = weighted average cost of capital with $500,000 of debt.

THE FCF METHOD

With $500,000 of 0.10 debt, the after-interest income to stockholders (before tax) is $103,846:

$$X - k_i B = \$153,846 - \$500,000(0.10) = \$103,846$$

The corporate tax is $0.35(103,846) = \$36,346$, and the after-tax, after-interest income to the stockholders is $67,500.

$$\$103,846 - 36,346 = \$67,500$$

The $67,500 is also used in the CCF method calculation. Since the after-tax stock equity income of $67,500 is a perpetuity, the value of the stock is the expected value of these incomes divided by the cost of levered equity.

$$S = \frac{\$67,500}{0.1421053} = \$475,000$$

The firm's value, V_L, is the sum of the values of the stock and the debt.

$$V_L = S + B$$
$$= \$475,000 + \$500,000 = \$975,000$$

The firm's value, V_L, can also be computed using equation (2.1). First calculate the firm's weighted average cost of capital, k_0, using equation (2.2).

$$k_0 = (475/975)(0.1421053) + (500/975)(1-0.35)(0.10)$$
$$= 0.0692308 + 0.0333333 = 0.1025641$$

The value of the levered firm is:

$$V_L = \frac{(1 - t_c)X}{k_0} = \frac{(1 - 0.35)\$153,846.15}{0.1025641} = \$975,000$$

This is the FCF method. The initial outlay required for the investment is $700,000. Of this, $500,000 is supplied by debt. The stockholders put in $200,000 and get benefits of $475,000 (present value), which is a $275,000 net present value. Adding the $500,000 debt to the $475,000 of stock, the levered firm's value is $975,000.

THE CCF CALCULATION: THE VALUE TO INVESTORS

The annual returns for debt and equity investors if there is $500,000 of 0.10 debt are:

Debt 500,000(0.10) = $50,000
Stock   = $67,500
Total   = $117,500

Using equation (2.5) we calculate the weighted average return required by investors, as follows: :

$$r^* = k_i \frac{B}{V_L} + k_e \frac{S}{V_L} = 0.10\left(\frac{500}{975}\right) + 0.1421053\left(\frac{475}{975}\right)$$

$$= 0.05128205 + 0.06923079 = 0.12051284$$

Using equation (6), the value of the total returns to all the investors using r^* is:

$$V_L = \frac{117,500}{0.12051284} = \$975,000$$

which is equal to the value of V_L previously computed using the free cash flow. Note that the 0.12051284 is r^* and does not reflect the tax shields of the financing method. The $117,500 of cash flows for all investors does incorporate the tax effects of the financing since they affect the calculation of $67,500 the income to stockholders.

ADJUSTED PRESENT VALUE

The cost of the stock equity capital if $500,000 debt is used has been assumed to be 0.1421053. With zero debt, the cost of equity is less than 0.1421053 because there is less risk for the stockholders than if there is debt outstanding. With zero debt the firm's cost of common stock is 0.125. Using the 0.125 cost of equity, the present value of the after-tax benefits ($100,000) of the before-tax cash flows ($153,846) is:

$$V_U = \frac{\$100,000}{0.125} = \$800,000$$

The $800,000 is the value of the equity with zero debt.

With $500,000 of debt the interest is $50,000. With a tax rate of 0.35, the tax saving of the $50,000 interest tax shield is $17,500 per year. If the risk of the tax savings is the same as the risk of the debt cash flows, then the tax saving has a present value of

$$\frac{\$17,500}{0.10} = \$175,000$$

using the 0.10 before-tax borrowing rate. Also, the tax savings are equal to $t_c B$ or 0.35($500,000) = $175,000.

The investment's adjusted present value is $975,000.

$$APV = \$800,000 + 175,000 = \$975,000$$

This is the same present value as we obtained with the previous calculations using the FCF and CCF methods.

Above, we assumed that, with zero debt (a capital structure of all stock equity), the cash flows should be discounted using 0.125. We know that the appropriate discount rate is larger than the debt rate of 0.10 and smaller than the stock cost of 0.1421053 with $500,000 of debt. If we use 0.125, the estimated value of the asset using APV is equal to the values using the FCF and CCF methods. The use of any other stock equity discount rate for the zero debt situation will result in a different present value.

EXAMPLE contd.

Consistent with the example assume the asset's present value, including the $175,000 value of the tax savings of the debt, is $975,000. The asset's value if financed entirely with stock equity must be $800,000. Since the after-tax benefits per year are equal to $100,000, the cost of equity with zero debt must be 0.125.

In general, the present value of the interest tax shields should be calculated using a discount rate appropriate for their risk. This example used the interest rate on the debt as the discount rate because the amount debt is a constant proportion of the project value and the project value is constant over time. If the project value varied over time and the proportion of debt to project value remained constant, then the discount rate for the unlevered equity cash flows would be appropriate for the interest tax shield.

COSTS OF FINANCIAL DISTRESS

How does a firm estimate the costs of financial distress? Consider the following several elements of financial distress:

1. inability to raise capital (thus the firm cannot undertake profitable investments);
2. the bankruptcy process (legal fees);
3. loss of customers;
4. loss of suppliers;
5. reduced ability to hire managerial (and other) talent.

All of the above are different depending on the situation. Thus it is more important to recognize that these costs exist and should be considered than to offer average estimates that will not apply to the next decision.

THE COSTS OF CAPITAL

Assume that an investor buys a specific portfolio consisting of $(1 - t_c)B$ of the debt and all the stock of a levered firm. The return from this specific portfolio of debt and stock should equal the return from investing in the equity of the unlevered firm. To see this, let $\tilde{X}$ be the actual earnings before interest and taxes to the equivalent unlevered firm (EBIT). The expected value of $\tilde{X}$ is $153,846, but the actual value in any particular year may be different. Because of the limited liability feature of common stock the value to the stockholders cannot be negative. The return to the stock of an unlevered firm used to value the firm will be $\tilde{X}(1 - t_c)$ if $\tilde{X} > 0$ and zero otherwise. For $\tilde{X}$ to be equal to the FCF, there can be no change in working capital.

29

Now consider the return to the specific portfolio of debt and equity of the levered firm. Three cases must be considered: $\tilde{X} \geq k_iB$, $k_iB > \tilde{X} \geq 0$ and $0 < \tilde{X}$. If $\tilde{X}$ is greater than or equal to k_iB, then the return to the specific portfolio will equal the return to all of the equity plus $(1 - t_c)$ of the return to the debt. Specifically, the return to the equity will be $(\tilde{X} - k_iB)(1 - t_c)$ and the return to the debt portion of the specific portfolio will be $(k_iB)(1 - t_c)$. The sum of these two components is $\tilde{X}(1 - t_c)$. In this case the payment to debtholders is equal to the amount promised them and the value of the portfolio (S plus $(1 - t_c)B$) is equal to the value of the unlevered firm.

If $\tilde{X}$ greater than equal to zero, but less than k_iB, then the return to the equity portion of the specific portfolio will be zero and all of the returns earned by the levered firm will go to the debt. However, the payment to the debtholders will be less than the amounts promised. To maintain the assumption that there is no year-to-year change in working capital, the shortfall in payments to debtors cannot create a short term liability. Therefore we must assume that the debt is an income bond such that debt payments are due only if earned. The specific portfolio will receive $(1 - t_c)$ of the total payment to the debt, which equals $\tilde{X}(1 - t_c)$. Thus the return to the specific portfolio in this case will be $\tilde{X}(1 - t_c)$ for any non-negative value of $\tilde{X}$. This is the same as the return to the equity of the unlevered firm.

Now consider the case in which $\tilde{X}$ is negative. There will be no return to either equity or debt. To maintain the assumption that there is no year-to-year change in working capital, there must be no tax-loss carryforward as well as no obligation to pay the missed interest payments. Thus in case three the return to stockholders of the unlevered firm and the return to the holder of the specific portfolio of the levered firm will be zero whenever $\tilde{X}$ is negative.

Under these conditions, the return to the stockholders of the unlevered firm is equal in every case to the return to the specific portfolio. The return in both cases is $\tilde{X}(1 - t_c)$ whenever $\tilde{X} \geq 0$ and zero whenever $\tilde{X} < 0$. Then the value of the specific portfolio, the sum of $(1 - t_c)B$ plus S, must in equilibrium be equal to V_u since the returns are equal. Thus the following equality must hold since the returns must be equal:

$$k_e(0) = k_i \frac{(1 - t_c)B}{V_u} + k_e \frac{S}{V_u} \tag{2.10}$$

For the above example using equation (2.10) we have

$$k_e(0) = 0.10 \frac{0.65(500,000)}{800,000} + 0.1421\left(\frac{475,000}{800,000}\right)$$

$$= 0.0406 + 0.0844 = 0.125$$

Thus the 0.125 value of the cost of equity with no debt is effectively defined by the 0.10 cost of $500,000 of debt and the 0.1421 cost of equity with debt. It is not an arbitrary number and it is not equal to the before-tax WACC as Ruback assumes in his classic (2002) paper. Given 0.125 we could also have computed k_e, the cost of equity with debt by re-arranging equation (2.10) to solve for k_e.

THE WACC WITH DEBT

Previously the WACC with debt was assumed to be 0.10256. The following relationship, which is derived from equations (2.2), (2.7), and (2.10) in the appendix to this chapter, can also be used to obtain the WACC with debt:

$$k_0 = k_e(0)\left(1 - t_c\frac{B}{V_L}\right) \qquad (2.11)$$

Note that the value of k_0 decreases as B increases. For the perpetuity example we have:

$$k_e(0) = 0.125$$
$$t_c = 0.35$$
$$B = \$500,000$$
$$V_L = \$975,000$$

Using equation (2.10) the value of the WACC with $500,000 of debt and the firm value of $975,000 is:

$$k_0 = 0.125\left(1 - 0.35\frac{500,000}{975,000}\right) = 0.10256$$

The WACC for the firm with $500,000 of debt can also be computed using the basic relationship of equation (2.2):

$$k_0 = (1 - t_c)k_i\frac{B}{V_L} + k_e\frac{S}{V_L} \qquad (2.2)$$

$$= (1 - 0.35)0.10\left(\frac{500}{975}\right) + 0.1421\left(\frac{475}{975}\right)$$

$$= 0.03333 + 0.06923 = 0.10256$$

The firm values and the costs of capital are all linked together with the values being determined by the values of the cost of equity with no debt, the cost of equity with

$500,000 of debt, the cost of debt and the expected cash flows generated by the project.

VALUATION: A SUMMARY

Above it was assumed that either the firm's earnings or cash flows can be used if the maintenance capital expenditures were exactly equal to the depreciation expense and there were no changes in required working capital. The cash flow measure implicitly assumed the maintenance capital expenditures had been deducted. We will continue these assumptions.

Let X be the expected earnings before interest and taxes and let the depreciation expense be equal to the maintenance capital expenditures. The corporate tax rate is t_c and the debt interest payment is I. The value of the stock is S, the value of the debt is B, the value of the unlevered firm is V_u and the value of the levered firm is V_L.

Three choices of amounts to be discounted are:

1	$X(1 - t_c)$	FCF. Interest expense, if any, is not subtracted.
2	$(X - I)(1 - t_c) + I$	CCF. I is the return to debt where $(I = k_i B)$ and $(X - I)(1 - t_c)$ is the return to stock equity.
3	$X(1 - t_c) + t_c I$	APV: There are two cash flow terms, FCF and the interest tax shield. Each term may have a different discount rate. These terms are the inputs to the APV calculation. The sum of the two terms is equal to the CCF. The sum of their PVs should be equal to the value of the levered firm.

In calculating the value of the FCF, interest expense, if any, is not subtracted before calculating income taxes, so that the tax shields from interest expense are excluded from the amount to be discounted.

While the second and third methods both reflect the tax shield of interest and they are equal mathematically, they differ in application. The second calculation, $(X - I)(1 - t_c) + I$ uses one discount rate (r^*) that does not reflect the interest tax shield. The third calculation $X(1 - t_c) + t_c I$ will use the cost of equity with zero debt, $k_e(0)$, to discount the Free Cash Flow component, $X(1 - t_c)$ and the cost of debt, k_i, to discount $t_c I$.

The five relevant discount rates for valuation are:

1    $k_e(0)$, the cost of equity with zero debt

2    $k_0 = (1 - t_c)k_i \dfrac{B}{V_L} + k_e \dfrac{S}{V_L}$ or   (2.2)

$$k_0 = k_e(0)\left[1 - t_c \frac{B}{V_L}\right], \text{ the WACC with } B \text{ debt} \qquad (2.11)$$

3   k_i the before-tax cost of debt.

4   $$k_e = k_e(0) + \frac{(1 - t_c)B}{S}[k_e(0) - k_i], \qquad (2.12)$$

the cost of equity with B debt outstanding. (This relationship follows from equations 2.7 and 2.10. The proof is in an appendix to this chapter.)

5   $r*$, the before-tax cost of capital, defined as

$$r* = k_i \frac{B}{V_L} + k_e \frac{S}{V_L} \qquad (2.5)$$

Alternatively, subtracting equation (2.2) from equation (2.5) and re-arranging we find an alternative expression for $r*$ which is computationally convenient.

$$r* = k_0 + \frac{t_c I}{V_L} \qquad (2.13)$$

It is necessary to match the discount rate with the amounts to be discounted, or the components of these amounts.

$X = \$200, t_c = 0.5, k_e(0) = 0.10$. If debt is issued in substitution for stock $B = \$600, k_i = 0.08, I = \$48$. The values of $k_e, k_0,$ and $r*$ will be computed below from this information.

WITH NO DEBT

With no debt and EBIT equal to X, the value of the unlevered firm is:

$$V_u = \frac{(1 - t_c)X}{k_e(0)} \qquad (2.8)$$

For the example:

$$V_u = \frac{(1 - 0.5)200}{0.10} = \$1,000$$

With no debt, the FCF equals the CCF and the WACC is equal to the cost of equity with no debt which is equal to the $r*$, the pre-tax cost of capital.

WITH $600 OF DEBT SUBSTITUTED FOR STOCK

With no costs of financial distress, no investor taxes, and constant perpetual leverage, the new firm value, using equation (2.7), is $1,300

EXAMPLE 2.2

with $600 of debt:

$$V_L = V_u + t_c B = 1,000 + 0.5(600) = \$1,300 \qquad (2.7)$$

The value of the equity in the levered firm is $S = \$1,300 - \$600 = \$700$. Using equation (2.12) we can now compute the cost of equity with $600 of debt as follows:

$$k_e = k_e(0) + \frac{(1 - t_c)B}{S}[k_e(0) - k_i]$$

$$= 0.10 + \frac{300}{700}[0.10 - 0.08] = 0.1085714 \qquad (2.12)$$

We can now use equation (2.2) to compute the firm's WACC.

$$k_0 = (1 - t_c)k_i\frac{B}{V_L} + k_e\frac{S}{V_L}$$

$$= (0.5)0.08 \frac{600}{1,300} + 0.1085714 \frac{700}{1,300}$$

$$= 0.0769231$$

As a consistency check, we can use equation (1) to verify the value of the levered firm:

$$V_L = \frac{X(1 - t_c)}{k_0} = \frac{200(1 - 0.5)}{0.0769231} = \$1,300$$

Note that the numerator is the after-tax earnings computed without reference to the amount of debt (it does not include the interest related tax savings). The WACC, k_0, reflects the tax savings of the interest.

WITH DEBT (USE OF APV)

An adjusted present value (APV) valuation with perpetuities using equation (9) is:

$$V_L = \frac{X(1 - t_c)}{k_e(0)} + \frac{t_c I}{k_i} = \frac{\$100}{0.10} + \frac{0.5(\$48)}{0.08} = \$1,000 + \$300 = \$1,300$$

The $X(1 - t_c)/k_e(0)$ is V_u, the $1,000 value assuming zero debt computed above. The value of the levered firm is again $1,300.

THE USE OF $r*$ (THE CCF METHOD)

The before-tax cost of capital $(r*)$ may be used to discount the total returns to all investors: The before-tax WACC $(r*)$ is by definition:

$$r* = k_i\frac{B}{V_L} + k_e\frac{S}{V_L} \qquad (2.5)$$

$$r* = 0.08\left(\frac{600}{1,300}\right) + 0.1085714\left(\frac{700}{1,300}\right)$$

$$r^* = \frac{48}{1,300} + \frac{76}{1,300} = \frac{124}{1,300} = 0.0953846$$

There are alternative but equivalent formulations for r^*. For example, two variations are:

$$r^* = k_0 + \frac{t_c I}{V_L} \qquad (2.13)$$

$$r^* = 0.0769231 + \frac{24}{1,300} = 0.0769231 + 0.0184615 = 0.0953846$$

$$r^* = k_0 \left[1 + \frac{t_c I}{(1 - t_c) X} \right] = 100 \left[1 + \frac{24}{100} \right]$$

$$= \frac{100}{1,300} \left(\frac{124}{100} \right) = \frac{124}{1,300} = 0.0953846$$

$$V_L = \frac{(X - I)(1 - t_c) + I}{r^*} \qquad (2.6)$$

$$V_L = \frac{(X - I)(1 - t_c) + I}{r^*} = \frac{76 + 48}{0.0953846} = \$1,300$$

or equivalently:

$$V_L = \frac{(1 - t_c)X + t_c I}{r^*} = \frac{(1 - 0.5)200 + 0.5(48)}{\dfrac{124}{1,300}} = \frac{124}{\dfrac{124}{1,300}} = \$1,300 \; (2.13)$$

CALCULATION OF DISCOUNT RATES

Above we assumed values of k_e, k_0, and r^*. Now assume we have $k_e(0) = 0.10$, $V_u = \$1,000$, $V_L = \$1,300$, $S = \$700$, $B = \$600$, and $k_i = 0.08$. The value of the cost of equity with debt (k_e) is:

$$k_e = k_e(0) + \frac{(1 - t_c)B}{S}[k_e(0) - k_i] \qquad (2.12)$$

$$k_e = 0.10 + \frac{300}{700}(0.10 - 0.08)$$

$$= 0.10 + \frac{6}{700} = \frac{76}{700} = \frac{0.76}{7}$$

The new WACC with debt is a weighted average of the cost of equity and the after-tax cost of debt.

$$k_0 = (1 - 0.5)0.08 \frac{600}{1,300} + \frac{0.76}{7} \left(\frac{700}{1,300} \right)$$

$$= \frac{24}{1,300} + \frac{76}{1,300} = \frac{100}{1,300} \qquad (2.2)$$

The WACC can also be computed starting with $k_e(0)$, the cost of equity with zero debt:

$$k_0 = k_e(0)\left[1 - \frac{t_cB}{V_L}\right]$$

$$= 0.10\left(1 - \frac{300}{1,300}\right) = \frac{100}{1,300} = 0.0769231 \qquad (2.11)$$

FINITE-LIVED ASSETS

Above we assumed a perpetuity and constant debt-equity ratio. With a finite-lived asset, it is more difficult to ensure that the valuation methods are being computed with the same implicit assumption regarding the capital structure through time. But with care, it can be done. If we assume that the costs of all the capital are determined by the firm's characteristics rather than the project's characteristics, it is easier to illustrate the equivalence, but more difficult to understand the underlying complexities.

The use of the firm's weighted average cost of capital remains a popular method of evaluating investments. It is intuitively appealing to define the firm's weighted average cost of capital as the hurdle rate that an investment with equivalent risk must overcome to be acceptable. Unfortunately, the exactness offered by the decision rule is an illusion. The firm's WACC can be used to give an impression of desirability, but should not be used as an absolute accept-or-reject device, unless it correctly reflects time value and risk for each period of the asset's life and the cash flow components all have the same risk.

GLOBAL BUSINESS ASPECTS

When business is conducted in a different currency than dollars, it is appropriate that the investment analysis be computed using the different currency (say, yen) as well as using dollars for a second calculation.

If yen is used for the investment analysis, then the discount rate being used must reflect the capital markets of the foreign country as well as the capital structure of the foreign operations.

Since the ultimate goal of any foreign investment is to increase the well being of the domestic investors, the final step of the investment analysis is to convert the expected terminal value from yen to dollars and compute the internal rate of return and NPV of the investment.

Since the above calculations must be done on an after tax basis, the decisions and tax implications must be correctly incorporated into the analysis.

CONCLUSIONS

Illustrated in this chapter are three primary methods of calculating present value. If the capital structure is kept constant, the FCF method gives a reliable measure of value if the WACC represents effectively both time value and risk of the project.

Both the CCF and APV methods are useful if the capital structure will not be constant. For the APV method, the after-tax benefits without tax shields of financing are discounted using the cost of equity (assuming zero debt) and to this value of the unlevered firm are added the present value of the tax savings associated with the debt type of financing that is being used. This latter calculation is simplified to t_cB if the amount of debt is constant and will be outstanding for perpetuity.

Normally, one project or even a set of projects does not affect the firm's capital structure targets and it is reasonable to use NPV (FCF method) with an assumption of a constant capital structure.

We have illustrated the valuation of a firm (or a project) using three different flows being discounted using different discount rates. We have omitted three complexities. One is the situation with a finite life. Secondly, we have not illustrated the situation with changing amounts of leverage. Both of these complexities can be solved but the solutions are complex and do not provide additional basic insights.

The third complexity that we have omitted in this chapter is the consideration of the costs of financial distress arising because of capital structure. As debt is substituted for stock the likelihood of a firm incurring costs from bankruptcy and operational disruptions increases. Estimation of these costs is difficult since the values are highly subjective.

In this chapter, we have omitted the valuation method using residual incomes (economic incomes) that will be covered in Chapter 13. The infinite life eliminates the depreciation deduction and end of life complexities. The economic income calculation is better illustrated with the asset having a finite life (or a terminal value).

All of the calculations assumed that the benefits, X, can be estimated. In this chapter, we assumed zero growth. When we apply the formulations of this chapter to the valuation of a firm or a project, the determination of X and its growth rate are two important stumbling blocks.

PROBLEMS

1 Assume a firm's cost of capital with zero debt is 0.15 and the cost of debt is 0.08. The value of the unlevered firm is

$$V_u = \frac{\$150,000}{0.15} = \$1,000,000$$

where $150,000 is the expected after-tax earnings, with zero debt. If $500,000 of debt is substituted for stock, determine the value of firm (no costs of financial distress and no investor taxes). The corporate tax rate is 0.35.

2 (*Continue 1*) Determine the value of the outstanding stock, after the debt issuance.

3 (*Continue 1*) Determine the cost of equity, after the debt issuance.

4 (*Continue 1*) Determine the weighted average cost of capital (WACC) with the debt.

5 (*Continue 1*) Compute the firm's present value using the FCF method.

6 (*Continue 1*) Compute the firm's present value using APV method.

7 (*Continue 1*) If $230,769 is the firm's expected EBIT, what annual returns will the firm's investors earn?

8 (*Continue 1*) What is the firm's before-tax cost of capital? Assume the cost of equity is 0.183704.

9 (*Continue 1*) Assume the total return to all investors is $164,000. Determine the firm's value.

10 (*Continue 1*) Assume the firm's EBIT is $300,000 and with the firm having zero debt the stockholder earns

$$300,000(1 - 0.35) = \$195,000$$

Now assume the firm has $500,000 of 0.08 debt and the investor buys

$$(1 - 0.35)\,500,000 = \$325,000 \text{ of debt and}$$
$$\$675,000 \text{ of stock}$$

If the firm's EBIT is $300,000, what dollar return does the investor earn? Compare your answer to $195,000 computed above.

11 Assume a 0.35 corporate tax rate.

   a. If the firm is unlevered, and the value of EBIT is $200,000, the investor will earn $_____ per year.

   b. Now assume the firm has $500,000 of 0.10 debt and $475,000 of equity, and the investor buys $(1 - t)B = \$325,000$ of debt and $475,000 of stock. Again assume EBIT = $200,000, the investor will earn $_____ per year.

   c. What are your conclusions?

DISCUSSION QUESTION

Equation (2.11) implies that as more debt is substituted for stock the value of the weighted average cost of capital will decrease. Do you agree?

BIBLIOGRAPHY

Brealey, R. and S. Myers, *Principles of Corporate Finance*, 6th edn, New York: McGraw-Hill Book Company, 2000.

Copeland, T. E. and J. F. Weston, *Financial Theory and Corporate Policy*, 3rd edn, Reading, MA: Addison-Wesley, 1988.

Fama, E. F. and M. H. Miller, *The Theory of Finance*, New York: Holt, Rinehart, and Winston, 1972.

Fernandez, Pablo, *Valuation Methods and Shareholder Value Creation*, Academic Press, 2002.

Fernandez, Pablo, "The Value of Tax Shields Is NOT Equal to the Present Value of Tax Shields," *Journal of Financial Economics*, 73, 1, 2004, pp. 145–65.

Inselbag, I. and H. Kaufold, "Two DCF Approaches for Valuing Companies under Alternative Financing Strategies and How to Choose Between Them," *Journal of Applied Corporate Finance*, 10, 1997, pp. 114–22.

Luehrman, T. A., "Using APV: A Better Tool for Valuing Operations," *Harvard Business Review*, 75, 1997, pp. 145–54.

Ross, S. A., R. W. Westerfield, and J. Jaffe, *Corporate Finance*, 4th edn, Chicago: Irwin, 1996.

Ruback, R. S., "Capital Cash Flows: A Simple Approach to Valuing Risky Cash Flows," *Financial Management*, summer 2002, pp. 85–103.

Van Horne, James C., *Financial Management and Policy*, 12th edn, Englewood Cliffs, NJ: Prentice-Hall, 2002.

Wonder, N., "Comment on the Value of Tax Shields is *Not* Equal to the Present Value of Tax Shields," *Quarterly Review of Economics and Finance*, 45, 2005, pp. 184–7.

APPENDIX DERIVATIONS

Equation (2.11)

Equation (2.11) can be derived from equations (2.2), (2.7), and (2.10) as follows.

Multiplying both sides of equation (2.2) by V_L gives:

$$k_0 V_L = (1 - t_c)k_i B + k_e S \tag{a}$$

Multiplying both sides of equation (2.10) by V_U gives

$$k_e(0)V_U = (1 - t_c)k_i B + k_e S \tag{b}$$

Since the right hand sides of equations (a) and (b) are equal, it follows that

$$k_0 V_L = k_e(0)V_U \tag{c}$$

Re-arranging equation (2.7) gives:

$$V_U = V_L - t_c B \tag{d}$$

Substituting the right hand side of equation (d) for V_U in equation (c) gives:

$$k_0 V_L = k_e(0)(V_L - t_c B)$$

Dividing both sides of the above by V_L gives equation (2.11)

$$k_0 = k_e(0)\left(1 - \frac{t_c B}{V_L}\right) \tag{2.11}$$

Equation (2.12)

Equation (2.12) can be derived from equations (2.2a), (2.7), and (2.10) as follows:

$$k_e(0) = k_i \frac{(1 - t_c)B}{V_U} + k_e \frac{S}{V_U} \tag{2.10}$$

Multiplying both sides of equation (2.10) by V_U and re-arranging gives

$$k_e S = k_e(0)V_U - (1 - t_c)k_i B \tag{e}$$

Equation (2.2a) states that $V_L = S + B$. Substitute the right hand side of equation (2.2a) for V_L in equation (d) and re-arrange to give the following:

$$V_U = S + (1 - t_c)B \tag{f}$$

Now substitute the right hand side of (f) for V_U in equation (e) and re-arrange.

$$k_e S = k_e(0)(S + (1 - t_c)B) - (1 - t_c)k_i B$$
$$= k_e(0)S + k_e(0)(1 - t_c)B - k_i(1 - t_c)B$$
$$= k_e(0)S + (1 - t_c)B(k_e(0) - k_i)$$

Dividing both sides of the above equation by S gives equation (2.12).

$$k_e = k_e(0) + (1 - t_c)\frac{B}{S}(k_e(0) - k_i) \tag{2.12}$$

Part II

Capital budgeting and valuation under uncertainty

Anyone who goes to a psychiatrist should have his head examined.
(Samuel Goldwyn, quoted by Anita Gates,
New York Times, October 6, 2001)

Once we introduce uncertainty the use of $(1 + r)^{-n}$ to compute present values, with the same r for all n, is limited to very well defined situations. With uncertainty, it is necessary to be concerned with the amount of risk aversion, the value of having alternatives (real options), the manner in which uncertainty affects the expected value through time, and the risk characteristics of each component of the cash flow stream. While each of these aspects is complex, an understanding is necessary if investment opportunities are to be reasonably evaluated.

Understand that not all the models illustrated in these chapters can be readily applied to practical business situations to obtain exact answers. However, they can be used to gain a better understanding of the elements of investment decisions.

Chapter 3

Capital budgeting with uncertainty

You see, Lewis, being so sure of my ground and my star so early in life, I was soon forced to choose between honest arrogance and a hypocritical humility. Well, the world knows I chose honest arrogance.

(Frank Lloyd Wright in a letter to Lewis Mumford)

We want to be able to make sensible investment decisions when there is uncertainty. The first step is to summarize the relevant measures of value and risk of the cash flows of an investment or a portfolio of investments. We next need to understand that the investors have attitudes toward risk and that this affects the amount of expected rewards they need to undertake a risky investment. Finally, we need to understand the interaction of time and risk and the fact that with uncertainty there are difficulties. If a firm justifies the undertaking or rejection of uncertain investments with a single summary measure of value (such as net present value or internal rate of return or payback or return on investment), that firm is likely to make errors. There is no single measure that allows us to make investment decisions with confidence if there are uncertainties. There are difficulties (measurement difficulties as well as theoretical difficulties) with all measures.

TREE DIAGRAMS

In Table 3.1, an uncertain investment is described by listing all the possible scenarios, the probability of each scenario, and the sequence of cash flows that would occur if the investment were accepted and that scenario occurred. In this example, there are six possible scenarios, and cash flows can occur at only three different times, so the complete description is manageable.

Table 3.1 An investment with uncertainty

Scenario	Probability of scenario	Cash flows in period		
		0	1	2
a	0.3	−$200	$110	$0
b	0.1	−200	110	121
c	0.1	−200	165	121
d	0.2	−100	55	60.5
e	0.1	−100	55	121
f	0.2	−100	110	242

A common and very useful means of describing the information contained in Table 3.1 is a tree diagram. Tree diagrams can be used to summarize the interrelationships between sequences of events. The tree diagram in Figure 3.1a shows the two possible events at time 0, an outlay of $100 or of $200. Each event has a probability of 0.5. The probabilities can be determined by summing the probabilities of the corresponding rows in Table 3.1. In the tree diagram each event is depicted by a branch that ends above the point on the time line at which the event will be observable. The cash flow corresponding to the event is shown below the branch near its end, and the probability that the event will occur is shown above the branch near its end. The probabilities of all branches originating from a common point must sum to 1.

In Figure 3.1b events that might be observable at time 1 have been added to the tree diagram in Figure 3.1a. All the events that are possible from a given starting point are shown as branches radiating from that starting point. Near the end of each branch, the cash flows that would occur are shown below the branch, and above the branch is the probability of the branch, given its starting point at the left-hand end of the branch. These are called conditional probabilities, since they give the probability of the branch given that the event depicted at the left end of the branch has occurred.

In Figure 3.1c the tree diagram is completed by adding the events that could occur at time 2. Tree diagram 3.1c and Table 3.1 contain identical information about the investment.

A limb in the tree diagram consists of a sequence of branches starting at the extreme left of the diagram and ending up at the extreme right. Each limb corresponds to a particular sequence of events, one at each point in time. Such a sequence of events is referred to as a *state of nature* or a *scenario*. To determine the probability of a scenario at the end of each path, multiply the probabilities of the corresponding branches. The circles at the beginning of each split in the branches indicates that a stochastic event (an outcome subject to a probability distribution) follows. The pluses at the right end of the trees in Figures 3.1a and 3.1b indicate that the tree does not end at that point in time. The probabilities shown at the end of the branches in Figure 3.1c are the probabilities of the corresponding scenarios.

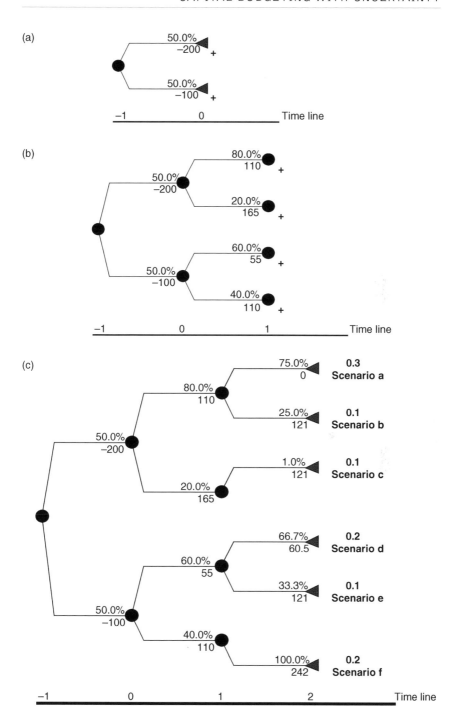

Figure 3.1 *Tree diagrams*

In this simplified example, in which there are only three periods and six scenarios, it is possible to depict all the possible scenarios. In practice with a real investment it may not be possible to depict on one page every possible scenario. Suppose that cash flows occur at 10 different times and that for each event for time $t - 1$ there are 10 different outcomes that can occur at each time t. Then a total of 10 billion different scenarios is necessary to describe completely an investment. Clearly, a method of summarizing the possible scenarios is necessary. The next sections of the chapter briefly introduce some strategies that have been used to summarize the possible scenarios associated with an uncertain investment.

PERIOD-BY-PERIOD SUMMARIES

A common approach for summarizing the cash flows associated with an uncertain investment is to write down a single number for each time period to represent the cash flow that it is "estimated" will be associated with the investment. Many investment decisions are based on the present value of these estimated cash flows.

An important type of estimated cash flow is the expected value which is a probability weighted average of all possible cash flows. Occasionally the single set of estimated cash flows may be supplemented by other possible scenarios that could occur. An example of this type of presentation is contained in lines 2 and 3 of Table 3.2. The first line is the "best" estimate of cash flows. The terms used in Table 3.2 do not have exact statistical interpretations.

The estimated cash flows are ordinarily accompanied by a table that gives one or more summary measures of investment worth based on the best estimate of cash flows, as illustrated in Table 3.3.

SENSITIVITY ANALYSIS

The summary measures included in Table 3.3 may be estimates that are conditional on certain assumptions. For example, the net present value calculation assumes a discount rate of 10 percent. All of the measures calculated assume that the life of the investment will be two years and that the initial outlay will be $150. The purpose of a sensitivity analysis is to determine how varying the assumptions will affect the measures of investment worth. Ordinarily the assumptions are varied one at a time. The results of the type of analysis are illustrated in Table 3.4. In the first panel of the table (A), the estimated cash flows are held constant, but the rate of discount used is varied (as when there is a difference of opinion as to what rate should be used). Note that the net present value is positive for the four rates used.

Table 3.2 *Period-by-period summary of the cash flow of an uncertain investment*

Line	Item	Periods		
		0	1	2
1	Best estimate of cash flows	−$150	$100	$100
2	Optimistic cash flow for each period	−100	165	242
3	Pessimistic cash flow for each period	−200	55	0

Table 3.3 *Summary measures of the worth of an uncertain investment, based on best estimate of cash flows*

Measure	Value
Net present value at 10%	$23.55
Internal rate of return	21.5%
Payback	1.5 years
Return on average investment	33.3%

Table 3.4 *Sensitivity analysis*

Assumption varied	Assumed level of variable	Net present value
A Discount rate	20%	$2.78
	15	12.57
	10	23.55
	5	35.94
B Estimated annual proceeds	$120	58.26
(initial outlay is $150 and a	100	23.55
0.10 discount rate)	80	−11.16
C Initial outlay	$200	−26.45
(annual proceeds are $100	150	23.55
and a 0.10 discount rate)	100	73.55

In the second panel (B), the discount rate is assumed to be 10 percent, and the initial outlay is assumed to be $150; holding these assumptions constant, the effect of changing the assumed level of the estimated constant annual proceeds is determined. In the third panel of the table (C), the effect of changing the level of the initial outlay is illustrated if the discount rate is 10 percent and annual proceeds are $100 per period.

47

SIMULATION

Simulation, sometimes called risk analysis, is intended to give the managers a better feel for the possible scenarios that can occur, so that they can use their judgment and experience with regard to whether or not the investment is acceptable. In practice, the possible scenarios are so numerous that listing all of them is not feasible, even with the help of a large-scale computer. Therefore, the analysis may be based on a sample of the possible scenarios. This approach is called simulation. If the process involves choosing scenarios randomly, the process is sometimes called the Monte Carlo method.

The steps involved in producing a risk analysis for a particular investment can be briefly summarized as follows. First, one or more measures of investment worth are selected, for example, net present value at 10 percent, net present value at 20 percent, breakeven time and internal rate of return. Second, a computer program is used to select a random sample from the population of all possible scenarios in such a way that the probability of a scenario being included in the sample is proportional to the probability of the scenario occurring. For example, if one were analyzing the investment previously referred to which had 10 billion possible scenarios, one might select a sample of 10,000 scenarios. For each scenario selected the probability of the scenario, the time sequence of cash flows for that scenario and the values of each of the selected measures of investment are calculated and saved in the computer. Third, for each selected measure of investment worth, the computer program would calculate and display a description of the corresponding sample values. For example, the computer program could calculate and display the probability weighted sample average and standard deviation, the maximum, minimum and median values, the 5th and 95th percentiles, and the inner quartiles. In addition it could draw a graph of the frequency distribution of each of the measures. This approach is called risk analysis. While carrying out such an analysis would be a daunting task if it were necessary to write a special computer program for the purpose, there are commercial programs that are specifically designed to facilitate risk analysis. With these programs, risk analysis is feasible even for complex projects.[1]

Assume that the scenarios for one investment project has been simulated a large number of times (say, 100,000). For 30,000 trials scenario A occurred. Table 3.5 assigns a 0.3 probability to scenario A. Table 3.5 gives the net present value, using a 10 percent discount rate, for each state of nature A to F. This table is consistent with the hypothetical investment of Table 3.1. Table 3.6 illustrates some of the ways a set of net present values could be summarized for management using the information of Table 3.5.

Monte Carlo is a process that generates scenarios using a computer and a probabilistic simulation model. Decisions are made by analyzing a sample of scenarios that have occurred only in a simulation.

---

1 Two of the best known programs are @*Risk* and *Crystal Ball*.

Table 3.5 Frequency distribution of net present values of an uncertain investment

Possible status of nature	Probability of state	Net present value at 10%
a	0.3	−$100
b	0.1	0
c	0.1	50
d	0.2	0
e	0.1	50
f	0.2	200

Table 3.6 Risk analyses of an uncertain investment based on net present value using a 10% discount rate

Expected net present value	$20
Modal net present value	−100
Maximum (with probability 0.2)	200
Minimum (with probability 0.3)	−100
Probability of zero or less	0.6
Probability of $200 or more	0.2

Assume a firm is considering introducing a new product. There is uncertainty regarding the size of the total market for the product; the market share the firm can obtain; the cost of producing the product; the selling price; and the life of the product.

While a decision could be made based on the expected values of all the above uncertain elements, management might be interested in the possible outcomes and their probabilities. For example, what is the probability that the NPV will turn out to be negative? Assume a 0.10 discount rate.

The first step is to assign a probability distribution to each uncertain element.

The second step to conduct a Monte Carlo simulation. For example, we might obtain a scenario characterized by the following values:

Size of total market	1,000,000 units per year
Firm's share (20%)	200,000 units per year
Selling price	$30
Cost (incremental) net	16
	$14
Annual proceeds	$2,800,000
Life of product	8 years
Cost of equipment	$10,000,000

The NPV of this scenario is:

$$NPV = -10,000,000 + 2,800,000 \, (5.3349)$$

where 5.3349 is the present value of an annuity for eight years using a 0.10 discount rate.

$$NPV = -10,000,000 + 14,900,000 = \$4,900,000$$

The simulation process is repeated and the following distribution of NPVs is obtained for 10,000 scenarios:

	Number of trials	Proportion
NPVs positive	9,145	91.45
NPVs negative	855	8.55

The managers would also like information regarding the dollar amounts of NPV. The final decision will be a judgment call on the part of management.

With any decision where there is uncertainty and a desire on the part of management to have more information than that supplied by computing an expected value, Monte Carlo is a useful tool.

RISK PREFERENCES

Some people like risk; others are risk neutral (they buy risky bonds and stocks but think the expected value is positive).[2] But most persons are risk averse; they require higher expected returns to accept risky investments.

Attitudes toward risk are an important factor that must be taken into account when considering investment opportunities that are subject to uncertainty. Suppose that a potential investor has $50,000 of cash. The investor considers that the probability is one that the assets held in a riskless investment account for one year will be worth $55,000 one year from now. There is a second investment opportunity that would require an immediate outlay of $50,000 and would return either $0 (with probability 0.2) or $100,000 (with probability 0.8) one year from now. If this opportunity is accepted, the expected cash flow one year from now will be $80,000 (that is, 0.2 × 0 + 0.8 × $100,000). The rate of return on the expected cash flows of this one-year investment will be 60 percent. This is an attractive expected rate of

---

2 People who gamble at race tracks and the casinos in Atlantic City despite negative expected values are not necessarily risk loving in the sense that is relevant to capital budgeting. Most recreational gamblers enjoy the excitement and control their bets so that they do not lose too much. They look upon the expectation of a small loss as a fair price to pay for the entertainment of gambling.

return by ordinary standards. However, we cannot use the expected rate of return to decide the acceptability of this investment for this potential investor. It is necessary to establish attitudes toward risk before we can decide whether the investor should accept or reject the investment if it must be financed with the investor's own funds.

One may be tempted to say that a reasonable way to make the decision is to compare the certain cash flow of $55,000 that would be realized if the investor kept the money in a savings account with the average or expected cash flow of $80,000 from accepting the risky investment. The difficulty with this approach is that it buries the fact that at the end of the year, the investor will have either $0 or $100,000 if the risky investment is chosen while the investor will certainly have $55,000 if the safe investment is chosen. The question that the potential investor cannot avoid is whether the dissatisfactions associated with the 0.2 possibility of having $0 next year, when a safe investment would lead to a sure $55,000, outweigh the satisfactions associated with the 0.8 possibility of having $100,000. Figure 3.2 shows the decision tree for the two choices.

The ability to make a decision under uncertainty depends on such comparisons and requires knowledge of attitudes toward risk. Different investors might answer questions regarding the acceptance of risk differently, in which case we shall say that they have different risk preferences. And the same investor may have different risk preferences at different stages of life or under different circumstances. Other investments already undertaken, the investor's state of health, the number of persons dependent on the outcome, the size of the investment relative to the investor's total wealth, and the chances of being unemployed next year are factors that one must take into account in making the decision.

A utility function can be used to describe an investor's risk preferences. Just as subjective probabilities can be used to describe a person's attitude about the likelihood that some scenario will occur, so a utility function describes risk preferences. A utility function assigns a number to each possible scenario of an uncertain investment. The expected utility of the investment is the expected value of the utility function calculated over all possible scenarios of the investment.

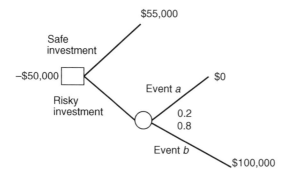

Figure 3.2 *Two choices and two outcomes*

The expected utility of an investment can be interpreted as an index of the relative attractiveness of that investment to the individual whose utility function is used. If the utility function of an individual accurately describes the individual's attitudes towards risk, then in choosing between mutually exclusive investments, the individual will tend to pick the investment alternative that has the highest expected utility. If the individual is risk averse, the alternative with the highest expected net present value will not necessarily be the alternative with the highest expected utility.

No matter how large the firm, there is some investment opportunity that it would not want to consider on a straight expected monetary value basis. The analysis of risk (i.e., incorporating the consequences of the scenarios) would be performed by a utility analysis or by some other means, but it must be recognized that we cannot expect one number, such as the internal rate of return of the expected cash flows or the expected net present value, to be the sole basis of an investment decision. It is necessary to consider the probabilities of all scenarios.

For giant corporations it is sometimes difficult to imagine an investment that we could not judge on a straight expected monetary value basis. But even for such corporations, there are investments (or classes of investments) of such magnitude that they give rise to the likelihood of events that could be disastrous to the firm. Boeing faced such a decision when it was deciding whether or not to develop an airliner that was significantly larger than its 747. Incorporating attitudes toward risk into the analysis, rather than just using the maximization of wealth (or the expected monetary value criterion), can be done by the use of a utility analysis. Assume that an investment has the characteristic of resulting in a doubling of the firm's income or reducing the firm's value to approximately zero. Should this type of investment decision be made on an expected monetary value basis?

The expected value decision criterion may at times be consistent with the wealth maximization objective, but several things should be noted. The consistency holds true only in the long run and assuming that we can repeat the trial many times. We are dealing with averages, and there is a very low or zero probability that the average event will actually occur on any trial. In some cases, following the expected monetary value criterion will lead to bankruptcy (i.e., ruin) and end of the "game." Where the possibility of this unhappy event is present, it is reasonable that this should affect the firm's decision process. The objective "maximize the expected wealth" ignores the fact that this is a maximization of an average amount. This is not a sufficient description of the objectives of the investor. The maximization goal is reasonable but the things being maximized should not be expected monetary values; rather it should be expected value with risk being considered.

CERTAINTY EQUIVALENTS

We can use certainty equivalents to take risk into consideration. This method uses a certainty equivalent of the cash flows of period t, CE_t rather than the expected value of the cash flow, $\overline{C}_t$, where CE_t is defined as the risk-adjusted equivalent of $\overline{C}_t$. The decision can be formulated in present value terms by using a "default-free" rate in the discounting process. Using this method, we would then calculate the net present value of the certainty equivalents,

$$P = \sum_{t=0}^{n} \frac{CE_t}{(1 + r_f)^t} \tag{3.1}$$

where, r_f is a default-free interest rate and n is the economic life of the project. The project would be deemed acceptable if P is positive.

The determination of certainty equivalents for a corporation, even for one-period investments, would not be easy. It would be necessary to determine the appropriate utility functions, and it is not clear that we know how to determine a corporation's utility function. In practice, the certainty equivalent approach is difficult to implement for most capital budgeting decisions. But the certainty equivalent approach underlies the popular methods used to analyze financial options.

It is possible to express the value of an asset by discounting its expected cash flows at a risk adjusted discount rate or by discounting the certainty equivalents of its expected cash flows using default free discount rates. Both approaches should produce the same value. Chapter 4 expands on the subject of certainty equivalents.

TIME AND RISK

A satisfactory definition of a discount rate to be used for time discounting would be helpful in guiding the internal investment policy of corporate management. The choice of investments frequently represents a strategic decision for the management of a firm, since in large part the choices made now will influence the future course of the firm's development. It is not surprising to find that implicit in any definition of a discount rate to guide investment policy is a judgment of the goals toward which the firm is or should be striving. The goals help to determine the appropriate definition of capital cost.

There are wide-ranging disagreements about the choice of the rate of discount to be used to evaluate investments. It is sometimes argued that the weighted average cost of capital of a firm may be used to evaluate investments whose cash flows are perfectly correlated with the cash flows from the firm's present assets. With perfect correlation between the cash flows of two investments, the risk is the same. But if the timing of the cash flows is not also the same, then the same discount rate cannot be used for both investments. This will be explained in the following paragraphs.

In choosing an appropriate discount rate three factors need to be considered. One factor is the nature of the uncertainty about the cash flows and how this may diminish their value because of the risk aversion of investors. A second factor is when the uncertainty about the cash flows is resolved. A third factor is the time period when the cash flows are received. The uncertainty about the cash flows may not be resolved until just before the cash is received. Alternatively, the uncertainty may be resolved in advance (either suddenly or gradually through time). All three of the above factors need to be considered in deciding what discount rate to use to discount the expected cash flows.

RISK ADJUSTED DISCOUNT RATES

In capital budgeting practice, a commonly used criterion for making accept or reject decisions is to compare the internal rate of return for an investment with the firm's weighted average cost of capital (WACC). The WACC represents the required rate of return for the firm as whole, and as its name suggests, it is an average. Those who advocate this procedure recommend accepting an investment if the internal rate of return of its expected cash flows exceeds or is equal to the firm's cost of capital. A more acceptable variation of this rule is to accept an investment if the internal rate of return of its expected cash flows exceeds the risk-adjusted discount rate appropriate for that specific investment.

Figure 3.3 illustrates a firm or an asset with a WACC of 0.15. Risk is measured on the X axis. The beta of an asset is one method of measuring risk. Other possibilities would be to use the standard deviation or variance of the distribution of net present values.

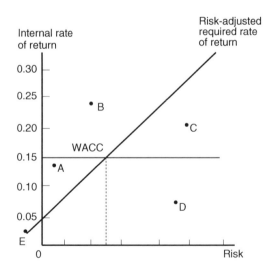

Figure 3.3 *Risk-adjusted required rate of return*

Figure 3.3 shows both the WACC and the risk-adjusted required-return lines. The two lines imply different investment criteria; in each case, the line is the boundary between the accept region (above the line) and the reject region (below the line).

For investments B and D, both criteria lead to the same decisions. For investments A, C, and E, contradictory recommendations would result. Investments A and E would be rejected by the WACC criterion but would be acceptable using the risk-adjusted discount rate approach, even though E yields less than the default-free return. Investment C would be accepted using the WACC but rejected using the risk-adjusted discount rate approach.

Figure 3.3 illustrates one important limitation of using a firm's WACC to evaluate investments. It would not take into account variations in the riskiness of different projects. The one-rate approach tends to reject some low-risk projects, like A and E, whose expected rates of return are less than the one-rate WACC but are large enough to compensate for the specific risk of the project.

The above discussion assumes that all of the cash flows from a project are equally risky. But most projects consist of a mixture of cash flows with different risks. To take this into account the present value of each cash flow component should be calculated using a discount rate appropriate for its risk. The present values of all of the cash flow components should be summed and projects should be selected using the present value criterion applied to the total present value of the project. This situation is considered in Chapter 8.

THE REQUIRED RETURN

A large chemical corporation has done very well for ten years. The average ROI earned during that time period was 0.25. Now, the CEO wants to use 0.25 as the hurdle rate for future investment projects. The firm's management has concluded that the firm's cost of capital is 0.10.

The 0.25 is not relevant in determining the cut-off for investments being considered. For example, if the firm had earned a zero ROI for ten years, it would not want to use a zero cut-off rate when it had a capital cost of 0.10.

DEFAULT-FREE RATE OF DISCOUNT

Many discount rates may be suggested for use in making investments decisions. The following are the two possibilities we shall consider in this section: (1) interest rate of US government securities and (2) interest rate of long-term bonds of the firm. The discussion in this section assumes that the debt has a fixed interest rate that is specified when the debt is issued and would require some modification for floating rate securities.

The term risk-free might be used to describe the US government interest rate. This is suggestive, but not strictly accurate. There are risks that cannot in practice be eliminated and that affect all interest-bearing securities to a greater or lesser extent. The interest rates we have in mind are those at which investors can lend money with no significant danger of default or at which they can borrow if their collateral is so good that their creditors feel that there is a negligible chance of default.

Even if the risk of default is practically negligible, there are other risks inherent in fixed money debt instruments as long as there is uncertainty about the future changes that might take place in the economy. One source of risk arises because of uncertainty about future real interest rates. Another source of risk occurs because of uncertainty about the future price level. Expectations about possible future price levels influence the market determination of interest rates. Domestic lenders will tend to be hurt if the price level rises; hence, they require a higher interest return with an expected price-level increase than with an expected price-level decrease, or with expected constant prices. Foreign lenders of US dollar denominated debt will be concerned about possible future decreases in the market price of the US dollar relative to the value of other currencies.

Another source of risk arises because of the possibility of changes in the level and structure of interest rates. Normally, the interest rate on bonds will vary with the number of years to maturity even when there is no risk of default. Bonds that mature in a few years will tend to have lower yields than bonds that mature in the more distant future. This is partially due to uncertainty about future re-investment rates, as described in the next paragraph. It may also reflect a liquidity price premium to short maturity bonds, since the transaction costs associated with buying or selling short term bonds are generally less than with long term bonds.

If there is no risk of default, the lender can always be sure of earning the current yield by buying a bond of given maturity and holding it until it matures. The possibility exists, however, that some other strategy would result in earning a high yield. If investors want to lend money for a 5-year period and expect a decline in interest rates, they may be able to earn a higher yield by buying a 15- or 20-year bond and selling it after 5 years than by buying a 5-year bond and holding it to maturity. When this former strategy is followed, however, there is no longer any guarantee that a certain minimum rate of interest will actually be earned.

The interest rates on US government debt constitute a reasonable choice of discount rates representing default-free lending opportunities. These rates represent actual market opportunities at which firms or individuals could lend money with essentially no risk of default. If a default-free rate is used to discount the certainty equivalents of the future cash flows, the resulting present value should be a good estimate of the current market value of the asset or investment opportunity. However if the default-free rate is used to discount the expected future cash flows, then it would then be necessary to subtract from the net present value a dollar amount for the asset's risk.

THE BORROWING RATE

Neither private corporations nor individuals can actually borrow money at default-free rates. The rates at which a corporation could actually borrow for a given term would be higher than the rates at which the government can borrow for loans of the same maturity.

The after-tax borrowing rate of a firm sets a minimum return target for an investment with certain cash flows. A firm would not want to borrow at 0.07 after tax, for the purpose of earning a certain 0.06 return. However, firms can and do rationally borrow money long term with the intention of holding it as cash (or cash equivalents). In this situation, the cost of borrowing long term is usually greater than the interest that will be earned while the cash is invested in short term liquid securities. However, the increased liquidity that results from borrowing long-term and investing the proceeds in short term securities may have a value exceeding the interest paid. It can allow the firm to quickly take advantage of attractive investment opportunities, or to reduce the costs of financial distress when unexpected difficulties occur.

Using the after-tax borrowing rate as a discount rate applied to the uncertain cash flows from an asset would give a net present value that did not reflect the risk of the asset; thus further adjustments for risk by subtracting a dollar risk premium would be necessary.

CHANGING THE UNCERTAINTY

It is possible for a company to follow courses of action that will decrease to some extent the degree of uncertainty connected with its operations. Increasing the information obtained prior to making a decision is one method of decreasing uncertainty. For example, thorough market research may make the outcome of a new product investment much less uncertain than if the product were launched without the market research.

Another method of changing uncertainty in some situations is by increasing the scale of operations. A large oil company faces less risk of 100 percent dry wells when it drills 50 oil wells than does a small group of investors banded together to drill one well.

Product diversification may also decrease a firm's uncertainty. A combined gas and electric company servicing a metropolitan city would have less uncertainty a than would a company specializing in either the electric or gas business. If major users switch from electricity to gas, the fortunes of the specialized companies will be drastically affected, whereas if there were only one company there would be less of a change in the company's profits. A combined grocery and machine equipment company would have less uncertainty as a result of changes in equipment technology than would a specialized machine equipment manufacturer. Risk can also be modified by the judicious use of derivatives, but the use of derivatives as speculations can also increase risk.

GLOBAL BUSINESS ASPECTS

It is important to understand the risk consequences of investing on an international basis.

There are two levels of risk that we will consider. First are the risks of the individual project, including the country's political and economic risk. Thus the investing firm can determine the nature of the project's risks.

But even more important is the second type of risk analysis. What does undertaking this foreign investment do to the firm's overall risk? How is the foreign investment correlated with the outcomes of the firm's domestic assets?

When Anheuser–Busch considered investing in a beer company in China, it was recognized that this was a very risky undertaking. But the correlation of the outcomes was essentially independent of A–B's domestic operations, thus there was no need to increase the discount rate used to evaluate the investment for the special risks associated with investing in a non-capitalistic non-democratic country with a different legal system.

CONCLUSIONS

Risk means different things to different people. The desirability of a risky investment for an individual decision-maker depends heavily on the preferences of that decision-maker. For example, if the amount of possible loss is small relative to the wealth position of the investor, the decision may be based purely on expected present value. For relatively large possible losses, risk aversion may lead to rejecting an investment despite a positive expected net present value. All shortcut methods of risk adjustment in which expected cash flows are reduced to "certainty equivalents" or discounted at risk-adjusted discount rates fail to capture some dimension of risk.

Simple decision rules such as "accept the investment if its net present value is positive" are not reliable if there is considerable uncertainty. Until more is learned about how an individual or a group perceives risk, the analyst can only describe the various outcomes to which the investor or the firm will be subject and the likelihood of their occurrence if a particular decision or set of decisions is reached.

For a publicly held corporation, an individual investment decision-maker should not impose a personal risk preference in the decision-making process. The firm's goal should be the maximization of the stockholders' wealth position and, for publicly held corporations, the wealth position is measured by the price of the stock. If there were perfect information, the real judge of an investment's worthiness would be the marketplace and how it would react to the news of the investment.

Business managers have a preference for easily understood, intuitively appealing, decision rules. The use of the weighted average cost of capital to evaluate investments is such a rule. If capital has a given cost (the weighted average cost of capital) then it would seem reasonable that an investment should be accepted if its return is higher than this cost. If the cost of capital reflects the risk of the investment being considered, it can be used as a hurdle rate in a capital budgeting decision. However the WACC combines in one measure time value considerations and risk attitudes, and this one measure is used for the all of the cash flows in all periods. Using one risk-adjusted discount rate to compute present value equivalents is not a reliable solution to the problems of time value and risk, but the method can be an usable approximation.

PROBLEMS

1   Assume a $1,000 outlay for an investment with two possible payoffs:
        0.4 probability of $500
        0.6 probability of $2,000
    The payoff are at time 1. The discount rate is 0.10.
    a.   Determine the expected net present value of the investment.
    b.   What is the NPV of the worst event? The probability?
2   (*Continue 1*)
    Assume that 1/2 of two identical investments (each costing $500) are undertaken.
    a.   Determine the expected net present value of the two investments.
    b.   Determine the NPV of the worst event? The probability?
3   Which numbers of problem 1 are subjective thus could be changed?
4   Assume there are two equally likely immediate outcomes $0 and $10. How little would the cost of the investment have to be to have you play the game?
5   Assume there are two equally likely immediate outcomes $0 and $100,000. How little would the cost of the investment have to be to have you accept the investment?
6   For questions 4 and 5 what amounts would make you indifferent to accepting or rejecting the investments.

59

7   Assume the following investment exists:

Probability	Outcome	Expected value
0.999	$0	$0
0.001	$100,000	$1,000

Would you pay $1,000 for the investment?

8   (*Continue 7*) Assume the payoff takes place at time 1 and that you would be willing to pay $800. What internal rate of return does that imply?

9   (*Continue 7 and 8*) Assume the payoff takes place at time 20 and that you would be willing to pay $249. The risk free rate is 0.06. What internal rate of return does the $249 price imply?

DISCUSSION QUESTION

Assume a corporation has a WACC equal to 0.10.

a.   If there is a very safe investment (compared to the firm's average investment) do you want to use 0.10 as a discount rate?

b.   If there is a very risky investment (compared to the firm's average investment) do you want to use 0.10 as a discount rate?

BIBLIOGRAPHY

Barberis, N., "Investing in the Long Run When Returns are Predictable," *Journal of Finance*, February 2000, pp. 225–64.

Crum, Roy L. and F. G. J. Derfinderen, *Capital Budgeting under Condition of Uncertainty*, Boston: Martinus Nijhoff, 1981.

Crum, Roy L., Dan J. Laughhunn, and John W. Payne, "Risk-Seeking Behavior and Its Implications for Financial Models," *Financial Management*, winter 1981, pp. 20–7.

Fama, E. F., "Risk Adjusted Discount Rates and Capital Budgeting Under Uncertainty," *Journal of Financial Economics*, June 1977, pp. 3–24.

Harris, Milton and Artur Raviv, "The Capital Budgeting Process, Incentives, and Information," *Journal of Finance*, September 1996, pp. 1139–74.

Holton, Glyn A., "Defining Risk," *Financial Analysts Journal*, November–December 2004.

Jagannathan, R. and I. Meier, "Do We Need CAPM for Capital Budgeting?" *Financial Management*, winter 2002, pp. 55–77.

Markowitz, Harry M., "Portfolio Selection," *Journal of Finance*, March 1952, pp. 77–91.

—— "Investment for the Long Run: New Evidence for an Old Rule," *Journal of Finance*, December 1976, pp. 1273–86.

May, Don O., "Do Managerial Motives Influence Firm Risk Reduction Strategies?," *Journal of Finance*, September 1996, pp. 1291–308.

Wright, Frank Lloyd and Lewis Mumford, *Thirty Years of Correspondence*, ed. Bruce Brooks Pfeiffer and Robert Wojtowicz, New York, Princeton Architectural Press.

Chapter 4

Elements of time and uncertainty

There's no good answer to a stupid question.

(A Russian proverb)

The capital budgeting process must take into consideration both time (the time value of money) and uncertainty (the future cash flows are very rarely known with certainty). In this chapter we want to consider the primary elements that must be considered in order to make capital budgeting decisions. These elements include:

1   Pure time value of money (the discount rate that would be used with no uncertainty; we will use the risk-free rate, r_f, to represent this factor).
2   The probabilities of the different outcomes (cash flows) for a given time period. We will use the expected value of the cash flow to include these probabilities in the calculation. The expected value of the cash flow X_i for period i is denoted $E(X_i)$.
3   The risk aversion of the investor. A measure of risk aversion enables the decision maker to convert an expected value to a certainty equivalent (CE). The term j_i is the risk aversion factor for the cash flows of period i. Assume j_i is greater than one, then:

$$CE_i = \frac{1}{j_i} E(X_i) \qquad (4.1)$$

and CE_i is less than $E(X_i)$
4   The period in which uncertainty is resolved.

We will consider two different time-risk models. One focuses on the risk preferences of the individual investor and uses the concept of the certainty equivalent. The certainty equivalent model is incorporated in most real world option pricing models used in practice. The second time-risk model makes use of the capital market to convert time-risk preferences into a relatively easily used calculation method.

THE INVESTMENT PROCESS

To evaluate the investments effectively management must take into consideration both the timing of the investment's cash flows and the amount of uncertainty.

It is sometimes stated that the weighted average cost of capital of a firm may be used to evaluate investments whose cash flows are perfectly correlated with the cash flows from the firm's present assets. With perfect correlation between the two sets of cash flows, the risk is the same. But if the timing of the cash flows is not also the same, the same discount rate may not be appropriate for both investments. The cost of capital combines in one discount rate an allowance for the time value of money and an allowance for risk. To apply the same cost of capital to cash flows that occur at different points in time, the magnitude of these allowances (i.e., the percent per unit of time) must remain constant over time.

Consider a situation where some gambles have payoffs of either $0 or $1,000, both with 0.5 probability. Thus the expected payoff for all of the gambles is $500. All of the gambles are perfectly correlated, and the outcome of the gambles will be known immediately. Assume one of the gambles will pay off one year from now, and an investor is indifferent between this gamble and $400 for certain now. The choice of $400 implies an average cost of capital of 0.25. (The expected value of the payoff is $500 and a 0.25 rate of discount would equate the present value of $500 to the $400 outlay.) A second identical gamble will pay off twenty years from today. If the discount rate of 0.25 is applied to the $500 expected value, we obtain $5.75 (0.0115 × $500). If the time value of money for a zero risk investment is 0.10, however, it is not clear that an investor would be indifferent between $5.75 and the gamble. The present value of the $1,000 discounted at 0.10 is $148.64. This is what the gamble will be worth if the outcome is favorable. Multiplying by the 0.5 probability, we obtain an expected value of $74.32. Most persons would pay more than $5.75 for a lottery ticket that is equally likely to be worth $148.64 or zero.

If the benefits from all investments are perpetuities, the use of different discount rates, where the rates increase with increased risk, may give an evaluation of investments using their present values that is consistent with their risks. For example, if all investments have expected cash flows of $1,000 per year and if there are three investments with different risks (high, medium, and low), we can use a high discount factor (say, 0.20) with the high risk, a medium discount factor (say, 0.10) with the medium risk, and a low discount factor (say, 0.05) with the low risk. The three different present values we obtain are as follows:

	Discount factor	Perpetual cash flow present value factors	Present value of $1,000 per year
High risk	0.20	5	$5,000
Medium risk	0.10	10	10,000
Low risk	0.05	20	20,000

Instead of being perpetuities the same general approach could be used if all the investments were finite-lived investments.

There is a $0.50 discount per dollar of proceeds for risk as we move from the low- to the medium-risk investment, and a $0.75 discount per dollar for risk as we move from the low- to the high-risk investment. These risk adjustments may not be correct, but at least the adjustment for risk is in the correct direction, and they apply in the same manner to all investments in the same risk class.

It is less obvious than with common stock, but the cost of corporate debt also includes an adjustment for risk, because there is generally the possibility of default. A bond yield of 0.07 is partially a result of time preference (say, 0.04) and partially a result of the risk of default. It may also include an allowance for the risk and dilution of value resulting from expected inflation or a possible change in interest rates.

As normally defined and computed, the cost of common stock equity funds and the yields of most debt instruments include an allowance for risk, but it does not necessarily follow that the use of a higher discount rate applied to future cash flows is a desirable way of determining the present value of an asset that is subject to risk.

We shall use two examples to illustrate the difficulty of predicting the effect of using different discount rates in an attempt to take risk into consideration.

EXAMPLE 4.1

Assume that we have two investments, the second more risky than the first. With the first investment we shall use a discount rate of 0.10, and with the second a discount rate of 0.20. The two investments have expected cash flows of $10,000 in years 1 and 50.

Note that the $9,091 present value of the cash flows of year 1 of the less risky investment is 1.09 times as large as the $8,333 present value of the cash flow of year 1 of the more risky investment. However, the present value of the cash flows of year 50 of the less risky investment is approximately 83 times as large.

EXAMPLE contd.

The use of a larger rate of discount for a more risky investment may move the decision in the correct direction (that is, the riskier the investment, the lower the present value of the future cash flows). However, it does this in an approximate and somewhat unpredictable manner. We cannot be sure of the impact of the risk discount added to the time value of money without considerable computation, and comparing two investments of different risk the effect of the risk discount will be different each year.

Year	Expected cash flows	Present value factor using 0.10	Present value using 0.10	Present value factor using 0.20	Present value using 0.20
1	$10,000	0.9091	$9,091	0.8333	$8,333
50	$10,000	0.0085	83	0.0001	1

The use of a risk discount rate assumes that the risk difference between the two investments is increasing as we move farther into the future. As we have already mentioned, this assumption may not be correct. Even if the assumption is correct, we still need to inquire whether the discount factor appropriately measures the disadvantage of the larger risk.

This difficulty with the use of a risk discount (that is, a larger interest rate) to take risk into consideration is not limited to situations involving long time periods.

EXAMPLE 4.2

Assume that we are given the opportunity to bet on a horse race being run today and the information we receive is so good that we consider the probability of obtaining $3 for each dollar invested to be 0.5. There remains a 0.5 probability of losing our entire investment, so we want to apply a large interest rate to take the risk into consideration. However, the benefits are zero time periods in the future. When the discount factor $(1 + r)^{-t}$ is computed for t equal to zero, we find the present-value factor is 1 and is independent of the choice of the discount rate, r.

We conclude that, for practical business decision-making with very short time periods, varying the rate of discount may not be a good way of accomplishing the objective of taking risk into consideration. It is true that most persons would require a higher return for risky investments than for less risky investments; however, determining the exact amount the rate of discount should be increased for different types of risk in different time periods is a difficult task.

EXAMPLE 4.3

Assume the following lottery taking place in year 30.

Event	Probability	Outcome
e_1	0.5	1,000,000
e_2	0.5	0
		E(Value) = $500,000

Assume the investor is averse to risk and would be indifferent to the lottery or receiving $300,000 for certain (define the $300,000 to be the certainty equivalent) at time 30.

E(Value) $500,000
Certainty equivalent $300,000
The lottery cost = $50,000
Default free discount rate = 0.05
Risk adjusted discount rate = 0.12

Two alternative present value calculations are:

1 Using the certainty equivalent and a default free rate:
   $PV = 300,000(1.05)^{-30} = \$69,413$
2 Using the risk adjusted rate:
   $PV = 500,000(1.12)^{-30} = \$16,689.$

The example illustrates the fact that the two calculations can lead to drastically different decisions. With a $50,000 cost for the lottery, the certainty equivalent calculation leads to an accept decision and the risk adjusted rate leads to a reject decision. A more realistic example would have to consider the effect of receiving some information in each of the 30 years.

In the next section the expected cash flows of each year will be converted into certainty equivalents and the nature of the discount rates leading to the same present values will be defined. One necessary condition for using a constant discount rate for each period will be established.

THE DISCOUNT RATE

The usual capital budgeting process assumes that an expected cash flow of $1 can be discounted back to time zero using

$$PV = (1 + r)^{-n} \tag{4.2}$$

for any time n. The discount rate r reflects both time value and risk aversion considerations. The use of the expected cash flow takes into consideration the probabilities of the outcomes.

If each time period has a different one period forward rate (consistent with a non-constant term structure), then the present value of a dollar of expected cash flow at time n is:

$$PV = [(1 + r_1)(1 + r_2)\ldots(1 + r_{n-1})(1 + r_n)]^{-1} \tag{4.3}$$

where r_i is the one period forward rate of i-th year. If all the forward rates are equal to r then:

$$PV = (1 + r)^{-n}.$$

In the examples to follow we will convert expected values to certainty equivalents and then discount certainty equivalents back to the present. Unfortunately, there is not an exact reliable method for converting expected values to certainty equivalents.

Nevertheless we consider this chapter to be comparable in importance to the introduction of the basic time discounting calculation $(1 + r)^{-n}$. Normal practices use a risk adjusted discount rate (r) and it is essential that managers understand the assumptions implicit in the use of a risk adjustment factor in a compound interest formula.

There would be no problem with the discount rate choice if there were no uncertainty or if the investors were not risk adverse. If there were no uncertainty the correct discount rate to apply to the known future cash flows would be the default free rate of r_f. If investors were not risk adverse, but there were uncertainty, then the default free rate could be used as a discount rate applied to the expected cash flows.

The interesting (and relevant) case is when there is both uncertainty and risk aversion since that is a fair description of the world in which managers operate. The primary importance of the certainty equivalent analysis to follow is that it forces us to come to terms with the fact that current practice is based on implicit assumptions. If these assumptions do not apply to the situation being analyzed, then the calculations that result are misleading and may result in incorrect capital budgeting decisions.

The use of the risk adjusted discount rate r and the time value factor $(1 + r)^{-n}$ for the cash flows of any time period n implicitly assumes that risk is increasing in a very systematic manner through time. The risk factor implicitly included in r is compounding through time. If the expected value of time one is converted to a certainty equivalent by dividing by j, the expected value of time n is converted to a certainty equivalent by dividing by j^n. If these adjustments are not appropriate then it is not correct to use $(1 + r)^{-n}$ to compute the present value of a period n cash flow, and to discount the expected cash flows a different risk adjusted rate should be used for each time period.

CONVERTING EXPECTED CASH FLOWS

The relationship of the certainty equivalent of period $i(CE_i)$ and the expected value $E(X_i))$ is:

$$CE_i = \frac{1}{j_i}E(X_i) \tag{4.1}$$

where $1/j_i = [(1 + r_f)/(1 + r)]^i$ is the assumed certainty equivalent factor and r is the risk-adjusted discount rate. Thus the expected cash flow is converted into a certainty equivalent by multiplying the expected value of year i by $[(1 + r_f)/(1 + r)]^i$ where r_f is the default free rate. Let $r_f = 0.05$, $r = 0.10$, $E(X_1) = \$110$ and $E(X_2) = \$121$. The certainty equivalents are:

Year	Expected value	Certainty equivalents
1	$E(X_1) = \$110$	$110(1.05/0.10) = 105$
2	$E(X_2) = \$121$	$121(1.05/0.10)^2 = 110.25$

Using certainty equivalents and the 0.05 default-free discount rate the present value is:

$$V_0 = \frac{105}{1.05} + \frac{110.25}{(1.05)^2} = \$200.$$

Using the expected cash flows and the risk adjusted discount rate $(r = 0.10)$ the present value is again $\$200$:

$$V_0 = \frac{110}{1.10} + \frac{121}{(1.10)^2} = \$200.$$

The use of the rate r for any period applied to the expected cash flows is justified if at time 0 we determine that for any period:

$$CE_i = \left(\frac{1 + r_f}{1 + r}\right)^i E(X_i) \tag{4.4}$$

This assumption is a necessary condition for the use of the same r for the cash flows of each period. But if

$$CE_i = \frac{1}{j}E(X_i) \tag{4.5}$$

and the certainty equivalent factor is any constant j and if a constant risk-adjusted interest rate r is used, different present values will result from using the certainty equivalent and the risk free rate r_f and from using the expected values discounted using the risk adjusted rate r. With a constant certainty equivalent factor such as one divided by j, a different risk-adjusted discount rate should be used for each time period.

THE DISCOUNT RATE ASSUMPTION

The usual capital budgeting process assumes that an expected cash flow of $E(X_n)$ can be discounted back to time zero using:

$$V_0 = (1 + r)^{-n} E(X_n) \tag{4.6}$$

for any time n. The discount rate r reflects time both time value and risk aversion considerations. The use of the expected cash flow takes into consideration the probabilities of the outcomes. If each time period has a different one period forward rate (consistent with a non-constant term structure) then the present value of a $E(X_n)$ expected cash flow at time n is:

$$V_0 = [(1 + r_1)(1 + r_2)\ldots(1 + r_{n-1})]^{-1} E(X_n) \tag{4.7}$$

where r_i is the one period forward rate of the i-th year. If all the forward rates are equal to r then $V_0 = (1 + r)^{-n}E(X_n)$. In this chapter we question the assumption that even if we assume a constant term structure one can always use $(1 + r)^{-n}$ to compute the present value of a cash flow for all values of n. Under what conditions of uncertainty can we appropriately use $(1 + r)^{-n}$ for all values of n?

CAPITAL BUDGETING WITH CONSTANT RISK AVERSION

Assume constant risk aversion. That is, the cash flow expected value $E(X)$ of any time period is multiplied by a constant $(1/j)$ that is less than one to obtain a certainty equivalent, and the factor $(1/j)$ is constant for all time periods.

Assume that an investment's expected cash flows of the n-th year are being discounted using a risk adjusted discount rate (r_n). This rate can be determined using the capital asset pricing model, the discounted cash flow dividend model, or

69

some comparable process. For an expected cash flow $E(X_n)$ to be received at time n the present value is:

$$PV = E(X_n)(1 + r_n)^{-n} = \frac{E(X_n)}{(1 + r_n)^n} \qquad (4.8)$$

The probability distribution of cash flow outcomes for any period can be translated to a certainty equivalent (CE). We assume that

$$CE = \frac{E(X)}{j} \qquad (4.9)$$

for the $E(X)$ of any period. This is the constant risk aversion assumption (at time zero j is the same for the cash flows of all the time periods). The CE of any time period can be discounted using the risk free rate (r_f) since the CE is by definition equivalent in value to a certain cash flow. For the present value of the CE_n received at time n we have

$$PV = CE_n(1 + r_f)^{-n} = \frac{CE_n}{(1 + r_f)^n} \qquad (4.10)$$

Equating the two present values of equations (4.8) and (4.10):

$$E(X_n)(1 + r_n)^{-n} = CE_n(1 + r_f)^{-n}$$

Since $j(CE) = E(X)$ for all time periods, substituting for $E(X_n)$ and dividing by CE_n we obtain:

$$j(1 + r_n)^{-n} = (1 + r_f)^{-n}.$$

If j is held constant then the discount rate (r_n) for a cash flow at time n for which the two present values are equal is:

$$r_n = (1 + r_f)j^{1/n} - 1 \qquad (4.11)$$

The value of r_n is different for all values of n. Table 4.1 shows the values of r_n for a constant $j = 1.1$ and $r_f = 0.04$ for different values of n.

Remember that $E(X)$ is an expectation of the cash flows and j only adjusts for risk aversion. Table 4.1 shows that if j is a constant for all time periods and larger than one that the discount rates r_n decrease as n increases. See the right hand column of Table 4.1. If the risk aversion factor is a constant, generalizations derived from Table 4.1 or its equivalent apply.

Table 4.1 Values of r_n given constant values of j; values of r_n if $j = 1.10$, $r_f = 0.04$

Time	$(j)^{1/n}$	$1 + r_f$	$r_n = (1 + r_f)(j)^{1/n} - 1$
1	1.1000	1.04	0.144
2	1.0488	1.04	0.091
3	1.0323	1.04	0.074
5	1.0192	1.04	0.060
10	1.0096	1.04	0.050
15	1.0064	1.04	0.047
20	1.0048	1.04	0.045
50	1.0010	1.04	0.041

CAPITAL BUDGETING WITH A CONSTANT RISK ADJUSTED RATE

Now assume that it is correct to use the 0.144 discount rate for each period. What is the implied value of j for each time n? Define j_n to be the appropriate risk aversion factor for cash flows at time n. Table 4.2 shows the value of j_n assuming that $j_n = [(1 + r_n)/(1 + r_f)]^n$ and $r_n = 0.144$ for all n.

The risk aversion factor (j_n) is implicitly assumed to increase geometrically if a constant value of r_n is assumed. Remember that if a risk adjusted discount rate is used it is applied to the expected cash flow. This expectation has to include the probability of the firm surviving to the time period when the cash flow is expected to occur. Is it reasonable to assume that the risk aversion factor increases geometrically?

Table 4.2 With implied values of the risk conversion factors (j_n); constant discount rate $(r_n = 0.144)$ and $r_f = 0.04$

Time	$(1 + r_n)^n$	$(1 + r_f)^n$	Implied j_n
1	1.1440	1.04	1.10
2	1.3087	1.0816	1.21
3	1.4972	1.1249	1.33
5	1.9594	1.2167	1.61
10	3.8394	1.4802	2.59
15	7.5230	1.8009	4.18
20	14.7408	2.1911	6.73
50	834.2596	7.1067	117.39

EXAMPLE 4.4

Consider the following investment where the outcomes and payments are all at time zero (initially, time value is not a factor).

Event	Probability	Outcome
e_1	0.5	$1,000
e_2	0.5	0
		$E(X) = \$500$

The value of $E(X)$ is $500. Assume $j = 1.1$ and that the $CE = \$454.545$:

$$CE = \frac{E(X)}{j} = \frac{500}{1.1} = \$454.545. \tag{4.9}$$

The value of the investment is $454.545 and there is no time discounting since the outcomes takes place at time zero.

Now assume the revelation of outcome and the payoff both take place at time one. Assume $r_i = 0.144$ and the risk free rate (r_f) is 0.04. For the example using the risk-adjusted discount rate of 0.144:

$$V_0 = \frac{E(X_1)}{1 + r_1} = \frac{500}{1.144} = \$437.06 \tag{4.8}$$

or equivalently using the certainty equivalent and the 0.04 default free rate:

$$V_0 = \frac{CE_1}{1 + r_f} = \frac{454.545}{1.04} = \$437.06 \tag{4.10}$$

Since $1/j_1 = 1 + r_j/1 + r_1$ and $r_1 = 1.04 (1.1)-1 = 0.144$ the two present values are equal.

Now assume the outcome is determined and the payoffs are made at time 2, and j is now equal to $1.1^2 = 1.21$. If we use $r_2 = 0.144$ and $E(X_2)$ to compute the V_0:

$$V_0 = \frac{E(X_2)}{(1 + r_2)^2} = \frac{500}{(1.144)^2} = \$382.05 \tag{4.8}$$

or equivalently using the certainty equivalent ($j_2 = 1.21$) of $413.223:

$$V_0 = \frac{CE_2}{(1 + r_f)^2} = \frac{E(X_2)}{j_2(1 + r_f)^2} = \frac{413.223}{(1.04)^2} = \$382.05 \tag{4.10}$$

The two present values are again equal. But if j_2 is equal to 1.1 rather than 1.21 for the second example then the certainty equivalent is $500/1.1 = \$454.5455$ and the present value using the certainty equivalent is:

$$V_0 = \frac{CE_2}{(1 + r_f)^2} = \frac{454.5455}{(1.04)^2} = \$420.25. \tag{4.10}$$

The use of $E(X_2)$ and r_2 leads to a present value of $382.05 but the use of the certainty equivalent with $j_2 = 1.1$ gives a present value of $420.25. If $j_2 = 1.1$

EXAMPLE contd.

is correct, then the use of 0.144 to discount a time 2 cash flow understates the present value. Solving for the appropriate risk adjusted rate with $j_2 = 1.1$ we have 0.0907612 for the risk adjusted rate.

$$r_n = (1 + r_f)(j)^{1/n} - 1$$

$$r_2 = (1.04)(1.1)^{\frac{1}{2}} - 1 = 0.0907612 \qquad (4.11)$$

Using the risk adjusted discount rate and the expected value to compute the present value of the time 2 cash flow:

$$V_0 = E(X_2)(1 + r_2)^{-2} = 500(1.0907612)^{-2} = 500(0.840506)$$
$$= \$420.25. \qquad (4.8)$$

This $420.25 present value obtained using the $500 expected value and $r_2 = 0.0907612$ is equal to the present value of the $454.5455 certainty equivalent obtained above using $r_f = 0.04$ and $j_2 = 1.1$.

A CAPITAL MARKET PERSPECTIVE

Up to this point the investor's risk aversion function has determined the appropriateness of the use of a constant discount rate. Now we will switch the focus to the importance of the capital markets as an explanation of the use of a constant risk-adjusted discount rate.

Three conditions must be satisfied in order to justify using the same risk-adjusted discount rate for different time periods to compute the present value of uncertain cash flows (assuming the relevance of the capital asset pricing model):

1   The same beta applies to all future time periods.
2   If an event occurs that changes the beta of one time period, the betas of all the other periods also change.
3   The investor is diversified so that the CAPM utilization is justified.

How reasonable are these assumptions? There are scenarios that are consistent with these assumptions, thus the use of $(1 + r)^{-n}$ to compute the present value of the cash flow of any time period n is reasonable in those situations.

If there is reason to expect the beta to change through time, then the use of a constant discount rate would not be appropriate. Also, if the investor is not well diversified, the CAPM might not apply and we have to consider the nature of the investor's risk aversion factor through time before using $(1 + r)^{-n}$ for all n.

A QUALIFICATION OF THE CAPM DECISION RULE

For a well-diversified investor, a corporation should accept all investments where the investment's return is larger than the required return of $\bar{r}_i$ where

$$\bar{r}_i = r_f + (\bar{r}_m - r_f)\beta_i \tag{4.12}$$

where β_i and $\bar{r}_i$ both apply to the specific investment being considered.

The assumption is that the cost of the capital being used reflects the project's risk and is less than the project's internal rate of return. But assume a situation where $\beta_i = 0$, $r_f = 0.04$ and an investment yields 0.05. While this project seems to be acceptable, assume it is to be financed with 0.06 debt. With these facts, the project must earn more than 0.06 or be rejected. This can be readily seen if the cash flows of the debt are subtracted from the investment's cash flows to obtain the stock equity cash flows. The present value of the cash flows will be negative since the investment yields 0.05 and debt costs 0.06, thus the investment is not desirable.

Why did the debtholders want 0.06 even though the theoretically correct required CAPM return is only 0.04? One possibility is that this riskless project is contaminated by the presence of other assets that are risky and the firm can only borrow at 0.06. A second explanation is that there are transaction costs. A third explanation is that there are relevant unsystematic risks. The conclusion is that there can be investments which satisfy the CAPM requirements, but which still should be rejected because of imperfections in the capital market or other factors that should be considered.

A solution for the first possibility would be for the corporation to isolate the project's cash flows so that 0.04 becomes the effective cost of capital and the project earning 0.05 can be accepted.

GLOBAL BUSINESS ASPECTS

All of this book applies globally as well as domestically. The models of this chapter apply to investment decisions, independent of the currency that is appropriate.

CONCLUSIONS

It is clear that one cannot automatically accept the use of $(1 + r)^{-n}$ with the same r for all time periods as being the correct method of converting a series of future expected cash flows to present values. It may be necessary to use $(1 + r_n)^{-n}$ where there is a different value of the risk adjusted discount rate (r_n) for each time period.

A different and decreasing r_n is consistent with the risk aversion factor j being constant and larger than one.

Fortunately, there are a set of conditions which if satisfied leads to the correct use of one discount rate for the cash flows of all time periods. With a well-diversified investor, if the same beta applies to all future time periods and a change in one beta leads to a change in the betas of all time periods, then the use of one discount rate is reasonable.

The analysis is more complex if the investor is not well diversified. We must consider how risk aversion changes through time. For one risk-adjusted discount rate for the expected cash flows of all time periods to be appropriate, risk aversion cannot be constant through time. The risk-free rate for comparable time periods establishes an absolute floor for the time discount factor, but we would expect some risk premium to be appropriate even for long time periods if there is risk aversion.

The certainty equivalent approach is offered as an assistance in understanding uncertainty. An expected value calculation may not be a sufficient measure of the value of a period's cash flow. Implementation of the certainty equivalent approach is very difficult and not likely to be feasible for a corporation, but understanding the certainty equivalent relationship is important.

QUIZ

Assume an investor who is not well diversified.
If the expected value of each period is multiplied by 0.75 to obtain the certainty equivalent and if the risk free rate is 0.05 what is the risk adjusted rate for year 1? For year 20? For year 50?

PROBLEMS

1   Assume the expected value of period i's cash flow is converted to a certainty equivalent by multiplying by $(1 + r_f / 1 + r)^n$. Assume
   $r_f = 0.04, r = 0.15$
   $E(X_1) = 161, E(X_2) = \$238.05$
   Convert the two expected values to certainty equivalents.

2   (Continue 1) Compute the present value using the 0.15 risk adjusted rate. Compute the present value using the 0.04 risk free rate and the certainty equivalents.

3   (Continue 1) Now convert the expected value to a certainty equivalent by multiplying the expected values by 0.8 for all periods.
   Convert the two expected values to certainty equivalents
   What discount rate should be used for the cash flows of period 1?

75

What discount rate should be used for the cash flows of period 2?

4 (*Continue 1 and 3*) Compute the present value using the risk adjusted rates $r_1 = 0.3$ and $r_2 = 0.16276$ and the expected cash flows.

Compute the present value using certainty equivalents and the 0.04 risk free rate.

Compute the present value using the expected cash flows and the 0.15 risk adjusted discount rate for both years.

5 (*Continue 1, 3 and 4*) Compute the appropriate risk adjusted rate assuming the cash flow is at time 20.

Compute the present value of $1,000 using a rate of 0.0517.

Compute the present value of $1,000 using the 0.15 discount rate.

6 (*Continue 1*) Compute the expected return on a $320 investment for year 1 and a $207 investment for year 2 as of time zero.

7 (*Continue 1*) Assume X_1 can take on the value $193.20 with 0.6 probability or $112.70 with a 0.4 probability.

What is the expected value of X_1?

8 (*Continue 7*) Assume that if $X_1 = 193.20$ then the value of X_2 is (with equal probability):

$$X_2 = 333.27(1.2) = 399.9424$$

or

$$X_2 = 142.83(1.2) = 171.396$$

What is the expected value of X_2 if $X_1 = 193.20$?

9 (*Continue 8*) What is the present value at time zero given that $X_1 = 193.20$ and $E(X_2) = 285.66$?

10 (*Continue 8 and 9*) What is the expected return on investment for the first period given $X_1 = 193.20$, $V_1 = \$248.40$ and $V_0 = \$384$?

DISCUSSION QUESTION

A corporation uses equation 12 to determine its hurdle rate to evaluate investments. What mistakes are possible (or implicit in its use)?

SOLUTION TO QUIZ

$$CE = \frac{1}{j}E(X_i)$$

$$\frac{1}{j} = 0.75 = \frac{3}{4}$$

$$j = \frac{4}{3}$$

For $n = 1$

$$r_n = (1 + r_f)(j)^{1/n} - 1$$

$$= (1.05)\left(\frac{4}{3}\right) - 1 = 0.40$$

For $n = 20$

$$r_{20} = 1.05\left(\frac{4}{3}\right)^{\frac{1}{20}} - 1 = 0.0652$$

For $n = 50$

$$r_{50} = 1.05\left(\frac{4}{3}\right)^{\frac{1}{50}} - 1 = 0.0561$$

BIBLIOGRAPHY

Bogue, M. and R. Roll, "Capital Budgeting for Risky Projects with 'Imperfect' Markets for Physical Capital," *Journal of Finance*, May 1974, pp. 601–13.

Brennan, M. J., "An Approach to the Valuation of Uncertain Income Streams," *Journal of Finance*, June 1973, pp. 661–74.

Fama, E. F., "Risk Adjusted Discount Rates and Capital Budgeting Under Uncertainty," *Journal of Financial Economics*, June 1977, pp. 3–24.

Hu, H. T. C., "Risk, Time, and Fiduciary Principles in Corporate Investment," *UCLA Law Review*, 38 (2), 1990.

Markowitz, H. M., *Portfolio Selection: Efficient Diversification of Investment*, New York: John Wiley & Sons, 1959.

Myers, S. C., "Interactions of Corporate Financing and Investment Decisions: Implications for Capital Budgeting," *Journal of Finance*, March 1974, pp. 1–25.

Ruback, R. S., "Calculating the Market Value of Riskless Cash Flows," *Journal of Financial Economics*, March 1986, pp. 323–39.

Rudd, A. and Barr Rosenberg, "The 'Market Model' in Investment Management," *Journal of Finance*, May 1980, pp. 597–607.

Sharpe, W., "Capital Asset Prices: A Theory of Market Equilibrium Under Conditions of Risk," *Journal of Finance*, September 1964, pp. 425–42.

Stapleton, R. C., "Portfolio Analysis, Stock Valuation and Capital Budgeting Decision Rules for Risky Projects," *Journal of Finance*, March 1971, pp. 95–117.

Stern, J. M. and D. H. Chew, Jr., *The Revolution in Corporate Finance*, 4th edn, Malden, MA: Blackwell Publishing, 2003, Chapters 5–7.

Van Horne, J. C., "An Application of the Capital Asset Pricing Model to Divisional Required Returns," *Financial Management*, spring 1980, pp. 14–19.

Weston, J. F., "Investment Decisions Using the Capital Asset Pricing Model," *Financial Management*, spring 1973, pp. 25–33.

Weston, J. F. and Nai-fu Chen, "A Note on Capital Budgeting and the Three Rs," *Financial Management*, spring 1980, pp. 12–13.

Chapter 5

The state preference approach

Theories that are right only 50 percent of the time are less economical than coin-flipping.

(George J. Stigler, *The Theory of Price*, Professor Stigler implicitly assumed decisions with two outcomes)

This chapter considers the state preference approach to capital budgeting. The state preference approach is a natural generalization to conditions of uncertainty of the present value approach under certainty.

If the state preference approach is interpreted literally, it would require treating separately each possible sequence of cash flows that could result from an investment. In any complex situation, this would be difficult, even with the help of computers. Nevertheless, there are several reasons for considering this approach. First, there are situations in which actual cash flows can be evaluated using this approach, either because the investments are not complex or because approximations can be used so that each possible cash flow does not need to be considered individually. Second, the state preference approach provides a great deal of intuition about how the characteristics of the cash-flow sequence affect the value of an investment. For example, the required rate of return can be derived for an investment, and the required return can be a function of the time and the state of the economy. Third, commonly used asset-valuation approaches, such as option-pricing theory and capital asset pricing model (CAPM), can be expressed in state preference terms, which provides valuable intuition.

PRICES WITH CERTAINTY

Consider an investment that will pay $100 for certain after one time period and $200 after two time periods. If the appropriate time-value factor is 0.05, then we know that a dollar due in one time period is worth $1/1.05 = 0.9524$ now. We can say that the "price" now of \$1 due in one time period is \$0.9524. In like manner, the price now of \$1 due in two time periods is $1/(1.05)^2 = \$0.9070$. Thus, the present value of the proceeds from the investment is

$$
\begin{array}{r}
\$100 \times 0.9524 = \;\;\$95 \\
\$200 \times 0.9070 = \underline{\$181} \\
\$276
\end{array}
$$

In a situation of certainty, we would be willing to pay as much as \$276 for the right to receive these proceeds.

If, instead of earning \$100 at time 1, the investment earned \$146, we would merely substitute \$146 for \$100 in the previous calculations. The 0.9524 present value factor would be unchanged, unless the time-value factor of 0.05 changed.

PRICES WITH UNCERTAINTY

We want to establish "prices" for future dollars when uncertainty exists. We will consider first a one-period horizon, where the only form of uncertainty that concerns us is uncertainty about the next period's cash flows. Suppose an investment has two possible cash flows (\$150 and \$80) next period. A tree diagram is a convenient way of illustrating the sequence of different possible outcomes that can occur. In this case, there are two branches with two different cash flows, as illustrated in Figure 5.1. Each branch in the tree diagram represents a different possible state of the world.

The previous section described an investment that could be evaluated by multiplying the cash flow that would occur at time 1 by a present value factor, 0.9542, which represents the price at time zero of \$1 in one period. In the next section the present value factor will be adjusted for uncertainty.

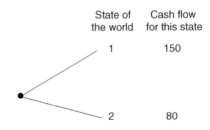

Figure 5.1 *Tree diagram of cash flow*

EXAMPLE 5.1

To evaluate investments under uncertainty, we suggest multiplying each of the possible cash flows that can occur by prices that represent the value now of a dollar to be received in a future period if a particular state of the world occurs. For example, suppose it was determined that $0.3204 was the right price at time 0 for a dollar to be received next period if state 1 occurred, while if state 2 occurred, the price is $0.6320. It is necessary that the sum of these prices be equal to the $0.9524 present value of a dollar using the 0.05 time value factor of the example. The investment evaluation process for the above example would be as follows:

(1) State	(2) Value of a dollar given the state (RAPVFs)	(3) Investment cash flow for the state	(4) Risk-adjusted present values
1	0.3204	$150	$48.06
2	0.6320	80	50.56
Totals	0.9524		$98.62

Using this approach, the total of the products in the last column, $98.62, would be the risk-adjusted present value of the cash proceeds.

To emphasize that this approach is a generalization of the use of present value factors under conditions of uncertainty, we recommend calling the prices in column 2 risk-adjusted present value factors, or RAPVFs. The products of column 2 and column 3 in column 4 are the risk-adjusted present values of the two states. The sum is the risk-adjusted present value of the investment.

Suppose an investment generates cash flows of $100 for certain at time 1. Remember that a certain dollar received at time 1 should be discounted using 0.05 and is worth $(1.05)^{-1}$ or 0.9524.

State	RAPVF	Cash flow	RAPV
1	0.3204	$100	$32.04
2	0.6320	100	63.20
Totals	0.9524		RAPV = $95.24

When the same flow is received in every state, the cash flows can be evaluated by summing up the RAPVFs over all the states (0.9524) and multiplying the total by the certain cash flow. The sum of the RAPVFs over all states is equal to the discount factor that would be applied to a certain cash flow at that time. This approach can be generalized to cover multiperiod investments. As will be shown next, the RAPVFs must be estimated in a systematic fashion to obtain meaningful results.

The state preference model assumes that if everyone agrees about (1) the states that are possible, and (2) the value today of $1 to be received in each state, there will be agreement about the value of an asset. Insurance policies are examples of assets that produce specified cash flows if some event occurs but zero cash flows if the event does not occur.

Investors will agree about the values of the RAPVFs for each state if there are markets in which the state conditional cash flows can be purchased or sold separately. Also, if these markets exist, investors and consumers in the economy will be able to allocate their wealth to a portfolio of assets that produces the optimal number of dollars in each state, subject to the decision maker's overall budget constraint. If markets exist and investors assign probabilities to each state, then for each investor, the RAPVF for each state can be decomposed into a product of three terms, as described in the next section.

THE THREE FACTORS

A risk-adjusted present value factor can be considered to be the product of three terms: the probability that the state will occur, the present value of $1 for certain, and a risk-adjustment factor appropriate for that state. One requirement is that the probabilities of all possible states must sum to 1 over all the states. Suppose, in Example 5.1 where there are two states, that the probability of the first state occurring is believed to be 0.7, and therefore the probability of the second state is 0.3. Using these values, we can calculate "expected" cash flow for the risky investment considered previously.

State	Cash flow	Probability	Expected cash flow
1	$150	0.7	$105
2	80	0.3	24
Totals		1.0	$129

The second term in the product is the present value factor, the meaning of which has already been explained. Assume the present value factor is 0.9524, which corresponds to the present value of $1 for one-period and an interest rate of 5 percent.

State	Cash flow	Present value factor	Present value
1	$105	0.9524	$100.00
2	24	0.9524	22.86
		Total expected present value	$122.86

The third term in the product leading to the RAPVFs is the risk-adjustment factor. For a given state it represents the value of a dollar in the state. Each state has its own risk-adjustment factor. Just as present value factors represent the price of certain dollars at different points in time, risk-adjustment factors represent the relative price of dollars in different states at the same time. As noted before, the probabilities of all of the states at a particular time must sum to one. Similarly, the sum over all possible states at a given time of the products of the probability of a state times the risk adjustment factor for that state, must be equal to one. We return to this point in the section on "The Expected Risk-Adjustment."

These risk-adjustment factors do not consider the time value of money. Ordinarily, we would expect that an additional dollar would be less valuable in states in which typical investors have larger incomes and wealth positions than in states in which they have smaller incomes and wealth positions. Therefore, in equilibrium the risk-adjustment factor would be below average in states in which most investors have above-average income and wealth and above average in states in which they have below-average income and wealth. The risk-adjustment factors are the relative prices at which investors can buy or sell state conditional dollars at a given time; they are objective facts not personal opinions.

Assume that state 1 in example 1 represents prosperity, and state 2 represents a severe depression. Assume a dollar in state 1 is worth $0.4806 at time 1 (the typical investor is rich), and a dollar in state 2 is worth $2.212 (the investor is poorer). These risk-adjustment factors are applied to the expected present value of the cash flows of each period. Continuing the calculations, we again have a risk-adjusted present value (RAPV) of $98.62.

State	Cash flow	Risk-adjustment factor	RAPV
1	$100	0.4806	$48.06
2	22.86	2.2120	50.56
		RAPV =	$98.62

Multiplying the three components, we obtain for the risk-adjusted present value factors for each state:

$$0.7 \times 0.9524 \times 0.4806 = 0.3204$$
$$0.3 \times 0.9524 \times 2.212 = 0.6320$$

which are the two "prices" we used previously.

We could also multiply each cash flow by the corresponding risk-adjustment factor and probability and sum the resulting products. The sum is called a *certainty equivalent*. The present value of the certainty equivalents at the default-free interest rate is equal to the risk-adjusted present value. In the above example, the certainty equivalent of the cash flows is $103.55. Multiplying by the present value factor, 0.9524 again gives the RAPV of the cash flows $98.62.

State	Cash flow	Risk-adjustment factor	Probability	Certainty equivalent
1	$150	0.4806	0.7	$50.46
2	80	2.2120	0.3	53.09
Totals			1.0	$103.55

THE EXPECTED RISK-ADJUSTMENT

So that the certainty equivalent of a certain dollar is equal to unity, the expected value of the risk-adjustment factor over all states must be equal to unity. This requirement is satisfied in this example, as $0.7 \times 0.4806 + 0.3 \times 2.212 = 1.00$.

It is important to recognize that the risk-adjustment factor associated with a state depends on the income and wealth position of the typical investor in that state relative to other states at the same time. It does not depend on the amount of cash generated by the asset during that state if the cash flows generated by any one asset are a very small part of the income or wealth of a typical investor.

The state-preference model is useful in analyzing the market value of an asset. Sometimes a single asset represents a significant portion of an individual's wealth. The state-preference model presented in this chapter would be applicable to determine the market value of such an asset for that individual, but it would not be useful for determining the subjective value of that asset for that individual. The risk-adjustment factor for the state would depend on the amount of cash generated in that state. A utility function approach would be more appropriate in that case.

COUNTERCYCLICAL ASSETS

While most assets generate more cash flows during prosperity (state 1) than during depressions (state 2), some countercyclical assets may be available. Suppose there was a countercyclical asset available whose cash flow pattern was as shown in Figure 5.2. The expected cash flow from this asset is $101.

State	Probability	Cash flow	Expected cash flow
1	0.7	$80	$56
2	0.3	150	45
			$101

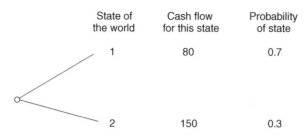

State of the world	Cash flow for this state	Probability of state
1	80	0.7
2	150	0.3

Figure 5.2 Cash-flow pattern of countercyclical asset

Using the RAPVF approach and the factors derived previously, the value of this investment would be $120.43:

State	RAPVF	Cash flow	RAPV
1	0.3204	$80	$25.63
2	0.6320	150	94.80
Totals	0.9524		$120.43

Although the cash flows associated with this investment are uncertain and have a lower expected value than the $129 of the investment on page 82 that we considered, the $120.43 risk-adjusted present value of this investment is greater. This is because the investment generates more of its flows during the states of nature in which the cash is most needed. Assets like this have some of the characteristics of insurance and are relatively attractive. The risk-adjusted present value ($120.43) is actually larger than the $101 expected cash flows.

REQUIRED RATES OF RETURN

Assume the assets have costs (required investments) equal to each asset's RAPV.

The required rate of return for an asset is defined as the risk-adjusted required return for the uncertain cash flows. In the state preference model, the state-conditional cash flows and RAPVFs determine the RAPV of an asset. If we also know the state probabilities, we can calculate the expected cash flow and determine the required rate of return.

For the first asset considered, the expected cash flows are $129, and the RAPV and the asset's cost is $98.62. Therefore, the required rate of return for this asset using $98.62 as the investment basis is 0.3081:

$$\frac{\$129}{\$98.62} - 1 = 0.3081$$

This is a "normal" asset whose uncertain cash flows are larger in good times than in bad times (that is, larger in prosperous states than in depression states).

For the countercyclical asset, the expected cash flows are only $101, but the RAPV and cost of the asset is $120.43. In this case, the asset costs more than its expected cash flows. The required rate of return for this asset is negative. The required rate of return using $120.43 as the investment basis is a negative 0.1613:

$$\frac{\$101}{\$120.43} - 1 = -0.1613$$

The negative required rate of return reflects the fact that the cash flows of the asset are larger in bad times (when cash is in short supply and therefore especially valuable) than in good times (when cash is relatively plentiful, since other assets have large cash payouts). The cost of the asset is larger than the expected value of its cash proceeds.

APPLICATION OF THE RISK-ADJUSTED PRESENT VALUE APPROACH

The risk-adjusted present value (RAPV) approach described in the previous paragraphs is a generalization of the net present value approach. The RAPV approach can be applied in at least two different ways. A direct application would involve defining states of nature, determining the cash flows that would be generated by projects in each state, and estimating the RAPVFs for each state. With these data, the value of a proposed project could be determined. In practice, this would require building a spreadsheet model of the project and using a Monte Carlo simulation to determine its value. The RAPV approach, however, even if not used to make the actual calculations, also offers some very useful insights into such vexing questions as how to compare the relative riskiness of two or more projects. The project that offers downside protection (and thus has more valuable cash flows) is relatively more valuable.

MULTIPERIOD INVESTMENTS

Figure 5.3 shows the probabilities for a two-period investment. The tree diagram provides a useful framework for analysis. For simplicity, only two outcomes are allowed for each node.

We will assume that the default-free one-period rates of interest are:

0.08 for the first time period;
0.08 for the second time period if starting from node (1.1);
0.03 for the second time period if starting from node (2.1).

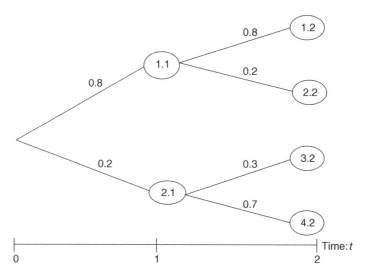

Figure 5.3 Probabilities for a two-period investment (tree diagram)

Each node is numbered with two numbers separated by a period. The first number is the node number (starting from the top) and the second number is the time period. Thus, node (3.2) is node 3 in time period 2. There is only one path through the tree diagram from the origin to a particular node.

We define s(n), the RAPVF for the nth node at time t, to be s(n, t), where n is the node number and t the time period. We assume that

$$s(1, 1) = 0.37037 \quad s(2, 2) = 0.55556$$
$$s(2, 1) = 0.55556 \quad s(3, 2) = 0.14563$$
$$s(1, 2) = 0.37037 \quad s(4, 2) = 0.82524$$

While we could use the s(n t) factors for single periods, it is somewhat easier to compute the RAPVFs that transform the cash flows of time t to present values at time 0. Define S(n, t) to be the risk-adjusted present value at time 0 of $1 received at node n and time t. For the example, we have

$$S(1, 1) = s(1, 1) = 0.37037$$
$$S(2, 1) = s(2, 1) = 0.55556$$
$$S(1, 2) = s(1, 1) \times s(1, 2) = 0.37037 \times 0.37037 = 0.13717$$
$$S(2, 2) = s(1, 1) \times s(2, 2) = 0.37037 \times 0.55556 = 0.20576$$
$$S(3, 2) = s(2, 1) \times s(3, 2) = 0.55556 \times 0.14563 = 0.08091$$
$$S(4, 2) = s(2, 1) \times s(4, 2) = 0.55556 \times 0.82524 = 0.45847$$

The logic of multiplying s(2, 1) times s(3, 2) to obtain S(3, 2) is the same logic whereby we multiply 0.9091 times 0.9091 (where 0.9091 is the present value of $1

87

due in one time period) to obtain the present value of $1 due in two time periods with a 0.10 discount rate. If $1 at node (3, 2) is worth 0.14563 at time 1, then it is worth 0.55556 times 0.14563, or 0.08091 at time 0; thus, $S(3, 2) = 0.08091$.

APPLYING THE RISK-ADJUSTED PRESENT VALUE FACTORS

Now that we have determined the $S(n, t)$'s, the evaluation of an investment is exactly analogous to the net present value calculation. Figure 5.4 shows the cash flows of an investment that costs $300.

The risk-adjusted present value of the positive cash flows is $365.

Node (n, t)	$S(n, t)$	Cash flow	RAPV
(1, 1)	0.37037	$432	$160
(2, 1)	0.55556	108	60
(1, 2)	0.13717	432	59
(2, 2)	0.20576	108	22
(3, 2)	0.08091	206	17
(4, 2)	0.45847	103	47
		RAPV =	$365

Since the risk-adjusted present value is $365 and the cost is only $300, the investment is acceptable.

In a world of uncertainty, the same term structure of interest rates could be used to evaluate different assets. Similarly, in a world of uncertainty, the same RAPVFs could be used to evaluate many different assets. In example 2, we use the RAPVFs previously derived to evaluate a new asset.

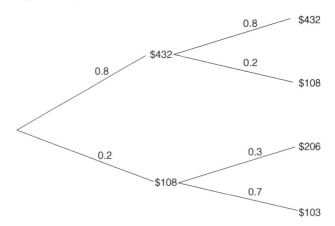

Figure 5.4 Cash flows of an investment that costs $300 (tree diagram)

EXAMPLE 5.2

Assume that an investment will generate in period 2 $108 at nodes 1 and 2 and $103 at nodes 3 and 4. These cash flows are represented in Figure 5.5. If node 1.1 occurs during period 1, the firm will know that it is to receive $108 for certain in period 2. It will also know the period 2 default-free interest rate, which will be 8 percent and if node 2.1 occurs, the default-free interest rate will be 3 percent and the outcomes at time 2 are $103.

If node 1.1 occurs, the future cash flows of $108 will be worth $100 at the end of period 1, using an 8 percent interest rate.

If node 2 occurs during period 1, the firm will know that it is to receive only $103 for certain in period 2. It will also know the period 2 default-free interest rate is 3 percent. So the future cash flows will also be worth $100 at the end of period 1, at node 2.

The value of the asset one period from now looks like Figure 5.6. Since the interest rate for period 1 is 8 percent, we would expect the asset to be worth

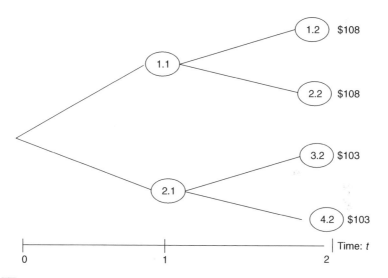

Figure 5.5 *Investment cash flows (tree diagram)*

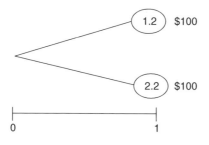

Figure 5.6 *Value of the asset one period from now (tree diagram)*

89

$100/1.08 = $92.59. The same answer could be reached using risk-adjusted present value factors on the period 2 cash flows.

Node (n, t)	$S(n, t)$	Cash flow	RAPV
(1, 1)	0.37037	$0	$0.00
(2, 1)	0.55556	0	0.00
(1, 2)	0.13717	108	14.81
(2, 2)	0.20576	108	22.22
(3, 2)	0.08091	103	8.33
(4, 2)	0.45847	103	47.22
			$92.59

Alternatively, we could apply RAPVFs to the end-of-period one-asset values.

Node (n, t)	$S(n, t)$	Value	RAPV
(1, 1)	0.37037	$100	$37.037
(2, 1)	0.55556	100	55.556
			$92.593

GLOBAL BUSINESS ASPECTS

The international decision problem has the same elements as those discussed in this chapter.

One complexity is added. If there is a desire to make the analysis using dollars instead of the local currency, then it is necessary to translate all transfers of cash to the parent into dollars. Given that the exchange rate will likely depend on the state of nature (the node) this can cause the calculations to be complex.

CONCLUSIONS

In principle, the application of the state preference model illustrated in this chapter enables us to compute risk-adjusted present value factors for different nodes through time. While the separate consideration of risk precludes the conventional compound interest present value calculations directly, we are taking into account the time value of money as well as the risk of the investment.

Once the RAPVFs have been computed, the calculations of the net value of an investment are analogous to the calculations that are made under the assumption of certainty. If the RAPV of the positive cash flows is greater than the cost of the investment, the risk-adjusted net-present value will be positive and the investment is acceptable. To apply the state-preference model in practice, it is necessary to generate a Monte Carlo simulation of the project that is consistent with the state-preference model.

PROBLEMS

1   Evaluate the following investment, assuming an interest rate of 0.10.

Time	Cash flow
0	−$8,000
1	10,000

2   (*Continue 1*) Instead of certain cash flows, assume the following time 1 outcomes exist.

State	Probability	Outcome
0	0.6	$5,000
1	0.4	17,500

Compare the expected value of the investment.

3   (*Continue 1 and 2*) Assume that a risk-adjustment factor of 0.8 applies to dollars received if state 1 occurs and 1.3 if state 2 occurs. The discount rate for the certain cash flows is still 0.10.
   Determine the RAPVFs for states 1 and 2.

4   (*Continue previous problems*) Given all the previous facts, evaluate the investment whose cash flows are described in 2.

5   Evaluate the following investment, assuming an interest rate of 0.10 per period and certain cash flows.

Time	Cash flow
0	−$11,000
1	+10,000
2	+5,000

91

6   (*Continue 5*) Instead of certain cash flows, assume the following outcomes
    are possible.

Period 1			Period 2		
State	Probability	Outcome	State	Probability	Outcome
(1, 1)	0.5	$4,000	(1, 2) and (3, 2)	0.4	$6,500
(2, 1)	0.5	16,000	(2, 2) and (4, 2)	0.6	$4,000

The outcomes of period 2 are independent of the outcomes of period 1.
Evaluate the investment, assuming a zero risk-adjustment.

7   (*Continue 5 and 6*) Assume that the following risk-adjustment factors apply:

    (1, 1) 0.8 (1, 2) and (3, 2) 0.9

    a.   Determine the risk-adjustment factors for states (2, 1), (2, 2), and (4, 2).
    b.   Determine the RAPVFs for all of the states.

8   (*Continue previous three problems*) Given all the previous facts, evaluate the
    investment.

9   Consider the investment described in Figure 5.7.

    In Figure 5.7 there are two numbers near the middle of each branch. The
    first is a one-period RAPVF for that branch. The second (in parentheses) is
    the conditional probability of the branch, given the previous node. Numbers

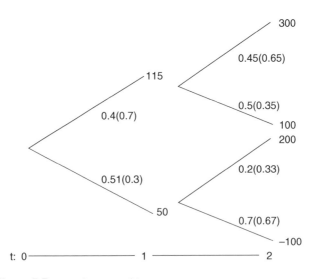

Figure 5.7 *Tree diagram of investment*

at the end of each branch are cash flows that will occur if the state corresponding to the branch occurs.

Data in Figure 5.7 apply to questions 9 through 11.

Find the RAPV at time 0 of an asset that will generate the cash flows described in the tree diagram for this problem.

10 (*Continue* 9) Find the required rate of return on the asset during period 1.

11 Figure 5.8 is a tree diagram that gives values of $s(n, t)$ single-period RAPVFs.

    a. Complete the following table:

t	n	$S(n, t)$
1	1	0.6050
1	2	0.3040
2	1	
2	2	
2	3	
2	4	

    b. Find the RAPVF of $1 at time 2 if "good times" occur. (Odd-numbered nodes are "good times.")

DISCUSSION QUESTION

The State Preference Approach has many merits. What are the primary objections to a firm implementing the process?

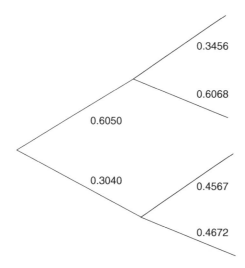

Figure 5.8 *Tree diagram of single-period RAPVFs*

Labels in figure: 0.3456, 0.6068, 0.6050, 0.3040, 0.4567, 0.4672

BIBLIOGRAPHY

Arrow, K., "The Role of Securities in the Optimal Allocation of Risk Bearing," *Review of Economic Studies*, April 1964, pp. 91–6.

Banz, R. W. and M. H. Miller, "Prices for State-Contingent Claims: Some Estimates and Applications," *Journal of Business*, October 1978, pp. 653–72.

Black, F. and M. Scholes, "The Pricing of Options and Corporate Liabilities," *Journal of Political Economy*, May–June 1975, pp. 637–54.

Breeden, D. T. and R. Litzenberger, "Prices of State-Contingent Claims Implicit in Option Prices," *Journal of Business*, October 1978, pp. 621–51.

Debreu, G., *The Theory of Value*, New York: Wiley, 1959.

Fama, E. F., "Risk-Adjusted Discount Rates and Capital Budgeting Under Uncertainty," *Journal of Financial Economics*, August 1977, pp. 3–24.

Hirshleifer, J., "Investment Decisions under Uncertainty: Choice Theoretic Approaches," *Quarterly Journal of Economics*, November 1965, pp. 509–36.

——, "Investment Decisions under Uncertainty: Application of the State Preference Approach," *Quarterly Journal of Economics*, May 1966, pp. 252–77.

Kraus, A. and R. Litzenberger, "Market Equilibrium in a Multiperiod State Preference Model with Logarithmic Utility," *Journal of Finance*, December 1975, pp. 1213–77.

Rubinstein, M., "An Aggregation Theorem for Securities Markets," *Journal of Financial Economics*, September 1974, pp. 225–44.

——, "The Strong Case for the Generalized Logarithmic Utility Model as the Premier Model of Financial Markets," *Journal of Finance*, May 1976, pp. 551–71.

——, "The Valuation of Uncertain Income Streams and the Pricing of Options," *Bell Journal of Economics*, fall 1976, pp. 407–25.

Stigler, George J., *The Theory of Price*, New York: Macmillan, 1966, p. 6.

Chapter 6

Resolution of uncertainty

A passage like that is not wrong, but it only appears to be saying something.

(Robert M. Solow, *New York Times,* July 12, 1987, Book Review section, p. 36)

How does the timing of the receipt of information affect the value of an asset and its expected rate of return? Traditional capital budgeting analysis focuses on the cash flows and their timing. It does not explicitly include quantitative inputs concerning the timing of information releases that partially or fully resolve the uncertainty about future cash flows. A better understanding of these topics helps determine the appropriate discount rate to use.

RISKS, RETURNS AND THE RESOLUTION OF UNCERTAINTY

An asset will be referred to as *risky* if some or all of its future cash flows are uncertain. In general, investors will demand a higher expected return to compensate for the systematic risk associated with the future cash flows of an asset. Systematic risks are risks that cannot be reduced or eliminated by diversification. Therefore an asset whose cash flows are exposed to positive systematic risks will have a lower price, and a higher expected rate of return than another asset whose cash flows are not exposed to systematic risks.

New information about the value of an asset is relevant if it permits a more accurate estimate of the asset's cash flows. If the new information is favorable, the value of the asset will increase. If it is unfavorable, the value of the asset will decrease. In any case, when relevant new information becomes available, there tends to be a reduction in the uncertainty about the value of the asset. The term "resolution of uncertainty" is used to refer to a situation in which the arrival of relevant new information reduces the uncertainty about the future value of an asset. Two consequences typically accompany the resolution of uncertainty. The first is less uncertainty about the value of the asset. The second is a change in the value of the asset. The change may be good or bad. The person who owns the asset when the new information is released bears the risk of this change in value.

There is a close connection between the amount and kind of uncertainty resolution expected for an asset in a particular period and the equilibrium expected rate of return of the asset during that period. There is also a close connection between the new information that occurs in the period and the realized rate of return that occurs during the period.

Assume no interim cash flows for the following three situations.

■ If no new information about the future cash flows is expected in a particular period, the equilibrium expected rate of return on the asset in that period will equal the default-free short term interest rate. If no new information is received in the period, the actual rate or return on the asset will equal the default-free short term interest rate.

■ If the new information expected in a particular period pertains only to non-systematic risks affecting the cash flows, the expected rate of return on the asset will equal the default-free short-term interest rate. However, depending on what new information is received, the realized rate of return during the period will usually not equal the short-term interest rate.

■ If the new information expected in a particular period includes information pertaining to systematic risks affecting the cash flows, the expected rate of return on the asset will differ from the default-free short-term interest rate by an amount that depends on the systematic risk to which the asset is exposed during the period. The realized rate of return will differ from its expected value by an amount that depends on the new information that actually occurs.

A risky asset may have periods during its life in which it functions as a safe or relatively riskless asset because little or no new information about its future cash flows is expected. There may be other periods in which an asset's risk is intensified because a great deal of new information will become available. For example, much of the uncertainty about how consumers will react to a new product or a new model of an established product is determined during the first few months after its introduction.

In practice, all cash flows from a project are conventionally discounted at the same discount rate. This chapter illustrates that different discount rates may be appropriate during different periods of an asset's life, if there are predictable differences in how uncertainty about the asset is resolved. Chapter 8 shows that different cash flow components should be discounted at different discount rates if their risk characteristics are different.

To help understand how resolution of uncertainty affects the expected rate of return of an asset, we consider several numerical examples. We start by considering three simple assets, each of which generates cash flows in only one period. The assets are similar in many ways but they differ in when their cash flows occur, and in when the uncertainty about the cash flows is resolved. We use state preference methodology to describe the assets and determine their value at each point in time and their expected rate of return in each period.

After analyzing the simple assets we will consider two capital budgeting projects, each of which is a combination of two of the three assets. Using the known characteristics of the assets, we calculate the expected rate of return of the projects in each period. The projects are analogous to investment portfolios and the underlying assets in the projects are analogous to the securities that make up an investment portfolio.

INTRODUCING THE THREE ASSETS

To keep the examples as simple as possible we limit ourselves to assets with at most a two period life. In each period there are two possible states of the economy, good or bad. Both states are assumed to be equally likely. The chance of the good state occurring in period 2 is the same regardless of whether the good or bad state has occurred in period 1.

Asset cash flows

Each asset generates cash flows of either $130 or $90 in one of the two periods. Asset A generates cash flows in period 1. For Asset A, the actual cash flows depend on the state of the economy in period 1. If the economy is in the good state Asset A generates $130; if the economy is in the bad state Asset A generates $90. Asset A generates no cash flows in period 2. Assets B and C generate cash flows in period 2 and no cash flows in period 1. The cash flows generated by Asset B depend on the state of the economy. The cash flows are $130 if the economy is in the good state and $90 if the economy is in the bad state in period 2. The cash flows generated by Asset C in period 2 depend on the state the economy in period 1. If the economy is in the good state in period 1, Asset C generates $130 in period 2. If the economy is in the bad state in period 1, Asset C generates $90 in period 2. These assumptions are summarized graphically in Figure 6.1.

To provide some intuition for these characteristics to think of the cash flow from Assets A and B as coming from sales of goods that are carried in inventory and are available for sale. By contrast, the cash flows from Asset C come from the sale of goods that are made to order. The goods are ordered in period 1 but produced and delivered in period 2.

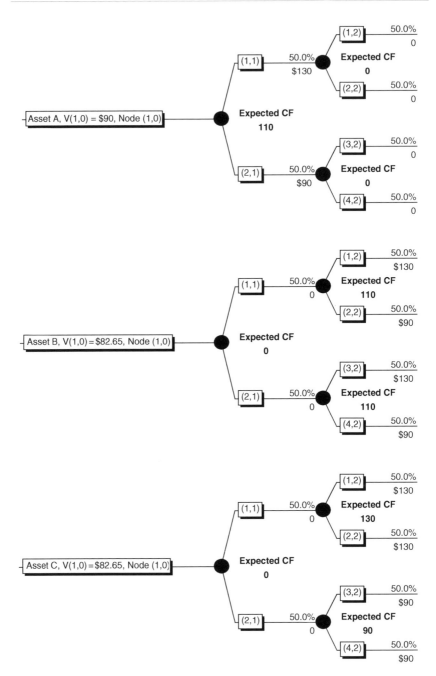

Figure 6.1 Assets A, B and C and their cash flows

Source: The tree diagrams in this figure were drawn with the help of PrecisionTree, a software product of Palisade Corps., Ithaca, NY; www.palisade.com

Economic environment: Explanations of Table 6.1

Table 6.1 provides a detailed description of the economic environment for Assets A, B and C. Each tree diagram in Figure 6.1 contains six branches, two in period 1 and four in period 2. Each of the six rows in Table 6.1 corresponds to one branch of the tree diagram. The node identifications in Table 6.1 use the notation introduced in Chapter 5 where n represents the node number at a given time, and t represents the time period. In each tree there is one node at time 0, two at time 1 and 4 at time 2. Each node at times 1 and 2 is connected to its originating node by a branch. Each branch carries the designation of the node it is heading for (to the right), the conditional probability of that branch given the originating node, and the cash flow that occurs at the ending node. For example, in the Asset A tree, the top branch from node (1, 0) is designated (1, 1). The (1, 1) branch is heading for node (1, 1). The probability of branch (1, 1) is 50 percent and the cash flow that occurs at node (1, 1) is $130. The branch (2, 1) is heading for node (2, 1), the probability of the branch is 50 percent and the cash flow at that node is $90.

For all examples in this chapter, branches emerge from three different nodes. These originating nodes are listed in column 1 of Table 6.1. The branches that emerge from each node are listed in column 2. Columns 3 through 8 describe the general economic conditions. These values are applicable for all three assets and for the two projects that will be created by combining the assets. Column 3, headed $p(n, t)$, gives the conditional probabilities of the branches. The conditional probabilities for all branches coming from a node sum to one. Column 4, headed pvf(n, t), gives the one period present value factor for default-free cash flows. For convenience, the value given is the same for both periods and corresponds to a default free

Table 6.1 Common economic environment for assets A, B and C

Originating node (n, t)	Branch (n, t)	Probability of branch p(n, t)	One period present value factor pvf(n, t) $(1.088889)^{-1}$	Risk adjustment factor raf(n, t)	Expected value of raf(n, t) eraf(n, t) Col.5 times Col.3	One-period risk adjusted present value factor s(n, t) Col.6 times Col.4	Time-zero risk adjusted present value factor S(n, t)
(1)	(2)	(3)	(4)	(5)	(6)	(7)	(8)
(1, 0)	(1, 1)	0.5	0.9184	0.40	0.2	0.1837	0.1837
(1, 0)	(2, 1)	0.5	0.9184	1.60	0.8	0.7347	0.7347
(1, 1)	(1, 2)	0.5	0.9184	0.40	0.2	0.1837	0.0337
(1, 1)	(2, 2)	0.5	0.9184	1.60	0.8	0.7347	0.1349
(2, 1)	(3, 2)	0.5	0.9184	0.40	0.2	0.1837	0.1349
(2, 1)	(4, 2)	0.5	0.9184	1.60	0.8	0.7347	0.5398

99

interest rate of 8.8889 percent. (The interest rate must be the same for all branches from a single node.) The interest rate could vary from one originating node to another. Column 5, headed raf(n, t), gives the risk-adjustment factor for each branch. The raf(n, t) measures the value of a dollar at that branch relative to the value of dollars at other possible branches that emanate from the same node. The risk adjustment factor is smaller for the nodes in which the economy is good and larger for those in which the economy is poor.

The values in columns 3, 4 and 5 define an economic environment for all three assets. Changing any of these values would change the numerical values in our examples, but would not change the substance of our general conclusions. The values in columns 6, 7 and 8 are derived from the values in columns 3, 4 and 5.

Column 6, headed eraf(n, t), is the product of the risk adjustment factor times the probability factor. The formula for this quantity is eraf$(n, t) = p(n, t) \cdot$ raf(n, t). For example, for row $(1, 1)$,

$$\text{eraf}(1, 1) = p(1, 1) \cdot \text{raf}(1, 1) = 0.5 \cdot 0.4 = 0.2.$$

The sum of the eraf(n, t) for all branches originating from a common node must equal one. For example two branches $(1, 1)$ and $(2, 1)$ emerge from node $(1, 0)$, The sum of the eraf(n, t) values of these two branches is $1.0 [= 0.2 + 0.8]$.

Multiplying the eraf of a branch by the cash flow of the branch and summing over all branches from a common node produces the certainty equivalent (CE) of the cash flows from that node. Figure 6.1 shows that for Asset A the cash flows associated with branches $(1, 1)$ and $(2, 1)$ are $130 and $90 respectively. The CE of the period 1 cash flows is $98 [= (0.2)\$130 + (0.8)\$90]$, where eraf$(1, 1) = 0.2$ and eraf$(2, 1) = 0.8$. Discounting the $98 certainty equivalent by the one-period default-free discount rate of 8.8889 percent gives $90, which is the risk-adjusted present value of Asset A's cash flows.

In column 7, the quantity $s(n, t)$ is the one-period risk-adjusted present value factor for node (n, t). The formula for $s(n, t)$ is $s(n, t) = p(n, t) \cdot$ pvf$(n, t) \cdot$ raf(n, t) or equivalently, $s(n, t) = $ eraf$(n, t) \cdot$ pvf(n, t). For $s(1, 1)$ we have $0.9184(0.2) = 0.1837$ and for $s(2, 1)$ we have $0.9184(0.8) = 0.7347$. Multiplying $s(n, t)$ by the value of the end-of-period cash flow from node (n, t) gives the risk-adjusted present value of the cash flow at the beginning of the node. The sum of the products of the period 1 cash flows of Asset A times the corresponding one period risk-adjusted present value factors, $s(n, 1)$, is $(0.1837) \cdot \$130 + (0.7347) \cdot \$90 = \$23.88 + \$66.12 = \$90.00$. This agrees with the calculation in the previous paragraph of Asset A's value at time zero using the product of the default free rate and the certainty equivalent of the cash flows. This relationship will be used repeatedly in later sections to determine the value of assets and projects.

In column 8, the quantity $S(n, t)$ is the multi-period risk-adjusted present value factor. Multiplying the end-of-period cash flow from node (n, t) by $S(n, t)$ gives the risk-adjusted present value of the cash flow at time zero (the beginning of the tree). For $t = 1$, $S(n, 1) = s(n, 1)$. For $t > 1$ the value of $S(n, t)$ is obtained by multiplying the values of the one-period risk-adjusted present value factors for all of the branches from the origin of the tree to the node in question. For example, the path for the outcome at the end of branch $(3, 2)$ goes through the lower branch $(2, 1)$, in period 1, and the upper branch, $(3, 2)$, in period 2. The risk-adjusted present value at time zero of a dollar that occurs at the end of branch $(3, 2)$ is $0.1349 [=$1.00(0.7347)(0.1827)]$ after correcting for error due to rounding.

ASSET VALUES BY NODE

The value of an asset at any node is the risk-adjusted present value of all of the future cash flows that can be generated starting from that node. Using the risk-adjusted present value factors of Column 7 in Table 6.1 we compute the value of the assets at time 0 and at both of the possible time 1 nodes. All of the assets have a zero value at all time 2 nodes, since there are no cash flows after time 2. The results are shown in Table 6.2. Following the table is a detailed explanation of how the results were computed.

We have already determined that the value of Asset A at time zero is $90. Its value at both time 1 nodes is $0 since Asset A generates no cash flows in period 2.

The value of asset B at node $(1, 1)$ e.g., if economic conditions are good during period 1, is given by the following:

$$V_B(1, 1) = X_B(1, 2) \cdot s(1, 2) + X_B(2, 2) \cdot s(2, 2) = \$130(0.1837)$$
$$+ \$90(0.7347) = X_B(1,2) \text{ is the cash flow at time 2 and path } (1,2).$$
$$= \$23.88 + \$66.12 = \$90.00$$

Table 6.2 Asset values by asset and node ($)

Asset	Node	Time 0	Time 1
	(1, 0)	(1, 1)	(2, 1)
A	90.00	0.00	0.00
B	82.65	90.00	90.00
C	82.65	119.39	82.65

If economic conditions are poor, the value of the asset at node $(2, 1)$ is as follows:

$$V_B(2, 1) = X_B(3, 2) \cdot s(3, 2) + X_B(4, 2) \cdot s(4, 2)$$
$$= \$130(0.1837) + \$90(0.7347) = \$23.88 + \$66.12 = \$90.00$$

Since B's cash flows at time one are zero, the value of asset B at time zero is the present value of the time two cash flows:

$$V_B(1, 0) = \{V_B(1, 1)\}s(1, 1) + \{V_B(2, 1)\}s(2, 1)$$
$$= \$90(0.1837) + 90(0.7347) = \$82.65^1$$

Next consider asset C. If economic conditions are good during period 1, asset C will generate cash flows of $130 at both of the possible period 2 nodes [(1, 2) and (2, 2)]. The value of Asset C at node (1, 1) is given by the following:

$$V_C(1, 1) = X_C(1, 2)\, s(1, 2) + X_C(2, 2)\, s(2, 2)$$
$$= \$130\,(0.1837) + \$130\,(0.7347) = \$119.39$$

where $s(n, t)$ is the one-period risk-adjusted present value factor for the end of branch (n, t). If economic conditions are poor during period 1, asset C will generate cash flows of $90 at both of the possible period 2 nodes [(3, 2) and (4, 2)]. The value of Asset C at node (2, 1) is given by:

$$V_C(2, 1) = X_C(3, 2) \cdot s(3, 2) + X_C(4, 2)\, s(4, 2)$$
$$= \$90\,(0.1837) + \$90\,(0.7347) = \$82.65$$

The value of asset C at time zero is given by

$$V_C(1, 0) = \{V_C(1, 1)\}s(1, 1) + \{V_C(2, 1)\}s(2, 1)$$
$$= \$119.39(0.1837) + 82.65(0.7347) = \$82.65$$

The state conditional asset values in Table 6.2 are presented graphically in Figure 6.2.

EXPECTED RATES OF RETURN BY ASSET AND NODE

We now calculate the expected rate of return on each of the assets for each node in which the asset value is not zero. The results are previewed in Table 6.3.

At time zero, the value of Asset A is $90. At the end of period 1 its cash flow will either be $130 or $90, depending on whether economic conditions are good or bad. Since each of the two states is equally likely, Asset A's expected cash flow at the end of period 1 is $110. Its value at the end of period 1 (after the cash flows

---

1 Corrected for rounding errors.

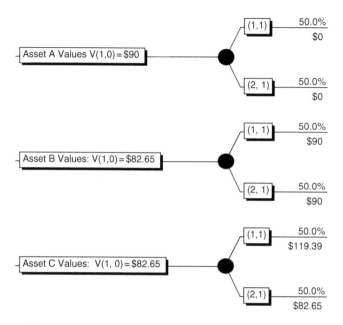

Figure 6.2 *Asset values by asset and node*

Source: The tree diagrams in this figure were drawn with the help of PrecisionTree, a software product of Palisade Corps., Ithaca, NY; www.palisade.com

have been received) is zero since there are no cash flows in period 2. Define the expected rate of return on the time zero asset value to be

($110 − $90)/$90 = 2/9 = 0.222222 = 22.22 percent.

Asset B's value at time zero is $82.65. No cash flows are expected during period 1. At the end of period 1, its value will be $90 for certain, since its value at both possible nodes, (1, 1) and (2, 1) is $90 (see Table 6.2.) Therefore the expected rate of return on the value of Asset B during period 1 is 8.89 percent [=($90 − $82.65)/$82.65 = $7.35/$82.65 = 0.088888]. At the beginning of period 2, Asset B looks like Asset A at time zero. Its value is $90. Its period 2 cash flows will be either $130 or $90 depending on what state occurs. At the end of

Table 6.3 *Expected rates of return by asset and node (%)*

Asset	Node		
	(1,0)	(1,1)	(2,1)
A	22.22	NA	NA
B	8.89	22.22	22.22
C	22.22	8.89	8.89

103

period 2, its value will be zero. Therefore Asset B's period 2 expected rate of return will be the same as Asset A's period 1 expected rate of return, namely 22.22 percent.

Asset C's value at time 0 is worth $82.35. It will generate no cash flows during period 1. At the end of period 1 it will be worth $119.39 if business conditions in period 1 are good or $82.65 if business conditions are poor. Since each of these scenarios is equally likely, the expected end-of-period-one value of Asset C is $101.02 [=($119.39 + $82.65)/2] and its expected rate of return is 22.22 percent [=$101.02 − $82.65)/$82.65]. At the end of period 1, the cash flows that Asset C will generate in period 2 are known. As shown in Table 6.2, if business conditions have been good in period 1, the value of the asset will be $119.39, its end-of-period cash flows will be $130 and its rate of return will be 8.88 percent [=($130 − $119.39)/$119.39 = $10.61/$119.39 = 0.088888 = 8.89 percent]. If business conditions have been poor in period 1, the value of the asset will be $82.65, its end-of-period 2 cash flows will be $90 and its rate of return will be 8.88 percent [=($90 − $82.65)/$82.65 = $7.35/$82.65 = 0.088888 = 8.89 percent].

These results about expected rates of return are summarized graphically in Figure 6.3.

CONCLUSIONS ABOUT THE THREE ASSETS

Assets A, B and C each generate cash flows in only one period. At time 0 there is uncertainty about the magnitude of the cash flows for each of the assets, but there is no uncertainty about when they will occur. The actual cash flows can be either $130 or $90; the two possibilities are equally likely and given the information available at time 0 the expected future cash flows from each asset are $110.

Asset A's cash flows occur in period 1. The value of Asset A is $90 at time 0 and its expected rate of return in period 1 is 22.22 percent. The actual rate of return is either 44.44 percent or 0 percent, depending on which state occurs. There is uncertainty about Asset A's cash flows at time 0 but at time 1 there is none. Therefore Asset A's uncertainty has been resolved in period 1.

Asset B's cash flows occur in period 2. There is uncertainty about the value of these cash flows at time 0 and at time 1 but not at time 2. Therefore for asset B there is no resolution of uncertainty during period 1 but there is during period 2. Asset B has an expected rate of return of 8.89 percent, during period 1 and 22 percent during period 2.

Asset C's cash flows occur in period 2. There is uncertainty about the value of these cash flows at time 0 and but not at time 1 or at time 2. Therefore for asset C there is resolution of uncertainty during period 1 but not during period 2. Asset C has an expected rate of return of 22 percent during period 1 and 8.89 percent during period 2.

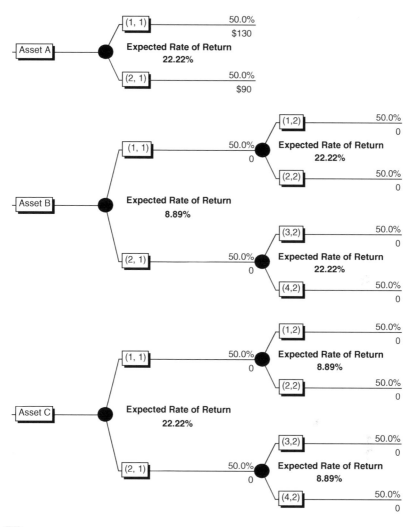

Figure 6.3 Expected rates of return by asset and node

Source: The tree diagrams in this figure were drawn with the help of PrecisionTree, a software product of Palisade Corps., Ithaca, NY; www.palisade.com

Assets A and B are similar in that no uncertainty about the magnitude of their cash flows is resolved before the cash flows actually occur. Asset C is like asset B in that its cash flows will occur in period 2. It is like Asset A in that the uncertainty about the cash flows is fully resolved during period 1.

The only expected rates of return possible with these three assets are 8.89 percent or 22.22 percent. In any given period uncertainty about the cash flows is either completely resolved or not resolved at all. The relationship between the expected rate of return and the resolution of uncertainty is summarized in Table 6.4. Since

105

Table 6.4 Uncertainty resolution and expected rate of return for assets A, B and C

Asset	Period	Uncertainty resolution?	Expected rate of return (%)
A	1	Yes	22
	2	NA	
B	1	No	9
	2	Yes	22
C	1	Yes	22
	2	No	9

asset A generates no cash flows after period 1, its value at the end of period 1 is zero, and it is not meaningful to talk about its rate of return during period 2.

AN ALTERNATIVE CALCULATION

The values of asset B and of asset C at time zero can be expressed as the present value of their period 2 expected cash flow discounted by two different interest rates. For both B and C

$$V(0) = \$110 \left(\frac{1}{1.08889} \right) \left(\frac{1}{1.2222} \right) = \$82.65$$

The 0.0889 discount rate is used for the period in which no uncertainty is resolved. The 0.2222 discount rate is used for the period in which uncertainty is resolved. This present value formula gives the correct expected value for each asset at time 1 if the expected cash flows are discounted using the appropriate discount rate. [$V_B(1) = \$82.65(1.08889)$. $V_C(1) = \$82.65(1.2222)$]. It is interesting to note that the IRR of both assets is equal to 15.37 percent which is equivalent to the following equation:

$$V(0) = \$110 \left(\frac{1}{1.1537} \right) \left(\frac{1}{1.1537} \right) = \$82.65$$

This equation incorrectly implies that the expected value of the asset at time 1 is $95.35 [$=\$82.65(1.1537)$] while the correct values are either $101.02 [$= (\$119.39 + \$82.65)/2 = \$82.65(1.2222)$] for asset C and $90 [$=\$82.65 (1.0889)$] for asset B.

In the next section we consider two capital budgeting projects that have a more complex structure. Each project consists of a combination two of the three assets analyzed above.

INTRODUCING THE TWO PROJECTS

To help understand how resolution of uncertainty affects the expected rate of return of an asset, we consider an example with two projects. The two projects generate cash flows for two periods. The projects will be referred to as Project 1 and Project 2. Project 1 is composed of Asset A and Asset B. Project 2 is composed of Asset A and Asset C. The value of a project at any node is the sum of the values of its components. The expected rate of return of a project at any node is a value-weighted average of the rates of return of its components at that node.

Projects 1 and 2 have identical cash flows in period 1. In both projects there is uncertainty about the period 1 cash flows at time zero and this uncertainty is resolved during period 1. These two projects differ in the extent to which period 1 events resolve uncertainty about the period 2 cash flows. The period 1 cash flows of Project 1 provide no information about its period 2 cash flows. Uncertainty about each period's cash flows is resolved during the period in which the cash flows occur. The period 1 cash flows of Project 2 are perfectly correlated with its period 2 cash flows. When the period 1 cash flows are realized they completely resolve the uncertainty about the period 2 cash flows.

Table 6.5 gives the value of both projects at each relevant node. Table 6.6 provides the expected rate of return for both of the projects at each node. The relationship between the expected rates of return of the two projects and the resolution of uncertainty at each node is summarized in Table 6.7. For project 1 during period 1, there is

Table 6.5 Project values by project and node ($)

Project	Node		
	(1,0)	(1, 1)	(2, 1)
1	172.65	90.00	90.00
2	172.65	119.39	82.65

Table 6.6 Expected rates of return by project and node (%)

Project	Node		
	(1,0)	(1, 1)	(2, 1)
1	15.84	22.22	22.22
2	22.22	8.89	8.89

107

Table 6.7 *Uncertainty resolution and expected rate of return for projects 1 and 2*

Project	Period	Uncertainty resolution?	Expected rate of return (%)
1	1	Partial	16
	2	Yes	22
2	1	Yes	22
	2	No	9

a partial resolution of uncertainty. The uncertainty about the period 1 rate of return is fully resolved, and the expected rate of return of that component of the project is 22.22 percent. On the other hand, there is no resolution of uncertainty about the period 2 cash flows of the project, and that component of the project earns 8.889 percent. The weighted average of the expected rate of return of these two components is 15.84 percent [$= (90/172.65)0.2222 + (82.65/172.65)0.8889 = 0.1584$]. This return is shown for project 1 for the return expected at node $(1, 0)$.

GLOBAL BUSINESS ASPECTS

Investments in international assets frequently are made with the intention of reinvesting proceeds in the foreign country and not returning the cash flows to the domestic country until a distant time period. The motivation may be to avoid high tax rates.

Assume a situation where the US corporate tax rate is much larger than that of the foreign country. There is a tax incentive to leave the funds invested in the foreign country.

In 2004, the US tax law was changed so that the tax rate on cash returned to the US was much lower than the normal 0.35 corporate tax rate. While there were limitations on how the returned cash could be used, many firms brought to the US the cash that had for many years resided in foreign countries.

If a firm expects that the cash will not be brought back for many years (e.g., until the tax rate is reduced), then there is considerable uncertainty for a long period of time since it is necessary to forecast an exchange rate of a long distant time period. This lack of immediate uncertainty resolution adds to the risk of foreign investments.

GENERALIZATIONS

Suppose that at time zero ($t = 0$) there is an asset that generates cash flows only at some fixed future date, T where $T > 1$. The timing of the resolution of uncertainty will affect how the value of the asset changes from time 0 to time 2.

Assets B and C illustrate this situation. Both assets have payoffs only at time 2 and at time 0 the probability distribution of the time 2 payoffs is the same for both. Both assets are expected to generate cash flows of $110 at time 2 and both assets have the same value at time 0, namely $82.65. But the timing of the resolution of uncertainty is different between them and the two assets do not necessarily have the same value at time 1. If all that one cares about is the present value of the asset at time zero, then this value can be expressed as

$$V_0 = \frac{\$110}{(1 + r_1)(1 + r_2)} = \$82.65$$

Any two values of r_1 and r_2 will work as long as the product $(1 + r_1)(1 + r_2)$ equals 1.3309. For example r_1 equal 0.08889 and r_2 equal 0.2222, or vice versa, or both values equal to 0.1537, or one value equal to 1.1 and the other equal to 1.2099 will work.

The reasoning in the above paragraph depends on two assumptions. One is that the owner of an asset can do nothing to affect the future cash flows. That may not be the case. For example, if the new information that arrives indicates a high probability of a negative cash flow, then the owner of the asset might decide to scrap it because the loss from scraping the asset may be less than the loss from operating it.

More importantly, most real projects have cash flows that arrive at multiple future periods. In this situation, we want an accurate value for the project as a whole. We can do this by finding the correct value for each component cash flow, and add up the values of the components, or by combining all the cash flows and discounting them by an average discount rate. Both of these approaches are likely to require taking the timing of the resolution of uncertainty into account.

PROBLEMS

1 Assume that there are complete markets available for selling uncertain outcomes, and that the investment can be scaled to any size. The certainty equivalent for this investment is equal to the expected value divided by 1.2. The default-free interest rate is 0.10. The investment pays off at time 2. Assume that the investor buys three claims with the following characteristics. The claims pay cash flows at time 2:

Payoff at time 2
$1,200 Mean cash flow
$1,320 Mean cash flow
$1,452 Mean cash flow

a.   What are the certainty equivalents of the cash flows?

b.   What should be the market values of each of the three investments?

2   (*Continue 1*) Divide the $1,320 cash flow of investment B into three components.

a.   Return of money invested.

b.   Return on money invested (0.10).

c.   Expected return for bearing risk.

3   (*Continue 1*) Assume the payoffs for three investments are as follows:

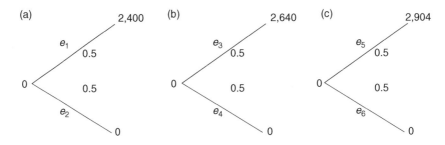

Investing in all three, what is the probability of a zero cash flow if the outcomes of all three investments are statistically independent?

4   Assume an asset will generate cash two periods from now. The certainty equivalent of the uncertain cash flows is $1,210. Assume the possible outcomes are:

Event	Probability	Outcome	Expectation
e_1	0.25	4,000	1,000
e_2	0.50	800	400
e_3	0.25	208	52
		Expected Cash Flow	1,452

The outcome of the investment is determined at time 2, immediately before the cash flows are received. The certainty equivalent is equal to the expected value divided by 1.2.

a.   What is the value of the certainty equivalent at time 1?

b.   With a 0.10 risk-free rate and complete markets, what is the value of the asset at time zero?

c.   What is the value of the asset at time 2 before the outcome is determined?

d.   What is the value of the asset at time 2 immediately after the uncertainty is resolved?

5   (*Continue 4*) What is the internal rate of return that the investors require if $1,000 is paid for the asset?

6 (*Continue 4*) Compute the asset's present value as of time zero and time one:
   a. Using a 0.205 discount rate applied to the expected value.
   b. Using a 0.10 discount rate applied to the certainty equivalent.
   c. Compare the present values for time zero and time one.

DISCUSSION QUESTION

Consider the drilling for oil. Describe how and when uncertainty is resolved. Is drilling for oil risky?

BIBLIOGRAPHY

Bierman, H. and W. H. Hausman, "The Resolution of Investment Uncertainty Through Time," *Management Science*, August 1972, pp. B654–B662.

Brenner, Menachem and S. Smidt, "A Simple Model of Non-Stationary Systematic Risk," *Journal of Finance*, September, 1977, pp. 1081–92.

Hausman, Warren H., "Sequential Decision Problems: A Model to Exploit Existing Forecasters," *Management Science*, October 1969, pp. 93–111.

Hertz, David B., "Investment Policies That Pay Off," *Harvard Business Review*, January–February 1968, pp. 96–108.

Hillier, Frederick S., "The Derivation of Probabilistic Information for the Evaluation of Risky Investments," *Management Science*, April 1963, pp. 443–57.

Naslund, Bertil, "A Model of Capital Budgeting Under Risk," *Journal of Business*, April 1966, pp. 257–71.

Pratt, John U., "Risk Aversion in the Small and in the Large," *Econometrica*, January 1964, pp. 132–36.

Robichek, A. A. and S. C. Myers, "Valuation of the Firm: Effects of Uncertainty in a Market Context," *Journal of Finance*, May 1966, pp. 215–27.

Salazar, R. C. and S. K. Sen, "A Simulation Model of Capital Budgeting Under Uncertainty," *Management Science*, December 1968, pp. 161–79.

Van Horne, James C., "The Analysis of Uncertainty Resolution in Capital Budgeting for New Products," *Management Science*, April 1969, pp. 376–86.

Weingartner, H. Martin, "Some New Views on the Payback Period and Capital Budgeting Decisions," *Management Science*, August 1969, pp. 594–607.

——, "Capital Rationing: Authors in Search of a Plot," *Journal of Finance*, December 1977, pp. 1403–32.

Wilson, Robert B., "Investment Analysis Under Uncertainty," *Management Science*, August 1969, pp. 650–64.

Chapter 7

Diversification and risk reduction

Ten percent of what I teach is wrong and should be ignored. The problem
is that I do not know which ten percent.

(Cornell University Professor)

A major objective of a capital budgeting analysis is to have the decision consistent with
how the market value of a firm will change if the firm accepts the capital project under
consideration. If the decision is to accept the project, the market value of the firm
must be expected to increase. In theory, the proposed capital investment project is
evaluated from the viewpoint of a representative investor who is free to buy or sell
additional shares in the firm that owns the project. Such an investor will tend to buy
additional shares and thus bid up the price of the stock if the new project is worth
more than it costs. Similarly, if the new project is worth less than it costs the investor
will tend to sell shares in the firm and thus reduce their price. While the actual
decision-makers in a firm may not always be able to determine whether the decision
is consistent with the objective of maximizing the market value of the firm, they
should be concerned with the potential effect of their capital budgeting decisions on
the firm's market value. Even if a firm is privately held, if the possibility exists that the
firm might someday go public or be sold to a public firm, or continue as a private firm,
managers will be concerned with how the decision affects the firm's future value.

The primary objective of this chapter is to clarify the nature of risk and what
can be achieved by diversification. Managers are naturally concerned with their
own interests, the interests of their operating units, the well-being of their firms,
and the well-being of the stockholders of their firms. It would be very surprising
if one measure of the investment's value evaluated perfectly the interests of all
these parties. Thus the objective is to understand the uses and limitations of several
measures of investment value given the presence of uncertainty.

Consider a situation where the NPV measure of a project is positive. In order to evaluate the project, given a considerable amount of uncertainty, the decision-maker might want to know the variance of the project's NPV's. Before buying a bond an investor will want to know the bond's yield to first call, yield to maturity, and compare these measures to the yield of a Treasury Bond.

SYSTEMATIC AND UNSYSTEMATIC RISK

We assume that the representative investors are risk averse. Risk averse investors are willing to hold securities that they perceive as high risk only if they expect to receive a sufficiently high return to compensate for the high risk. Since risk tends to reduce market value, other things being equal, to be attractive riskier investments must have higher expected returns.

It is normally advantageous for investors to diversify. Modern capital markets make diversification easy and inexpensive for investors. Some types of risk associated with individual securities tend to become less important when the securities are part of a diversified portfolio. If the risk of the security is independent of the risks of a well diversified portfolio it need not add to the concern of the owner of the portfolio. Risks that tend to disappear in well diversified portfolios are referred to as diversifiable or non-systematic risks. Other risks persist without reduction in diversified portfolios. Such risks are referred to as un-diversifiable or systematic risks. When a security with systematic risk is added to a diversified portfolio, the additional systematic risk is added to the risk of the portfolio.

These considerations regarding risk have profound consequences for the pricing of securities and for the evaluation of capital investment projects. Well diversified investors should attempt to consider only systematic risk when deciding which securities to include in their portfolio.

Given the ability of investors to diversify, it is important to distinguish between systematic and non-systematic risks when analyzing a capital budgeting project. When it comes to estimating how the project will affect the market value of the firm, it is theoretically appropriate for the well diversified investor to ignore non-systematic risks. Frequently the mangers who will make the ultimate decision about whether to accept or reject the project are also affected by the outcome of the project. Their reputation, compensation and perhaps even their continued employment may depend to some extent on the success of the project. In these circumstances, the managers will want to understand how accepting or rejecting the project will impact their personal situation. In addition, non-systematic risks can affect the ability of the firm to execute its strategic plans successfully. For these reasons, both the systematic and non-systematic risks associated with the capital budgeting project are relevant. The important point is that managers who must make decisions about a project often have different points of view and may reach a different conclusion relative to a project than well-diversified stockholders.

A very large can corporation organized a capital budgeting seminar for its management. The professor gave a brilliant lecture describing the relevance of systematic risk and the lack of relevance of non-systematic risk. He illustrated this point with an example where there was a large probability of losing a lot of money, but the risk was all non-systematic risk.

The manager of the steel division made it clear, with very strong language, that he would not accept the investment with a large probability of a large loss. He did not care (he used stronger language) that this risk was not systematic.

DIVERSIFICATION

Normally, it is not a desirable strategy for individual investors who are risk averse to put all their funds into the one best stock or bond or into securities with highly similar risk characteristics. The disadvantage of an investor buying investments with similar risk characteristics is that if some unfavorable event occurs that greatly affects some of the investments, it is likely to affect all the investments in the same way, and it may have a drastic effect on the investor's total financial situation.

Stock market investors typically attempt to spread their investments in common stocks over a large number of different companies in different industries. When this strategy is followed, an unfavorable event specific to a firm, adversely affecting the value of that firm's common stock, will have a relatively small effect on the value of the entire portfolio. This is non-systematic risk. The risk affects only a specific firm or a small group of firms and therefore has little effect on the average results of all of the firms in the market.

The collection of marketable stocks and other marketable securities held by an individual investor is a portfolio. The portfolio problem might be defined as the problem of choosing a collection of securities that, taken together, has desirable characteristics with respect to risk and expected rate of return where there is a trade-off between risk and return. As is customary, we use the standard deviation or variance of the rate of return from a portfolio of securities to measure portfolio risk.

Two basic assumptions of portfolio analysis are that investors dislike risk and prefer higher returns to lower returns. It follows that investors will attempt to reduce risk without reducing expected returns, whenever it is possible. There is an incentive to use diversification to reduce the risk of a portfolio.

Although expected return is used to measure the benefits and the standard deviation or variance of return to measure the risk of a portfolio, it can properly be argued that other statistical measures are also of interest to investors. While using only two measures (two moments of the probability distribution of returns) is an approximation, it is a way of achieving a workable solution to a very complex problem.

INTRODUCTION TO PORTFOLIO ANALYSIS

Suppose an investor who already owns some assets is considering the purchase of an additional asset. The natural tendency is for the investor to focus on the risk of the individual asset being acquired. However, this may be misleading. The correct question is "How will the new asset affect the risk of my portfolio?" An asset that looks risky when viewed in isolation may or may not add to the risk of a portfolio. We will illustrate an extreme situation in which acquiring an asset that appears to be risky can actually reduce the risk of the investor's portfolio. This is an extremely important point that is not always fully appreciated in practice.

Figure 7.1 illustrates two assets that are available to the investor who has $900,000 of cash available for investment. Asset A is a project that requires an outlay of $400,000 and has two equally likely outcomes and expected benefits of $500,000. Assume that the benefits will result one year after the initial outlay has been made. The expected rate of return on an investment in the asset A is 25 percent. Based on the expected values, the project is apparently acceptable. Note that the outcomes are either $0 if event e_1 with 0.5 probability occurs or $1,000,000 if event e_2 with 0.5 probability occurs. Asset B costs $500,000 and has an expected payoff of $500,000 and an expected rate of return of zero. Any funds not invested in A or B can earn a zero risk rate of 5 percent.

Both assets A and B are capital budgeting types of real projects that can either be accepted or rejected. The investor cannot choose half of A or a quarter of B. A and B are economically independent projects. Accepting or rejecting A does not affect the payoffs of B and accepting or rejecting B does not affect the payoffs of A.

Projects A and B are economically independent but they are not statistically independent. The expected proceeds of each of the projects is $500,000. If event e_1

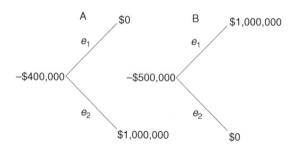

Figure 7.1 *Available investments*

occurs project A has a payoff of zero and investment B has a payoff of $1,000,000, so that the payoff of one project is determined by the payoff of the other project. This creates the statistical dependence. If the two projects were statistically independent, then knowing the payoff to one project would provide no information about the possible payoffs to the other project.

If we think about the projects one at a time, many of us would reject project A because of excessive risk. There is a 0.5 probability of losing $400,000. In rate-of-return terms, the expected rate of return of 25 percent earned by an investment in A is attractive; but the standard deviation of 125 percent is scary. Therefore, if you think about projects one at a time you are likely to find this investment very unattractive.

Now consider project B. It has a $500,000 outlay followed one year later by $500,000 of expected benefits. The expected rate of return on this project is zero, and the standard deviation of its rate of return is 100 percent. Accepting this project seems to add risk and no expected return, producing an infinite risk/reward ratio. If you disliked project A based on this type of logic, you should hate project B. Thus looking at individual projects, an investor is likely to reject both projects A and B.

If investments are made by looking at how accepting an investment affected the payoffs from the resulting portfolios, then very different investment decisions might result.

Accepting both projects A and B results in a $1,000,000 of proceeds for either event. The expected proceeds are $1,000,000 and the standard deviation of the proceeds is zero. The outlay is $900,000. The expected rate of return of the $900,000 portfolio is 11.1 percent and the standard deviation of the rate of return is zero. With a time value factor of less than 11.1 percent this portfolio (A plus B) is acceptable. Undertaking both projects is preferred to the 5 percent risk free return since the two projects return 11.1 percent with no risk.

THE PORTFOLIO PROBLEM IN PERSPECTIVE

The above simple example focuses on relationships that exist in more complex and hard to understand forms in real situations. Keeping the example simple clarifies some essential relationships between risk and return.

In the above example an investor starts with $900,000 of cash and is given an opportunity to acquire either or both of two risky projects. We showed that an investor who focused on the risks and rewards of individual investments, as measured by the expected value and standard deviations of the projects' rate of return, would be inclined to reject both of the projects. By contrast, an investor who focused on the risk and reward of the portfolios that are created by accepting or rejecting the two projects would be inclined to accept both of them. In this example, accepting the two risky investments creates a portfolio that has an 11.1 percent certain return and no risk. This is better than the 5 percent risk-free return.

One important conclusion from this example is that to make satisfactory investment decisions, it is necessary to know how accepting an individual investment will affect the risk and return of the relevant portfolio. It is relatively easy to measure how accepting an investment will change the expected benefits of the corresponding portfolio whether benefits are measured in present values or in rates of return. By contrast, the relationship between the risk of a project and the risk of the corresponding portfolio is much more complex. Because our example is simple, we can directly calculate the risk of all of the possible portfolios; there were only three different assets (including the risk-free alternative) and two different uncertain events. In a realistic situation, there might be hundreds or even thousands of potential assets and millions of events. Direct calculation of the risk characteristics of all of the possible portfolios that could be formed is not practical.

A measure of the risk of an individual investment is needed that describes how much risk the investment would add to a portfolio. We accept the portfolio's rate of return's standard deviation as an acceptable measure of portfolio risk. However, the standard deviation for an individual project is not an acceptable measure of how adding that project to a portfolio would change the risk of the portfolio. To develop an appropriate risk measure for individual investment project, we must first understand the co-variance concept.

THE CO-VARIANCE

The co-variance is a useful means of measuring how two random variables react to events. When the value of one investment is large, will the value of the other tend to be large or small? Three possible relationships between the two random variables X and Y shown in Figure 7.2.

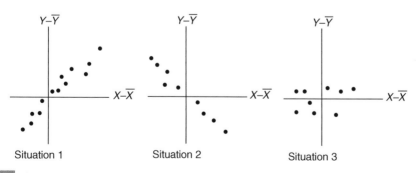

Figure 7.2 *Examples of co-variation*

In Figure 7.2 the X and Y axes have been shifted. Instead of the X axis being drawn where Y is equal zero, it is drawn where Y equals the expected value of Y. Similarly, the Y axis is located where X equals the expected value of X. As a result of these shifts, points at which both X and Y are above their average values lie in the upper-right quadrant and points in which both variables are below their average values lie in the lower left quadrant.

Situation 1 in Figure 7.2 illustrates positive co-variation. If one of the variables has an above (below) average value, the other tends to deviate in the same direction. Situation 2 in the figure illustrates negative co-variation. If one of the variables tends to be above average the other tends to be below average. Finally, situation 3 illustrates zero co-variation. Knowing that one of the variables is above (below) average provides no information about whether the other variable is likely to be above its mean or below its mean.

Suppose that X and Y represent rates of return on two different securities with similar expected values and standard deviations. We are interested in comparing the risk of a portfolio containing only X with the risk of a portfolio containing equal quantities of X and Y. Understanding which situation best describes the type of co-variation between X and Y would be helpful. The risk of the portfolio containing X and Y will be greatest if situation 1 applies, and least if situation 2 applies and at some intermediate level if situation 3 applies.

The co-variance is a quantitative measure of the co-variation between two random variables. The sign of the co-variance depends on the sign of the product of two deviation terms (the value of the random variable from the mean). If both of the deviation terms tend to have the same sign, as in situation 1 in Figure 7.2, then the product of the two deviation terms will tend to be positive. If the two deviations tend to have the opposite signs, as in situation 2, then the co-variance will tend to be negative. If situation 3 applies, the co-variance, will tend to be close to zero.

The co-variance is affected by the scale used to measure the variables. The correlation coefficient $(\rho_{x,y})$ is invariant to scale and is obtained by dividing the co-variance by the product of the two standard deviations for the two random variables

$$\rho_{x,y} = \frac{\text{cov}(X,Y)}{\sigma_x \sigma_y} \tag{7.1}$$

The correlation coefficient $\rho_{X,Y}$ can take on values between -1 and $+1$. The subscripts on the correlation coefficient are commonly omitted if the variables to which it refers are clear.

Using the co-variance, there is an exact formula connecting the variance of the value of a portfolio and the properties of its components. Let Z be the sum of the two random variables X and Y. The variance of Z is

$$\text{var}(Z) = \text{var}(X + Y) = \text{var}(X) + \text{var}(Y) + 2\text{cov}(X,Y) \tag{7.2}$$

The risk of undertaking both projects X and Y is equal to the individual risk of X plus the individual risk of Y, plus two times the co-variance of X and Y. If we have three random variables (X_1, X_2, and X_3), then

$$\text{var}(X_1 + X_2 + X_3) = \text{var}(X_1) + \text{var}(X_2) + \text{var}(X_3) + 2\text{cov}(X_1, X_2)$$
$$+ 2\text{cov}(X_1, X_3) + 2\text{cov}(X_2, X_3) \qquad (7.3)$$

Note that with three securities there are three different co-variances each of which carries a weight of two. There are six co-variances.

To understand the computation of the variance of the payoff of a portfolio, one can use a table of variances and co-variances that gives one line and one column for each of the assets in the portfolio. This table is a generalization of the formulas given in equations 7.2 and 7.3. For N assets there are N^2 entries in the table. All entries on the diagonal boxes are variances of the rates of return of the individual assets, and all other entries are their co-variances. The entries in the upper right-hand half corner (with the table split by the diagonal) mirrors the lower left-hand half. For three assets we have:

	1	2	3
1	$\text{Var}_{1,1}$	$\text{Cov}_{1,2}$	$\text{Cov}_{1,3}$
2	$\text{Cov}_{2,1}$	$\text{Var}_{2,2}$	$\text{Cov}_{2,3}$
3	$\text{Cov}_{3,1}$	$\text{Cov}_{3,2}$	$\text{Var}_{3,3}$

With N assets there are N^2 cells in the table. Of these, N are variances on the diagonal, and $N^2 - N$ are co-variances. Since each co-variance appears twice because ($\text{cov}_{i,j} = \text{cov}_{j,i}$) and there are N variances, there are $(N^2 - N)/2$ different co-variances.

With 100 different assets, there are 10,000 separate cells in the table, 100 variances and 9,900 co-variances. Each of 4,950 different co-variances are entered into the table twice. Note that there are many more co-variances than variances. With many different investments in the portfolio, the co-variances tend to be more heavily weighted than the variances (there are more of them) in determining the risk of the portfolio. The importance of the co-variance terms can be seen in the following formula

$$\text{Var (Portfolio)} = N(\text{Average variance}) + (N^2 - N)(\text{Average co-variance}) \qquad (7.4)$$

The portfolio being analyzed may be a collection of securities or of real assets. The same basic relationships apply. However, the co-variances may be different depending on whether the asset is being added to a division of a firm (how is the project correlated with the other assets of the division?) or is being added to a portfolio of securities (how is the rate of return correlated with that of the other securities of the portfolio?).

THE EFFICIENT FRONTIER OF INVESTMENT ALTERNATIVES

Figure 7.3 shows three portfolios. The expected rate of return is measured on Y axis, and the standard deviation of the rate of return is measured on the X axis. Using Figure 7.3 we conclude that

1   Portfolio 2 is better than portfolio 1 (same risk and higher mean return).
2   Portfolio 3 is better than portfolio 1 (same expected return and smaller risk).

Any portfolio that lands within the area bounded by the two vectors is better than (dominates) portfolio 1. It is desirable to move up, to the left, or up and to the left. If we compare portfolios 2 and 3, we cannot make a definite choice between them. Portfolio 2 has a larger expected return, but it also has more risk than portfolio 3. The choice will depend on the investor's preferences as to risk-return trade-off.

Taking all portfolios that are not dominated by other portfolios, we can form an efficient frontier of portfolios. All the portfolios on the efficient frontier are eligible for consideration. So far, the portfolios 2 and 3 would be on the frontier but portfolio 1 would not. The choice of a specific portfolio on the efficient frontier will depend on the investor's preferences and the availability of a risk-free investment alternative.

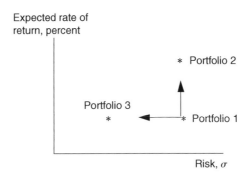

Figure 7.3 *Choosing portfolios*

PERFECT POSITIVE CORRELATION

Figure 7.4 shows the rates of return of two perfectly correlated ($\rho = 1$) assets, A and B. At point A 100 percent of the value of the portfolio is invested in asset A.

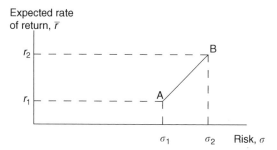

Figure 7.4 *Perfect linear dependence*

All combinations of asset A and asset B lie on the straight line connecting points A and B. As we substitute asset B for asset A, we move up the straight line AB toward point B.

PERFECT NEGATIVE CORRELATION

Figure 7.5 shows that if the rates of return of assets are perfectly negatively correlated (the correlation coefficient is equal to -1) then it is possible to attain a zero-risk portfolio. If we start with 100 percent of an investment in asset B, we are at point B. As we substitute some asset A for B, both the risk and the expected return decrease. At the point C the portfolio has zero risk. If still more asset A is introduced then the investor slides down line CA. There is increasing risk and decreasing expected rate of return (this is not desirable).

Any point on line CA is dominated by one or more points on line CB. No investor would want to have an amount of asset A that causes a portfolio to lie on line CA if it is feasible to acquire more of investment B.

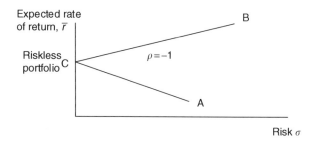

Figure 7.5 *Perfect negative correlation*

IMPERFECT CORRELATION

The correlation coefficient can take on any value between -1 and $+1$. Figure 7.6 shows the feasible portfolios resulting from different mixtures of A and B. If ρ is greater than minus one and less than plus one the locus of feasible portfolios is a curve inside the ABC triangle. If one starts with a portfolio consisting of 100 percent of security A and ρ is less than one, and begins to substitute security B for security A then the point representing the portfolio moves up and to the left of the AB line. The upward movement reflects the increase in the expected return of the portfolio. This is not surprising, since B has a higher expected return than A. Second, the risk of the portfolio may decrease if the value of ρ is small enough. The fact that the portfolio's expected rate of return and risk stays to the left of the AB line reflects the fact that the correlation coefficient between A and B is less than one.

Diversification allows one to substitute some B for A, increasing the expected return and at the same time may reduce risk if the assets are not perfectly correlated.

We will consider three cases: two are extremes. The first extreme case is perfect positive correlation. The second extreme case is perfect negative correlation. The third case is imperfect correlation. The two extreme cases are interesting because they set the boundaries for what is possible.

The construction of an efficient frontier of investments (portfolios) makes use of the concepts illustrated in Figure 7.6. Assets are combined to form portfolios that have less risk than the risk of its most risky components. By changing the composition of the portfolio, you can change its expected rate of return. If the correlation coefficient is equal to -1, it is possible for the portfolio to have zero risk.

THE POWER OF DIVERSIFICATION: INDEPENDENT INVESTMENTS

We want to show the advantages of diversification if investments are statistically independent so that the correlation coefficient is equal to zero.

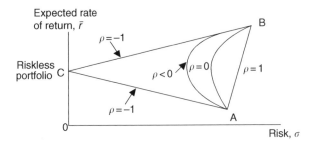

Figure 7.6 Two securities and different values of ρ

Consider investment E of Figure 7.7. With the outcomes at time zero, the investment has a $400 expected value and a 40 percent expected immediate return. It is desirable to a risk-neutral investor, but a risk-averse investor might reject it because there is a 0.5 probability of losing $1,000. Any fraction of E can be purchased.

Investment F is identical to E except that its outcomes are independent of the outcomes of E. The $1,000 is now split between E and F. The outcomes of investing $500 in E with 0.5 probability of winning $1,400 and investing $500 in F are shown in Figure 7.8. Now there is only 0.25 probability of losing $1,000. Some of the probability of the two extreme outcomes has been shifted to the less extreme net outcome of $400. The variance of outcomes has been cut in half with no change in the expected value.

If there were additional independent investments, we could further reduce the risk. In fact, we could make the probability of a loss approach zero if we had enough independent investments with identical characteristics.

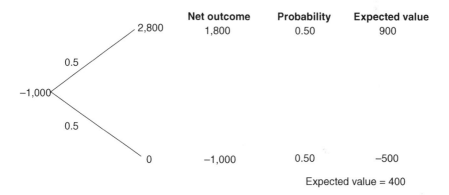

Figure 7.7 *One investment: investment E*

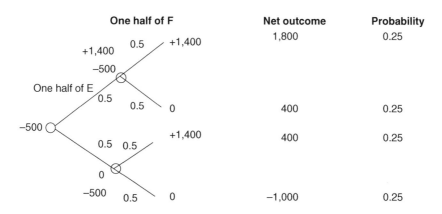

Figure 7.8 *Two independent investments (half of E and half of F)*

123

We shall generalize the situation in which we can invest in more than one statistically independent investments. For simplification of the conclusions, we assume that all the investments have the same variance.

The variance of the portfolio when one-*n*th of its value is in each of *n* independent investments, is one-*n*th of the variance of the individual investment.

$$\text{var}(R_p) = \frac{\text{var}(R)}{n} \qquad (7.5)$$

As the number of independent investments, *n*, approaches infinity, $\text{var}(R_p)$ approaches zero. This is consistent with equation (7.5).

Assume that with one security, the risk measure (the variance) is 0.04. With the investment spread over 10 statistically independent securities, the variance is reduced by 90 percent to 0.004. This is illustrated graphically in Figure 7.9 for $\rho = 0$. The corresponding reduction in the standard deviation is from 0.2 to 0.0632.

POSITIVELY CORRELATED INVESTMENTS

The previous results apply to portfolios of securities whose rates of returns are statistically independent. When securities exhibit positive correlation the risk of

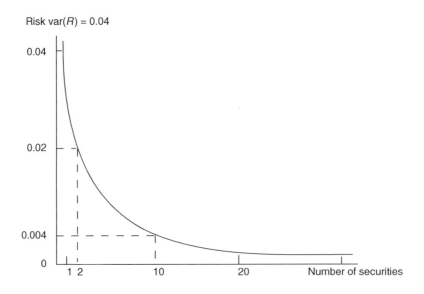

Figure 7.9 *Risk and number of securities*

the portfolio can be divided into two components, a systematic component and an unsystematic component. The risk reduction behavior illustrated in the previous section applies to the unsystematic component, but not to the systematic component. As the number of securities becomes very large, the amount invested in each security becomes very small and the portfolio's unsystematic risk in total approaches zero.

Assume the rate of return of each security has the same variance equal to $var(R)$, but $\rho \geq 0$. All pairs of investments have the same correlation coefficient. If n is infinitely large, the variance of the portfolio is:

$$var(R_\rho) = \rho \, var(R_\rho) \qquad (7.6)$$

Therefore if $\rho = 0.80$ and $var(X) = 0.04$, the minimum variance of a portfolio and an infinite number of securities is 0.032.

Table 7.1 shows the variance for different numbers of securities if the variance of the security is 1. Notice that with $\rho = 1$ there is no risk reduction. With the other values of ρ there are different amounts of risk. The minimum amount of variance is always $\rho \, var(R)$. The variance cannot be reduced below the value $\rho \, var(R)$. While the amount of risk reduction for a given number of securities depends on the value of ρ, the fraction of risk reduction is independent of ρ, as long as $\rho \geq 0$, but is a function of the number of securities in the portfolio.

For $n = 10$, 90 percent of the maximum feasible risk reduction is achieved. Increasing the number of securities to 100 increases the risk reduction to 99 percent of the maximum feasible risk reduction. If $\rho = 0$, it is possible to reduce the risk to zero with a very large number of securities.

These formulations all made simplifying assumptions so that we could obtain definite conclusions. If we drop the assumptions, the mathematical presentations and conclusions are more complex and less exact, but the same general type of observations remains. Risk can be reduced by an intelligent theoretically sound

Table 7.1 Portfolio variance as fraction of individual security variance where var(R) = 1 and the number of securities is changed

Number of securities in the portfolio	Correlation between securities (ρ)					% of risk reduction
	1	0.8	0.5	0.1	0	
1	1	1	1	1	1	0
2	1	0.9	0.75	0.55	0.50	1/2
10	1	0.82	0.55	0.19	0.10	9/10
100	1	0.802	0.505	0.109	0.01	99/100
∞	1	0.800	0.500	0.100	0.00	1

diversification policy, but there is a limit to the amount of achievable risk reduction, unless the correlation coefficient is equal to or less than zero.

OBSERVATIONS REGARDING DIVERSIFICATION

We have highlighted the fact that the average correlation of the rates of return of the assets held by the investor (or firm) is very important in evaluating the risk of holding the investment from the point of view of the investor (or firm). The co-variance is the crucial building block in evaluating the effect on risk of adding an asset to a portfolio of asssets. The riskiness of the portfolio is evaluated using the standard deviation or the variance of the portfolio's rates of return.

The riskiness of a single investment cannot be evaluated in a meaningful way by looking only at the possible outcomes of the investment taken by itself. In evaluating the riskiness to a corporation of a new asset to be acquired by the corporation, one should take into account how it will affect the dispersion of possible outcomes for the corporation as a whole. Similarly, the common stock of a particular corporation is seldom the sole asset in the portfolio of an investor. The majority of the common stock of large corporations is held by institutions and individuals whose portfolios contain dozens and sometimes hundreds of other securities. Investors who purchase mutual funds are likely to have a significant degree of diversification.

A corporation should take into consideration the nature of the risk associated with the investment and its interaction with the risks of other investments. The process by which risk is incorporated into the decision can be complex. The existence of security markets helps to simplify the decision process tremendously. If we assume that the decisions of the firm are not affected by non-systematic risk and that the investors are able and willing to diversify, the only risk components that need be taken into account by the corporation (from the point of view of stockholders) are those that the investors cannot eliminate by diversification. This suggests that many investments that have been traditionally considered to be highly risky, such as exploring for new reserves of oil, may turn out to be relatively riskless for a large corporation owned by diversified investors.

Self-interested corporate management may wish to apply a significant risk premium to large investments that could jeopardize the existence of the firm or their jobs. If managers have special skills and experience that make them more valuable to their present employer than to other firms, and if they derive a large fraction of their income from this employment, they are less able than most stock-holders to diversify against events that could threaten the continued existence of the firm or their continued employment. Also, investments with a large amount of non-systematic risk are likely to affect the firm's ability to execute its strategic plans successfully, and this risk should be considered.

A non-diversified investor who is not well diversified may be adversely affected by a decision that fails to consider firm-specific risk. A corporation may try to take into consideration the affairs of this investor. However, doing this is likely to reduce the market value of the firm's stock.

THE RISK-FREE ASSET

The previous section presented the basic portfolio analysis but there was no opportunity to invest in a risk-free asset (or, more exactly, a default-free asset). When that opportunity is included in the analysis, we can derive a theory called the capital asset pricing model (CAPM). The CAPM is an extension of the basic portfolio model. The main change is that when we use the CAPM to choose the optimum portfolio, we implicitly make use of the prices that the market is setting for return-risk trade-offs rather than using subjective measures of attitudes toward risk (such as the risk preferences of specific investors). The investor does choose the mix of risky portfolio and risk-free asset that is optimum (for that investor). It is necessary to know the willingness of investors to exchange risk for expected return.

The capital asset pricing model is a major contribution to modern business finance theory and practice. Wall Street analysts construct portfolios using the theories and models presented in this chapter and corporations use it to evaluate alternatives.

THE ASSUMPTIONS

The CAPM is a single-period model with no assumptions being made about the interaction of return and risk through time. It is assumed that the market is only interested in the expected return and standard deviation (or variance) of the portfolio's outcomes. For some probability distributions, this ignores other information that an investor might consider to be relevant, but the expected value and variance does define exactly a normal probability distribution.

It is assumed that all investors must be persuaded to take more risk by the prospect of a higher expected return (they are risk averse). The actions of any one investor do not affect price. The investors are "price takers." The investors can invest at the default-free rate (r_f), and generally we assume that they can borrow at the same risk-free rate, but this assumption is easily dropped. Investors can sell securities they do not own; that is, they can borrow securities to sell them (this is called a short sale). All investors agree about the expected rate of return and variance of all securities (they have homogeneous expectations), and they are all perfectly diversified. Securities are infinitely divisible; any dollar amount can be purchased. There are no transaction costs or taxes.

Many of these assumptions could be dropped, and a model very much like the conventional CAPM would be derived. One important function served by the above set of assumptions is a simplification of the model so that we are not distracted by elements that are not crucial to our understanding.

A risk averse investor requires a larger expected return as risk (defined as the standard deviation of outcomes) is increased. We assume utility-maximizing investors who (1) are risk averse, (2) measure the risk of an investment portfolio by the standard deviation of its rate of return, and (3) have indifference curves (different combination of expected return and standard deviation for which the investors are different).

PORTFOLIO ANALYSIS WITH A RISKLESS SECURITY: THE CAPITAL ASSET PRICING MODEL

If we assume the existence of a riskless security and extend portfolio analysis theory to cover that situation, we obtain some useful insights. Marketable government debt instruments that mature in one period are essentially riskless assets. Therefore, every investor has a riskless security available. "Riskless" as used here refers only to the risk of default and not to other types of risk.

Suppose an investor has two securities available. One is a riskless security earning a pure time value of money rate, r_f (such as the yield of a US Treasury bill). The second is a portfolio of marketable risky securities, denoted as M, with an expected return of $\bar{r}_m$ and standard deviation of σ_m. The portfolio M of risky assets is picked so that it is on the efficient frontier determined without considering the risk-free asset at a point where the straight line connecting the points of r_f and M is tangent to EE, the efficient frontier of risky portfolios. This is shown in Figure 7.10. The line r_fM is called the capital market line (CML).

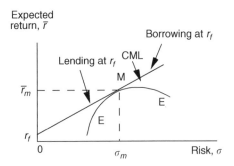

Figure 7.10 The capital market line

If 100 percent of the investor's portfolio is invested in portfolio M, the investor will earn $\bar{r}_m$ with risk σ_m. If 100 percent of the investor's portfolio is invested in the risk-free security, the investor will earn r_f with no risk. By varying the proportion of the risk free asset from zero to 100 percent and investing the balance in M, an investor can attain any point on the line segment r_fM.

If the investor borrows funds at a rate of r_f and invests them in portfolio M, the right-hand extension of the line r_fM defines the expected return-risk possibilities. The funds are being borrowed at r_f and invested to earn $\bar{r}_m$. Since $\bar{r}_m$ is larger than r_f, borrowing increases the portfolio's expected profit, but it also increases its risk. Thus by holding the risky portfolio M and either investing in the riskless asset or borrowing at the riskless rate an investor can attain any risk and return combination on the CML.

Choose any point on curve EE (the efficient frontier without the riskless asset) other than M. Note that for the same risk, a higher expected return can be earned by a point on the Capital Market Line. The CML offers a set of investment opportunities that is at least as desirable as the efficient frontier (the set of efficient investment opportunities that excludes the risk-free asset).

Different investors (with differing degrees of risk aversion) will have optimal portfolios that lie on different points on the capital market line, but all optimal portfolios will consist of the riskless asset and the portfolio M, which is called the market portfolio.

There are two steps in the determination of the investor's optimum portfolio. Step 1 determines point M, the market portfolio. Assuming that all investors have the same expectations, all investors hold the same market portfolio. The second step is to determine the optimum point on the Capital Market Line. This is the optimum mix of the portfolio M and the risk-free asset. The theory (originated by Tobin) supporting this two-step process is called the separation theorem.[1]

The market portfolio consists of all risky assets held in the same proportions as their relative total market value. Investors whose common objective is to achieve the maximum amount of diversification would include in their portfolio every security available. Securities are defined here to include common stock, warrants, convertible bonds, and preferred stock issues and would be included in the market portfolio.

We shall assume that because of the diversification characteristics of the market portfolio and the risk aversion of most investors, the prices of the securities in the market portfolio have adjusted so that an investor could not earn a higher rate of return for the same or a lower level of risk in some other form of investment. The level of risk associated with the market portfolio may be too high or too low for a particular investor, however. Investors can lower the level of risk to which they are exposed and still invest in the market portfolio by buying some of the risk-free asset.

---

1 See James Tobin, "Liquidity Preference as a Behavior Towards Risk," *Review of Economic Studies*, February 1958, pp. 65–86, for a discussion of the states of nature and modes of investor behavior that imply this assumption.

Whether the investor borrows (moves to the right of M) or invests in a riskless security (moves to the left of M) depends on the investor's risk preferences. But all investors will own some of the market portfolio except for those investors who only want the risk free security.

THE EXPECTED RETURN

Assume that an investor owns the market portfolio. In equilibrium if we add a very small amount of a new security i, the expected return-risk trade-off that results from the inclusion of i must equal the market's current trade-off rate. For this to happen, it is necessary that security i's expected return be equal to

$$\bar{r}_i = r_f + (\bar{r}_m - r_f)\beta_i \tag{7.7}$$

where

$\bar{r}_i$ = the equilibrium expected return of security i (the security's required rate of return)
r_f = the return from the risk-free asset
$\bar{r}_m$ = the expected return from investing in the market and σ_m^2 its variance
β_i = the beta of security i, where $\beta_i = \text{cov}(r_i, r_m)/\sigma_m^2$

The term $(\bar{r}_m - r_f)\beta_i$ is an adjustment to the risk-free rate for the risk of security i. Equation (7.7) is referred to in the finance literature as the security market line.

The beta of a security measures the amount of its systematic risk, that is, the risk arising for this security because of fluctuations in the market return. There is no adjustment to the required rate of return for risk specific to the firm (unsystematic risk). In the CAPM, it is assumed that investors can reduce the unsystematic risk of their portfolios to essentially zero by including in their portfolios a sufficiently large number of investments whose unsystematic return components are statistically independent. The beta of a security measures how the security's return is correlated with the market's return; it is the only measure of a security's risk that is needed in the CAPM to estimate the security's required rate of return.

The security market line is the major mathematical relationship of the capital asset pricing model. It determines the equilibrium required rate of return of a security as a function of the characteristics of the security (its beta) and the characteristics of the market, (the risk-free rate and the risk premium). If the beta, of a security is one, then the expected return of the security is $\bar{r}_m$ which is the same as the expected return of the market portfolio. If a security has more systematic risk than the market (a beta greater than one) the market will require a higher expected return.

We are interested in the expected rate of return the market requires for a given amount of risk. To determine this, we need to know the risk premium $(\bar{r}_m - r_f)$ as well as how the systematic risk of a specific security compares to the risk of the market (the security's beta). The model needs the estimated values of beta and the risk premium in order to be used correctly. However, usually data based on past events are used to estimate the values of beta and the risk premium. One problem is that the values of beta, and of the risk premium may change through time. In addition, the value of r_f will depend on the maturity of the government security that is used. It is not easy to use the CAPM in an exact manner.

USE OF THE CAPM

Even though the assumptions on which the CAPM is based limit the generality of the model, it is still widely used. Among the uses are

1   To estimate the cost of equity capital: using

$$\bar{r}_i = r_f + (\bar{r}_m - r_f)\beta_i \tag{7.7}$$

These estimates were widely in regulatory proceedings for public utilities when prices in these industries were set by public utility commissions. They are also commonly used to determine the hurdle rates (the required return) that must be earned by real investments in many corporations.

2   To form portfolios of securities. The beta of a portfolio is a value-weighted average of the betas of all the securities in the portfolio.

3   To evaluate securities: If the expected rate of return of a security is larger than its required rate of return, $r_f + (\bar{r}_m - r_f)\beta_i$, then the security is a "bargain." If a security has a larger expected return than the return indicated by the CAPM, investors will buy it until its expected return is lowered to be equal to

$$\bar{r}_i = r_f + (\bar{r}_m - r_f)\beta_i \tag{7.7}$$

In like manner if a security i is expected to earn less than $r_f + (\bar{r}_m - r_f)\beta_i$, then rational investors will be reluctant to buy the security (some will sell it short), its price will decrease, and the security's expected return will increase.

All securities are contained in the market portfolio in proportion to their market value. The beta of the market portfolio is 1.

SYSTEMATIC AND UNSYSTEMATIC RISK

It is conventional practice to separate risk into two components. One component is systematic risk or market risk that represents the change in value resulting from market value changes. Systematic risk can be somewhat reduced by the choice of securities (including low-beta securities in the portfolio). However, reducing systematic risk in this way may increase total risk, since the investor's portfolio will not be perfectly diversified. Alternatively, the level of systematic risk in a portfolio can be changed by changing the proportions of the risk free asset and the market portfolio. The second type of risk is residual or unsystematic risk. This risk is specific to the company (or asset) and is independent of what happens to the market. If the investor's portfolio consists of a very large number of securities each with a risk of $var(x)$ with no security being a large percentage of the portfolio, then this residual risk is equal to $var(X)/n$. If n is very large, this unsystematic risk can be made to approach zero by this strategy of diversification. Figure 7.11 shows the effect on total risk and unsystematic risk of adding securities.

Since the costs of diversification are relatively low, investors will not be willing to pay more for a security simply because it carries a relatively low burden of unsystematic risk (which can be diversified away). Similarly, securities that carry a large amount of unsystematic risk will not suffer a serious price disadvantage. To the extent that security prices are determined by the activities of the investors who can diversify their portfolios at low cost, the prices of securities will be set in such a way that differentials in expected rates of return will reflect primarily differences in the amount of systematic risk to which the securities are exposed.

While a middle manager might find the risk of a specific asset to be of interest, the top management of a firm will want to know the effect of the asset on the overall risk and value of the firm. Managers are likely to be interested in the effect of the specific asset on the risk to their careers and the ability of the firm to execute its strategic plan. At the investor level, well-diversified investors should be more interested in the effect of the specific asset on the riskiness of their portfolios than in the risk of a specific asset.

For convenience we will assume that only systematic risk is relevant for a perfectly diversified investor (this is only an approximation, since non-systematic risk may affect a firm's value by affecting its ability to carry out its plans).

The beta of a security measures its systematic risk. This is the risk associated with changes in the market's excess return. Most common stocks have beta values

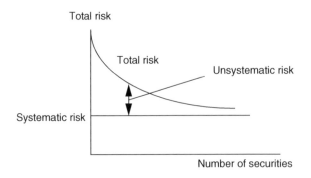

Figure 7.11 Risk reduction by diversification

between 0.8 and 1.2. Since most investors want extensive diversification it is difficult to reduce the systematic risk of a common stock portfolio by changing the composition of the common stocks in the portfolio (by definition the beta of the market is 1.0). Changing the systematic risk of a portfolio is best accomplished by varying the proportion of the risk free asset in the portfolio.

Unsystematic risk can be diversified away because each security's unsystematic risk is independent of the unsystematic risk of other securities. If the portfolio consists of a very large number of securities with each security being a very small proportion of the portfolio, the unsystematic risk of the portfolio will approach zero.

A beta coefficient of unity indicates that a security has the same amount of systematic risk as the market portfolio. A beta coefficient greater (less) than unity indicates the security is riskier (safer) than the market portfolio. Betas based on actual data are prepared by Merrill Lynch, Wells Fargo Bank, and the Value Line investor service as well as others. These are called historical betas. Fundamental betas would be ex ante estimates of beta based on the capital structure and operating characteristics of the firm.

IMPLICATIONS FOR CORPORATE INVESTMENT POLICY

The portfolio problem can be developed in a context of investments in stocks and bonds or business capital expenditures. However, there are significant differences between an investment in securities and an investment in real assets. One difference is the relevant time horizon and transaction costs. The transaction costs associated with purchasing or selling most stocks and bonds are a relatively small fraction of their value. Thus the holder of these assets can make decisions within the framework of a relatively short time horizon. By contrast, the transaction costs associated with buying or selling real assets may be a large fraction of their value. When acquisition of such assets is under consideration, the relevant time horizon is often the life of the asset.

A second difference is the divisibility of the investments. You cannot buy half a steel mill or two-thirds of a lathe, but you can buy securities that represent ownership interests in a very small fraction of a very large collection of real assets. The real assets themselves are not easily divisible into convenient sizes for consumer ownership, but the securities are customarily issued in relatively small denominations so that investors can buy the number of ownership units they desire.

Another important difference is the nature of the economic dependency of the cash flows from the investments. The expected cash flows from a portfolio consisting of two securities can be obtained by adding the expected cash flows of the two securities. But the expected cash flows to a firm from owning a blast furnace and a rolling mill are often greater than the total amount that could be earned from each of the assets by itself because of economic efficiencies (sometimes called synergy).

UNSYSTEMATIC RISK

From a strict CAPM viewpoint, unsystematic risk is not a relevant factor in a firm's investment decisions. But there are two exceptions that require consideration.

First, the existence of unsystematic risk might prevent the firm from obtaining the capital necessary to undertake desirable projects. The inability to complete desirable projects can reduce the firm's value.

Secondly, unsystematic risk is not relevant for a perfectly diversified investor. An investor who is not perfectly diversified might conclude that this risk is relevant. An important group of less than perfectly diversified investors are the firm's employees. They invest their capital as well as their careers. For this group, unsystematic risk is relevant.

The conventional CAPM formulation does not include a term for unsystematic risk. If it is concluded that a specific project has relevant unsystematic risk, then there has to be added a factor to the normal CAPM cost of equity for the abnormal unsystematic risk. We do not have a recommendation on how large the amount of adjustment should be.

GLOBAL BUSINESS ASPECTS

A risky foreign investment might actually reduce the risk to the firm. Assume the outcomes of the foreign investment are independent of the outcomes of the current investments. For example, Anheuser–Busch might assume that there is no correlation between the amount of beer (brand of Tsingtao) that is bought in China and the amount of beer (brand of Budweiser) that is bought in the US.

Assume the variance of a new domestic investment is 100 (perfectly correlated with the present assets) and the variance of the investment in a foreign country is 500 (there are political and economic risks). The firm's current variance is 2,500. The variance of the firm with the foreign investment (the two investments are independent) is:

$$\text{Variance with foreign investment} = 2{,}500 + 500 = 3{,}000$$

If the domestic investment (variance of 100) is undertaken instead of the foreign investment:

$$\begin{aligned}\text{Variance with domestic investment} &= 2{,}500 + 100 + 2(50)(10)\\ &= 3{,}600\end{aligned}$$

where 50 is the standard deviation of 2,500 variance and 10 is the standard deviation of 100 variance.

The domestic investment results in more risk than the foreign investment despite the fact that on a stand alone basis the foreign investment with a 500 variance is five times more risk than the domestic investment with a variance of 100.

CONCLUSIONS

Investors have available a market basket of risky securities and the opportunity to invest in securities with no risk of default. Risk preferences of investors can lead to a combination of the market basket of the risky securities and the riskless securities. In equilibrium, the expected rate of return of any security must be such that the investor expects to earn a basic rate of return equal to the rate of return on a default-free security plus an adjustment that is heavily influenced by the "correlation" between the security's rate of return and the market's rate of return. If the rates of return from the investment are positively correlated with the market rates of return, the equilibrium expected rate of return will be larger than the default-free return. If the correlation is negative, the equilibrium expected rate of return will be smaller than the default-free rate of return.

At best, the net present value measure is a prediction of how the market value of a firm would change if the investment were accepted. The rule that investments should be accepted if their net present value is greater than zero is consistent with profit maximizing behavior for the firm. But this is not a prediction about how managers will actually behave. It is well known that objectives of firms and managers are multidimensional and that there will be a reluctance for management to ignore a risk just because it does not affect the well-diversified investor. The so-called "unsystematic" risk is not something that is likely to be ignored by a management that includes among its objectives the continuity of existence of the firm and equally important, the continuity of their employment.

Industry tends to use a "cost of capital" or a "hurdle rate" to implement the discounted cash flow capital budgeting techniques. Both of these measures are "averages" reflecting average risks and average time value conditions and cannot be sensibly applied to unique "marginal" situations. There is no reason to think that the firm's weighted average cost of capital can be inserted in a compound interest formula and then be applied to all future cash flows of a project to obtain a useful measure of net present value that correctly takes both the time value and risk of the investment into consideration.

The models we have used here are somewhat simplified. Investors are much more complex in their behavior and markets are less than perfect. Nevertheless, the conclusions reached are relevant and are the foundation for a great deal of financial investment decisions. Investment decision-making under uncertainty is not an easy task, but uncertainty is a characteristic of the world and the problem must be faced.

We now have the following important conclusions:

1   The cash flows of a project and their riskiness cannot be used, solely, to determine whether a project is acceptable
2   It is necessary to consider how undertaking the project affects the portfolio's return (both the expected return and the standard deviation) where the term portfolio applies to the assets of any or all of the above following, corporate division, or other corporate unit, corporation, managers, or shareholders.

REVIEW PROBLEM 1

Asumme the market portfolio had an historically based expected return of 0.085 and a standard deviation of 0.03 during a period when risk-free assets yielded 0.025. The 0.06 risk premium is thought to be constant through time. Riskless investments may now be purchased to yield 0.08.

A security has a standard deviation of 0.07 and a 0.75 correlation with the market portfolio. The market portfolio is now expected to have a standard deviation of 0.035.

a.   What is the market's return-risk trade-off now?
b.   What is the security's beta now?
c.   What is the equilibrium required expected return of the security?

REVIEW PROBLEM 2

With a total investment of $5,000 the rate of return of each of 10 $500 investments has a variance of 100 and each one has a 0.5 correlation coefficient with every other one. What is the variance of the rate of return of a portfolio of the 10 investments?

REVIEW PROBLEM 3

Assume two investments with two possible outcomes:

Event	Probability	Outcome (rate of return)	
		Investment 1	Investment 2
e_1	0.6	0.20	0
e_2	0.4	0.05	0.30

Compute the expected rates of return, variances, standard deviations, and the co-variance.

PROBLEMS

1 Two investments have the following cash flows for the next period:

	Expected cash flow	Variance	Standard deviation
Investment A	$1,000	$100	10
Investment B	2,000	900	30

For an outlay of $800 in each of the two investments ($1,600 in total), compute:

a. The expected total cash flow.

b. The variance of the total cash flow if the correlation coefficient is 0.8.

c. The variance of the total cash flow if the correlation coefficient is −0.8.

d. The variance of the total cash flow if the investments are statistically independent.

2 The outcomes of investment C are as follows:

Event	Outcome	Probability
e_1	$200	0.4
e_2	100	0.5
e_3	−100	0.1

Compute the expected value and variance of the investment outcomes.

3 All you are told about an investment is that there is an outlay of $100 and that the returns (net of outlay) have an expectation of $120 and a variance of $7,600.

Would you accept this investment? Explain.

4 Two investments have the following returns for the two events indicated:

Event	Probability	Value of investment	
		D	F
e_1	0.6	$600	−$100
e_2	0.4	−400	500

a. Compute the expectation and variance of the return of each investment and their co-variance of the two investments.

b. Compute the correlation coefficient of the returns of the two investments.

137

5 (Problem 4 continued) What is the expected value and variance of the total return of investment in both D and F?

6 An investment ABC has the following net return for the two events indicated:

Event	Probability	Value
e_1	0.6	$500
e_2	0.4	100

Compute the expectation and variance of investment in the net return of ABC.

7 Consider a portfolio consisting of 0.6 of security G and 0.4 of security H that have rates of return that are independent.

	Expected rate of return(%)	Standard deviation(%)
Security G	20	5
Security H	10	3

a. The portfolio has an expected rate of return of _____ percent and a standard deviation of _____ percent.

b. If the two securities had rates of return that are perfectly positively correlated, then the expected rate of return on the portfolio _____ is percent. The standard deviation of the portfolio's return is _____.

c. If the correlation coefficient of the returns is 0.7 the variance of the portfolio is _____ percent.

8 Securities 1 and 2 (Figure 7.12) are to be combined into a portfolio.
a. If point A results, the correlation coefficient is _____.
b. If point E results, the correlation coefficient is _____.

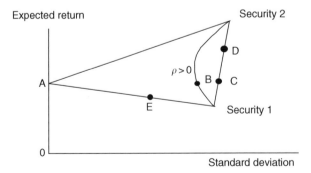

Figure 7.12 Expected return and risks for different portfolios

c. If point C results, the correlation coefficient is _____.

d. If point D results, the correlation coefficient is _____.

9 There are two investments with the following characteristics:

Investment	Expected return	Variance
A	0.10	0.09
B	0.20	0.25

The correlation coefficient is -0.5.

If 0.4 is invested in A and 0.6 in B;

a. The portfolio's expected return is _____.

b. The variance of the portfolio's return is _____.

c. The co-variance is _____.

10 Suppose that an investor has the following information for two securities:

Security	$\bar{r}_i$	σ_i
A	0.05	0.02
B	0.12	0.06

The correlation coefficient between A and B is 0.2.

Compute the expected return and variance of the following portfolios.

a. All invested in A.

b. All invested in B.

c. 0.5 invested in A and 0.5 invested in B.

d. 0.1 invested in A and 0.9 invested in B.

11 If there are four securities in a portfolio, how many different co-variances will there be?

12 If there are 100 securities in a portfolio, how many co-variances will there be? What does this tell you about the importance of the co-variances in determining the value of the portfolio's variance?

13 Assume that a small firm has enough funds to drill one oil well and that the cost of drilling a well is $1 million. A large firm has enough funds to drill 50 wells.

a. What is the maximum loss of the small firm?

b. What is the maximum loss of the large firm?

c. Which of the two firms has more risk?

14 An investment firm conducts a contest where the person who recommends 20 stocks that perform the best over a given period wins a prize.

What investment strategy would you recommend to win the contest?

15 Assume that you are approached about the possibility of investing in a Broadway play. After conducting some research, you find that the expected

profits are $800,000 per play and that approximately 25 percent of the plays that open on Broadway show a profit.

Explain whether you would be willing to invest in a play being prepared for Broadway.

16 Answer the following two questions as you would if *you* were faced with the betting situations. Assume that the bets are legal and moral.

  a. *Situation 1*: A fair coin will be tossed fairly. If a head appears, you will receive $5. If a tail appears, you will receive nothing. How much would you pay to participate in this game?

  b. *Situation 2*: Two evenly matched basketball teams are playing this Saturday. You will receive $5 if you pick the winner, $0 otherwise. How much would you pay for this gamble?

17 The Boeing Company was faced with a major decision: To what extent should it independently develop a supersonic air transport? The estimates of the cost of developing such a plane ranged up to $10 billion. During the period of decision other companies (in other countries) were acting jointly in the development of such a plane.

   If you were advising the president of Boeing, what would you suggest?

DISCUSSION QUESTION

CAPM is based on the assumption that non-systematic risk is not relevant to a well-diversified investor.

  Should managers be indifferent to non-systematic risk?

SOLUTION TO REVIEW PROBLEM 1

a. Market's return-risk trade-off $= \dfrac{\bar{r}_m - r_f}{\sigma_m}$ $\bar{r}_m = 0.06 + 0.08 = 0.14$

$$= \dfrac{0.14 - 0.08}{0.035} = 1.714$$

b. $\beta_i = \dfrac{\text{cov}(r_i, r_m)}{\sigma_m^2} = \dfrac{\rho \sigma_i \sigma_m}{\sigma_m^2} = \dfrac{0.75 \times 0.07 \times 0.035}{0.035^2} = 1.5$

c. $\bar{r}_i = r_f + (\bar{r}_m - r_f)\beta_i = 0.08 + (0.06)1.5 = 0.17$

It is difficult to decide which estimates of market return, risk premium, and market standard deviation to use.

SOLUTION TO REVIEW PROBLEM 2

Using Table 7.1, the portfolio variance is $0.55(0.0625) = 0.034375$ since $n = 10$ and $\rho = 0.5$.

The variance is reduced from 0.0625 to 0.034375, a reduction of 0.028125. The maximum reduction is $0.0625 - 0.034375 = 0.03125$; $0.028125 / 0.03125 = 0.9$ of the maximum reduction has been achieved with 10 securities.

SOLUTION TO REVIEW PROBLEM 3

Investment 1

e_i	r_1	$p(e_i)$	Product	$(r_1 - \bar{r}_1)$	$(r_1 - \bar{r}_1)^2$	$p(r_1 - \bar{r}_1)^2$
e_1	0.20	0.6	0.12	0.06	0.0036	0.00216
e_2	0.05	0.4	0.02	-0.09	0.0081	0.00324
			$\bar{r}_1 = 0.14$		Var $(r_1) =$	0.00540
					$\sigma_1 =$	0.07348

Investment 2

e_i	r_2	$p(e_i)$	Product	$(r_2 - \bar{r}_2)$	$(r_2 - \bar{r}_2)^2$	$p(r_2 - \bar{r}_2)^2$
e_1	0	0.6	0	-0.12	0.0144	0.00864
e_2	0.30	0.4	0.12	0.18	0.0324	0.01296
			$\bar{r}_2 = 0.12$		Var $(r_2) =$	0.02160
					$\sigma_2 =$	0.1470

Computation of Covariance

e_i	$p(e_i)$	r_1	r_2	$(r_1 r_2)$	$p(r_1)(r_2)$
e_1	0.6	0.20	0	0	0
e_2	0.4	0.05	0.30	0.015	0.006
					$E(r_1 r_2) = 0.006$

$$cov(r_1, r_2) = E(r_1 r_2) - \bar{r}_1 \bar{r}_2$$
$$= 0.006 - (0.14)(0.12) = 0.006 - 0.0168 = -0.0108$$

141

The correlation coefficient is

$$\rho = \frac{cov(r_1, r_2)}{\sigma_1 \sigma_2} = \frac{-0.0108}{0.07348 \times 0.4170} = -1.0$$

BIBLIOGRAPHY

Bierman, H. and J. E. Hass, "Capital Budgeting Under Uncertainty: A Reformulation," *Journal of Finance*, March 1973, pp. 119–29.

Brealey, R. A. *An Introduction to Risk and Return from Common Stocks*, Cambridge, MA: M.I.T. Press, 1969; 2nd edn, 1983.

Fama, E, "Risk, Return, and Equilibrium: Some Clarifying Comments," *Journal of Finance*, March 1968, pp. 29–40.

Graham, John R., Michael L. Lemmon, and Jack G. Wolf, "Does Corporate Diversification Destroy Value?" *Journal of Finance*, April 2002, pp. 695–720.

Hamada, R. S, "Portfolio Analysis, Market Equilibrium and Corporation Finance," *Journal of Finance*, March 1969, pp. 13–31.

Harris, Robert S., Thomas J. O'Brien, and Doug Wakeman, "Divisional Cost-of-Capital Estimation for Multi-Industry Firms," *Financial Management*, summer 1989, pp. 74–84.

Hyland, David C. and J. David Diltz, "Why Firms Diversify: An Empirical Examination," *Financial Management*, 31, spring 2002, pp. 51–81.

Jin, Li, "CEO Compensation, Diversification, and Incentives," *Journal of Financial Economics*, 66, October 2002, pp. 29–63.

Lamont, Owen A. and Christopher Polk, "Does Diversification Destroy Value? Evidence from the Industry Shocks," *Journal of Financial Economics*, 63, January 2002, pp. 51–77.

Markowitz, H. M. *Portfolio Selection: Efficient Diversification of Investments*, Monograph no. 16, New York: Cowles Foundation, 1959.

——, "Markowitz Revisited," *Financial Analysts Journal*, September–October 1976, 3–8.

Modigliani, Franco and Gerald A. Pogue, "An Introduction to Risk and Return," *Financial Analysts Journal*, March–April 1974, pp. 68–80, and May–June 1974, pp. 69–86.

Mossin, J. *Theory of Financial Markets*. Englewood Cliffs, NJ: Prentice-Hall, 1973.

Robichek, A. A, "Risk and the Value of Securities," *Journal of Financial and Quantitative Analysis*, December 1969, pp. 749–56.

Robichek, A. A. and S.C. Myers, "Valuation of the Firm: Effects of Uncertainty in a Market Context," *Journal of Finance*, May 1966, pp. 215–27.

Ross, S. A, "The Arbitrage Theory of Capital Asset Pricing," *Journal of Economic Theory*, December 1976, pp. 341–60.

Sharpe, W. F, "Capital Asset Prices; A Theory of Market Equilibrium Under Conditions of Risk," *Journal of Finance*, September 1964, pp. 425–42.

——, *Investments*, 2nd edn, Englewood Cliffs, NJ: Prentice-Hall, 1981.

——, *Portfolio Theory and Capital Markets*, New York: McGraw-Hill, 1971.

Tobin, J, "Liquidity Preference as Behavior Towards Risk," *Review of Economic Studies*, February 1958, pp. 65–86.

APPENDIX: STATISTICAL BACKGROUND

The formulas in this appendix are presented, without proof, as a review. The following notation is used: X, Y, Z, W, and X_i are random variables, $E[.]$ is the a and w_i. are scalar constants or parameters. The symbol $\equiv$ indicates that the relationship on the right is the definition of the symbol on the left.

$$E[aX] = aE[X]$$

$$E[X + Y] = E[X] + E[Y]$$

$$\text{var}(X) \equiv E[(X - E[X])^2]$$

$$\text{var}(X) = E[X^2] - E[X^2] = \sigma_x^2$$

$$\text{var}(aX) = a^2\text{var}(X)$$

$$\text{cov}(X,Y) \equiv E[(X - E[X])(Y - E[Y])]$$

$$\text{cov}(X,Y) = E[XY] - E[X]E[Y]$$

$$\text{cov}(X,X) = \text{var}(X)$$

$$\rho \equiv \frac{\text{cov}(X,Y)}{\sigma_X \sigma_Y}$$

$$\text{cov}(X,Y) = \rho\sigma_X\sigma_Y$$

$$\text{cov}(aX,Y) = a\text{cov}(X,Y)$$

$$\text{var}(X + Y) = \text{var}(X) + \text{var}(Y) + 2\text{cov}(X,Y)$$

$$W \equiv \sum_{i=1}^{N} X_i$$

$$\text{var}(W) = \sum_{i=1}^{N}\sum_{j=1}^{N} \text{cov}(X_i,X_j)$$

$$\text{var}(W) = \sum_{i=1}^{N}\text{var}(X_i) + 2\sum_{i=2}^{N}\sum_{j=2}^{i-1}\text{cov}(X_i,X_j)$$

$$Z = \sum_{i=1}^{N} w_i X_i$$

$$E[Z] = \sum_{i=1}^{N} w_i E[X_i]$$

$$\text{var}(Z) = \sum_{i=1}^{N} w_i^2 \text{var}(X_i) + 2 \sum_{i=2}^{N} \sum_{j=1}^{i-1} w_i w_j \text{cov}(X_i, X_j)$$

Chapter 8

Projects with components having different risks

At the end of the day, the benefits of new technologies can be realized only if they are embodied in capital investment, defined to include any outlay that increases the value of the firm.

(Alan Greenspan, from a talk on
the revolution in information technology
Boston College Conference on the New Economy
March 6, 2000)

Conventional capital budgeting practice is to calculate the expected cash flows for an investment project on a year-by-year basis. One discount rate is used to calculate the present value of each year's expected cash flow; the present values for each year are summed to obtain the net present value of this cash flow sequence. We will refer to this as the *project cash flow* procedure for calculating net present values.

The use of a single discount rate for all of the project cash flows is appropriate if all of the components of the cash flows have identical risk characteristics and if the term structure of interest rates is flat. For simplicity, we will assume that the term structure of interest rates is flat. However, most projects consist of a mixture of cash flow components with different risks. For example, contribution margins and depreciation tax shields have different risk characteristics. This chapter considers the procedures that should be used to determine the present value of a project that consists of a mixture of cash flows with different risks. We conclude that it is more accurate to discount each cash flow component with its own risk-adjusted discount rate and to sum the present values of the component cash flows to obtain the project present value. We refer to this procedure as the *component cash flow* procedure for calculating net present values.

This chapter will assume that the appropriate discount rate for each component of the cash flow is known (there are some risks reflected in the discount rates) in order to focus on the distortions that arise when applying one constant discount rate to a project with a mixture of cash flows with different risks.

For simplicity and clarity it is initially assumed that the tax rate is equal to zero. Later in the chapter we consider how the discount rates should be adjusted to reflect tax considerations.

EXAMPLE 8.1

A NEW PRODUCT PROJECT WITH TWO DIFFERENT CASH FLOW COMPONENTS

Assume a company is considering developing a new product. We designate this as project A. The product development phase will require outlays of $120 million per year for the next three years (the first payment at time one). The product is expected to generate cash proceeds of $250 million per year for the following two years (starting in year 4). These cash proceeds consist of revenues from the sale of the product less the variable costs of production. The project cash flows, measured as of the end of each year, are shown in Table 8.1.

Assume the product development outlays have zero systematic risk. The new product combines well-known proven technologies in an innovative way. It is just a question of time and money to engineer the new product configuration. No new production facilities will be needed for the new product, since production will be out-sourced. The major risk associated with the new product is its demand. Demand is expected to be sensitive to business conditions during the lifetime of the project.

The cash proceeds and the cash outlays do not have the same risk in this example. The proceeds are subject to systematic risk, while the outlays of the first three years have no systematic risk. Therefore, it is appropriate to use a higher discount rate for the cash proceeds than for the cash outflows. The appropriate discount rates are assumed to be 6 percent for the cash outlays and 12 percent for the cash proceeds.

At time zero, the present value of the future cash proceeds, discounted at 12 percent is $300.74 $[= 250(1.12)^{-4} + 250(1.12)^{-5}]$ and the present value of the future cash outlays, discounted at 6 percent is $-\$320.76$ $[= -120(1.06)^{-1} - 120(1.06)^{-2} - 120(1.06)^{-3}]$. The net present value of the project at time zero is equal to the present value of the proceeds plus the present value of the outlays which equals a negative $20.02.

Table 8.1 Project A: cash flow

Cash flow components/years	1	2	3	4	5
Cash proceeds				250	250
Cash outlays	−120	−120	−120		
Net cash flows	−120	−120	−120	250	250

Table 8.2 shows the present value of the proceeds, the present value of the outlays and the net present value of the project, calculated using the component cash flow procedure.

Table 8.2 *Project A: present value using the component cash flow procedure*

Cash flow components/years	Discount rates(%)	Present values($)	1	2	3	4	5
Cash proceeds	12	300.74				250	250
Cash outlays	6	−320.76	−120	−120	−120		
Net cash flows			−120	−120	−120	250	250
Net present values		−20.02					

CALCULATING THE VALUE OF AN ASSET BY DISCOUNTING ITS NET CASH FLOW

We have been considering a project that has two cash flow components with different risks. To find the value of the project, we used a different discount rate for each of the two cash flow components. This is the approach we recommend. Financial theorists always recommend using different discount rates for cash flows with different risk characteristics. However, the current business practice is to use one discount rate to discount all of the project's cash flows. Business practice refers to this discount rate as the hurdle rate or the required rate of return. An estimate of the firm's weighted average cost of capital (WACC) is one commonly used hurdle rate. The hurdle rate is usually determined in advance, and applied to a group of projects. Frequently there is one hurdle rate for the entire firm. Sometimes there is a separate hurdle rate (and a separate WACC) for each division or for each Strategic Business Unit. For the new product example we assume that the applicable firm-wide hurdle rate is 10 percent.

There are two basic methods, NPV and IRR, for using hurdle rates to make capital budgeting decisions. With independent investments, they frequently give identical results. The NPV method uses the project cash flow procedure to calculate the project NPV using the project's hurdle rate as the discount rate. With that method, the project is considered to be acceptable if the NPV is positive and is greater than the NPV of any mutually exclusive alternative project. The calculation of the NPV using this variant of the project cash flow procedure is illustrated in Table 8.3. Using a 10 percent hurdle rate, the NPV is positive. Therefore, this project would be considered to be acceptable if there were no mutually exclusive alternatives with a higher NPV.

Table 8.3 *Present value of project A using the project cash flow procedure with a 10% hurdle rate*

	Discount rate(%)	Present value($)	1	2	3	4	5
Cash proceeds			0	0	0	250	250
Cash outlays			−120	−120	−120	0	0
Net cash flows			−120	−120	−120	250	250
Net present value	10.00	$27.56	−$109.09	−$99.17	−$90.16	$170.75	$155.23

It is instructive to examine more closely why the project is accepted using a 10 percent hurdle rate, but is rejected using the component cash flow procedure. Using a discount rate of 10 percent for the net cash flows is equivalent to using the component cash flow procedure with a 10 percent discount rate for both the cash proceeds and the cash outlays of this project. The 10 percent discount rate assigns present values of $326 to the cash proceeds and $298 to the cash outlays. Subtracting $298 from $326 gives the project's net present value of $28.

In this example it is intuitively appealing that the cash proceeds, which consist of the net amounts of the variable revenues and the variable costs, have more systematic risk than the cash outlays. Even if 10 percent is in some sense, a good average rate, the rate for the cash proceeds should be higher, and the rate for the cash outlays should be lower. If we raise the discount rate for the proceeds, we reduce the present value of these cash flows; since the cash proceeds are positive, reducing the PV of this item will reduce the NPV. Similarly, if we reduce the discount rate applied to the cash outlays, we will increase the absolute present value of these outlays, and since their absolute amount is subtracted in computing the NPV, we will reduce the NPV of the project. As can be seen in Table 8.4, in this example, using the component cash approach reduces the PV of the proceeds by $25.25 and increases the PV of the cash outlays (a negative amount), by $22.34. Together, this sum explains the reduction in the project NPV if we use the component cash flow procedure (CCFP) instead of the project cash flow procedure (PCFP).

Table 8.4 *Comparison of the project A NPVs that result from using the project cash flow procedure (PCFP) and the component cash flow procedure (CCFP) ($)*

	PCFP	CCFP	CCFP − PCFP
Cash proceeds	325.98	300.74	−25.25
Cash outlays	−298.42	−320.76	−22.34
Net present value	27.56	−20.03	−47.59

Another method for using the hurdle rate is to calculate the internal rate of return (IRR) of the project and then compare the IRR to the hurdle rate. We will illustrate this approach and also point out some of its limitations.

The IRR for the net cash flows shown in Table 8.1 is 13.88 percent. Table 8.5 shows that the present value of these cash flows at 13.88 percent is equal to zero. Calculation of the IRR is ordinarily a trial and error process, but with modern spreadsheet programs, the IRR function supplied with the spreadsheet will readily compute the project's IRR.

Traditionally, the IRR is used to make accept or reject decisions. The logic is that if the IRR is greater than the hurdle rate, if the cash flows are conventional, and if there are no better mutually exclusive alternatives, then the project is acceptable. In the project A example, the cash flows are conventional because there are periods with negative cash flows followed by years with positive cash flows. With a conventional cash flow pattern there will be one and only one IRR. In addition, with Project A the IRR is greater than the hurdle rate. Therefore, if there are no better mutually exclusive alternatives, according to the traditional logic, the project is acceptable.

The traditional argument for the project cash flow procedure implicitly assumes all of the project's cash flow components are equally risky. If this assumption is true, then the component cash flow procedure (CCFP) and the project cash flow procedure (PCFP) will both produce the same project NPV provided the same discount rate is used for all cash flow components in the CCFP and for the project cash flows in the PCFP.

When all of the project cash flows have the same risk, the riskiness of the cash flows, described in terms of a hurdle rate, provides a useful standard that can be compared with the IRR to determine if the project was acceptable. But if a project contains cash flow components with different risks, there is no easily determined single hurdle rate that can be compared with the project IRR to make a reliable accept or reject decision.

Table 8.5 Project A present value using the project cash flow procedure with a 13.88% hurdle rate

Cash flow components/ years	Discount rate(%)	Present value($)	1	2	3	4	5
Cash proceeds			0	0	0	250	250
Cash outlays			−120	−120	−120	0	0
Net cash flows			−120	−120	−120	250	250
Net present value	13.88	0.00	−$105.37	−$92.53	−$81.25	$148.63	$130.51

INCREASING THE PROCEEDS

Now assume the benefits from project A are estimated to be $275 per year instead of $250 (an increase of 10 percent). Using the component cash flow procedure, the present value of the proceeds (discounted at 12 percent) increases by $30.07 to $330.81 from $300.74, a 10 percent increase. The NPV at time zero increases to $10.05 from −$20.02, which is also an increase of $30.07. The increase in the proceeds flows directly to the NPV bottom line. The absolute amount of the change in the NPV is the same as the absolute amount of the change in the present value of the proceeds.

There are two interesting features of this project. First, there are substantial cash outlays before the first cash inflows. Second, the discount rate used for the cash outlays is substantially lower than the discount rate used for the cash inflows. The use of different discount rates for different cash flow components may be unusual, but it is not a new idea having been used for buy versus lease decisions for many years.[1]

EXAMPLE 8.2

A NEW MARKET FOR AN OLD PRODUCT

In the previous example, the asset has two types of cash flows with different risks. But in any given period all of the cash flows were of the same type. This is convenient for introducing some of the concepts and procedures that are helpful in analyzing projects that contain cash flow components with different risks. But usually the cash flows from a project will contain more than one type of cash flow in each period. It will be helpful to consider an example of this type. Suppose a company is considering whether to introduce an old product into a new market. We refer to this as Project B. The company has decided to use a five-year horizon to evaluate this opportunity. Sales in the new market are expected to be constant each year over this period. All monetary amounts are in millions of dollars. The contribution margin is expected to be $150 per year. Product will require fixed outlays of $100 per year, to cover the costs of leasing the production facilities, and of providing basic advertising and various administrative costs. The values for each cash flow component are shown in Table 8.6.

Assume the cash proceeds and cash outlays have different systematic risks. The contribution margins are more subject to changes in business conditions than are the cash outlays. The appropriate discount rates are 12 percent and 6 percent for cash proceeds and outlays respectively. Table 8.7 illustrates the calculation of the present value of the project using the component cash flows procedure.

---

1 "Each distinct cash flow stream should, in general, be discounted at a different rate." Stewart C. Myers, David A. Dill, and Alberto J. Bautista, "Valuation of Financial Lease Contracts," *Journal of Finance*, 31, June 1976, 799–819. A simple buy versus lease example is presented later in this chapter.

Table 8.6 Project B cash flows

Cash flow components/years	1	2	3	4	5
Cash proceeds	150	150	150	150	150
Cash outlays	−100	−100	−100	−100	−100
Total cash flows	50	50	50	50	50

Table 8.7 Project B present value using the component cash flow procedure mutually exclusive alternative to project B

Years	Discount rates (%)	Present values ($)	1	2	3	4	5
Cash proceeds	12	540.72	150	150	150	150	150
Cash outlays	6	−421.24	−100	−100	−100	−100	−100
Total cash flows			50	50	50	50	50
Net present value		119.48					

Suppose that there is a mutually exclusive alternative to Project B, which we denote as project B-1. Project B-1 is a more automated version of Project B. It has higher fixed cash outlays, and lower variable costs. Many investment projects that increase the degree of automation of a process have the characteristic that they both increase fixed costs and decrease variable costs. It turns out that for Project B-1, the increase in the annual fixed costs is exactly equal to the increase in the annual contribution margin, so that the total cash flows in each period remain unchanged. If the project cash flow procedure were used for both projects, with a common discount rate then the NPV of projects B and B-1 would be identical. But with the component cash flow procedure, adding a dollar of high-risk contribution margin does not fully offset the simultaneous addition of a dollar of low-risk costs. The net effect is to reduce the NPV of the project from $119.48 to $89.10. This is shown in Table 8.8, which shows the computation of the NPV of project B-1 assuming the annual contribution margin and annual cash outlays both increase by $50 compared to project B.

Table 8.8 Project B-1 present value using the component cash flow procedure. Project B-1 is a mutually exclusive alternative to project B

Years	Discount rates (%)	Present values ($)	1	2	3	4	5
Cash proceeds	12	720.96	200	200	200	200	200
Cash outlays	6	−631.85	−150	−150	−150	−150	−150
Total cash flows			50	50	50	50	50
Net present value		89.10					

EXAMPLE Contd.

DISADVANTAGES OF USING A SINGLE DISCOUNT RATE

In general, it is possible to find a composite discount rate for a project that gives the same NPV for the project as the NPV derived from the component cash flow procedure. The net cash flows can be determined that gives the same present value as the sum of the present values of the component parts. But there are at least three problems in applying one discount rate to the sum of the cash flows.

1   Any change in assumptions about the project will tend to lead to a change in the composite discount rate. Changing the life of the project or the proportion of any of its cash flow components would likely require a different composite discount rate for the total cash flows.
2   If the correct composite discount rate is applied to the net cash flows of a project, then although the net present value of the project will be correct, the present values assigned to the cash flow components using this rate will be inaccurate. For example, the present value of the depreciation tax shields will usually be underestimated. In addition, the present value of the total cash flows in a particular year or a particular period will usually be inaccurate. This may lead to errors in decisions, such as estimating the value of the project at various future dates.
3   If the cash flow mixture is changed, the present value calculated using the previous composite discount rate would not produce accurate present values. This is particularly important in making choice between mutually exclusive alternatives that frequently involve a change in the mixture of cash flows, for example, the substitution of capital for labor.

A few generalizations can be made about how to find a composite discount rate for a project, and about the relationships between the composite discount rate and the corresponding component cash flows and their discount rates. It will be helpful to illustrate these generalizations in the context of some simple examples.

FINDING THE COMPOSITE DISCOUNT RATE FOR PROJECTS WITH A FINITE LIFE

We first illustrate finding a composite discount rate for a project with a one-year life. If the positive cash flows are discounted at 12 percent and the negative cash flows at 6 percent, at what rate should the net cash flows be discounted in order to get the same present value?

Consider the following example using the component cash flow procedure:

	Year 1	Discount rate (%)	PVF	PV
Cash proceeds	$1,120	12	0.8929	$1,000
Cash outlay	−106	6	0.9434	−$100
Net cash flows and NPV	$1,014			$900

To find the composite discount rate that makes the present value of the time one cash flow of $1,014 equal to $900 we solve the following equation for r.

$$\frac{1,014}{1 + r} = 900$$

$$r = \frac{1,014}{900} - 1 = 0.1267$$

Note that the composite discount rate for the net cash flows is larger than the 12 percent discount rate for the positive cash flow component. Intuitively what is happening is that the low-risk cash outlays provide operating leverage to the high-risk cash proceeds. With a one period example, the present value factor for the composite discount rate, r, can be expressed as a weighted average of the present value factors for the cash proceeds and the cash outlays.

Now suppose that the project has a life of 5 years, with the cash proceeds and cash outlays at the same level as the above example every year. We designate this as Project C. Table 8.9 shows the computation of project C's PV using the component cash flow procedure.

To find the composite discount rate that makes the present value of the net cash flows equal to the present value found using the component discount rate procedure, one can use the IRR function in the computer spreadsheet. The IRR of the following cash flow sequence is the composite discount rate that we are seeking.

Time	0	1	2	3	4	5
Cash flows	−$3,590.84	$1,014	$1,014	$1,104	$1,104	$1,014

Table 8.9 Project C present value using the component cash flow procedure

Years	Discount rate (%)	Present values ($)	1	2	3	4	5
Cash proceeds	12	4,037.35	1,120	1,120	1,120	1.120	1.120
Cash outlays	6	−446.51	−106	−106	−106	−106	−106
Total cash flows			1,014	1,014	1,014	1,014	1,014
Net present value		3,590.84					

153

In this example, the IRR is 12.72 percent. This is the composite discount rate that makes the project's net cash flows equal to the NPV calculated using the component cash flow procedure. There are some general conclusions that can be derived from this example that are worth noting.

- The composite discount rates for the five-period example and for the one-period example are not identical even though the annual cash flows are identical in both examples. The life of the project makes a difference.
- In both examples, the composite discount rate is greater than the discount rate of the cash proceeds. This occurs because of the operating leverage effects created by the low risk cash outlays.
- If the project life is finite and greater than one year, then finding the composite discount rate of a project requires finding an IRR. There may be projects for which an IRR does not exist, or is not unique. For those projects, there may be no composite rate, or the composite rate may not be unique.

BUY VERSUS LEASE

The buy versus lease decision illustrates well the desirability of using different discount rates for cash flows with different characteristics. The use of different discount rates for different cash flow components is a widely accepted practice in analyzing this problem.

Assume a firm can lease an asset for three years at a cost of $33,049 per year (the payment at the end of each year). This is a financial lease; the lessee firm cannot cancel the lease. The alternative is to buy the asset at a cost of $90,000. The firm can borrow $90,000 at a cost of 0.06. In three years, the asset's residual value is estimated to be $5,000.

The firm has a weighted-average cost of capital of 0.10. Assume a zero tax rate for simplicity. Two sets of cash flows require discounting:

1   lease flows of $33,049;
2   residual value of $5,000.

Let $B(n, r)$ be the present value of annuity of n years at a discount rate of r. Discounting the lease flows using the 0.06 borrowing rate:

$$PV = \$33,049 \; B(3, 0.106) = \$88,340$$

Using the WACC of 0.10:

$$PV = 33,049 \; B(3, 0.10) = \$82,188 \text{ (this calculation is not recommended).}$$

Discounting the residual value (0.20 is a risk adjusted rate).

Using $0.06 = 5,000(1.06)^{-3} = \$4,198$
Using $0.10 = 5,000(1.10)^{-3} = \$3,757$
Using $0.20 = 5,000(1.20)^{-3} = \$2,894$

The net cost of buying (the cost of buying minus the present value of residual value):

Using $0.06 = 90,000 - 4,198 = \$85,802$
Using $0.10 = 90,000 - 3,757 = \$86,243$
Using $0.20 = 90,000 - 2,894 = \$87,106$

Using the one discount rate (WACC $= 0.10$) for leasing and buying:

Cost of leasing $= \$82,188$
Cost of buying $= \$86,243$

Using the WACC $= 0.10$ as the discount rate, leasing has a lower cost and appears to be more desirable. But we do not advocate using a higher rate than the borrowing cost to compute the present value of the cost of leasing.

If we use the 0.06 borrowing rate for the cost of leasing (to compute the debt equivalent of leasing) and 0.20 for the high risk residual value we obtain:

Cost of leasing $= \$88,340$
Cost of buying $= \$87,106$

Now buying has a lower cost and is more desirable. The 0.20 is a reasonable discount rate for the high-risk residual value, but buying is the better choice since the debt flows of leasing should be discounted at the borrowing rate.

If the leasing arrangement is the equivalent to borrowing money then using the WACC of 0.10 or the risk adjusted rate of 0.20 to compute the present value of leasing is not attractive. If someone insisted on using the WACC of 0.10 to compute the present value of leasing then the necessary next step would be to use a 0.10 discount rate to compute the present value of the 0.06 debt used to finance the buying of the asset. This would add dollars to the buy analysis. Each of the cash flow components of the buy versus lease decision requires a different discount rate. The recommended analysis is summarized in Table 8.10, utilizing a variation of the component cash flow procedure.

A zero tax rate has been assumed. If the normal tax rate for corporations applies then the tax savings from depreciation deductions also requires its unique discount rate.

Table 8.10 *Buy versus lease: summary of recommended analysis*

Cash flow component	Discount rate	Present value factor	Cash flows	Present value
Buy				
Initial outlay	NA	1.0000	−90,000	−90,000
Residual value	20.00%	0.5787	5,000	2,894
				−87,106
Lease				
Lease flows	6.00%	2.6730	−33,049	−88,340

DISCOUNT RATES AND CORPORATE INCOME TAXES

This section assumes that a corporation is subject to non-zero corporate income tax rates and that the corporate income tax laws permit a tax deduction for corporate interest payments but not for dividends on stock. This creates a tax advantage to using debt financing relative to equity financing. It also means that the value of an asset depends not only on the future operating cash flows that it will generate, but also on how the asset has been financed. To estimate the market value of an asset in this kind of tax system, some assumption must be made about how much debt is used to finance the asset, and some procedure must be used to estimate how the use of debt affects the value of the asset.

A number of approaches are used to estimate the tax advantages of debt when all of the investment cash flows from a firm are equally risky. The most common approach is to use the WACC as the discount rate. This approach starts with the before-tax discount rate, which depends on the risk characteristics of the firm's assets. The before-tax discount rate is then reduced by an amount that is a function of the proportion of debt used to finance the firm, the corporate tax rate, and the interest rate on the debt.

Instead of a WACC for the firm as a whole, we will calculate a tax-adjusted discount rate for each cash flow component. This tax-adjusted discount rate for a cash flow component can be thought of as being analogous to the WACC for a firm that had assets that generated only this one cash flow component. Let r_i^* be the after-tax discount rate for the ith cash flow component. To calculate the tax-adjusted discount rate we need the following inputs:

r_i = the before-tax discount rate for ith cash flow component;

L_i = the proportion of the ith cash flow component's value that is debt financed;

k_i = the interest rate on the debt of the ith cash flow component; and

t_c = the corporate income tax rate.

Using this notation, the value of the after-tax discount rate for a cash flow component can be expressed as follows:

$$r_i^* = r_i - L_i t_c k_i$$

A derivation of this formula is contained in the appendix.

To implement the component cash flow procedure, we need an appropriate before-tax discount rate for each cash flow component stream, an estimate of the proportion of debt financing appropriate for that component, the cost of that debt, and the marginal corporate tax rate.

Much of the necessary information has to be estimated and the estimations are not likely to be exact. For convenience, the maximum statutory tax rate for corporations is normally used unless there is a reason to think its use is inappropriate (as when the corporation is not expected to have taxable income).

The examples have assumed that the split between debt and equity, the cost of debt and the cost of equity are all known for each cash flow component stream. Thus we determine the discount rate. All of these measures are estimates and could be different with different assumptions or calculation techniques.

THE PRESENT VALUE CALCULATION TECHNIQUE USED

The net present value calculations assume the after-tax cash flows are estimated as if all of the capital is equity. The WACC computed assuming some debt, gives rise to a tax shield. Thus the after-tax debt cost with a before tax yield of k_i, and a tax rate of t, is $(1 - t)k_i$. Investors buying the debt will earn k_i if the debt payments are made as contracted. If k_e is after corporate tax cost of equity, then k_e is the return that equity holders require.

An alternative calculation would be to add to the after-tax cash flow, as previously computed, the tax savings from having interest as a tax shield to obtain the cash flows. The discount rate is then computed as if debt does not create a tax shield. This is the Adjusted Present Value (APV) calculation.

Thus the tax saving may be reflected in the discount rate (the WACC calculation). This NPV calculation is done in the examples in this chapter. The APV alternative calculation adjusts the cash flows for the interest tax savings but uses a discount rate that does not include the tax savings of debt. See Chapter 2 for a more complete explanation.

GLOBAL BUSINESS ASPECTS

In a limited sense the analysis of any international project is an example of the application of this chapter's conclusion that each cash flow component, with a

157

different risk, should have a different discount rate. Because of the fact that where an investment in a foreign country has different risk characteristics than a domestic investment, a different discount rate is used. The next step would be to study the cash flow components of the foreign investment to determine if their differences imply the use of different discount rates of each component.

CONCLUSIONS

To value a project by discounting its component cash flows requires an estimate of the appropriate discount rate for each different cash flow component. The approach of valuing a project by discounting its total cash flows requires an estimate of the project's cost of capital. Under the conventional procedure management solves the complexity problem by choosing a "cost of capital" and the range of projects to which it applies. Frequently one cost of capital is applied to all projects in a company. Sometimes different discount rates are used in different divisions. Sometimes the same discount rate is applied to all divisions even though there are large differences in risk between the divisions in order to avoid the politically difficult task of assigning specific discount rates to different divisions.

Under the procedure we recommend, management would announce a classification of cash flow components and a discount rate for each component. For example, the discount rate could be 18 percent for contribution margins of projects in Division A, 12 percent for contribution margins of projects in Division B, 9 percent for overhead expenses, and 7 percent for depreciation tax shields. Managing a capital budgeting analysis system with different discount rates for different cash flow components is more complicated than just relying on a one discount rate fits all cash flows approach. But we believe that, in many circumstances, the improved quality of decisions would more than justify the extra complexity.

PROBLEMS

1   Assume a project with the following expected cash flows.

Time	Cash flow
0	−210.46
1	120
2	144

The internal rate of return (IRR) is 0.16.

a.   Compute the present value of the project at times, 0, 1 and 2 using the IRR.

b. Define value depreciation to be the change in value (using the IRR). Compute the depreciations, incomes, and ROI for each year.

2 (*Continue 1*) Now assume the cost of money is 0.10. Compute the NPV using 0.10.

3 (*Continue 1 and 2*)

a. Compute the project's present value at times 0, 1, and 2.

b. Compute the incomes for periods 1 and 2 using the value depreciations based on a 0.10 discount rate.

c. Compute the ROI of each year.

d. If the equity investment is $17.64 at time zero, what return does the equity investor earn?

e. What return does the $210.46 investment earn?

f. What percentage of the capital is assumed to be debt?

4 Assume a project with the following expected cash flow.

Time	Cash flow
0	−227.59
1	−200
2	269.12
3	312.18

The two outlays are certain with a 0.05 discount rate and the two positive cash proceeds are risky with a 0.11 discount rate.

Compute the conventional IRR for the cash flows.

5 (*Continue 4*)

a. Compute the debt equivalent for the two outlays.

b. Compute the IRR based on the investment being equal to the debt equivalent.

6 (*Continue 4*)

Compute the NPV using 0.05 for the two outlays and 0.11 for the risky cash proceeds.

7 (*Continue 4, 5, and 6*)

Assume equity investment at time 0 is $28.62 and the liability is $418.07.

a. What is the project's equity at time one?

b. What income does the equity earn in the first time period?

c. What percentage return on equity is the income?

8 (*Continue 4, 5, 6, and 7*)

a. What percentage of the capital is assumed to be debt at time zero?

b. What percentage of the capital is assumed to be debt at time one?

c. What would you expect to happen to the cost of equity capital through time?

DISCUSSION QUESTION

Consider the drilling of an oil well. This is a very risky undertaking. Can you apply the concepts of this chapter to the decision to drill an oil well?

BIBLIOGRAPHY

Bierman, H., Jr., "Analysis of the Buy-Lease Decision: Comment," *Journal of Finance*, September 1973, pp. 1019–21.

Bower, R. S., "Issues in Lease Financing," *Financial Management*, winter 1973, pp. 25–34.

Grenadier, S. R., "Valuing Lease Contracts: A Real Options Approach," *Journal of Financial Economics*, July 1995, pp. 293–331.

McConnell, J. and J. S. Schallheim, "Valuation of Asset Leasing Contracts," *Journal of Financial Economics*, August 1983, pp. 237–62.

Miller, M. and C. Upton, "Leasing, Buying and the Cost of Capital Services," *Journal of Finance*, June 1976, pp. 761–86.

Myers, S. C., D. A. Dill, and A. J. Bautista, "Valuation of Financial Lease Contracts," *Journal of Finance*, 31, June 1976, pp. 799–820.

Roenfeldt, R. L. and J. S. Osteryoung, "Analysis of Financial Leases," *Financial Management*, spring 1973, pp. 74–87.

Schall, L. D., "The Lease-or-Buy and Asset Acquisition Decisions," *Journal of Finance*, September 1974, pp. 1203–14.

APPENDIX: DERIVATION OF THE FORMULA FOR THE AFTER-TAX DISCOUNT RATE FOR A CASH FLOW COMPONENT

Let

r_i = the before-tax discount rate for the ith cash flow component,

r_i^* = the after-tax discount rate for the ith cash flow component (i.e. the weighted after-tax average cost of capital for this cash flow component),

L_i = the proportion of the value of this cash flow component financed with debt,

k_i = the promised interest rate on the debt used to finance the ith cash flow component,

r_{iE} = the expected rate of return on the "equity" of the ith cash flow component when the proportion of debt financing is γ_i, and t_c = the marginal corporate tax rate.

We assume that the values of r_i, k_i, L_i and t_c are known. Then the before-tax expected rate of return on the ith cash flow component can be expressed as follows:

$$r_i = (1 - L_i)r_{iE} + L_i k_i$$

Re-arranging the above to solve for r_{iE} we have

$$r_{iE} = \frac{r_i - L_i k_i}{1 - L_i}$$

The after-tax weighted average cost of capital for this cash flow component is:

$$r_i{}^* = (1 - L_i)r_{iE} + L_i(1 - t_c)k_i$$

By substituting the previously derived expression for r_{iE} into this expression we have

$$r_i{}^* = (r_i - L_i k_i) + L_i(1 - t_c)k_i$$

Simplifying gives

$$r_i{}^* = r_i - L_i t_c k_i$$

which is the expression given in the chapter body.

161

Chapter 9

Practical solutions to capital budgeting with uncertainty

Good intentions are not enough. You need hard cash.
(Margaret Thatcher, *The Wall Street Journal*,
Thursday, November 29, 1990)

With certainty, the value of an investment can be described in terms of the present value of its future cash flows using a default-free discount rate. This approach is theoretically correct since there is only one possible cash flow, and the appropriate discount rate is well defined. This chapter presents brief discussions of techniques for dealing with capital budgeting under uncertainty. With uncertainty, many alternative sequences of cash flows could occur if an investment were accepted. The decision-maker does not know in advance which sequence will actually occur. The goals are still the same as with certainty; we would like to know if the market value of the firm will increase if the investment were accepted. However, the estimation process is much more complex than with certainty.

THE TWO BASIC APPROACHES

We will describe two basic types of approaches for coping with uncertainty. There are many variations of each type. The two basic approaches to be discussed are:

1   Calculate measures such as the payback period, the present value profile and sensitivity analyses (e.g. Monte Carlo simulation) to help the decision-makers evaluate the desirability of the project.

2   Calculate the expected cash flows, and discount them using an appropriate risk-adjusted discount rate or rates (RADR).

The first method aims to describe the relevant characteristics of assets. The second method does provide an asset valuation.

The two approaches can be used in a complementary manner. Any investment decision under uncertainty involves a great deal of judgment. To make good decisions, the decision-maker must understand the characteristics of the investment projects under consideration. The first approach helps in this regard. Applying some of the descriptive methods, such as sensitivity analysis and the present value profile, can help identify investments characteristics that may be helpful as a supplement to the formal valuation methods in deciding whether or not to accept an investment. For example, the present value profile may reveal that the investment results are not sensitive to the choice of discount rate. The sensitivity analysis might reveal that the investment results are very dependent on the state of the economy.

The second method provides an estimate of the value of the investment project. In principle, the second method is a special case of the state-preference method. The second method assumes that the essential characteristics of a project's cash flows can be accurately summarized by specific characteristics, such as NPV using the expected free cash flow in each period, and the beta of the project.

APPROACH 1: USING PAYBACK, PRESENT VALUE PROFILE, AND SENSITIVITY ANALYSIS

All of the theoretical frameworks that might be used for the valuation of a project require that the persons making the valuation have a thorough understanding of the project being proposed. The cash flow framework is convenient for studying a project and for assembling and summarizing project-related information. Project analysts who have done their job properly know much more about a project than is indicated by a single set of cash flow estimates. In fact, one of the most important results of a capital budgeting study is the knowledge gained by the firm about the nature of the possible outcomes.

One difficult problem is communicating the analyst's conclusions to higher levels of management, without overwhelming busy executives with more detail than they can reasonably handle. There are a number of techniques that can be used in practice to help the analyst understand the project and to communicate that understanding in a concise way to management. Among the most important techniques is sensitivity analysis. This is a way of showing how key factors could influence the value of a project. Basically, it involves varying the level of variables such as the cost of a key raw material or the demand for the final product and showing how the changes affect the cash flows, the internal rate of return and the net present value estimates. Other important considerations are the project's flexibility (the extent to which it allows management to adjust to different conditions rather than committing management to a predetermined course of action) and the relationship of the project to the firm's strategic objectives.

The present value profile is a graph showing the NPV of the project as a function of the discount rate used. Essentially it is a way of presenting a sensitivity analysis of the project to changes in the discount rate.

The payback calculation is an effective way of communicating how rapidly the investment recovers its initial outlay. While an investment with a thirty-year payback may be desirable, management is warned that analysis is required to verify that the projected long-term benefits are likely to be realized.

APPROACH 2: CALCULATE THE NET PRESENT VALUE OF THE EXPECTED CASH FLOWS

The second approach for dealing with uncertainty is based on describing the investment project in terms of some summary characteristics that are sufficient to determine its value. The relationship between the assumed characteristics of the project and its economic environment and the conversion of this information into a decision model can be referred to as a valuation model. The primary valuation model is the use of the net present value of expected cash flows. Most capital budgeting techniques popular with practitioners fall into this category. The choice of the discount rate is an important consideration. Two of the more popular alternatives are the use of the weighted average cost of capital (WACC) or a risk adjusted discount rate (RADR). The two major tasks are estimating the expected cash flows of the asset and choosing an appropriate discount rate. In Chapter 6 we point out that the discount rate for a given set of cash flows need not be the same every year. In Chapter 8 we pointed out that different discount rates may be appropriate for different cash flow components in a project. One advantage of the net present value approach is that it can easily accommodate these modifications.

We will illustrate different approaches that could be used to adjust for risk when using expected cash flows to estimate the value of an asset. For this illustration, suppose a firm has the opportunity of acquiring an asset that is expected to generate $100 per year for the next three years. The default-free rate of interest is 5 percent. The present value of the $100 expected cash flows for three years at 5 percent is $272.32. This would be an appropriate estimate of the asset's value if the cash flows were certain. But with uncertainty, investors require some procedure reflecting the uncertainty about its ultimate value.

The approach most frequently used by practitioners to adjust for risk is to increase the discount rate that they apply to the expected cash flows to compute the present value. This is the risk-adjusted discount rate (RADR) method. The amount added to the default-free rate to allow for risk is called a risk premium. Suppose it is determined (somehow) that the appropriate risk premium in this case is 6 percent, and therefore that the appropriate rate of discount for this asset is 11 percent. Discounting the cash flows at 11 percent produces a risk-adjusted present value (RAPV) of $244.37. This is a decrease of $27.95 compared to the present value at the default-free rate.

The $27.95 difference between the present value at the default-free rate and the present value at the correct risk-adjusted rate may be called the risk adjustment of the asset. In this example, the risk-adjusted present value of the asset ($244.37) is about 90 percent of its present value at the default-free rate ($272.32).

A second way of adjusting for risk is to subtract a dollar risk adjustment. The risk-adjusted present value (RAPV) of the investment is $244.37.

$$RAPV = \$272.72 - \$27.95 = \$244.37$$

Just as using a risk-adjusted discount rate implies a risk adjustment, so estimating a risk adjustment implies a risk premium to the discount rate. If the dollar risk adjustment were estimated directly, it is possible that the estimate would turn out to be different than $27.95.

Both of the methods used above combine all of the cash flows in each period and use a single average discount rate. However, suppose that the expected cash flow of $100 per year consists of an expected after tax variable contribution (revenues minus variable costs minus the applicable income tax) of $147 and expected fixed after-tax fixed outlays of $47. The variable contribution amount is considered to be riskier than the fixed outlays. Therefore the discount rates used are 11 percent for the $147 per year of expected variable contributions and five percent for the $47 per year of expected fixed outlays. The present values are $359.23 for the contribution and −$127.99 for the outlays. The net present value for the project is the sum of these two amounts, namely $231.23. Adjusting for risk by applying different discount rates to cash flow components with different risks is a useful way of calculating the present value of the expected cash flows.

WACC: THE WEIGHTED AVERAGE COST OF CAPITAL

The most commonly used approach for calculating present values is to discount the expected cash flows using a discount rate that allows for both the time value of money and the riskiness of the cash flows (the second approach). The discount rate used is most commonly described as the weighted average cost of capital (WACC) of the firm in which the project will operate. There are variations, such as using the WACC for an industry, or for a division of a conglomerate firm, or for the project being considered (a RADR).

A substantial part of the remainder of this chapter is devoted to explaining in detail the WACC concept. We do this because the WACC is so heavily relied on in practice as the appropriate discount rate for capital budgeting analysis. While we do not recommend the general use of the firm's WACC, the WACC of a project or a cash flow stream is useful. There are significant flaws in the logic for using the firm's WACC as the discount rate for making capital budgeting decisions. Most important, there are easy to implement alternatives that are likely to produce better valuations and better insights into the characteristics of the project. The firm's WACC is also useful in considering the optimal capital structure for a firm. It is still useful for this purpose, although this is not the primary focus of this book.

A satisfactory definition of a discount rate that is universally useful would be helpful in guiding the internal investment policy of corporate management. The choice of investments frequently represents a strategic decision for the management of a firm, since in large part the choices made will influence the future course of the firm's development. Implicit in any definition of a discount rate to guide investment policy is a judgment on the goals toward which the firm is or should be striving. The corporate goal that has been conventionally adopted in discussions of this kind and accepted by us is that the corporation seeks to maximize the economic well-being of present stockholders. In attempting to work out a definition of a discount rate based on the goal of maximizing the economic interests of present stockholders, we do not mean to deny the existence or the importance of other goals. If other goals are in competition with the goal of maximizing present stockholders' economic interest, the development of an investment policy based on stockholders' interest may help us understand the extent to which the various goals are in conflict.

We will briefly describe the basic elements of computing the costs of different types of capital and the effect that a firm's changing its capital structure has on its weighted average cost of capital. We will then evaluate the use of the firm's weighted average cost of capital as a discount rate for measuring the desirability of corporate investments.

We assume here that it is the expected free cash flows from the proposed investment that are being discounted. Not surprisingly, if there is a change in the definition of the quantity being discounted, there must be a corresponding change in the discount rate.

Funds to finance an investment proposal may be obtained by a firm in a variety of ways: by borrowing from banks, by allowing short-term liabilities to expand, by selling marketable securities such as government bonds, by selling other assets or parts of its business, by issuing additional securities (for example, bonds, preferred stock, or common stock), or by committing funds generated by operations. These are only some of the more important sources. For certain types of these sources of cash, such as bank loans, there is a generally accepted definition of the cost of funds obtained. For other sources, such as funds generated by operations, there is less agreement. We must consider the opportunity cost to shareholders of retaining these funds. This cost is referred to as the cost of retained earnings.

THE COST OF RETAINED EARNINGS

The costs associated with retaining some part of the current earnings are not always obvious. The question must be asked, "Will the benefits be great enough to cover the opportunity cost of the funds?"

There are two kinds of opportunities for the use of corporate earnings. They may be retained within the corporation, or they may be distributed to stockholders.

If earnings (or some part of earnings) are retained within the corporation, stockholders are deprived of the current dividends or other distributions that could have been paid with those earnings. This is a cost to the stockholders. On the other hand, there are some benefits, the valuation of which will depend on what the corporation does with the funds. Suppose the corporation retains the cash flows from operations. If, as a result, there is an immediate increase in the value of the stock that more than offsets the lower current dividend, stockholders will be better off than if the funds had not been retained and they had received the cash dividends. Retained earnings have a cost and this cost should be measured by the alternative after-tax returns the shareholders can earn.

There are problems with determining the cost of retained earnings when there are differences in the income tax status of the firm's stockholders. Whether a particular stockholder will be better or worse off as a result of a somewhat smaller dividend and a somewhat larger rise in the price of the stock will depend on the income tax rates on ordinary income and on capital gains to which the stockholder is subject. Stockholders differ widely in this regard. Some are subjected to high marginal tax rates, and others, such as pension funds and universities, are not subject to income taxes. Thus there is no one minimum yield at which stockholders are better off if the corporation reinvests earnings instead of paying greater dividends since there are many groups of stockholders whose personal interests may be different.

An investor who is not subject to income taxes (for example, a university endowment fund or a pension fund) may be indifferent to the extra dollar in dividends and or the extra dollar of capital gains. An investor who has to pay a large tax on ordinary income and a smaller tax on capital gains may be willing to sacrifice a dollar in dividends in order to gain less than a dollar in capital gains. A change in the tax code might change the above conclusions.

The Internal Revenue Code is only one of many factors that create conflicts of interest among stockholders. At the same time that some stockholders are attempting to increase their investment portfolios, others are withdrawing a part of their investments for consumption. Even if neither group was subject to taxes, the first would tend to prefer retained earnings because it would thereby avoid the transaction costs required to convert dividends into additional stock holdings. The second group would tend to prefer dividends so as to avoid the expenses and inconvenience of selling a part of its holdings periodically.

If the stock of corporations were distributed between investors in some random manner, the conflicts of interest between investors could be of great practical importance. However, the securities of listed corporations tend to flow into the portfolios of investors whose personal or institutional investment goals are more or less consistent with the known policies of the companies whose stock they hold. Thus conflicts of interest between stockholders of widely held corporations are somewhat reduced by the ease with which stock may be purchased and sold.

COSTS OF RETAINED EARNINGS AND OF EQUITY WITH INVESTOR TAXES

The cost of common stock with investor taxes is complex (it depends on assumptions) so we will only consider the two simplest situations. In this section we assume zero transaction costs but explicitly consider the investor's income taxes. Let

> r_p be the investor's after-tax return on investments of comparable risk (this is the investor's opportunity cost)
> t_p be the investor's tax on ordinary dividend income
> r_c be the required return that the corporation must earn.

It is assumed that all values are known. The results would not hold if r_p and r_c were the expected values of random variables.

COSTS OF RETAINED EARNINGS WITH INVESTOR TAXES

If the firm pays $1 dividend, the investor nets $(1 - t_p)$.

If the firm retains the $1 and earns r_c, then after one year the firm can pay $(1 + r_c)$ and the investor nets (after tax):

$$(1 - t_p)(1 + r_c)$$

with a present value of:

$$(1 - t_p)(1 + r_c)(1 + r_p)^{-1}$$

Equating the value from a dividend and the value from retention, we have:

$$(1 - t_p) = (1 - t_p)(1 + r_c)(1 + r_p)^{-1}.$$

Simplifying the equation, the present value from retention for one year is equal to the value from an immediate dividend if $r_c = r_p$. Thus the return earned by the firm from retained earnings must equal the after-tax return the investor can earn on alternative investments of equivalent risk.

Instead of one year assume the investment is for n years. Investing the $(1 - t_p)$ in the market the investor has after n years

$$(1 - t_p)(1 + r_p)^n$$

With the firm reinvesting the $1 for n years and then paying a dividend that is taxed at t_p the investor nets:

$$(1 - t_p)(1 + r_c)^n$$

The two values are equal if $r_c = r_p$. To justify retention if all distributions are dividends the firm must earn the return (after investor tax) that the investor can earn.

COST OF NEW EQUITY CAPITAL WITH INVESTOR TAXES

Now we want to determine the cost of new equity capital. The new capital invested by the firm will earn r_c which is then taxed at a rate of t_p, and then the investor will have $1 + (1 - t_p)r_c$ after one year. The present value must equal $1.

$$1 = (1 + (1 - t_p)r_c)(1 + r_p)^{-1}$$

and solving for r_c:

$$r_c = \frac{r_p}{1 - t_p}$$

The cost of capital for new capital is larger than the cost of retained earnings. Assume $t_p = 0.15$ and $r_p = 0.10$, then the cost of new capital is

$$r_c = \frac{0.10}{1 - 0.15} = 0.1176$$

while the cost of retained earnings is 0.10 for this example.

An investment of $100 in the market will give the investor $110 after one year since $r_p = 0.10$.

An investment of $100 in the Corporation earning 0.1176 will give the investor $111.76 but the $11.76 of income will result in a $0.15(11.76) = \$1.76$ of tax and the investor again nets $110. The Corporation must earn a 0.1176 return to justify raising new equity capital when the market gives an after-tax return of 0.10.

Instead of one year, assume a perpetuity. Investing in the market the investor earns r_p each year. Assume a distribution of r_c the investor nets $(1 - t_p)r_c$ each year. Equating the two returns:

$$r_p = (1 - t_p)r_c$$

or

$$r_c = \frac{r_p}{1 - t_p}.$$

Now assume a n year horizon. Investing the $1 in the market the investor has

$$(1 + r_p)^n$$

Invested in the corporation, the value at time n is:

$$1 + (1 - t_p)r_c B(n, r_p)(1 + r_p)^n = 1 + (1 - t_p)r_c\left(\frac{(1 + r_p)^n - 1}{r_p}\right)$$

Equating the two values:

$$(1 + r_p)^n = 1 + (1 - t_p)r_c\left[\frac{(1 + r_p)^n - 1}{r_p}\right]$$

$$(1 + r_p)^n - 1 = \frac{(1 - t_p)r_c}{r_p}\left[(1 + r_p)^n - 1\right]$$

and

$$r_c = \frac{r_p}{1 - t_p}$$

More complex models can be created by assuming the firm retains earnings for n years and then the gain to the investor is taxed at a capital gains rate.

This section has considered the effect of investors' income taxes on the cost of capital. We assume that there are no transaction costs, but we explicitly consider the income taxes that stockholders pay on taxable dividends from corporations.

Our main conclusions are as follows:

1   If the alternative to undertaking the new investment is to return the funds to stockholders as a taxable dividend, the minimum required rate of return on new investments is the after-tax rate of return the investor can earn on investments of comparable risk.
2   If undertaking the new investment requires raising new equity capital, the minimum required rate of return on new investments is the after-tax rate of return the investor can earn on investments of comparable risk divided by one minus the investor's tax rate on corporate dividends.
3   Capital gains taxation or uncertainty about future returns results in complex models.

DEBT AND INCOME TAXES

In computing the effective cost of debt, the interest payments must be adjusted to compensate for the fact that debt interest is deductible for tax purposes. For example, suppose that the yield of the debt outstanding is 10 percent, the tax rate for the corporation is 35 percent, and the corporation has taxable income. Because the interest is deductible for corporate income tax purposes, $1 of interest will reduce taxes by $0.35 and effective interest cost will therefore be $0.65 per dollar of interest. The effective interest cost is 0.65×10 percent, or 6.5 percent, instead of the 10 percent yield of the debt. If a firm does not have taxable income, the effective cost of the interest payments becomes the contractual rate, not adjusted for income taxes. This possibility, if taken into consideration, would tend to make the effective interest cost higher than 6.5 percent. Also, the above calculation assumes the debt was issued at par.

THE RELEVANT SOURCE OF FUNDS

If an investment proposal is to be financed by borrowing, is the interest rate on the specific loan the relevant discount rate for this investment? Would a second investment financed by common stock then have a different discount rate? If this approach were consistently followed, the cost of capital would be an erratic quantity, fluctuating up or down as the firm obtained additional increments of capital from varying sources. Although there are situations in which a particular investment can be related to a specific source of financing, more commonly there exists, on the one hand, a group of apparently desirable investment proposals and, on the other, a variety of sources of additional capital funds that, taken together, could supply the financing for the increased investment.

171

In taking the time value of money into account we do not in general advocate a procedure where the analysis would be influenced by the type of financing specific to the project. Recognizing, however, that there must be some stock equity capital if there is going to be debt issued and that these securities lead to payments that are treated differently from a tax standpoint, we want the after-tax cost of capital to reflect the mixture of debt and common stock that will be used by the firm.

GLOBAL BUSINESS ASPECTS

A firm engaged in international business must determine where funds should be borrowed. There are tax implications regarding the source of borrowed funds. A tax law might require that interest be allocated to be used against the income of a specific foreign operation, or an interest allocation might not be allowed.

Interest expense from US debt is allocated to foreign income. This reduces that foreign tax credit that is allowed by the US, thus it might not be desirable to borrow marginal funds in the US.

Obviously, someone in the corporation (or available to the firm's management) must be knowledgeable about the domestic and foreign tax laws to determine where funds should be borrowed.

COMPUTING THE FIRM'S WEIGHTED AVERAGE COST OF CAPITAL

The cost of capital of a firm may be defined as a weighted average of the cost of each type of capital. The weight of each type of capital is the ratio of the market value of the securities representing that source of capital to the market value of all securities issued by the company. The term *security* includes common and preferred stocks and all interest-bearing liabilities, including notes payable.

Suppose the market value of a company's common stock is $4.5 billion. The market value of its interest-bearing debt is $3 billion and the average before-tax yield on these liabilities is 10 percent per year, which is equivalent on an after-tax basis to 6.5 percent per year (equal to 10 percent times 0.65, assuming a 35 percent corporate tax rate).

Assume that the company described in the preceding paragraph is currently paying a dividend of $8 per year and that the stock is selling at a price of $100. The rate of growth of the dividend is projected to be 6 percent per year. Thus the cost of the common stock equity is

$$k_e = \frac{\$8}{\$100} + 0.06 = 0.08 + 0.06 = 0.14 \text{ or } 14 \text{ percent}$$

The average cost of capital for the company as a whole could be estimated as shown in Table 9.1.

The preceding example is expressed in terms of the required rate of return for present debt and the present common stock. If we were considering the raising of new capital to finance additional investments, it would be more accurate to speak in terms of the rate of return that would be required if a mixture of additional debt and common stock were to be issued. The word *average* that is used in the term *weighted average cost of capital* refers to a weighted average of marginal costs for debt and stock.

While the calculations are normally for a firm, they could be redefined to apply to a division, plant, or a project.

CAPITAL STRUCTURE AND THE EFFECT ON THE WACC

Without investor taxes and costs of financial distress a firm's WACC is reduced by the addition of debt. Let:

k_0 be the firm's WACC
$k_e(0)$ be the firm's WACC and cost of equity with zero debt
t_c be the corporate tax rate
B be the amount of debt[1]
V_L the value of the firm with B of debt.

It can be shown that:

$$k_0 = k_e(0)\left[1 - \frac{t_c B}{V_L}\right]$$

Table 9.1 Estimate of weighted average cost of capital

Capital source	Proportion of total capital	After-tax cost	Weighted cost
Equity	0.60	0.14	0.0840
Interest-bearing debt	0.40	0.065	0.0260
Average cost of capital			0.1100

---

1 We assume the market value of the debt is equal to its book value and that the debt is a perpetuity so that $B = I/r$ where I is the annual interest payment on B debt.

For example, assume with zero debt that $k_e(0) = 0.12$. Now if B/V_L 0.5 and $t_c = 0.35$ we have

$$k_0 = 0.12[1 - (0.35)0.5] = 0.099$$

The use of 50 percent debt in the capital structure reduces the firm's WACC from 0.12 with zero debt to 0.099 because of the corporate tax savings associated with debt.

THE OPTIMUM CAPITAL STRUCTURE

There are times when a company will consider a permanent change in its capital structure because management believes that changes in the relative cost of source of capital, or changes in the business risks faced by the company, would make a different capital structure more desirable.

If we recognize the existence of costs of financial distress, then the WACC does not decrease for all amounts of debt. There might be a minimum WACC and an optimum amount of debt. Modigliani and Miller (1958) proved that under certain conditions that the entire WACC curve is horizontal and there is not one minimum cost of capital, but rather that all combinations of debt and common stock are equally desirable. Modigliani and Miller required the absence of income taxes and of costs of financial distress to reach this conclusion.

Even a company financed only with funds obtained from stockholders may eventually have to cease operations because a combination of operating losses and poor investments has exhausted its funds, but debt increases the risk of bankruptcy. With debt it is possible equity-holders may lose their interest in a company that may again become a profitable operation. It is frequently assumed that, with a well-managed and profitable company, the introduction of a small amount of non-equity capital presumably will not increase the risks of bankruptcy appreciably. Any increase in debt, however, increases the risks of bankruptcy. A very small increase in the chance that a firm may eventually become bankrupt can have a noticeable effect on the price that investors are willing to pay for its common stock, because if bankruptcy occurs, common stockholders are likely to lose their entire investment.

Even without bankruptcy the addition of debt can increase the costs of financial distress. These are the costs associated with disruption of business activity because customers and suppliers fear the possibility of bankruptcy. Thus, even if bankruptcy does not occur, a firm can lose value because of the adverse effect on operations of financial distress or the fear of financial distress.

One advantage of debt capital comes from the financial leverage it provides for the remaining equity capital. An increase in the debt ratio, however, generally has two effects on the earnings per share available to common stockholders: it tends to change the average earnings per share; and it tends to increase the year-to-year variability of earnings per share (including negative earnings arising from bankruptcy or near bankruptcy). If expected earnings per share increase, this is likely to increase the price per share that investors are willing to pay; the increase in variability is likely to decrease the price per share that investors are willing to pay.

An important advantage of debt is that interest is deductible for purposes of computing corporate taxable income, whereas dividends on common stock are not deductible. With high corporate tax rates, there is a very real tax incentive for firms to use debt as a major component of their capital structure.

There is an important non-financial cost associated with the use of debt. This category of costs is the result of limitations on management's freedom of action, which are usually included as part of the debt agreements. Provisions requiring that sinking funds be accumulated, limiting the conditions under which the corporation can acquire additional debt, and restricting the directors' freedom to declare dividends are examples. These limitations are frequently of importance, but they are difficult to quantify, and they must be taken into account on a judgment basis.

It is impossible to give any simple rules for determining in advance the optimum capital structure for a particular firm. Theoretically, the optimum structure is reached when an additional debt issue, in substitute for stock equity, will result in a decrease in the sum of the new market value of the common stock plus the market value of the debt. The capital structure just prior to the issue of that debt is the optimum capital structure. In determining whether a company's capital structure is optimum, management must to some extent rely on the intuitive judgment of well-informed persons.

It is important to keep in mind the fact that any increase in the percentage of debt used increases both the cost of the next dollar of debt and expected return required by stockholders (there is more risk). If before the issuance of debt the debtholders required 10 percent and the stockholders required an expected return of 14 percent, after the issuance we can expect both of these costs to increase. Since the percentage of debt is also increasing, we cannot predict the effect of the change of the weighted average cost of capital without more information. But we can conclude that the firm's average cost of debt is affected by tax factors (interest deductibility) and the costs of financial distress (bankruptcy).

THE FIRM'S WACC AND INVESTMENTS

The firm's weighted average cost of capital (WACC) at a given moment reflects both the average risk of the existing assets owned by the firm and the capital structure of the firm. In this section we focus on changes brought about by changing the composition of the assets, and assume that the firm achieves the best possible capital structure for whatever set of assets it owns at a particular time.

In principle, the acquisition of a new asset by the firm could change the capitalization of the firm (the total market value of its debt and equity) and its WACC. In practice, if a firm makes substantial investments whose characteristics are very different from the firm's average, the firm's cost of capital is likely to change as a result.

If the outlay required to acquire a new asset is less than the asset is worth, then the total capitalization of the firm will increase. If the outlay is greater than the asset's worth, the capitalization of the firm will decrease. Ordinarily it will be the firm's stockholders, as the residual claimants, who will benefit most from increases in capitalization and be hurt the most by decreases of capitalization. The point of the NPV rule for evaluating investments is to guide the firm to selecting investments that are worth more than they cost, e.g., that have a positive NPV and therefore a favorable effect on firm capitalization and on stockholder wealth.

If the new asset that is acquired is riskier than the firm's existing assets, the acquisition will tend to increase the firm's cost of capital. If the new asset is less risky than the average existing assets, the acquisition will tend to decrease the firm's average cost of capital. There is no necessary benefit to stockholders to decreasing a firm's WACC by selling off assets with above average risk. Nor is there any necessary harm to stockholders to increasing the firm's WACC by acquiring new assets that are riskier than the average old asset.

Suppose, for simplicity, that all of the cash flows from a single asset have the same risk. A specific new asset being considered might have a smaller or larger discount rate. The firm's WACC is the correct discount rate only for one level of risk. A project being evaluated is likely to have a different risk.

There is no reason to believe that any specific investment proposal being considered is exactly average with respect to risk or the timing of the cash proceeds. To the extent possible, the managers of a firm should attempt to use discount rates that reflect the actual risk of the investment being considered. If a given investment project has cash flow components with different risks, the discount rate used should reflect the risk of that cash flow component, not the average risk of the project or the average risk of the firm. The relationship between the amount of risk and the project's required return is shown in Figure 9.1. The firm's weighted average cost of capital represents an averaging of all risks of the firm. It would be incorrect to assume that the same rate of discount should be used for a marginal investment as required on the average for the present investments.

The firm's weighted average cost of capital can be used to evaluate investments in much the same manner that the payback method can be used. It gives some insights and, as long as it is not the final step in the analysis, it can be useful. One basic problem is that a WACC incorporates a risk adjustment, which is then inserted into a compound interest formula, and we do not know that risk

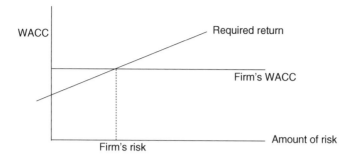

Figure 9.1 *Relationship between amount of risk, the required return, and the weighted average cost of capital (WACC)*

compounds evenly through time for all investments at the same rate. A second problem is that using the firm's WACC as a discount rate applied to all cash flows of all projects assumes that all of the project cash flows have the same risk, and that this risk is the same for all projects. A third problem is that using the WACC as the discount rate assumes that the project's risk is the same every year of its life, and this may not be the case.

THE PROJECT'S WACC

When a project has a different risk than the overall risk of the firm, then the project's risk (and costs of capital) should be used rather than the firm's risk and the firm's costs of capital.

There is a problem in determining the costs of capital of a sub-unit of a corporation. One common solution to this problem is to use the pure play method to calculate the costs of capital.

THE PURE PLAY

Assume a steel company owns an oil operation. The steel company's cost of equity does not apply to the oil division's operations.

A conventional solution is to find an oil company that is doing the same type of oil operations as the firm's oil division. The second step is to determine the oil company's cost of equity and weighted average cost of capital. These measures are then assumed to apply to the oil operations of the steel company.

A pure play of exactly the same characteristics as the operations requiring capital costs might not be easily found.

Secondly, there might be difficulties determining the cost of equity and the weighted average cost of capital of the pure play and translating these to the capital structure appropriate for the operating division.

Thus, the pure play approach is widely used, but it is not without its difficulties.

DEFAULT-FREE RATE OF DISCOUNT

There are several situations in which it is desirable to use a discount rate that reflects as nearly as possible the pure default free time value of money, and not include an adjustment for any associated risk. One such situation is the discount rate used in calculating the present value of a series of certainty equivalents. The certainty equivalents reflect the project's risk. Another situation is that in which one wants to construct a risk adjusted discount rate by adding a risk premium to pure time value of money rate. There are many discount rates that have been suggested for these purposes. Among them are the two possibilities we shall consider in this section: (1) interest rate of government securities, and (2) interest rate of long-term bonds of the firm.

The term *risk-free* might be used to describe the interest rate of government securities. This is suggestive, but not strictly accurate. There are certain risks that cannot in practice be eliminated and that affect all interest-bearing securities to a greater or lesser extent.

One source of risk arises because of uncertainty about the future price level. Expectations about possible future price levels influence the market determination of interest rates. Buyers of bonds will tend to be hurt if the price level rises; hence they require a higher interest return with an expected price-level increase than with an expected price-level decrease, or with constant prices.

Another source of risk arises because of the possibility of changes in the term structure of interest rates. Normally, the interest rate on bonds will vary with the number of years to maturity even when there is no risk of default on the bonds. Bonds that mature in a few years may have higher (or lower) yields than bonds that mature in the more distant future. If there is no risk of default, the lender can always be sure of earning the going yield by buying a default-free bond of given maturity and holding it until it matures. The possibility exists, however, that some other strategy would result in earning a higher yield. If investors want to lend money for a five-year period and expect a decline in interest rates, they may be able to earn a higher yield by buying a fifteen- or twenty-year bond and selling it after five years than by buying a five-year bond and holding it to maturity. When this strategy of investing in long-lived securities is followed, however, there is no longer any guarantee that a given minimum rate of interest will actually be earned for the shorter holding period.

A lender wishing to avoid the uncertainty that results from the possibility of changes in the term structure of interest rates may be unable to do so. An investment in short-term debt instruments, such as treasury bills, will lead to uncertainty about the rates that will be earned when the time for reinvesting these funds arises. An investment in longer-term securities will lead to uncertainty about the actual return that will be realized if the securities must be liquidated before they mature.

In spite of these limitations, the interest rates on government debt constitute a reasonable choice of discount rates representing default-free lending opportunities. These rates represent actual market opportunities at which firms or individuals could lend money with essentially no risk of default.

Unfortunately, neither private corporations nor individuals can actually borrow money at the same rate as the federal government, even with the best available collateral. For various reasons, the rates at which a private entity could actually borrow for a given term would be higher than the rates at which the government can borrow for loans of the same maturity. Thus the default-free rate (the rate on a Federal Government security) can only be used where the firm has excess cash, not where the firm must borrow to finance the investments.

If a default-free rate of discount is used to compute the present values of a risky project, then before a decision can be made, a dollar amount must be subtracted to take into consideration the riskiness of the cash flows. Unfortunately, the determination of the dollar risk-adjustment for a corporate investment is an art and not a science. Thus while application of a default-free rate of discount to the expected cash flows is not complex, the determination of the dollar risk-adjustment is a major obstacle to applying this technique with confidence.

DISCOUNTING STOCK EQUITY FLOWS

Instead of discounting an investment's cash flows, some managers and decision-makers prefer to discount the stock equity cash flows using the cost of equity capital. This type of analysis is frequently done in analyzing real estate investments, but it is also done when corporations are evaluating investments in joint ventures and in other situations.

Assume an investment is to be financed with a mixture of debt and common stock. For the given capital structure and the given risk, both the debtholders and the common stockholders have specified their required returns. We will assume that both time value and risk are being taken into consideration in a reasonable manner by these required returns. For simplicity of presentation we will assume zero taxes. The firm should be able to either discount the total investment cash flows using the project's weighted average cost of capital or discount the net of debt cash flows to the stockholders using the cost of equity capital for the project. Although the firm can discount the investment cash flows at the project's weighted average cost of capital the use of the cost of equity capital applied to the stock equity cash flows requires carefully specified assumptions.

Assume a firm uses equal amounts of debt and equity to finance an investment and that with that capital structure the cost of equity is 0.12 and the cost of debt is 0.08. With zero taxes the weighted average cost of capital (WACC) will be 0.10:

$$\text{WACC} = \frac{1}{2}(0.12) + \frac{1}{2}(0.08) = 0.10$$

An investment has the following cash flows and present values if the debt is adjusted annually to be equal to 0.5 of the present values:

Time	Cash flows	Present value (0.10)	Debt (0.5 of present value)
0	-$3,000	$3,513.1510	$1,756.58
1	1,600	2,264.46	1,132.23
2	1,400	1,090.90	545.46
3	1,200		
NPV(0.10) =	$513.15		

The stock equity cash flows with $1,756.56 of initial debt after the necessary debt payments are:

Time	Cash flows	Interest (0.08)	Principal	Stock equity flows
1	$1,600	$140.53	$624.35	$835.12
2	1,400	90.58	586.77	722.65
3	1,200	43.64	545.46	610.90

Using the 0.12 cost of equity consistent with equal amounts of debt and equity, the stock equity flows have a present value (PV) of

$$PV = \frac{\$835.12}{1.12} + \frac{\$722.65}{(1.12)^2} + \frac{\$610.90}{(1.12)^3} = \$1,756.56$$

Adding the stock equity's present value of $1,756.56 to the $1,756.58 present value of the debt we again obtain the $3,513.14 present value of the investment. Thus we can either discount the investment's free cash flows at the project's WACC or we can discount the common stock flows at the cost of equity and add this amount to the amount of debt. These calculations are consistent with each other. The calculations become flawed if the capital structure is not adjusted annually to maintain the equality of stock and debt.

180

To illustrate the problems that can arise, assume no debt is retired in the first time period and $645.47 is retired in the second. The stock equity cash flows are now:

Time	Cash flows	Interest (0.08)	Principal	Beginning debt	Stock equity flows
0	$1,600	$140.53	$0	$1,756.58	$1,459.47
1	1,400	140.53	645.47	1,756.58	614.00
2	1,200	88.89	1,111.11	1,111.11	0

The present value of the stock equity flows is

$$PV = \frac{\$1,459.47}{1.12} + \frac{\$614.00}{(1.12)^2} + 0 = \$1,792.58$$

The stock equity measure is now larger than the previous calculation. This arises because more debt is being used after the first time period, but with the use of more debt we did not adjust upward the cost of equity or the cost of debt.

The use of the cost of equity and stock equity cash flows requires that the capital structure implicitly being used in the stock equity cash flow calculation be consistent with the capital structure used in the weighted average cost of capital calculation. If the capital structure measures are consistent, the same net present value will be obtained using the WACC applied to the investment flows as will be obtained by the use of the cost of equity applied to the stock equity cash flows and the debt rate applied to the debt. In practice, this requirement is not always consistently applied.

SIMULATION AND THE MONTE CARLO METHOD

The concept of probability is a means of describing the likelihood of the different possible outcomes. If the outcomes are described in numerical terms, whether as cash flows, net present values, internal rates of return, or some other measure, the expected value, variance and standard deviation can be used to help summarize the possible outcomes.

Using these concepts, there are two main strategies for summarizing the possible outcomes of an uncertain investment. One strategy is based on looking at the cash flows on a period-by-period basis. The cash flows may represent a guess at the expected cash flows or an estimate conditional on a particular scenario occurring. A sensitivity analysis is frequently used to supplement the period-by-period cash flow estimate. To produce a sensitivity analysis, the assumed value of one factor is varied, and the resulting variations in estimated cash flows are recorded. A second strategy is to simulate the possible cash flows and summarize the results. This is called a risk analysis using simulation or the Monte Carlo method. The term Monte Carlo applies to the process since outcomes are selected randomly.

The purpose of a sensitivity analysis is to determine how varying the assumptions will affect the measures of investment worth. Ordinarily, the assumptions are varied one at a time. For example, assume the estimated cash flows are held constant, but the rate of discount used is varied (as when there is a difference of opinion as to what rate should be used).

Now assume, the discount rate is assumed to be constant, and the estimated annual cash flows are assumed to be subject to a stochastic process. The initial outlay can also be assumed to be stochastic.

Risk analysis is intended to give the managers a better feel for the possible outcomes that can occur, so that they can use their judgment and experience with regard to whether or not the investment is acceptable. In practice, the possible outcomes are so numerous that listing all of them is not feasible, even with the help of a large-scale computer. This approach is called simulation. If the process involves choosing outcomes randomly, the process is sometimes called the Monte Carlo method.

The steps involved in producing a risk analysis can be briefly summarized as follows. First, a measure of investment worth is selected, for example net present value or internal rate of return. Second, for each set of decisions a computer program is devised that will sample from all possible outcomes. For each outcome selected the probability of the outcome and the value of the investment are computed. Third, the results of the simulation are summarized and presented to management. The final summary might consist of drawing a histogram or calculating the mean and variance (or other measures of central tendency and dispersion) for whatever measure or measures of investments worth that were selected in the first step. This approach is called risk analysis.

Assume that the outcomes for one set of decisions has been simulated a large number of times (say, 100,000). For 30,000 trials outcome a occurred. Table 9.2 assigns a 0.3 probability to outcome a. Table 9.2 also gives the net present value, using a 10 percent discount rate, for each state of nature a to f.

Table 9.2 Frequency distribution of net present values of an uncertain investment

Possible states of nature	Probability of state	Net present value at 10%
a	0.3	−$100
b	0.1	0
c	0.1	50
d	0.2	0
e	0.1	50
f	0.2	200

Some investments available to a corporation may be more risky than other investments that is, there is a higher degree of uncertainty. The introduction of uncertainty opens up the possibility of losses, which in turn forces us to measure the relative importance of the possibility of large profits compared with the possibility of large losses.

It is suggested that management should consciously consider the possibility of not realizing the forecasted results and should incorporate this into the analysis. There remains the question of the psychological impact on business managers and investors of losses and gains. This type of analysis is still in its infancy. Finally, consideration must be given to the alternatives that are available to investors and how these alternatives affect the investment decisions of the firm. One technique used to evaluate the risk "Value-at-Risk."

VALUE-AT-RISK

Value-at-risk (VAR) techniques are marketed by financial advisors using different names and different computational techniques. But they all look at the client's past or different economic situations (e.g. interest rates) in order to determine the probability of different outcomes in the future, especially the probabilities of different losses.

If the future is exactly typical of the past then we can use the past history to predict the future. If however, the future is not exactly consistent with the past then the future may hold surprises. For example, assume a study of interest rates shows that the largest increase in interest rate over the period of a month is 400 basis points and financial decisions are made on this information. Now assume in the next month interest rates increase by 600 basis points. The losses can be large.

Instead of interest the value-at-risk analysis might involve stock prices, rate of inflation, oil prices, or a variety of other factors.

Value-at-risk is a useful tool but the probabilities presented for financial loss should be accepted with a grain of salt. Unusual events that did not happen in the past can and will happen in the future.

CONCLUSIONS

The decision-maker should understand the uses and limitations of each approach to evaluating investments under uncertainty. The fact is that while theory offers several different useful approaches and enables us to label some practices as being incorrect, we do not have one simple calculation that can be reliably used in all situations.

Unfortunately, once uncertainty is recognized, we no longer can offer a simple, always correct, method of evaluating investments. We know that we must estimate future cash flows, the value of the cash for different states of nature, the probabilities of different outcomes, the appropriate time discount rate, and adjustments for risk preferences of the investors and decision-makers. While two or more of the above considerations may be combined (as with state-conditional present value factors) all the factors must be considered. A single measure of value for the project may not be a feasible means of evaluating the investment.

When cash flows are discounted at a default-free interest rate, the resulting net present values adjust the cash flows for differences in timing, but not for risk. If any higher discount rate is used, there is an implicit risk allowance, and decision-makers must ask themselves whether the appropriate risk allowance has been made. Is the quantification of risk reasonably correct? Some firms may prefer to use the rate at which they can borrow long-term funds as a discount rate. If their credit rating is good, this rate will not be far above the default-free rate, and it may be easier to explain and justify to management. One alternative is to use a default-free interest rate and make risk adjustments separately. Both of these methods would require that a dollar risk adjustment be deducted from present value because of the existence of risk.

There are two basic methods of taking into consideration the time value of money and risk preferences. The generally accepted financial theory advocates the adjustment of the discount rate to take time value and risk into consideration in one calculation using $(1 + r)^{-n}$ where risk is the risk adjusted discount rate (RADR). The second method uses a default-free interest rate or the firm's borrowing rate to take time value into consideration and computing a present value, but then subtracting a dollar amount to take the project's risk into consideration. This dollar risk adjustment is not easily determined.

PROBLEMS

1   Assume that only two states of nature, A and B, are possible at time 1. The one-period default-free rate of interest is 0.07. The risk-adjusted present value of a dollar if state A occurs has been determined to be 0.500000.
    What is the present value of a dollar if state B occurs?

2   *(Continue 1)*
    a.   What is the present value of $1 to be received for certain at time 1?
    b.   What is the present value of an investment that will pay $1 if either event A or B occurs?

3   The XYZ Company has net income of $50,000,000 per year on stock equity of $500,000,000. The firm has a chance to invest $80,000,000 in an

investment that has an expected internal rate of return of 0.50. If the project is successful it will earn $40,000,000 per year for perpetuity. The probability of being successful is 0.20. If the investment is not successful it will earn zero cash flows. There is a 0.8 probability it will not be successful. A loss of $80,000,000 would be awkward but the firm could probably survive.

Should the investment be accepted?

4   The L Oil Company is considering purchasing a tract of land. The company requires a 0.20 internal rate of return on investments. There are zero taxes. The tract of land will be financed with 60 percent 20-year debt costing 0.12. The debt is a balloon payment type of debt. The land costs $10,000,000 and offers an annuity of $1,500,000 per year for 20 years. The land is expected to be worth $20,000,000 at the end of 20 years. The following cash flow analysis has been prepared:

Year	Investment	Debt	Net
0	−$10,000,000	+$6,000,000	−$4,000,000
1–20	+1,500,000	−720,000	+780,000
20	+20,000,000	−6,000,000	+14,000,000

The net present value using 0.20 is:

$$NPV = -\$4,000,000 + \$780,000(4.8696) + \$14,000,000(0.0261)$$
$$= -\$4,000,000 + \$3,798,000 + \$365,000 = +\$163,000$$

a.   Should the investment be accepted?

b.   Should the investment be accepted if the 0.12 debt is paid off using equal annual payments?

5   The ABC Company has net income of $50,000,000 per year on stock equity of $500,000,000. The firm has a chance to invest $800,000,000 in an investment that has an expected internal rate of return of 0.20. If the project is successful it will earn $200,000,000 per year for perpetuity. The probability of being successful is 0.8. If the investment is not successful it will earn zero cash flows. There is 0.2 probability it will not be successful. A loss of $800,000,000 would jeopardize the existence of the corporation.

Should the investment be accepted?

DISCUSSION QUESTION

Assume corporations can be expected to earn 0.10 (after corporate tax) in the future. Investors in the common stock of these corporations have an opportunity cost that is higher/lower than 0.10. Explain.

BIBLIOGRAPHY

Crum, Roy L. and F. G. J. Derfinderen, *Capital Budgeting Under Condition of Uncertainty*, Boston: Martinus Nijhoff, 1981.

Fama, E. F., "Risk Adjusted Discount Rates and Capital Budgeting Under Uncertainty," *Journal of Financial Economics*, June 1977, pp. 3–24.

Fama, E. F. and K. R. French, "Industry Costs of Equity," *Journal of Financial Economics*, February 1997, pp. 153–95.

Forham, David R. and S. Brooks Marshall, "Tools for Dealing with Uncertainty," *Management Accounting*, 79, September 1997, pp. 38–43.

Harris, Milton and Artur Raviv, "The Capital Budgeting Process, Incentives, and Information," *Journal of Finance*, September 1996, pp. 1139–74.

Liberatore, Matthew J., Thomas F. Monahan, and David E. Stout, "A Framework for Integrating Capital Budgeting Analysis with Strategy," *Engineering Economist*, 38, Fall 1992, pp. 1–18.

Markowitz, Harry M. "Portfolio Selection," *Journal of Finance*, March 1952, pp. 77–91.

——, "Investment for the Long Run: New Evidence for an Old Rule," *Journal of Finance*, December 1976, pp. 1273–86.

Robichek, A. A. and S. C. Myers, "Conceptual Problems in the Use of Risk-Adjusted Discount Rates," *Journal of Finance*, December 1966, pp. 727–30.

Part III

Option theory as a capital budgeting tool

There is less in this than meets the eye.

(Attributed to Tallulah Bankhead)

Imagine a situation where an alternative is accepted at time zero and there is no opportunity to depart from the chosen path. Now imagine an alternative situation where the initial outlay can be delayed, the method of operation can be modified, and at the end of each period there are alternative uses for the resources. In this second situation, there are "options." It is useful to be able to value these options.

Chapter 10

Real options and capital budgeting

> He shows not only that winning isn't everything, it's not even what it's cracked up to be.
>
> (Allen St. John's Review of *When Pride Still Mattered: A Life of Vince Lombardi*, quoted in *New York Times Book Review*, September 17, 2000, p. 40)

There are at least four common capital budgeting situations where real option considerations can affect the valuation. More than one of these situations may be applicable to the same capital budgeting project. These situations are:

1   The firm can wait before investing;
2   There will be an opportunity to increase or reduce the scale of the project in the future;
3   There will be an opportunity to sell a part of the project or to use the project in another way;
4   Future investment opportunities will be created that would not be available if the initial investment had not been undertaken. (The investment facilitates the undertaking of the next generation of investments.)

Triantis and Borison (2001) studied the use of real options by 39 individuals from 34 companies in seven different industries. They found that the companies (p. 23) "are actively adopting the real options approach." Real options offer (p. 23) "a general way of thinking and, in a more rigorous and intensive way, as an organizational process." Graham and Harvey (2002) also found widespread use of real options (p. 12) "Somewhat surprisingly, more than one-fourth of the companies claimed to be using real options (RO) evaluation techniques."

In general, real options are associated with a capital budgeting project whenever there will be a chance to make value enhancing decisions about the project in the future based on better information than is available today. The present value (PV) of a capital investment project that ignores the value of these options will be called the PV without flexibility. The PV without flexibility plus the value of options gives the PV with flexibility. Thus we have:

$$\text{PV with flexibility} = \text{PV without flexibility} + \text{Value of options} \qquad (10.1)$$

The value of an option reflects the value of the cash flows that will be generated if the option is optimally exercised. If the cash flows from a proposed investment depend in part on future decisions, and if it is believed that future management will be capable of making these future decisions correctly, then in valuing the investment we should assume that the future decisions are made correctly and value the resulting cash flows. The value of the investment with the future cash flows correctly evaluated is the PV with flexibility.

One way to calculate the PV with flexibility is to use the *direct* method. The direct method requires that the investment cash flows must be the cash flows that result from the correct future decisions, and that these cash flows must be valued correctly. Alternatively, we can calculate a PV by projecting and valuing the cash flows from the initial project as if no future decisions are possible. This is the PV without flexibility. We can then calculate and value the incremental cash flows from the correct future decisions. This is the value of options. As indicated in equation (1), the sum of the PV without flexibility plus the Value of options equals the PV with flexibility. When we add the PV without flexibility and the value of options to calculate the PV with flexibility, we are using the *indirect* method to calculate the PV with flexibility.

In principle, both the direct and indirect methods of estimating the PV with flexibility should give identical answers. In practice, there may be a reason for preferring one method of estimation or the other. The valuation technique that is commonly used to value capital investment projects is to discount the expected cash flows from the project at a constant discount rate that is supposed to adjust for both time value and risk. This approach does not work well with options. It also does not work well if the project cash flows include the cash flows from real options. For that reason, it is sometimes more practical to value the project without flexibility by discounting its expected cash flow, and then to use specialized valuation techniques to value the option.

The net present value, NPV, of a project is equal to the PV with flexibility minus the cost of the project.

$$\text{NPV} = \text{PV with flexibility} - \text{Cost of project} \qquad (10.2)$$

The value of an option is never negative. Therefore if the NPV of a project without flexibility is positive and the investment is deemed to be acceptable, it is not necessary to consider the value of any options to make an accept-or-reject decision about the project; the option values could only make the NPV more positive. If the proposed investment is one of a set of mutually exclusive alternatives, then the NPV with flexibility is needed in order to determine which investment in the set is preferred. It might be desirable to undertake the investment now, but it might be more desirable to delay the investment one or more time periods. Or the proposed investment might be desirable (NPV $>$ 0), but an initial investment of a smaller or larger scale might be more desirable. Whenever there are mutually exclusive alternatives, the values of any options should be considered.

The application of option theory to capital budgeting decisions is a major development in capital budgeting, and managers involved in a firm's capital budgeting process should understand when these concepts could usefully be applied.

It is helpful to distinguish three types of option-valuation situations. One is where the cash flows from the option being evaluated can be exactly duplicated by the cash flows from a portfolio of marketable assets. This situation will be discussed first. It is the easiest way to introduce some important ideas that apply to all options and modern option valuation techniques were developed to solve this type of option valuation problem. Also, options of this type have become an important feature in modern highly developed financial markets. In the second situation, a portfolio of marketable assets cannot exactly duplicate the payoffs from the alternative being evaluated. However, the payoffs from the option can be duplicated, in principle, by a portfolio consisting of the payoffs from some marketable assets and the payoffs from a fractional interest in a real or hypothetical capital investment project. This approach assumes that the value of the capital investment project (without flexibility) can be determined by conventional capital budgeting techniques. In the third situation, the existence of the options can be established but there is no accepted procedure for determining their value. Even in this case, option theory makes an important contribution by calling attention to the existence of the alternatives and of the resulting flexibility.

Black and Scholes (1973) opened the way to modern option pricing procedures by showing how to value options whose payoffs could be replicated by a portfolio of marketable assets. Their work was based on advanced mathematical techniques that are difficult for the average practitioner but fortunately the application of the Black–Scholes formulation does not require any mathematical sophistication. William Sharpe, who is best known as one of the discovers of the capital asset pricing model, CAPM, made an important contribution to option pricing theory by showing that a relatively simple technique based on the binomial process could be used to achieve the Black and Scholes results. Cox, Ross, and Rubinstein (1979) and Cox and Ross (1985) publicized Sharpe's idea. Copeland and Antikarov (2001) suggest procedures for valuing real options whose payoff does not directly depend on the value of another traded asset. This chapter is based on these seminal works.

Our objective is to value the options that are associated with investment projects, but we will begin by considering procedures for valuing a call option for common stock. This will introduce the basic option valuation concepts.

TWO TYPES OF STOCK OPTIONS

Call options

A call option on common stock is a contract giving its owner the right to buy a fixed number of shares of a specified common stock at a fixed price during a certain period of time.[1] To describe fully a particular common stock call option, we need to specify the key provisions of the contract. These include at least the following:

1 the number and type of common shares that can be purchased;
2 the price at which the shares can be purchased;
3 the last date at which they can be purchased;
4 whether or not the shares can be purchased only on the last date or on any date up to and including the last date;
5 who is obligated to sell the shares?

Call option owners who take advantage of their right under the contract to buy the common stock are said to be *exercising the option*. The common stock that can be purchased, such as the stock of General Motors, Consolidated Edison, and so on, is called the *underlying asset*. The purchase price is called *the strike price* or *the exercise price*. The last date on which the stock can be purchased is the *maturity date* of the contract. Contracts that can be exercised only on the maturity date are *European options*; contracts that can be exercised at any time up to and including the maturity date are *American options*. The party on the other side of the contract (who has an obligation to sell when the owner exercises the call) is *the writer*. The owner has the right to buy, and the writer has an obligation to sell at the owner's request at the exercise price. Once the contract is in existence it is an asset to the owner and a liability to the writer. Typically the owner makes a payment to the writer to induce the writer to enter into the option contract.

Put options

A *put option* gives its owner the right to sell an asset at a given price. Specifically, a put option is a contract giving its owner the right to sell a specified asset at a fixed

---

1 John C. Cox and Mark Rubenstein, *Options Markets* (Englewood Cliffs, NJ, Prentice-Hall, 1985) p. 1.

price on or before a specified date. Just as there are American and European call options, there are American and European put options. An American put gives the owner the right to sell at any time before the specified date. An European put gives the owner the right to sell only on the specified date. The writer of a put option has the obligation to buy at the put owner's request and at the price specified in the contract.

VALUING CALL OPTIONS ON COMMON STOCK

An option cannot have a negative value because the owner of the option has the right to make a given decision, but is not obligated to make that decision. Owners will exercise options only if they are better off as a result of exercising. Otherwise they will do nothing, which they could have done without the option. Therefore an option will have a positive value as long as there is a positive probability that it will be exercised. If there is a zero probability of exercise, the value of the option is zero.

The exact value of a common stock call option depends on factors such as the probability that the option will be exercised, the dividends that might be paid by the stock before the option is exercised, the volatility of the underlying stock and the rate of interest on debt.

In the evaluation of stock options we shall assume that an option gives the owner a right to acquire *one* share of common stock. Although options may be for more or less than one share, the assumption enables us to simplify notation and the example somewhat.

THE VALUE OF A CALL OPTION ON COMMON STOCK: A NUMERICAL EXAMPLE

The basic approach for valuing stock options is similar for all types of stock options. A replicating portfolio of marketable securities is defined that would have the same payoff as the option. The value of the option is equal to the value of the corresponding replicating portfolio. The seller of an option may create and hold the corresponding replicating portfolio. Because the combination of a short position in the option and a long position in the replicating portfolio creates a perfect hedge, the replicating portfolio is also known as a *hedge* portfolio. If the writer of an option actually wishes to create a hedge it is not sufficient to buy and hold the hedge portfolio through time. Rather the writer will need to periodically adjust the composition of the hedge portfolio as the price of the underlying stock changes and as the maturity dates approaches. We will illustrate these points with numerical examples later in the chapter. Sometimes, instead of actually creating the hedge portfolio, a mathematical model can be used to estimate the value of the option. It is beyond the scope of this book to consider the mathematical details of these valuation models, but the basic concept will be introduced, as they are very useful in capital budgeting applications. We will first give a numerical example to illustrate the procedure for valuing a call option by using a replicating portfolio. Then we will present the general formulas that can be used.

We want to value a call option that gives the owner the right to buy one share of a particular company's stock at a price of $120. The stock price is now $100. The option matures in one period. We assume that at maturity, the stock price will be either $150 or $100.

The assumption that the stock price can take on only two possible values is an example of the application of the binomial process referred to above. This assumption is clearly an unrealistic simplification, but it is sufficient to introduce the basic concepts that are used in valuation. In an appendix to this chapter we show how dividing the time to maturity into many short intervals can eliminate the numerical errors in valuation that may result from this simplification.

If the stock price were $150 at maturity, the owner of the call would exercise the option to buy the share at $120. Once acquired, the share could be sold in the market for $150, generating a positive net cash flow of $30. If the stock price at maturity were $100, the owner of the call would not exercise it. Therefore the payoff from the option at maturity will be either $30 (if the stock price is $150) or $0 (if the stock price is $100).

We want to determine a value for the option when the stock price is $100 and the option has not expired. At that point in time we know the possible payoffs for the option, but we don't know which of the payoffs will occur. To value the option we identify a portfolio of traded assets that will have the same payoffs as the option. This portfolio is called the *hedge portfolio* or the *replicating portfolio*. If the market is in equilibrium, the law of one price will apply and the value of the option and the net value of the replicating portfolio will be identical since they have the same payoffs. The replicating portfolio will consist of m shares of the underlying stock, which is now selling for $100 per share, and B dollars of default-free debt costing 10 percent per year. The value "m" is called the hedge ratio. It gives the number of shares of the underlying stock that must be held in the replicating portfolio to have the same value as a call on one share. The value of m will be positive and less than or equal to one. The value of B represents the amount of debt in the replicating portfolio. A negative value of B means that the hedge portfolio owes money; a positive value means that it is owed money. We want to determine values of m and B that will make the payoffs from the replicating portfolio equal to the payoffs from the option.

Since the value of an option is always positive, the net value of the hedge portfolio must be positive. This means that if B is negative, the value of the stock position must be greater than the value of the debt owed. In others words, any debt in the hedge portfolio will be fully collateralized. The fact that the debt in the hedge portfolio is fully collateralized justifies the assumption that the interest rate on the debt is equal to the risk free rate.

If the price of the stock goes up to $150 and the value of the call option is $30, the payoff from the replicating portfolio is

$$m(150) + B(1.1) = \$30$$

If the price of the stock goes down to $100, the value of the call option is zero, and the payoff from the replicating portfolio is

$$m(100) + B(1.1) = 0$$

This gives us two equations and two unknowns. Solving this system of equations, we find that $m = 0.6$ and $B = -\$54.55$. Therefore to form the replicating portfolio at time zero, buy 0.6 shares of the common stock, costing $60, and borrow $54.55, using the stock as collateral. The value (and net cost) of the replicating portfolio at time zero is $60 - \$54.55 = \$5.45$.

Since the replicating portfolio has the same two outcomes as the call option, the market value of the option should be the same as the value of the replicating portfolio. If the option and the hedge portfolio do not have equal market values, then arbitrageurs will have an incentive to enter the market and buy whichever is less expensive, and to sell whichever is more expensive, and thereby lock in a riskless profit. Arbitrageurs will drive the option price to the equilibrium level.

Arbitrage occurs when a security is bought in one market and immediately sold for a profit in another market. (*Arbitrageurs* are traders who specialize in arbitrage.) If the same security is available in two or more different markets, arbitrage will ensure that it has essentially the same price in all markets. If arbitrageurs are interested only in the cash payoffs of a security, then a call option and its replicating portfolio are essentially identical securities whose prices will be kept in line by arbitrage. Thus, there is a strong market force that keeps the price of call options in line with the market values of their replicating portfolios. Black and Scholes showed how to price stock options by using a formula that is the equivalent of calculating the value of the replicating portfolios.

FORMULAS FOR CALL OPTION VALUATION

The procedure for valuing a one-period call option using the replicating portfolio approach can be summarized in a few formulas. The approach is sometimes referred to as the binomial option pricing procedure because it relies on the assumption that the underlying stock price can have only two possible values in the next period, given its value in the previous period. In the numerical example just considered, in order to calculate the value of a one period call option, we introduced assumptions about the initial value of the underlying stock, the values the stock would have next period in the up and down states, the default free rate of interest, and the strike price of the call option. Table 10.1 presents the variable names we will use for these quantities as well as the values of these variables in our example.

For a meaningful example, the values chosen must satisfy certain conditions. The value of V must be greater than zero and the value of K must be greater than or equal to zero. Also, the value of r must be between the values of u and d and the value of d must be non-negative.

$$0 < d < r < u \tag{10.3}$$

If d were negative, the value of the underlying stock would be negative. If r were less than d, the worst outcomes from owning stock would be better than the certain return from debt; no one would own debt. If r were greater than u, the best outcomes possible from owning stock would be worse than the certain return from debt; no one would own stock. Given that the above conditions are satisfied, the composition of the replicating portfolio, and the value of the call option can be found.

FORMULAS FOR COMPOSITION OF THE REPLICATING PORTFOLIO

To value the option we need to define a replicating portfolio consisting of m shares of stock, with each share having a price of V, and a one period debt of B that will have the same payoff as the option. Let C represent the value of this replicating portfolio and therefore the value of the option.

$$C = mV + B \tag{10.4}$$

Table 10.1 *Variables for stock option valuation example*

Variable	Value	Explanation
V	100	Price of one share of common stock at start
u	1.5	One plus the rate of return on the stock in the up state
d	1	One plus the rate of return on the stock in the down state
r	1.1	One plus the default free interest rate
K	120	Option strike price

The characteristics of the replicating portfolio are determined by the values of m and B. Let C_u and C_d represent the option payoffs in the event the stock goes up or down respectively. The values of C_u and C_d are determined by the following formulas using values of the variables in Table 10.1.

$$C_u = \text{Max}(uV - K, 0) \qquad (10.5)$$
$$C_d = \text{Max}(dV - K, 0) \qquad (10.6)$$

In these equations the symbol Max stands for a function whose value is equal to the largest value in the subsequent parentheses. To ensure that the time one value of the replicating portfolio is equal to the time one value of the call option, the following two equations must be satisfied.

$$C_u = muV + rB \qquad (10.7)$$
$$C_d = mdV + rB \qquad (10.8)$$

If equation (10.7) is satisfied, the value of the replicating portfolio will equal the value of the option payoff if the stock goes up. If equation (10.8) is satisfied, the value of the replicating portfolio will equal the value of the option payoff if the stock goes down. The values of the variables u, d, r and V in these equations are assumed known. All of these variables are in Table 10.1. The values of the variables C_u and C_d have been determined to be $30 and $0 using the values of the variables in Table 10.1. The only variables in equations (10.7) and (10.8) whose values are not known are m and B. We can solve the two equations (10.7 and 10.8) for the values of m and B. Subtracting equation (10.8) from equation (10.7) eliminates B. Re-arranging the resulting equation gives the following expression for m:

$$m = \frac{C_u - C_d}{(u - d)V} = \frac{30 - 0}{(1.5 - 1)100} = \frac{30}{50} = 0.6 \text{ of a share of common} \quad (10.9)$$

Substituting the right hand side of equation (10.9) in place of m in equation (10.8) and re-arranging gives the following expression for B:

$$B = \frac{uC_d - dC_u}{(u - d)r} = \frac{1.5(0) - 1(30)}{0.5(1.1)} = \frac{-30}{0.55} = -\$54.55 \qquad (10.10)$$

If we use these expressions in place of m and B in equation (10.4) we guarantee that the payoffs of the replicating portfolio are equal to the payoffs of the option and therefore that the value of the replicating portfolio is equal to the value of the option. Using equation (10.4):

$$C = mV + B = 0.6(100) - 54.55 = \$5.45$$

The value of the call option for a share is $5.45.

Substituting the expressions for m and B from the right hand sides of equations (10.9) and (10.10) into the right hand side of equation (10.4) and eliminating the value of V which occurs in the numerator and denominator of the first term in the equation gives the following expression for the value of the call option in terms of the variables whose values are given in Table 10.1.

$$C = \frac{C_u - C_d}{(u - d)} + \frac{uC_d - dC_u}{(u - d)r} \tag{10.11}$$

Substituting numerical values from Table 10.1 into equation (10.11) we again obtain a $5.45 value for the option.

$$C = \frac{30 - 0}{1.5 - 1} + \frac{1.5(0) - 1(30)}{(1.5 - 1)(1.1)} = \frac{30}{0.5} + \frac{-30}{0.55} = 60 - 54.55 = \$5.45$$

CERTAINTY EQUIVALENT FORMULAS FOR THE VALUE OF AN OPTION

Another approach to valuing options, which is mathematically equivalent to the portfolio replication method but is often easier to implement, is called the Certainty Equivalent (CE) method.

The practical advantage of the Certainty Equivalent method is that in some situations, particularly those involving more than one period, much less arithmetic is required to value multi-period options. We first introduce the CE method and apply it to the single period example that we have already considered. Then we will use both the CE method and the portfolio replication method to solve a multi-period problem.

To derive the Certainty Equivalent formula we re-arrange the right hand side of equation (10.11) to make the variable r a common denominator for both terms and we rearrange the numerator so that the values C_u and C_d occur only once. After doing this, the value of C can be written as follows:

$$C = \left[\left(\frac{r - d}{u - d} \right) C_u + \left(\frac{u - r}{u - d} \right) C_d \right] \Big/ r \tag{10.12}$$

This formula has a simple intuitive interpretation. Designate the coefficient of C_u as q, so that

$$q \equiv \frac{r - d}{u - d} \tag{10.13}$$

The value of q will be positive and less than one if assumption (10.3) is true. Also the coefficient of C_d will also be positive and equal to $(1 - q)$. Writing the expression of C in terms of q, gives (remember $r = 1.10$):

$$C = [qC_u + (1 - q)C_d]/r \qquad (10.14)$$

The quantity q is defined in the real option literature to be the risk neutral probability (RNP) of the up state. The quantity $(1 - q)$ is the RNP of the down state. The numerator of the right hand side of equation (10.14) is the Certainty Equivalent (CE) of the end-of-period cash payoffs from the option. Using this terminology, equation (10.14) states that the value of the option is equal to the Certainty Equivalent of the option payoffs discounted at the default free rate. Substituting the values from Table 10.1 into equation (10.14), we find that the value of the numerator, the CE, is 60 and the value of the call option is again $\$5.45$ ($= 6/1.1$).

Note that the value of q depends only on the values of u, d and r, but not on the magnitude of the cash flows. One way to calculate the value of an option, or any other asset, is to calculate the certain equivalent of its cash flows and discount the certainty equivalent at the default free rate. Since the certainty equivalent valuation formula [equation (10.14)] was derived from the replicating portfolio valuation formula [equation (10.11)] both formulas give the same asset values. We will illustrate in the next section that the certainty equivalent formula extends easily to multi-period situations.

A MULTI-PERIOD CALL OPTION

To illustrate the valuation of a multi-period call option, assume that the option gives the owner the right to buy one share of stock for $\$120$ two years from now. The stock is currently selling for $\$100$ and in each of the next two years; the stock can either increase by 50 per cent ($u = 1.5$), or have no change in price ($d = 1$). The default free interest rate is 10 percent per year ($r = 1.1$).

Figure 10.1 shows the possible values of the stock at the end of period 1 and the end of period 2. The stock will either be worth $\$225$, $\$150$, or $\$100$ at the end of period 2. With a $\$120$ exercise price the corresponding option payoffs are $\$105$, $\$30$, or $\$0$. We will first value this two-period option using the replicating portfolio method. Then we will use the certainty equivalent method.

THE REPLICATING PORTFOLIO METHOD
FOR A TWO-PERIOD OPTION

The replicating portfolio method allows us to calculate the value of an option at a given time if we know the option payoffs at the end of the next period. To apply

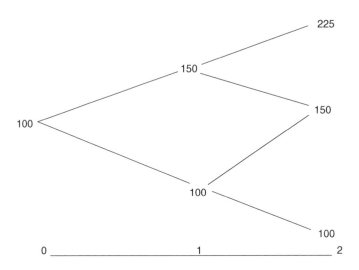

Figure 10.1 *The underlying stock prices over two periods*

this to a multi-period situation we must use a rollback procedure. We know the option payoffs in the last period, given the price of the stock in that period, and the terms of the option contract. From this we can find the value of the option at each possible state in the next-to-last period. We repeat this process as many times as necessary to find the value of the option at the initial period.

If the stock price is $150 at time one, the end-of-year-two cash flows from the option to buy at $120 will be either $105 or $30, depending on whether the stock price increases to $225 or remains constant at $150 during the second year (Figure 10.1). Using equations (10.9), (10.10), and (10.4) in this situation we can determine the appropriate hedge ratio, the amount of debt and the value of the option in this state as follows:

$$m = \frac{105 - 30}{(1.5 - 1)150} = \frac{75}{75} = 1$$

$$B = \frac{1.5(30) - 1(105)}{(1.5 - 1)1.1} = \frac{-60}{0.55} = -109.0909$$

$$C = 1(150) - 109.0909 = 40.9091$$

Similarly, if the stock price is $100 at time one, the end-of-year-two cash flow from the option will be either $30 or $0, depending on whether the stock price increases to $150 or remains constant during the second year. We have already found that the value of a one period option with these characteristics is $5.4545.

To value the option at time zero (the beginning of period 1), we again use equations (10.9), (10.10) and (10.4), but this time we allow the end-of year option payoffs to be either 40.9091 or 5.4545.

$$m = \frac{C_u - C_d}{(u - d)\, V} = \frac{40.9091 - 5.4545}{(1.5 - 1)100} = \frac{35.4546}{50} = 0.70909$$

$$B = \frac{uC_d - d\, C_u}{(u - d)r} = \frac{1.5(5.4545) - 1(40.9091)}{(1.5 - 1)1.1} = \frac{-32.7274}{0.55} = -59.5043$$

$$C = mV + B = 0.70909(100) - 59.5043 = 11.405$$

Therefore using the replicating portfolio method, the value of the two-period call option at time 0 is $11.405.

THE CERTAINTY EQUIVALENT METHOD FOR A TWO-PERIOD OPTION

At maturity there are three possible option payoffs, $105, $30 or $0 if the exercise price is $120. The $105 value occurs only if there are two consecutive up states. Using equation (10.13) the value of q, RNP for the up state is 0.2.

$$q = \frac{r - d}{u - d} = \frac{1.1 - 1}{1.5 - 1} = \frac{0.1}{0.5} = 0.2$$

Since the values of r, u and d are the same in periods one and two, the value of q will be the same in both periods. The probability of two up states in a row is 0.04 ($= 0.2^2$) since the probability of an up state in a given period is assumed to be independent of the state that occurred in the previous period. The $0 state occurs only if there are two consecutive down states. The RNP for each down state is 0.8 [$= (1 - q) = 1 - 0.2$] and the probability of two consecutive down states is 0.64 ($= 0.8^2$).

The $30 payoff occurs if there is one up state and one down state on the path from origin to the period-two state. The probability of each path is 0.16 ($= 0.2$ times 0.8). But there are two separate paths that lead to the $30 outcome (up then down, and down then up). So the probability of a $30 period-two payoff is the sum of the probabilities of all of the paths that lead to that payoff, or 0.32.

Table 10.2 uses these results to calculate the Certainty Equivalent of the cash flows at time zero. The CE is $13.80. To find the value of the option, we discount the CE back two periods using the risk free rate. The result is $11.405 ($= 13.8/1.21$). This is exactly the same value that was found using the replicating portfolio method. The advantage of the CE method is that the RNPs are the same

Table 10.2 Calculation of the certainty equivalent at time 2

State	RNP	Payoff	RNP Payoff
1	0.04	$105	$4.20
2	0.32	$30	$9.60
3	0.64	$0	$0.00
Totals	1.00		$13.80

at every node, and therefore need to be calculated only once. By contrast, the relevant replicating portfolio is in general different at each node.

NUMBER OF PERIODS

To keep the arithmetic simple, the example illustrated assumed that the stock price change can occur only once a period and that each period is one year long. Thus for the option maturing at the end of two years there are only three possible stock prices at maturity. The arithmetic simplicity in the example comes at a cost in accuracy. In practical applications, the year would be divided into many more periods. The binomial assumption that there are two possible stock prices at the end of each period for every stock price at the beginning of the period is maintained. The details of how to increase accuracy by increasing the number of periods per year are considered in Appendix A.

It turns out that the certainty equivalent calculations generalize easily as the number of periods per year increases. Thus, in practice, option valuation calculations nearly always use versions of the certainty equivalent formulas. For valuation purposes, that is all that is needed. Some additional calculations are necessary if it is necessary to actually maintain a hedge portfolio.

VALUING REAL OPTIONS

In the previous sections we have introduced the concept of an option and we have explained how the value of a financial option can be determined. In this section we build on these concepts and apply them to the valuation of real options.

We will describe situations in which there are real options associated with a capital investment project. The real options add flexibility to the project, and this flexibility has value. Sometimes, recognizing the value of flexibility will make a difference in whether the project is accepted or rejected. To value the flexibility associated with a real option, the decision-maker must determine in advance the most economical way to take advantage of this flexibility. In other words, to value a real option, a decision-maker must develop a rational strategy for managing the underlying asset as future uncertainties evolve into today's realities. Developing such a strategy in advance makes it less likely that a firm will continue bad projects when they should have been abandoned, or expand good projects when an expansion is not justified. Our aim is to introduce and illustrate some of the basic concepts involved without considering all of the mathematical and other complexities that can arise. This is an introduction to the topic of real options, not a comprehensive treatment.

The following sections provide examples of the process of evaluating real options. The underlying asset being considered is a new factory. There are two real options associated with the factory. One option is to abandon the factory at the end of year two, or earlier, if the factory results are disappointing. A second option is to expand the factory if demand is greater than expected. We first value each of these options separately, as if the other did not exist. Then we value the portfolio of options taking into account the fact that both of them exist.

Real options analysis involves two major steps. The first step is to establish the present value of the underlying asset without flexibility. This is what the underlying asset would be worth if there were no real options associated with it. The techniques used are those used in conventional capital budgeting analyses, namely estimating the expected cash flows from the asset and discounting them at an appropriate risk adjusted discount rate or cost of capital. However, this first step must go beyond conventional capital budgeting analysis in analyzing the uncertainty associated with the underlying asset. It is necessary to determine a reasonable description of how the value of the asset might change over time.

The second step is to analyze the real options associated with the underlying project. We must identify the major real options, determine the conditions under which each option would be exercised, and estimate the additional cash flows that will be generated as a result of exercising these options. Finally, the certainty equivalents of each option's cash flows will be estimated, and discounted at the default free rate to establish the value of the option. The value of the option is the value of flexibility. The present value of the project taking flexibility into account is the sum of the value of the project without flexibility plus the value of the options. We will consider two options associated with the same underlying asset. We begin with a description of the underlying asset.

DESCRIPTION AND VALUATION OF THE UNDERLYING ASSET WITHOUT FLEXIBILITY

A firm has to decide whether to build a new factory. The relevant WACC for this factory is 12 percent and the default free interest rate is 5 percent. There will be no net cash flows from the factory during the first two years, but the expected value of the factory (without flexibility) at the end of year 2 is $1,254.41. Discounting this expected value at the factory's WACC of 12 percent for two periods gives the value of the factory without flexibility, $1,000.

$$V = \frac{1,254.41}{1.12^2} = \frac{1,254.41}{1.2544} = \$1,000$$

The possible values of the factory over the next two years without taking flexibility into account are illustrated in Figure 10.2.

Because of uncertainty about demand and costs, the value of the factory could increase by 15 percent ($u = 1.15$) or decrease by 13.04 percent ($d = 1/u = 0.8696, d-1 = -0.1304$) in any given year. Assume the probability of an increase is 0.8930 and the probability of a decrease is 0.1070.

We need the probabilities for states D, E, and F.

States	Probability of state	Probability of state
D	0.8930(0.8930)	0.7975
E	0.8930(0.1070) + 0.1070(0.8930)	0.1911
F	0.1070(0.1070)	0.0114

The factory value at time 0 is $1,000. The Values for the States D, E, and F:

Value for state $D = 1,000(1.15)(1.15) = \$1,322.50$
Value for state $E = 1,000(1.15)(0.8696) = \$1,000.00$
Value for state $E = 1,000(0.8696)(1.15) = \$1,000.00$
Value for state $F = 1,000(0.8696)(0.8696) = \$756.20$

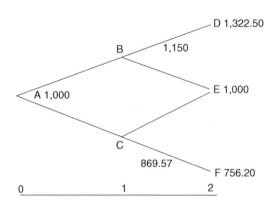

Figure 10.2 Underlying asset

In the table below we verify that the expected value of the factory at the end of period two is $1,254.40. We have already shown that the present value of $1,254.41 discounted for two periods at the WACC of 12 percent is equal to $1,000.

States	Factory value	Probability	Expected value
D	$1,322.50	0.7975	$1,054.69
E	$1,000.00	0.1911	$191.10
F	$756.15	0.0114	$8.62
Totals		1.0000	$1,254.41

Using equation (10.13), the risk neutral probability, q, of the up state for this factory is 0.6434.

$$q = \frac{r - d}{\mu - d} = \frac{1.05 - 0.8696}{1.15 - 0.8696} = 0.6434$$

Table 10.3 gives the values for r, d, and μ.

The RNP for the down state, $1 - q$, is 0.3566 ($= 1 - 0.6434$). These RNPs are consistent with the values shown in Figure 10.2. For example, inserting the RNPs and the end-of-period one values of the factory shown in Figure 10.2 into equation (10.14), the value of the factory at time zero can be calculated as follows:

$$C = [qC_u + (1 - q)C_d]/r \qquad (10.14)$$

Using the information from Table 10.3:

$$C = \frac{(0.6434)(1,150) + (1 - 0.6434)(869.57)}{1.05}$$

$$= \frac{739.91 + 310.09}{1.05} = \$1,000$$

Table 10.3 Variables for real option valuation example

Variable	Value	Explanation
V	$1,000	Value of factory without flexibility at time zero
u	1.15	One plus the rate of increase in the value of the factory in an up state
d	0.8696	One plus the rate of decrease in the value of the factory in a down state
r	1.05	One plus the default-free rate of interest
WACC	1.12	One plus the WACC for the factory without flexibility
q	0.6434	Risk neutral probability of an up state
p	0.8930	Probability of an up state

The options associated with this factory have not been taken into account in calculating the $1,000 value. We shall describe and evaluate two of these real options. We assume that these options expire during the first two years of the factory's life.

AN OPTION TO ABANDON

At the end of period one or period two, the firm can abandon the factory by removing the machinery, selling it in the secondhand market, and dismantling the factory building. The expected net proceeds from this salvage operation are $900. The option to abandon is an American put option. It is an American type option because it can be exercised before the time the option expires. It is a put option because by exercising the right to sell the asset the firm receives the exercise price, $900, and disposes of an existing asset, the factory. Figure 10.3 summarizes the values of the factory taking the existence of this put option into consideration. Note that the $900 put value replaces the $756.20 of Figure 10.2 at node F.

To assign values to each node in this decision tree we first began with the three end-of-period two nodes that describe the possible situations when the option is about to expire. At each end-of-period two node, the decision-maker will compare the going concern value of the factory with its salvage value. If the going concern value is greater, the abandon option will not be exercised. But if the going concern value is less than $900, the firm will abandon the factory. Thus the end-of-period two value of the factory is $\text{Max}(V_2, 900)$. In this formula V_2 is

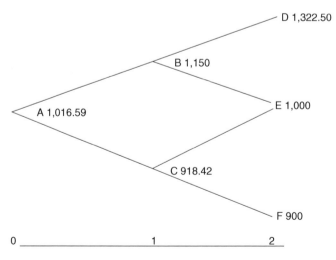

Figure 10.3 Decision tree for the option to abandon

the value taken from the corresponding nodes in Figure 10.2. The values of V_2 at these nodes are $1,322.50, $1,000 and $756.15. The factory will be abandoned only at node *F* since only at that node is the salvage value of the factory greater than its going concern value.

Since this is an American put option that could be exercised at any time, we need to consider the possibility that the option would be exercised at the time one or time zero nodes. To value the factory at nodes *B* and *C* at time one we use Max $(V_1^*, 900)$, where V_1^* is equal to the going concern value of the factory at that node. This going concern value is equal to the present value of the period-two successor nodes, evaluated using RNPs and equation (10.14).

Node *B* is followed by nodes *D* and *E*. The value of the factory at these nodes is $1,322.50 and $1,000 respectively. The certainty equivalent of these amounts using the RNP of 0.6434 is $1,207.5 [= (1,322.50(0.6434) + 1,000 (1 − 0.6434)]. The present value of $1,207.50 discounted at 5 percent is $1,150. Since the going concern value of the factory at node *B* is greater than its $900 salvage value, the abandon option will not be exercised at this node.

Next consider node *C*. The successor nodes to node *C* are *E* and *F*. The value of the factory at these nodes is $1,000 and $900 respectively. The $900 reflects the fact that if the factory is not abandoned at node *C*, and conditions worsen, it will be abandoned at node *F*. The certainty equivalent of the node *C* successor nodes is $964.34 [= (1,000(0.6434) + 900(1 − 0.6434)]. The present value of this amount discounted at 5 percent is $918.42. Therefore, since the value of factory as a going concern at node *C* in Figure 10.3 is greater than its $900 salvage value, the option to abandon will not be exercised at node *C*.

We can also consider whether it is logical to abandon the factory at node *A*. To determine the going concern value node *A* we use RNPs and equation (10.14).

$$V_0 = \frac{0.6434(1,150) + 0.3566(918.42)}{1.05} = \frac{1,067.42}{1.05} = 1,016.59$$

Since the going concern value of $1,016.59 is greater than the $900 abandonment value, the put option will not be exercised. Thus the present value of the factory, taking flexibility provided by the abandonment option into account is $1,016.59.

To determine the value of the abandonment option, we can utilize equation (10.1), which says that the value with flexibility equals the value without flexibility, plus the value of the option. We have already determined that the value of the factory with flexibility is $1,016.59 and the value without flexibility is $1,000. Solving equation (10.1) for the value of the abandonment option and inserting the values of the factory with and without flexibility, we have:

$$\text{Value of option} = \text{PV with flexibility} - \text{PV without flexibility}$$
$$= 1,016.59 - 1,000 = 16.59 \tag{10.15}$$

This is an example of the indirect method of calculating the value of the investment with flexibility.

The process of evaluating the factory taking the flexibility of the abandonment option into account is summarized in Table 10.4. Each row in the second column of the table shows the value of the factory without flexibility at the node shown in the first column. For nodes D, E, and F, the end-of-period two nodes, these values come from Figure 10.2. For nodes A, B, and C, these values are calculated by using the default free rate to discount the certainty equivalent of the value of the firm in the next period successor nodes. Each row in the third column of the table shows the value that would result if the abandonment option were exercised at that node. The fourth column shows the maximum of the third and the fourth columns. The fifth column designates whether or not the option was exercised at that node. The value at node A represents the value of the investment taking flexibility into account. Discounting the expected value of nodes D, E, and F at the factory's WACC would be an example of an incorrect direct calculation.

The value of the abandonment option, considered apart from any interaction with other real options is $16.59. We have previously calculated this option value as the difference between the value of the asset at node A when abandonment is considered and its value at that node without flexibility. The value of the abandonment option can also be calculated directly by calculating the certainty equivalent of the value that is created by exercising the option. The abandonment option will be exercised only in node F. As a result of exercising the option the value at that node increases from $756.14 to $900, an increase of $143.86 but the value at time zero only increases by $16.59. The RNP of reaching node F from node A is 0.1274 ($= 0.3566^2$). The value of the abandonment option is the present value discounted at the default free rate of the certainty equivalent of the gain from exercising the option.

$$\text{Value of abandonment option} = \frac{(0.1274)143.86}{(1.05)^2} = \frac{18.29}{1.1025} = 16.59$$

Table 10.4 Valuing the investment with the abandonment option

Nodes	Factory value without flexibility	Factory value after exercising abandonment option	Maximum value	Exercise option?
(1)	(2)	(3)	(4)	(5)
D	1,322.50	900.00	1,322.50	No
E	1,000.00	900.00	1,000.00	No
F	756.14	900.00	900.00	Yes
B	1,150.00	900.00	1,150.00	No
C	869.57	900.00	918.42	No
A	1,000.00	900.00	1,016.59	No

AN OPTION TO EXPAND

Assume that at the end of periods 0, 1 or 2 the firm can expand its factory by 25 percent at a cost of $150. Only one expansion is possible. The factory cannot be expanded at time one and then expanded again at time 2. This is an American call option. It is American option because it can be exercised at the end of any period. It is a call option because exercising the option requires a cash outlay and results in the acquisition of a new asset.

To value the expansion option we begin by considering the decisions that will be made at the expiration of the option. At node D, if the option is not exercised, the value of the factory is $1,322.50 (see Figure 10.2). If the option is exercised at this node, the gross value of the factory increases by 25 percent to $1,653.13 but after the required outlay of $150, the net value is $1,503.13. Since this is greater than the value of the factory with no expansion, the option will be exercised at this node if it has not previously been executed. The results of similar calculations for all three expiration period nodes are summarized in Table 10.5.

Next, consider the nodes at times one and zero. If the option is exercised at node B, the value of factory will be 1,287.5 (= 1.25(1,150) − 150 = 1,437.5 − 150). This is shown in line B of Table 10.6. If the option is not exercised, the value of the factory is $1,150. The value of the factory is greater if the option is exercised at node B. The results of similar calculations for nodes C and A are summarized in Table 10.6. The value of the expansion option, considered apart

Table 10.5 Calculating factory values at the expiration with an expansion option

Nodes	Factory value without flexibility	Factory value after exercising expansion option	Maximum value	Exercise option?
(1)	(2)	(3)	(4)	(5)
D	1,322.50	1,503.13	1,503.13	Yes
E	1,000.00	1,100.00	1,100.00	Yes
F	756.14	795.18	795.18	Yes

Table 10.6 Calculating factory values prior to expiration with an expansion option

Nodes	Factory value without flexibility	Factory value after exercising expansion option	Maximum value	Exercise option?
(1)	(2)	(3)	(4)	(5)
D	1,150.00	1,287.50	1,294.64	No
E	869.57	936.96	936.96	Yes
F	1,000.00	1,100.00	1,100.00	Yes

209

from any interaction with other real options is $100, the difference between the value of the factory when the expansion option is considered ($1,100), and its value without flexibility ($1,000).

MULTIPLE OPTIONS ON THE SAME ASSET

We have valued options one at a time. But frequently there are multiple real options associated with a single real asset. The value of a portfolio of real options on the same real asset may be different than the sum of the values of the options considered one at a time if the options interact. In the current example, for example, a factory could not be simultaneously expanded and abandoned. But our previous analyses, considering only one option at a time, showed that both the expansion and the abandonment option would be exercised at node *F*. Appendix A in this chapter illustrates the valuation of the factory illustrated in Figure 10.2 when both the option to abandon and the option to expand exist simultaneously.

CONCLUSIONS

In many capital budgeting projects, there are future operating decisions that can be deferred until a later date when more relevant information will be available. The flexibility that this provides may add value to the project. The purpose of real option analysis (ROA) is to assign a reasonable value to this flexibility. The techniques for valuing real options are an extension of the techniques used to value financial options.

Although ROA can increase the accuracy of a project valuation, it also increases the complexity of the analysis. In conventional capital budgeting, the expected cash flows from a project for each period are discounted at an appropriate discount rate to estimate the NPV of the project. To do a ROA, it is necessary to explicitly take into account the fact that in any given period there are many different cash flows that can occur. The cash flows in a given period may differ from their expected value because of external events over which management has no control, such as the state of the economy.

The value of flexibility can be estimated using ROA; but frequently a quantitative valuation will be extremely complex. Sometimes it will be necessary to substitute a qualitative input for an explicit quantitative analysis. An appreciation of the process by which real options are evaluated can enhance the decision-maker's intuition about the value of a project even when an explicit ROA is not computed. The purpose of this chapter is to introduce the reader to the basic concepts that underlie the evaluation of real options.

PROBLEMS

1   The XYZ Company has the opportunity to invest $32,000,000. At time 1 it
    will earn either a 0.30 return ($41,600,000) or a 0.05 return
    ($33,600,000). Debt costs 0.11. The company needs to avoid the possibility
    of earning only 0.05. For an expenditure of $3,000,000, it can obtain the
    right to sell the asset for $41,600,000.
    a.   Is the investment desirable without the $3,000,000 expenditure?
    b.   Is the investment desirable with the $3,000,000 expenditure?

2   The ABC Company has an opportunity to invest $32,000,000 for a year.
    While there is a large probability of earning 0.30 for the year if there are
    no trade restrictions, there is some probability that only 0.05 will be
    earned with trade restrictions. The firm will borrow $30,545,000 to finance
    the investment. Since debt costs 0.11, the earning of 0.05 could be a bad
    event. The firm could not survive with a 0.05 return.
       An investor has offered to advance $4,000,000 for the project. The investor
    will be paid $8,000,000 at the end of the year if there are no trade
    restrictions; otherwise, the investor receives nothing.
       Should the ABC Company go ahead with the project?

3   A stock is now selling at $80 per share. You buy a put to sell the stock at
    $75. The cost of the put is $4. The stock goes down to $72 just before the
    put expires.
       What was the profitability of buying the put?

4   Assume that an investor has $10,000 to invest. Stock can be purchased at
    $20 per share (500 shares can be purchased). Call options to purchase
    shares at a price of $25 can be purchased for $5 per option (options to
    purchase 2,000 shares can be purchased).
       Compare the change in the investor's wealth from buying the stock and
    buying the options if the stock price at the expiration of the option is:
    a. $35.
    b. $24.

DISCUSSION QUESTION

A firm uses a 0.15 rate to evaluate risky assets. The risk-free rate is 0.05.
    The firm can buy information that will reduce (essentially eliminate) the risk
for a long-lived project.
    What discount rate should the firm use to compute the project's benefits?

BIBLIOGRAPHY

Abel, Andrew B., "Optimal Investment Under Uncertainty," *American Economic Review*, March 1983, pp. 228–33.

Bartlett, I., *Familiar Quotations*, Boston: Little Brown, 1955, p. 941.

Bernanke, Ben S., "Irreversibility, Uncertainty, and Cyclical Investment," *Quarterly Journal of Economics*, February 1983, pp. 85–106.

Black, F. and M. Scholes, "The Pricing of Options and Corporate Liabilities," *Journal of Political Economy*, May 1973, pp. 637–59.

Brennan, M. J. and E. S. Schwartz, "Evaluating Natural Resource Investments," *Journal of Business*, January 1985, pp. 135–57.

Brennan, M. J. and E. S. Schwartz, "A New Approach to Evaluating Natural Resource Investments," *Midland Corporate Finance Journal*, spring 1985, pp. 37–47.

Copeland, T. and V. Antikarov, *Real Options*, New York: Texere, 2001.

Cox, J. C. and M. Rubenstein, *Option Markets*, Englewood Cliffs, NJ: Prentice-Hall, 1985.

Cox, J. C., S. A. Ross, and M. Rubenstein, "Option Pricing: A Simplified Approach," *Journal of Financial Economics*, September 1979, pp. 229–63.

Dixit, A. K. and R. S. Pindyck, *Investment Under Uncertainty*, Princeton, NJ: University Press, 1994.

Dukierman, Alex, "The Effects of Uncertainty on Investment Under Risk Neutrality with Endogenous Information," *Journal of Political Economy*, June 1980, pp. 462–75.

Graham, J. and C. Harvey, "How Do CFOs Make Capital Budgeting and Capital Structure Decisions?" *Journal of Applied Corporate Finance*, spring 2002, pp. 8–23.

Jarrow, R. and A. Rudd, *Option Pricing*, Homewood, IL: R. D. Irwin, 1983.

Kensinger, J. W., "Adding the Value of Active Management into the Capital Budgeting Equation," *Midland Corporate Finance Journal*, spring 1987, pp. 31–42.

Kulataka, N. and A. J. Marcus, "Project Valuation Under Uncertainty: When Does DCF Fail," *Midland Corporate Finance Journal*, fall 1992, pp. 92–100.

McDonald, Robert and Daniel R. Siegel, "Investment and the Valuation of Firms When There is an Option to Shut Down," *International Economic Review*, October 1985, pp. 331–49.

Majd, S. and R. S. Pindyck, "Time to Build, Option Value, and Investment Decisions," *Journal of Financial Economics*, March 1987, pp. 7–27.

Margrabe, W., "The Value of an Option to Exchange One Asset for Another," *Journal of Finance*, March 1978, pp. 177–86.

Mason, S. P. and R. C. Merton, "The Role of Contingent Claims Analysis in Corporate Finance," in E. I. Altman and M. G. Subrahmanyam (eds), *Recent Advances in Corporate Finance*, Homewood, IL: Irwin, 1985, pp. 7–54.

Merton, R. C., "The Relationship Between Put and Call Option Prices: Comment," *Journal of Finance*, March 1973, pp. 183–4.

——, Theory of Rational Option Pricing," *Bell Journal of Economics and Management Science*, spring 1973, pp. 141–83.

Myers, Stewart C., "Financial Theory and Financial Strategy," *Midland Corporate Finance Journal*, 5(1), 1987, pp. 6–13.

Pindyck, R., "Uncertainty and Exhaustible Resource Markets," *Journal of Political Economy*, December 1980, pp. 1203–25.

——, "Irreversible Investment, Capacity Choice, and Value of the Firm," *American Economic Review*, 78(5), 1988, pp. 969–85.

Robichek, A. and J. Van Horn, "Abandonment Value and Capital Budgeting," *Journal of Finance*, December 1967, pp. 577–90.

Sick, G., *Capital Budgeting with Real Options*, Monograph Series in Finance and Economics, New York: Stern School of Business, New York University, 1990.

Siegel, D. R., J. L. Smith, and J. L. Paddock, "Valuing Offshore Oil Properties with Option Pricing Models," *Midland Corporate Finance Journal*, spring 1987, pp. 22–30.

Smith, C. W., "Option Pricing: A Review," *Journal of Financial Economics*, March 1976, pp. 3–51.

——, "Applications of Option Pricing Analysis," in J. L. Bicksler (ed.), *Handbook of Financial Economics*, Amsterdam: North Holland, 1979, pp. 80–121.

Sturtz, R., "Options on the Minimum or Maximum of Two Risky Assets: Analysis and Applications," *Journal of Financial Economics*, January 1982, pp. 161–85.

Titman, S., "Urban Land Prices Uncertainty," *American Economic Review*, June 1985, pp. 505–14.

Triantis, A. and A. Borison, "Real Options: State of the Practice," *Journal of Applied Corporate Finance*, summer 2001, pp. 8–24.

Trigeorgis, L., "Option Interactions and the Valuation of Investments with Multiple Real Options," Boston: Boston University School of Management, October 1990.

Trigeorgis, L. and S. P. Mason, "Valuing Managerial Flexibility," *Midland Corporate Finance Journal*, spring 1987, pp. 14–21.

APPENDIX A: INCREASING ACCURACY BY USING A LARGE NUMBER OF SHORT PERIODS

The examples in the chapter assume that the time to maturity of the option is one or two years, and that the time to maturity is divided into periods one year long. The examples also assume that the value of the stock price or the underlying investment changes only once per period. The accuracy of an option valuation calculation will increase if the time to maturity of the option is divided into many shorter periods of time and the value of the stock price or underlying investment is allowed to change during each of these shorter periods. As the time to maturity is divided into more and more periods, the magnitude of the risk-free interest rate and stock price change parameters must be adjusted.

This appendix provides some basic results for increasing the accuracy of the calculations by increasing the number of periods and decreasing their length. Our formulas assume that the underlying asset pays no dividends, has a constant underlying rate of return and variance, and that the rate of return of the asset follows a lognormal distribution. The life of the options under consideration is t years. The default-free rate of interest is known and constant for this t year horizon. In the examples in the text, the values of u and d were given. In this appendix, we derive appropriate values of u, and d from the above assumptions.

A calendar year is divided into n equally long sub-periods. The option under consideration expires after t years, which is equivalent to $m = t(n)$ sub-periods. For example, if $n = 10$ and $t = 1.5$, then $m = 15$. The (instantaneous) expected rate of return on the stock is μ, and its standard deviation is σ, and one plus the annual default-free discount rate is r. We will present the appropriate values of u, d, and q based on these assumptions.

The discount rate for one sub-period that is $(1/n)$ years long is γ as given in the following formula.

$$\gamma = r^{1/n} \tag{10A.1}$$

The value of u applicable to each sub-period should be

$$u = e^{\sigma\sqrt{1/n}} \tag{10A.2}$$

and the value of d should be

$$d = 1/u = e^{-\sigma\sqrt{1/n}} \tag{10A.3}$$

Finally, the value of q, the RNP of an up state in each sub-period should be:[2]

$$q = 0.5 + (0.5)(\mu/\sigma)\sqrt{1/n} \tag{10A.4}$$

We want to determine the value at time zero of a call option that expires at time t. Since we assume that the underlying asset has no intermediate cash flows (e.g. a non-dividend paying stock) an American option would never be exercised before maturity and the values of an American and European options are the same. In this formula, K is the exercise price of the option and V is the initial value of the underlying asset and C is the value of the call option.

---

2 For the derivations of these equations see Cox and Rubinstein (1985), pp. 196–200.

$$C = \sum_{j=0}^{m} \left\{ \left(\frac{m!}{j!(m-j)!} \right) q^j (1-q)^{m-j} Max(0, u^j d^{m-j} V - K) \right\} \Big/ \gamma^m \qquad (10A.5)$$

In this formula, $m!$, (pronounced m factorial) has the following meaning. $m! = m(m-1)(m-2)\ldots(3)(2)(1)$, for m greater than or equal to 1, and $m! = 1$ if $m = 0$. Excel and many other spreadsheets have built in functions to evaluate m factorial. While equation (10A.5) may look rather forbidding, it has a simple intuitive explanation and it is not all that difficult to program a spreadsheet to evaluate it.

The numerator on the right hand side of the equation is the Certainty Equivalent of the value of the asset at maturity. The asset V follows a binomial process. The values of u and d have been picked so that there will be $m + 1$ different nodes at the end of m periods. The summation from $j = 0$ to m sums over these $m + 1$ nodes. Each of the $(m + 1)$ nodes is uniquely characterized by j, which represents the number of up states that must be traversed to reach that node. The value of j can be as high as m and as low as zero. Each term in the summation can be thought of as a product of three values. The parenthetical expression $(m!/j!(m-j)!)$ describes the number of different paths through the event tree that end up at the jth node. The value $q^j(1-q)^{m-j}$ represents the probability of each path to the jth node. Finally, the value of the Max function represents the dollar value of the underlying asset in the jth mode after optimal exercise of the option.

The denominator on the right hand side of the equation is the present value factor for m periods at the default free rate. Thus the right hand side of the equation is simply the CE of the time t value of the asset, after optimal exercise of the option, discounted to the present at the default free rate.

In more complex situations, such as put options, multiple options on the same asset, or where early exercise is possible, equation (10A.5) could be modified to represent a direct calculation of the value of the underlying asset with flexibility at time t. To do this, the Max function would be replaced by an appropriate expression for the value of the underlying asset at node j at time t.

APPENDIX B: VALUATION WITH MULTIPLE OPTIONS ON AN ASSET

To illustrate the process of evaluating multiple options on the same asset, we consider the value of flexibility when both abandonment and expansion options exist.

The overall process for evaluating multiple options is similar to the process used when there is only one option. Begin with the situation at maturity. For each node, determine the optimal decision and the value of the asset if that decision is made. Then move backward and repeat the process in the previous period, valuing the factory in each node as the present value of its subsequent values. It should be noted that our example has some special features that might not always be present. First, the two different options expire on the same date. Second, the two options are mutually exclusive: at the same node, you cannot simultaneously expand a factory and abandon it.

We begin with the nodes at the common expiration time, period 2. With two options there are three alternatives available: expand (exercise the expansion option), abandon (exercise the abandon option) or neither (do not exercise either option). If the options were not mutually exclusive, the alternative of exercising both options would also be included. The values associated with these three alternatives at node D are $1,503.13, $900, and $1,322.50. Since the expansion decision has the highest value, it will be chosen. The results of similar calculations for nodes D, E and F are summarized in the following table.

Nodes (1)	Expand (2)	Abandon (3)	Neither (4)	Maximum (5)	Decision (6)
D	1,503.13	900.00	1,322.50	1,503.13	Expand
E	1,100.00	900.00	1,000.00	1,100.00	Expand
F	795.18	900.00	756.14	900.00	Abandon

Next consider node B at time 1. The alternatives are expand, abandon or neither. The value of the factory if the expansion option is exercised is $1,287.50 [$= 1.1*(1,150) - 150$]. The value of the factory if the abandon option is exercised is $900. The value of the factory if neither option is exercised if the present value of the factory values in the succeeding nodes, $1,294.64. The calculations for the neither alternative are shown in the following equation.

$$V = \frac{0.6434(1,503.13) + (1 - 0.6434)(1,100)}{1.05} = 1,294.64$$

Since exercising neither option in this node has produced the highest value, this alternative will be chosen. Using a similar procedure, the results for nodes B, C and A are shown in the following table.

Nodes (1)	Expand (2)	Abandon (3)	Neither (4)	Maximum (5)	Decision (6)
B	1,287.50	900.00	1,294.64	1,294.64	Neither
C	936.96	900.00	979.70	979.70	Neither
A	1,100.00	900.00	1,126.03	1,126.03	Neither

The value of the asset at node A when the optimum decision is made at each node is $1,126.03. This represents a direct calculation of the present value of the asset with flexibility. The present value of the asset without flexibility is $1,000.

Therefore the value of the portfolio of options is $126.03.

The option to expand is worth $113.95 by itself, and the option to abandon is worth $16.59 by itself; the sum of their individual values is $130.54. This is $4.51 more than the value of a portfolio consisting of both options.

Intuitively, the reason for this result is that in this context, the two options are competitors. In this example, the competition occurs at node F. If only the option to abandon existed, then the optimal decision at node F would be to abandon. This would raise the value of the factory at that node from $756.14 to $900, an increase of $143.86. If only the option to expand existed, then the optimal decision at node F would be to expand. This would raise the value of the factory at that node from $756.14 to $795.14, an increase of $39.04. If both options exist and are mutually exclusive, the optimal decision is abandon. The $39.04 increase in node F that would occur if the expanding were the only alternative does not occur if both options are possible. The present value of $39.04 in node F is $4.50, as shown in the following equation.

$$\left(\frac{1-q}{1+r}\right)\left(\frac{1-q}{1+r}\right) 39.04 = (0.3396)^2 \, 39.04 = \$4.50$$

Adding the values of each option double counts the $39.04. The process of evaluating a portfolio of options eliminates this erroneous double counting. That is why the portfolio is worth less in this example than the sum of the values of the individual options.

Applications of capital budgeting

Bill Tierney, the successful coach of Princeton's lacrosse team asked about his master plan stated, "If I can create master plans, I should be doing something more important than coaching lacrosse."
(From an article by Frank Litsky, *New York Times*, May 29, 2001)

Part IV contains a wide range of applications of the basic time value concepts. Once an investment is accepted and undertaken, the investment's performance must be measured.

Chapter 11 discusses the issues of growth constraints.

Chapters 12 and 13 deal with alternative methods of valuing a firm. While the valuation of a firm is similar to valuing a project, there are enough differences so that the valuation deserves its own chapters.

Chapter 13 introduces the concept of present value accounting and Chapter 14 expands on this topic. The topic of present value accounting leads logically to Chapter 15 and performance measurement. Present value accounting is not likely to be part of generally accepted accounting principles in the near future, but understanding the basic concepts enables a manager to better work with conventional accounting.

The sequencing of the book's final chapters is arbitrary. Chapter 16 deals with the problem of fluctuating rates of output. Chapter 17 deals with investment decisions with additional information. It is a real option type of problem. Chapter 18 covers the classic problem of timing of investments. Chapter 19's subject is buy versus lease. Buy versus lease is an excellent example of where knowing how to apply a discount rate to a future cash flow is not sufficient to ensure a correct decision.

Chapter 11

Growth constraints

It's not that I'm so smart, it's just that I stay with problems longer.
(Albert Einstein. Quoted by Simon Singh,
The New York Times, January 2, 2005)

We have implied that firms should accept all independent investments with a positive NPV. However, we know that corporations do not always accept all projects with a positive NPV. Among the factors limiting a firm's growth and leading to a rejection of seemingly positive NPV projects are the following:

1 Capital rationing where the capital cannot be obtained in the capital markets at stated rates. This is "external" capital rationing.
2 Capital rationing where management decides to limit the amount invested. This is "internal" capital rationing.
3 While the capital is available, other factors of production may not be available, thus "good" investments must be rejected.

EXTERNAL CAPITAL RATIONING

There are times where the capital market cannot or will not supply the capital needed by a firm, even though the firm is willing to pay the stated market price. These events are rare, but they do occur when credit is rationed by the market.

Obviously, the market price is not really the market price in this situation or the capital would be forthcoming. Assume a situation where an investment grade firm (BBB) would like to raise capital and to pay the BBB bond rate. The banks and investment banks tell the corporation that it cannot issue bonds at this time at that rate.

If the corporation were willing to pay the rates of BB or B bonds it could probably raise the capital, but a BBB firm is generally reluctant to pay BB or B level rates.

Also, it is possible that during this period less than investment grade or low investment grade corporations cannot issue bonds. The market will not accept them.

Now consider a situation where the firm can borrow money at 0.10 (the BB rate) but it can only earn 0.07 (the BBB rate) on investments that are consistent with its present risk. While rejection of the 0.07 investments can be called capital rationing, we prefer to define it as a situation where the 0.10 effective cost of debt and equity is larger than the investment return that can be earned.

The term *borrow* is used here when a firm obtains capital from the market in such a way that the borrowing firm's capital structure is not changed. Thus, borrowing would normally involve issuing both debt and equity securities. Lending means acquiring a portfolio of securities or other assets that has approximately the same average risk characteristics as the assets presently owned by the firm. The borrowing and investing does not change the risk characteristics of the firm's assets compared to expanding the firm's operations by investing internally.

If capital markets were such that a firm could lend or borrow as much money as it desired at the going rate of interest, this rate of interest would be the same for both the borrowing and lending transactions. Why is there a difference between the borrowing rate and the lending rate? One explanation is that the firm has transaction costs if it raises additional capital. There are costs of raising capital. Aside from transaction costs one would expect the lending and borrowing rates for a corporation to be approximately equal if the risks are comparable.

INTERNAL CAPITAL RATIONING

There are two types of internal capital rationing. With the first type, the firm sets an investment cutoff rate that is higher than the firm's computed capital cost. With the second type, the firm decides to limit the total amount of funds committed to investments in a given year to a fixed sum. If these actions lead to investments having positive present values at the project's cost of capital being rejected, this is internal capital rationing.

Although a definite cutoff rate is available with the second type of internal capital rationing the logic of using that rate to discount cash flows is not completely correct. The rate of discount used should measure the alternative uses of funds available to the firm. The cut-off rate in the future may be different than the cut-off rate of this year. The appropriate discount rates in future periods are relevant to decisions made in the present because they affect the profitability of funds reinvested at those times. Cash flows expected in each future time period should be discounted at the rate of discount that will apply in that period. We must predict future opportunity costs for capital if managers are applying internal capital rationing.

If a company is in a situation of capital rationing, it may be useful for the top management to predict the appropriate cut-off rate that will apply in future years.

By this means, the investment planning in various parts of the organization can be coordinated in terms of the best available estimates of future cash needs and requirements for the company as a whole.

SCARCE FACTORS OF PRODUCTION

A firm's discount rate (or hurdle rate) may be increased because top management wants to decrease the amount of eligible investments, because various factors of production are in scarce supply. The shortages might be:

1   managerial talent;
2   skill sets (such as design or computer expertise);
3   some part of the current capital equipment or plant is close to capacity.

Rather than increase the hurdle rate for all investments it would be better to estimate the cost of the management component or any other labor group that will be utilized. Estimating the dollar cost is a more accurate adjustment than increasing the discount rate. It is difficult to adjust the discount rate by the right amount when it is really a cost factor that will be utilized and is affecting cash flows. Estimating the cost of adding a manager is more likely to take into consideration the economic consequences to the firm of undertaking a project than adding 300 basis points (0.03) to the discount rate.

RANKING OF INVESTMENTS

When not all desirable investments are to be accepted there is a tendency for management to want to rank the acceptable investments so that it can chose the best of the alternatives available.

There are several procedures that seem to give a reliable ranking of investments, but that appearance of reliability is an illusion. There is no reliable quantitative technique for the theoretically correct ranking of independent investments. The problem is that the ranking and its use implies the use of a cut-off rate above the cost of money and a rejection of investments that would be acceptable except for the rationing situation. This implies that the opportunity cost for funds will be higher than the firm's discount rate. Also, the opportunity cost of future time periods may well be different from that of the present.

We cannot supply a reliable quantitative model for ranking investments. However, in the same sense that we can determine the 10 best books of the last decade, we can define which $100,000,000 of investments are best for a firm, but it is likely that we cannot prove they are best.

We can use the net present value method to choose the best of a set of mutually exclusive investments if the rate of discount used is an appropriate opportunity cost (the cost of capital). As soon as we use the net present value method to rank independent investments (some investments with positive present values will be rejected), the rate of discount previously used in computing the net present values becomes an inappropriate rate to use because the firm's opportunity cost is higher than the cost of capital.

PROGRAMMING SOLUTIONS

There exist a large number of programming solutions to the capital-rationing situation. A typical solution is to maximize an objective function that consists of a sum of present values of future dividends. But to solve the programming problem, we not only need the information concerning currently available investments but also what investments will be available in the future.

The basic structure of the programming solution is to maximize the present value of the future dividends (or net cash flows) subject to the summations of all of a period's cash flows (positive and negative) minus a period's dividend that is equal to or less than the cash available from all the sources. These inequalities must hold for all time periods. There could be additional constraints that would insure that only one of a set of mutually exclusive investments is accepted.

Because of the immense information requirements (including knowledge of future investments), we are not enthusiastic regarding programming solutions to capital rationing situations. We do not know of any corporation that has successfully applied programming techniques to solving capital-rationing problems.

GLOBAL BUSINESS ASPECTS

In the past, corporate growth has been limited by a reluctance of management to invest in a country where a different language was spoken. This reluctance has universally disappeared. There are no large corporations that do not invest in and do business in a wide range of countries around the world. In fact, more and more small corporations are finding it profitable to do likewise. Global business is the norm and not the exception.

CONCLUSIONS

Many firms have growth constraints. Capital rationing in one form or another exists to some extent in most corporations. We may distinguish among minor and severe cases of capital rationing. Fortunately, in the minor cases of capital rationing the net present value rules recommended in this book may be used.

The net present value method cannot be used to rank independent investments where that ranking will be used to eliminate some independent investments with positive net present values. A reasonable (not exactly correct) ranking can be obtained using the internal rates of return of the investments. If desired, the net present values of different sets of investments can be computed and an attempt made to maximize net present value (but remember, the discount rate should represent the opportunity cost of funds).

Our preference is to eliminate the internal type of capital rationing, but include estimates of costs that will be increased so that the NPV's of the projects reflect all costs.

External capital rationing is likely to be rarely encountered. Normally, the gap between lending and borrowing rates is not large and can be ignored for purposes of evaluating alternative investments at little cost.

PROBLEMS

1   The ABC Company is planning its investment budget. Currently, it can raise money at a cost of 0.06. It assumes that its stockholders are able to invest funds so as to earn 0.04. There are also opportunities for the company to lend its funds and earn 0.04.

    a.   Assume that the company expected a large amount of investment opportunities. What discount rate should it use in making investment decisions?

    b.   Assume that the company expected a large amount of cash compared to internal investment opportunities. What rate of discount should it use in making decisions?

    c.   Assume that the company expected a shortage of cash for the coming 24 months but then expected a surplus amount of cash. What does this imply about the rate of discount to be used?

2   The president of the CDE Company wants a ranking of three investments. The firm considers its cost of money to be 0.05. The following three independent investments are ranked:

Investment	Cash flows of period			Net present value, using 0.05	Ranking
	0	1	2		
A	−$1,000	$1,120		$66.69	3
B	−1,000		$1,210	97.47	1
C	−1,000	400	775	83.89	2

The firm has $1,000 of uncommitted funds available (without borrowing) for investments. Based on the preceding ranking, the president decides to accept investment B. It is then revealed that, because investment B has an IRR of 0.10, this could be considered to be the investment cut-off rate (other investments that have already been approved have higher IRRs). Evaluate the decision process.

3   The RST Company has opened 100 new stores. It has incurred a great deal of expenses associated with opening the stores, and the stores have not yet built up enough clientele to be profitable. However, the stores are operating at profit levels exceeding expectations, and there are indications that they will be very profitable in the future. It is obvious that the stock market has not yet digested this latter fact, and the stock of the company is currently depressed compared to management's appraisal of value. The company has the opportunity to acquire an additional fifty stores this year, but to do so will require new stockholder capital acquired from the market (it has borrowed all it feels it is prudent to borrow and cannot obtain more capital from its current stockholders). Without the new capital, the stockholders can expect to earn an equivalent annual yield of 0.15 on the current market value of their investment (assume that there is $100 million of common stock outstanding). The stock is currently selling at $100 per share and paying a $6-per-share dividend. The earnings are $7.50 per share ($7.5 million in total).

The new investment would require $10 million to be obtained by issuing 100,000 new shares of common stock. The investment would return $1.2 million per year available for dividends for perpetuity. The stockholders desire a 0.08 return per year on their incremental investments.

a.   Should the corporation issue the new shares and undertake the investment?

b.   What would be your recommendation if the corporation had the necessary cash already available?

4   Change the statement of problem 3 so that the present stockholders can expect to earn dividends of $6 per share or an equivalent annual yield of 0.06 for perpetuity unless the new investment is undertaken. Should the new investment be undertaken?

5   Change the statement of problem 3 so that the present stockholders can expect to earn $8 million, or an equivalent return of 0.08 per year on the current market value of their investment, if the new investment is not undertaken. Should the new investment be undertaken?

6   The CDE Company can borrow and lend funds at an interest rate of 0.08. It can invest $11 million in a risky project that on the average will generate net cash flows of $1 million per year. A consultant has suggested that the firm use its cost of capital of 0.10 in computing the present value of the

investment. The investment's life is extremely long. Insurance can be purchased that will guarantee the $1 million per year.

Should the investment be undertaken? How much could the firm afford to pay for the insurance?

7   The WXY Company has a borrowing rate of 10 percent. It has an opportunity to invest in an asset that yields 8 percent and has the following cash flows:

Time	Cash flows
0	−$10,000
1	5,608
2	5,608

While this investment would ordinarily be rejected, the analyst has computed the return on reinvested funds (the opportunity cost) to be 20 percent, thus, the $5,608 can be reinvested at time 1 to earn $6,730 at time 2. With $12,338 now being received at time 2, this is an 11 percent internal rate of return, thus the firm has decided to accept the investment.

Evaluate the decision.

DISCUSSION QUESTION

The CEO wants to raise the cut-off rate for investments from 0.10 (the estimated cost of capital for the project's risk) to 0.15 because he thinks the firm's overheads will increase. Evaluate the suggestion.

BIBLIOGRAPHY

Baumol, W. and R. Quandt, "Investment and Discount Rates Under Capital Rationing: A Programming Approach," *Economic Journal*, June 1965, pp. 317–29.

Bernhard, Richard H., "Mathematical Programming Models for Capital Budgeting: A Survey, Generalization, and Critique," *Journal of Financial and Quantitative Analysis*, June 1969, pp. 111–58.

Carleton, W. T., "Linear Programming and Capital Budgeting Models: A New Interpretation," *Journal of Finance*, December 1969, pp. 825–33.

Forsyth, J. D. and D. C. Owen, "Capital Rationing Methods," in R. L. Crum and F. G. J. Derkinderen (eds.), *Capital Budgeting Under Conditions of Uncertainty*, Boston: Martinus Nijhoff Publishing, 1981, pp. 213–35.

Weingartner, H. M., "Capital Rationing: n Authors in Search of a Plot," *Journal of Finance*, December 1977, pp. 1403–31.

Chapter 12

The valuation of a firm

It does make me marvel that a $1.99 box of stationery with some typing on it can turn into a national event.

(Avery Corman, author of *Kramer versus Kramer,*
New York Times, January 13, 1980)

At one level, the valuation of a firm is identical to the valuation of a project. Compute the present value of uncertain future cash flows taking into consideration both the time value of money and risk. But there is one major difference. A firm has a past history of earnings and cash flows that can be used as the basis of forecasting the future and to help value the firm. A project normally has only cash flow projections into the future. The possibility of being able to use actual objective quantitative measures instead of only having projections is a major difference between the valuation of a firm and the valuation of a project.

We will illustrate a wide range of techniques that can be used to value a firm. The methods of calculation include:

1　PV of dividends and other cash distributions assuming perpetuity.
2　PV of earnings minus new investments.
3　Using PVGO where PVGO is the present value of growth opportunities.
4　PV of cash distributions for *n* years plus present value of the firm's value at time *n* (possibly determined using a multiplier). *n* stage growth models.
5　Multipliers times E, EBIT, NEBIT, EBITDA, NEBITDA (with most multipliers the analyst must subtract debt and CAP-EX). Multiplier times sales, Multiplier times book value, Multiplier times number of customers. The "N" of NEBIT and NEBITDA stands for the next period's flows.
6　Free cash flows.
7　Book value.

8 Market capitalization: Stock price $\times$ Number of outstanding shares.
9 $V_L = V_u + tB$. Value of a firm with initial value of V_u assuming substitution of B debt for equity:
10 $V_L = V_u + tB +$ operations improvements.
11 Option theory.
12 Present value of residual income (or economic income or economic value) and terminal value.

EXAMPLE 12.1

The following example will be used to illustrate the above valuation techniques.

EBIT $= \$100 =$ Earnings before interest and taxes
Corporate tax rate $= t = 0.35$
Retention rate $= b = 0.4$
Accounting depreciation $= \$50$
After-tax earnings $= E = \$65$
Cash distribution $= D = \$39$
Cost of equity with zero debt $k = k_e(0) = k_0(0) = 0.12$
Return on new investments $= r = 0.25$
Growth rate $= g = 0.10$ (in the simplest form equal to $rb = 0.25(0.4) = 0.10$)

Assume that the maintenance cap-ex is $50, thus equal to the $50 of accounting depreciation expense.

PRESENT VALUE OF DIVIDENDS

If we define dividends to be the transfer of any cash flow from the firm to its shareholders, the value of a firm is equal to the present value of dividends.
Let

D be the next year's dividends ($D = \$39$)
k be the discount rate used by the market ($k = 0.12$)
g be the expected growth rate in dividends ($g = 0.10$)
P be the firm's value today.

Then since k is larger than g and the growth is constant and perpetual:

$$P = \frac{D}{k - g} = \frac{39}{0.12 - 0.10} = \$1,950. \tag{12.1}$$

This is a widely used relationship but the numerical valuation is suspect when used in the real world because:

1 the assumption of perpetual constant growth;
2 the value is very sensitive to the estimate of growth (g) and the cost of equity (k), and neither of these measures is known with certainty.

PRESENT VALUE OF EARNINGS MINUS NEW INVESTMENT

The present value of earnings minus new investment is (note that $D = (1 - b) E$):

$$P = \frac{(1 - b)E}{k - g} = \frac{E}{k - g} - \frac{b E}{k - g} \tag{12.2}$$

where b is the retention rate, bE is the incremental investment, and $\frac{bE}{k - g}$ is the present value of the firm's growing investment.

For the example:

$$P = \frac{65}{0.12 - 0.10} - \frac{26}{0.12 - 0.10} = 3{,}250 - 1{,}300 = \$1{,}950.$$

This formulation has the same weaknesses as the dividend valuation model.

PRESENT VALUE OF GROWTH OPPORTUNITIES

Define the value of the firm as an earnings perpetuity plus the present value of the growth opportunities (PVGO) where

$$\text{PVGO} = \frac{E(g - bk)}{k(k - g)} = \frac{65(0.10 - 0.4(0.12))}{0.12(0.02)} = \$1{,}408 \tag{12.3}$$

and

$$P = \frac{E}{k} + \text{PVGO} = \frac{65}{0.12} + 1{,}408 = 542 + 1{,}408 = \$1{,}950 \tag{12.4}$$

The growth has a positive present value since new investments earn 0.25 and the cost of equity is only 0.12. Remember that $g = rb$ and in this example $g = 0.25(0.4) = 0.10$.

A TERMINAL VALUE MODEL

Instead of assuming perpetual growth of 0.10 assume the firm's value at time 10 is $5,057.80 with a present value of $1,628.48. There is zero growth after ten years.

$$\$5,057.80(1.12)^{-10} = \$1,628.48.$$

The present value of the first ten years' dividends growing at 0.10 is $321.52.

Present Value of Growth $= 1,950 - 1,628.48 = \$321.52$

The stock's value is:

$$P = 1,628.48 + 321.52 = \$1,950.$$

To obtain the $5,057.80 value at time 10 we need the dividend at time 11 assuming growth of 0.10 per year for ten years.

$$\text{Div}_{11} = 39(1.10)^{10} = \$101.16.$$

The firm's value at time 10 assuming a constant growth of 0.10 for perpetuity is:

$$P_{10} = \frac{101.16}{0.12 - 0.10} = \$5,057.80$$

with a present value at time zero of $1,628.48. Adding the $321.52 present value of the first ten years' dividends, we again have $1,950.

The growth rate assumptions can be changed to determine the effect on the price at time zero.

MULTIPLIERS

A popular method of valuation is to use the operating results times multipliers obtained from comparable firms. The multipliers may be applied to:

earnings (E);
earnings before interest and taxes (EBIT);
earnings before interest, taxes, depreciation and amortization (EBITDA);
free cash flow.

Instead of using the period's results sometimes the results of next period are used (but these are estimates, thus less reliable). Also, sometimes the multiplier is applied to basic measures such as the number of subscribers or total revenue.

Multipliers are normally obtained from observing the transactions involving other firms. These "comparables" may be based on a few or a large number of observations. A common technique is to compute a range of values.

Behind each multiplier is a theoretically correct explanation. For example, consider the price-earnings multiplier (M_0) where

$$P = M_0 E \quad \text{or} \quad M_0 = \frac{P}{E}$$

where E is the earnings and P is the price. We know that:

$$P = \frac{D}{k - g} = \frac{(1 - b)E}{k - g} \tag{12.1}$$

Dividing both sides by E:

$$\frac{P}{E} = M_0 = \frac{1 - b}{k - g} \tag{12.5}$$

For the example with perpetual 0.10 growth and $b = 0.4$, we have

$$M_0 = \frac{1 - 0.4}{0.12 - 0.10} = 30.$$

Using the price earnings multiplier of 30 and earnings of $65, the firm's value is again $30(65) = \$1,950$.

There are comparable calculations for the other multipliers (EBIT, EBITDA, etc.).

In practice, the multipliers are not computed using fundamentals but rather they are based on observing the price and flows of comparable firms. Finding comparable firms and reconciling differences is very difficult.

FREE CASH FLOW

Free cash flow is also used for valuing a firm. The two basic valuation methods are to use a comparable firm multiplier and to use a conventional present value calculation. The third free cash flow calculation is analogous to sustainable dividends (however, financial transactions are omitted). Unfortunately there are several definitions of free cash flow, among these are:

1 cash flow from operations (income plus depreciation and amortization);
2 cash flow from operations minus maintenance capital expenditures (Maintenance Capex);

3 cash flow from operations minus all capital expenditures;

4 cash flow from operations minus all capital expenditures and minus the dividends on equity securities.

Interest on debt is normally subtracted for all the above calculations if the value of the common stock equity is being computed.

The multiplier that is used should depend on which of the free cash flow calculations is being used. For many valuation calculations, the free cash flow definitions that are most useful are "Cash flow from operations minus maintenance CapEx" or "Cash flows from operations minus CapEx."

BOOK VALUE

Book value is the result of accounting rules and conventions and there is a collection of non-relevant sunk costs. If the book value is a reasonable estimation of replacement costs, then the measure is of some use (but it is the replacement costs, not the book value that is relevant).

Thus book value is normally not a significant measure of value, but each situation is unique and deserves analysis.

VALUE WITH ZERO DEBT

Define NOPAT to be net operating income after tax assuming all equity financing. If k is the firm's cost of capital (with no debt), and if there is zero growth, and if the sum of depreciation expense and amortization expense (Dep) is equal to the firm's capital expenditures (CapEx), then the firm's value at time zero (V_0) is:

$$V_0 = \frac{\text{NOPAT}}{k} \tag{12.6}$$

With zero change in working capital define free cash flow (FCF) to be:

$$\text{FCF} = \text{NOPAT} + \text{Dep} - \text{CapEx} \tag{12.7}$$

then since it is assumed Dep = CapEx, FCF equals NOPAT and there is zero growth:

$$V_0 = \frac{\text{FCF}}{k} \tag{12.8}$$

233

Also since with zero growth there are zero retained earnings and all NOPAT is paid as dividends (Div) we also have:

$$V_0 = \frac{\text{Div}}{k} \tag{12.9}$$

Now assume there is a constant growth rate (g) in earnings and g equals rb where r is the return on new investment and b is the retention rate (retained earnings additions divided by the year's earnings).

The dividend rate is $(1 - b)$ and the new firm value is:

$$V_0 = \frac{(1 - b)\text{NOPAT}}{k - g} \tag{12.10}$$

If we define $(1 - b)$ NOPAT to be equal to FCF then:

$$V_0 = \frac{\text{FCF}}{k - g} \tag{12.11}$$

We have defined FCF to be:

$$\text{FCF} = \text{NOPAT} + \text{Dep} - \text{CapEx} \tag{12.7}$$

We can expand $(1 - b)$ NOPAT to be:

$$(1 - b)\,\text{NOPAT} = \text{NOPAT} - b\,(\text{NOPAT}).$$

The Cap Ex or total investment (including maintenance CapEx) is equal to:

$$\text{CapEx} = b\,(\text{NOPAT}) + \text{Dep}$$

Substituting in (12.7) for CapEx:

$$\text{FCF} = \text{NOPAT} + \text{Dep} - b\,(\text{NOPAT}) - \text{Dep} = (1 - b)\,\text{NOPAT} \tag{12.12}$$

therefore

$$V_0 = \frac{\text{FCF}}{k - g} \tag{12.11}$$

or

$$V_0 = \frac{\text{Div}}{k - g} \tag{12.1}$$

EXAMPLE 12.2

NOPAT = \$65, Dep = \$8, CapEx = \$34, $k = 0.12$
Maintenance CapEx = \$30, $r = 0.25$

The portion of NOPAT that is invested is $\dfrac{34 - 8}{65} = 0.40$ therefore $b = 0.4$ and $(1 - b) = 0.6$ and $g = 0.25(0.4) = 0.10$

$$FCF = NOPAT + Dep - CapEx \qquad (12.7)$$
$$= 65 + 8 - 34 = \$39$$

$$V_0 = \frac{FCF}{k - g} = \frac{39}{0.12 - 0.10} = \$1{,}950 \qquad (12.11)$$

or

$$V_0 = \frac{(1 - b)NOPAT}{k - g} = \frac{0.6(65)}{0.12 - 0.10} = \$1{,}950 \qquad (12.10)$$

Note that with the above assumptions the \$30 of maintenance capital expenditures does not enter the solution. It is assumed that $g = 0.10$. But assume g is not 0.10 but rather the net investment contributing to growth is $34 - 30 = 4$ and the effective retention rate for the growth calculation is:

$$b = \frac{4}{65} = 0.0615$$

and if r is till 0.25 (it could be larger), the growth rate is now 0.0154:

$$g = rb = 0.25 \, (0.0615) = 0.0154$$

and now with the lower growth rate:

$$V_0 = \frac{39}{0.12 - 0.0154} = \$373$$

It seems reasonable that the magnitude of the maintenance CapEx should affect the growth rate. For example, if the dividend were \$39 but if \$39 of capital in excess of depreciation expense were needed to maintain the basic cash flow there would be zero investment for growth and the expected growth rate would be zero. Following this logic the retention rate is:

$$b = \frac{CapEx - Maintenance \ Cap \ Ex}{NOPAT} \qquad (12.13)$$

When CapEx = \$34, Maintenance CapEx = \$30

NOPAT = \$65, Div = \$39 or DIV = $65 + 8 - 34 = \$39$

$$b = \frac{34 - 30}{65} = 0.0615 \qquad (12.13)$$

EXAMPLE contd.

Using NOPAT in the numerator we have:

$$b = \frac{\text{NOPAT} + \text{Dep} - \text{Maintenance} - \text{CapEx} - \text{Div}}{\text{NOPAT}}$$

$$= \frac{65 + 8 - 30 - 39}{65} = \frac{4}{65} = 0.0615$$

The \$65 plus \$8 gives the cash flow being generated. The \$30 is the maintenance CapEx and the \$39 is the cash outlay for the dividend. The residual amount of \$4 is the cash invested to generate earnings growth.

MARKET CAPITALIZATION

The market capitalization (of common stock) is equal to the number of common stock shares outstanding times the market stock price. For many purposes this product is a reasonable measure of the value of the firm's stock equity since it reflects the weighted judgment of a very large number of investors.

SUBSTITUTION OF DEBT FOR EQUITY

With no investor taxes and no costs of financial distress, if B of debt is substituted for equity we have:

$$V_L = V_u + tB \tag{12.14}$$

where V_u is the market value of the common stock of an unlevered firm.

V_L the value of the levered firm, has a second meaning. In addition to being the new value of the firm it is also the new value of the initial shareholders' total wealth (not the shareholders' investment in the firm) assuming the entire amount equal to the new debt, B, is distributed to the shareholders.

The value of the stock (S) after the debt issuance is

$$S = V_L - B.$$

EXAMPLE 12.3

Above for the basic example we obtained a stock value of $1,950. Now assume $1,500 of debt is substituted for $1,500 of stock. If the entire $1,500 of debt proceeds is given to the stockholders, the new firm value is:

$$V_L = 1,950 + 0.35(1,500) = \$1,950 + 525 = \$2,475. \qquad (12.14)$$

The value of the stock is:

$$S = V_L - B = 2,475 - 1,500 = \$975$$

The firm's capital is now:

Debt (B)	$1,500
Stock (S)	975
V_L	= $2,475

The stockholders receive $1,500 from the debt and have an equity investment of $975 in the firm thus have total wealth of $2,475 (equal to V_L).

OPTION THEORY

The value of the stock is equal to the value of an option on the firm's assets with the exercise price equal to the debt value. This method of valuation can be import-ant. Consider a firm whose only value consists of real estate. The value of the real estate has recently decreased so that now the value is less than the present value of the debt (but the firm is still meeting its legal debt obligation). Does the firm's stock have a value? If the real estate value stays depressed the stock will be worthless. If the real estate market rebounds, the stock can have a large value. The "option" on the firm's assets (the common stock) has value.

PRESENT VALUE OF ECONOMIC INCOME

Rather than computing the present value of cash flows we can compute the present value of economic incomes (or economic values added). The following calculations must be part of the present value calculation using economic incomes:

1 present value of economic incomes;
2 the book value is added at time zero;
3 the present value of the residual value has to be added and the present value of the book value at the end of the horizon has to be subtracted.

While it might seem book value is relevant to the present value calculation, the sum of the book value, depreciation expenses, interest expenses on capital, and the

237

end of period book value have a zero present value, with the result they do not affect the firm's values. This subject is expanded on in the next chapter.

VALUATION FOR ACQUISITION

Assume a firm wants to value a target firm. There are two different viewpoints that can be the basis of the valuation.

One viewpoint can be that of the seller. What is the firm's value if it continues to operate as a separate entity? Both the buyer and seller are interested in this value.

The second viewpoint is to value the target assuming it is integrated into the acquirer's operation. The two different viewpoints might result in two highly different valuations. One would assume that the successfully completed transaction will be computed at a value that is between the two extreme values, thus both parties (the seller and buyer) expect to be better off as a result of the acquisition.

DCF VERSUS COMPARABLES

Comparables are very useful since they are reasonably objective and are applied to a reasonably objective measure. Finding comparable firms and transactions may be very difficult. Also, translating the data into one set of comparable measures that can be used for valuation is complex.

DCF requires assumptions as to how the project or firm will perform in the future. DCF requires the application of imagination (estimating the future). With new plant and equipment there are frequently only estimates of the future and no past history, thus the use of DCF is reasonable. With the valuation of a firm, market values and measures of effectiveness of operations are normally available and should be used. This does not mean that the basic principles of DCF should not also be used to value a firm, but that they tend to be subordinate to the use of comparables and multipliers in practice.

MERGERS AND ACQUISITIONS

A firm might buy an entire firm rather than individual real assets. The acquisition of a firm by another firm is analogous to the purchase of plant and equipment. It differs because there is more information (e.g., market prices and past performance). Acquisitions of firms occur for many different reasons ranging from the desire for risk reduction to the necessity of doing something with extra cash currently held. Many specific reasons are given for acquisitions. For example, if a firm wants to start a new activity, an acquisition may be quicker than doing it from scratch.

One of the more important reasons for an acquisition of a firm is that it will lead to the obtaining of resources such as

1   management talent;
2   markets;
3   products;
4   cash or debt capacity;
5   plant and equipment (the cost of replacing is more than the price of the firm);
6   raw material;
7   patents;
8   know-how (processes).

Another reason for acquisitions is diversification for risk reduction. Since individual investors can diversify for themselves, a corporation does not have to diversify for its investors – the investors can diversify relatively cheaply. On the other hand, managers and labor find it difficult to diversify their careers, since they are generally tied to a firm and an industry. Also, risk reduction might enable the firm to do things that would otherwise be too risky.

A popular reason offered for acquisitions is that the two firms joined together will be more valuable than the sum of the values of the two independent firms. There will be synergy.

A form of synergy can be derived from the market's respect for size. A firm of large size tends to be able to obtain capital at a lower cost and the market may pay a higher P/E for the stock of a larger, less risky firm.

With the acquisition of a firm whose stock is traded on a market, the present and past stock prices are relevant. Investors will consider any offer in relation to the current stock price and are likely to compare any offer to the recent past prices (even though past prices are not relevant in a theoretical economic sense).

FORECASTING THE POST-ACQUISITION PRICE

Consider the following facts where Co. P is acquiring T. This follows the structure of the real world situation where Starwood acquired ITT.

Co. T

9,900	Shares
× $40	Market price (a 10 times P/E)
$396,000	Market cap

239

<u>Co. P</u>

100	Shares
× $90	Market price (a 60 times P/E)
$9,000	Market cap

If Co. T's stock is selling at $40 and Co. P's stock is selling at $90 before the merger announcement, and if P acquires T for 9,900 shares of P, we cannot assume the price being paid is

$$9,900(90) = \$891,000.$$

The exchange offer of one share of P (or 9,900 shares in total) appears to be worth $90 per share for one share of T. But is the projected value of a P share $90?

Assuming zero synergy from the merger, the projected price of the P stock after the acquisition is:

$$\text{Stock price} = \frac{396,000 + 9,000}{10,000} = \$40.50$$

It is reasonable to conject that P is paying $40.50(9,900) = \$400,950$ for T. Assume the earnings of T are $39,600 and P are $150.

<u>Co. T</u>

Earnings = $39,600
EPS = $4

<u>Co. P</u>

Earnings = $150
EPS = $1.50

Merged firm (10,000 shares outstanding)

Earnings = $39,750

$$\text{EPS} = \frac{39,750}{10,000} = \$3.975 \qquad P/E = \frac{40.50}{3.975} = 10.19$$

The new P/E is 10.19. Weight the initial P/E of 10 for Co. T and 60 for Co. P and we obtain the new P/E of 10.19:

$$P/E = 10\left(\frac{39,600}{39,750}\right) + 60\left(\frac{150}{39,750}\right) = 9.96 + 0.23 = 10.19$$

240

The new P/E is a weighted average of the initial P/E's.

The new stock price is equal to the new P/E times the new EPS of $3.975:

$$P = 10.19(3.975) = \$40.50$$

GLOBAL BUSINESS ASPECTS

Since the valuation of a firm must be on an after-tax basis, it is necessary that the value computations be done consistent with the tax law of the host country.

If the valuation is being done with the objective being the acquisition of a firm, then the legal acquisition rules of the host country must be understood and complied with.

CONCLUSIONS

We have illustrated twelve different methods of valuing a firm. The first method explained computed the present value of cash distributions with retention and growth. In Chapter 2 we considered different combinations of cash flows or earnings and discount rates to obtain present values. The conclusions are relevant for both the valuation of firms and projects.

PROBLEMS

1 Assume:

$X = \$1,538.146$

$t = 0.35, b = 0.4, k = 0.10$

Return on new investment = 0.15

Depreciation is equal to maintenance CAPEX of $350.

What is sustainable growth rate?

What is the dividend?

2 (*Continue 1*) What is the firm's value?

3 (*Continue 1*) What is the present value of the earnings?

What is the present value of future investments?

4 (*Continue 1*) What is the present value of the firm's growth opportunities?

5 (*Continue 1*) What will be the dividend at time 21?

What will be the firm's value at time 20?

6 (*Continue 1, 2 and 5*) Using the information from 2 and 5 what is the present value of the dividends for the firm's next twenty years?

241

7   (*Continue 1 and 2*) What is a reasonable *P/E* multiplier for this firm?

8   (*Continue 1*) What is the firm's free cash flow?

9   (*Continue 1 and 2*) If $10,000 of debt is substituted for the equity what is the value of the firm? Assume no costs of financial distress and no investor taxes.

10 (*Continue 1 and 9*) After the debt is substituted, what is the value of the shareholders' investment in the firm?

11 An investment of $6,500 has a life of two years. The cash flows are $5,500 for year 1 and $3,630 for year 2 plus a residual value of $726 at time 2. Depreciation expense will be $3,000 per year. Use a 0.10 discount rate. What is the present value using cash flows?

DISCUSSION QUESTION

How does the valuation of a project differ from the valuation of a public corporation?

BIBLIOGRAPHY

Copeland, T., T. Koller, and J. Murrin, *Valuation: Measuring and Managing the Value of Companies*, 2nd edn, New York: John Wiley, 1996.

Danielson, M., "A Simple Valuation Model and Growth Expectations," *Financial Analysts Journal*, 54 (3), 1998, pp. 50–7.

Fairfield, P., "P/E, P/B and the Present Value of Future Dividends," *Financial Analysts Journal*, 50 (4), 1994, pp. 23–31.

Fama, E. and K. French, "The Equity Premium," *Journal of Finance*, 57 (2), 2002, pp. 637–59.

Leibowitz, M., "Spread-Driven Dividend Discount Models," *Financial Analysts Journal*, November–December, 2000, pp. 64–81.

Palepa, K., V. Bernard and P. Healy, *Business Analysis and Valuation: Using Financial Statements*, Cincinnati, OH: South-Western, 1996.

Ruback, R. S., "Capital Cash Flows: A Simple Approach to Valuing Risky Cash Flows," *Financial Management*, summer 2002, pp. 85–103.

Soffer, L. C., "SFAS No. 123 Disclosures and Discounted Cash Flow Valuation," *Accounting Horizons*, June 2000, pp. 169–89.

Weaver, S. C., "Measuring Economic Value Added: A Survey of the Practices of EVA Proponents," *Journal of Applied Finance*, 11 (1), 2001, pp. 50–60.

Chapter 13

Using economic income (residual income) for valuation[1]

When Einstein resisted Heisenberg's uncertainty principle by arguing
that "God does not throw dice" Bohr responded "Nor is it our
business to prescribe to God how He should run the world."
(Richard Rhodes in a review of *Niels Bohr's Times,*
In Physics, Philosophy and Policy, by Abraham Pais,
New York Times Book Review, January 26, 1992, p. 3)

While conventional accounting does not include a deduction for the cost of equity
capital, economic income includes this deduction. We want to explain the use of
economic income as a measure to evaluate investments.

The normal capital budgeting method uses cash flows and discounts the cash
flows to compute a present value. But managers like to think in terms of income
and have some difficulty reconciling the cash flows of the investment decision and
the incomes of the resulting performance measures. Thus we normally have cash
flows used to evaluate investments and income and return on investment to evaluate
performance. Cash flow return on investment sometimes is used (frequently
incorrectly) to evaluate performance once the investment begins operations.

While adjustments can be made to the accounting income measure if the analyst
thinks the measure is flawed, we will consider only one necessary adjustment to
convert the accounting income to economic income for valuation purposes. An
estimate of the dollar cost of equity capital used as well as the cost of debt capital
will be deducted from accounting income to obtain the economic income. The

---

1 Some inaccurately refer to economic income as economic value added (EVA). The calculation being
illustrated does not lead to a measure of value added, but it is a reasonable income measure, especially
if economic income is combined with economic (present value) depreciation.

results of operations are assumed to add to the stockholders' economic position only after there is a charge for the equity capital management uses.

We will use the economic income valuation techniques to value a firm, but all the calculations apply to investments in specific real assets with minor changes in definitions of terms (for example, dividends become cash flows). There are two basic methods for valuing a firm's equity using a forecast of future operations and time discounting. The conventional method used by finance theorists is to compute the present value of future dividends and other cash distributions or a comparable calculation based on cash flows (or free cash flows). The second method computes the present value of future economic incomes or residual earnings. There are no theoretical advantages for choosing one model over the other. With both methods the accounting information regarding the balance sheet and income statement is relevant as the basis of estimating the future growth rate of dividends and earnings.

THE DISCOUNTED CASH FLOW MODEL ACCEPTED BY FINANCE THEORISTS

There is general agreement in the finance academic community that the value of a share of stock is equal to the present value of all the firm's future cash distributions to the shareholders. For simplicity, we assume the firm has only equity capital. Let D_i be the firm's cash distribution in period i, and let k be the cost of capital for the firm. Then the value of the firm at time zero can be written as

$$P_0 = \sum_{i=1}^{\infty} \frac{D_i}{(1 + k)^i} \qquad (13.1)$$

Assuming a constant growth rate (g) for perpetuity that is smaller than the cost of equity capital (k) and with the next distribution equal to D, then the value of the firm (P_0) is:

$$P_0 = \frac{D}{k - g} \qquad (13.2)$$

THE ECONOMIC INCOME MODEL

It can be shown that equation (13.1) or equation (13.2) can be transformed to:

$$P_0 = B_0 + \sum_{i=1}^{n} \frac{Y_i}{(1 + k)^i} + \frac{G_n}{(1 + k)^n} \qquad (13.3)$$

where

Y, is the economic income, equal to the accounting income (E_i) minus the capital charge on the beginning of the year book value ($k\,B_{i-1}$).

G_n is equal to the residual value (R_n) minus the book value (B_n) at time n.

B_0 is the initial book value.

Equation (13.3) indicates that the value (P_0) is the sum of the initial book value (B_0) plus the present value of the economic incomes and the present value of the difference between the terminal value of the firm and the terminal book value. The terms residual income, economic income, and economic value added may be used interchangeably. There is an assumption that only equity capital is being used. This eliminates the complexities introduced by different capital structure decisions.

We should not conclude that P_0 depends on the initial book value. Equation (13.3) can be misleading to a casual reader. An expansion of equation (13.3) shows the relevant factors that affect value. All the measures relating to the book values and other accounting measures wash out (their present values sum to zero).

We will use three simple numerical examples to illustrate why B_0 and the other measures related to book value are not relevant to the valuation. Assume a three year life, $k = 0.10$, $B_0 = \$3,000$ and $1,000 per year straight line depreciation expense and zero residual value and zero terminal book value. The present value of all the terms containing B_0 in equation (13.3) or are based on B_0 is:

$$PV = 3,000 - \frac{0.10(3,000) + 1,000}{1.10} - \frac{0.10(2,000) + 1,000}{(1.10)^2}$$

$$-\;\frac{0.10(1,000) + 1,000}{(1.10)^3}$$

$$PV = 3,000 - \frac{1,300}{1.10} - \frac{1,200}{(1.10)^2} - \frac{1,100}{(1.10)^3} = 0$$

The $3,000 is the value of the initial book value (B_0) in equation (13.3). The three terms that are subtracted from $3,000 are the inputs into the calculation of Y_i. For the first negative term (for year 1):

0.10(3,000)   is the interest on the beginning of the year investment

1,000   is the depreciation of the first year (using straight line depreciation)

These two values are discounted back one year consistent with equation (13.3).

Since the PV of all of the terms that contain book value is equal to zero, the value of B_0 does not affect the value of the stock. In this example, the terminal real value and the terminal book value are both equal to zero (G_3 is equal to zero).

Now assume accelerated depreciation (sum-of-the-years-digits) instead of straight line depreciation:

$$PV = 3,000 - \frac{0.10(3,000) + 1,500}{1.10} - \frac{0.10(1,500) + 1,000}{(1.10)^2}$$

$$- \frac{0.10(500) + 500}{(1.10)^3} = 3,000 - \frac{1,800}{1.10} - \frac{1,150}{(1.10)^2} - \frac{550}{(1.10)^3} = 0$$

The change in the method of computing the value of accounting depreciation does not change the present value. The zero present value of all terms containing elements of the book value term is independent of the method of accounting and the initial book value. Both the interest on the investment and the depreciation change, but the changes balance each other and the *PV* is again zero. Now assume the depreciation per year is $800 (there is $600 of terminal book value and zero residual value at time 3). We have:

$$PV = 3,000 - \frac{0.10(3,000) + 800}{1.10} - \frac{0.10(2,200) + 800}{(1.10)^2}$$

$$- \frac{0.10(1,400) + 800}{(1.10)^3} - \frac{600}{(1.10)^3}$$

$$PV = 3,000 - \frac{1,100}{1.10} - \frac{1,020}{(1.10)^2} - \frac{1,540}{(1.10)^3} = 0$$

While equation (13.3) clearly includes B_0 as a positive amount it also includes as negative amounts the present values of the interest deductions implicit in the present values of the residual incomes, the present value of the depreciation deductions, and the present value of the remaining book value at the end of the time horizon (implicit in the value of G_n). The present value of the sum of the three negative components (interest, depreciation, and remaining book value) and the one positive component (initial book value) is equal to zero so that the value of B_0 in equation (13.3) has no effect on the value of the stock calculation.

VALUATION USING ECONOMIC INCOME

We want to compute the present value of a firm (or a firm's equity or of an investment in real assets) using the firm's cash flows and then using the economic incomes (also known as the residual incomes). We will see that the two present values must be equal.

Assume the book value (B_0) is \$3,000. The dividends or cash flows to be earned by investors over the next three years are:

Year	Cash flows
1	1,210
2	1,331
3	1,331

The firm's present value as of time 0 using positive cash flows beginning at time 1 and a 0.10 discount rate is:

$$PV = \frac{1,210}{1.10} + \frac{1,331}{(1.10)^2} + \frac{1,331}{(1.10)^3} = 1,100 + 1,100 + 1,000 = \$3,200$$

Assume the net revenues equal the cash flows. The capital charge, an allowance for the cost of the equity capital employed, is 10 percent of the beginning of the period book values. The initial book value is \$3,000. The economic incomes, arbitrarily assuming \$1,000 depreciation per year, are:

	Year 1	2	3
Net revenues	1,210	1,331	1,331
Depreciation	1,000	1,000	1,000
Capital charge	300	200	100
Economic incomes	−90	131	231

The present value of the economic incomes, using 0.10 as the discount rate is \$200. Adding the \$3,000 initial book value and assuming zero residual value and zero terminal book value:

$$P_0 = B_0 + \sum_{i=1}^{n} \frac{Y_i}{(1 + k)^i} = 3,000 + 200 = \$3,200$$

The same \$3,200 value is obtained using the cash flows (equivalent to dividends) and using the economic income approach. Note that the book value is added to the present value of the economic incomes, but the present value of book value plus the other book value related deductions (obtained from the above table) is equal to zero:

$$PV = 3,000 - \frac{1,300}{1.10} - \frac{1,200}{(1.10)^2} - \frac{1,100}{(1.10)^3} = 0$$

The assumption of $3,000 of book value does not affect the firm's value. For example, assume the initial book is $1,500 and the annual depreciation is $500. We now have:

	Year		
	1	2	3
Net revenues	1,210	1,331	1,331
Depreciation	500	500	500
Interest	150	100	50
Economic incomes	560	731	781

The present value of the economic incomes is now $1,700, but P_0 again equals $3,200.

$$P_0 = B_0 + \sum_{i=1}^{n} \frac{Y_i}{(1 + k)^i} = 1,500 + 1,700 = \$3,200$$

The firm's value (or value of the equity) is not affected by the book value measure or other accounting measures. The annual measures of economic incomes could be improved by a better depreciation method (present value depreciation is explained in Chapter 14), but the firm's present value would not be affected.

OTHER METHODS OF VALUATION

This chapter has focused on the present value of economic incomes (or equivalently the present value of residual earnings). There is a popular valuation method using free cash flows. If free cash flow is equivalent to the firm's cash distributions then there is no difficulty reconciling the two methods. If free cash flow has a different definition then one has to be careful that reinvested funds and the terminal values are incorporated into the calculations in a theoretically correct manner. A popular solution in practice for valuing a firm is to compute cash flows before taxes and interest and use a multiplier to obtain the firm's value. Normally, debt must be subtracted to compute the value of the stock. The usual caveats associated with multiplier models are applicable.

The main objective of the above examples is to illustrate two basic methods of valuation; one uses cash flows and the second uses projected earnings. If the analyst wants to use projected earnings for valuation, then the accounting incomes must be converted to economic incomes by deducting an interest cost on all capital used, include the initial book value and the ending book value (as well as real residual value). The application of equation (13.3) will lead to a reasonable value measure that, if computed correctly, will be equal to the value measure obtained using the cash flow method of calculation. Multiplier models can be used with either approach. They are a convenient rule of thumb, but are susceptible to misuse if the conditions under which they were derived no longer apply.

COMPARING ROI AND ECONOMIC INCOME

Economic Income offers several significant advantages over ROI as a performance measure. First, and most importantly, the use of ROI might discourage division managers from accepting investments that offer returns that are larger than the firm's required risk adjusted returns, but that are less than the ROI the division is currently earning. If the new investment is accepted the division's ROI will be decreased.

A division is now earning $30,000,000 (a perpetuity) on an investment of $100,000,000.

$$\text{ROI} = \frac{30,000,000}{100,000,000} = 0.30$$

The division can invest an additional $50,000,000 and earn 0.15 ROI or $7,500,000 per year (a perpetuity) on this investment. The firm's required return for this investment is 0.10, thus the investment is economically desirable. Should the division accept the new investment? If it is accepted the division's ROI is reduced to:

$$\text{ROI} = \frac{37,500,000}{150,000,000} = 0.25$$

Based on the adverse effect on the division's ROI, a manager might reject this economically desirable investment. This problem does not arise if economic income is used.

The economic income before the new investment is:

Initial economic income = 30,000,000 − 10,000,000 = $20,000,000

The capital charge is 0.10 of $100,000,000 or $10,000,000. Note that the capital charge is computed on the total investment, not just the portion financed by debt. After the $50,000,000 investment, the economic income increases by $2,500,000:

New economic income = 37,500,000 − 15,000,000 = $22,500,000

EXAMPLE 13.1

EXAMPLE contd.

Based on economic income, there is an incentive for the division manager to accept the desirable investment.

The second problem with ROI is related to the first. ROI gives faulty evaluations of relative division performance. Consider two divisions, one with a ROI of 0.30 and the second with a ROI of 0.25. Which of the two division managers is doing the better job? Above, we showed that accepting the economically desirable investment reduces the division's ROI from 0.30 to 0.25. The division earning 0.25 is being managed better than the division that earns 0.30 and that rejects good investments. Using economic income to measure performance solves this problem that exists with ROI.

The third advantage of economic income is that it allows more flexibility. For example, if short-term interest rates are 0.20 and long-term rates are 0.12 (the pattern of 1980), the 0.20 interest rate could be used for working capital items in computing economic income. The ability to use different capital charges for assets with different risks introduces a flexibility that ROI lacks.

GLOBAL BUSINESS ASPECTS

Economic income is a great example of a global principle. Equity capital has a cost and to fail to recognize this cost is a deficiency, anywhere on the globe.

CONCLUSIONS

Accounting income omits a capital cost for equity capital. Economic income includes a capital cost for all capital. The same present value is obtained using cash flows or economic incomes.

There remains the problem that the incomes of individual years may be inconsistent with the overall profitability of the asset. This problem can be solved by the use of present value (economic) depreciation (see Chapter 14).

An intelligent well-educated manager might be able to overcome the limitations of conventional accounting using brilliance. Adjusting the accounting to be consistent with the underlying economics of the asset is more reliable and in many cases is likely to be easier.

PROBLEMS

1 The ABC Company uses ROE to measure performance and requires a 0.30 ROE. The following is the forecast for the next year.

Revenue	$10,000
Expenses	7,750
Interest	250
Income	2,000
Liabilities	2,500
Stock equity	7,500

$$ROE = \frac{2,000}{7,500} = 0.267$$

Incremental debt would cost 0.10.

What do you recommend to increase the ROE is above 0.30, assuming there are no incremental efficiencies or investments?

2 The XYZ Company uses ROA to measure performance. The firm is currently earning 28.33 percent. The CEO wants to earn 30 percent. There are three equal sized divisions with the following ROA's.

Division	ROA
A	0.35
B	0.30
C	0.20

Assume there are no incremental efficiencies or investments.

What should the management do to satisfy the CEO's wishes?

3 The RST Company has defined ROI as Y/C where Y is the income after interest and C is the investment. The following facts apply (these investments are financed 100 percent with debt).

$$ROI(A) = \frac{100}{100} = 1.0$$

$$ROI(B) = \frac{100}{200} = 0.5$$

The firm requires a 0.10 return.

A new desirable investment available to the Div A earns $20 (after interest) and $40 before interest on an investment of $200.

If A accepts the investment it will earn:

$$ROI(A) = \frac{120}{300} = 0.40.$$

A's performance would then be inferior to B.

What do you recommend?

4 Consider two alternatives with the following average ROI's:

	Average ROI
A	0.25
B	0.75

Which alternative do you prefer?

5   Assume the ABC Company's stock has the following record:

Time	Price	Dividend	Price change	Total return
0	$50			
1	40	2.00	−10.00	−8.00
2	45	2.10	5.00	7.10
3	50	2.30	5.00	7.30
4	60	2.50	10.00	12.50
	Total	8.90	10.00	18.90

a.   What IRR did the holder of a share earn?

b.   What other information would you want to know before reaching a conclusion as to how well management performed?

6   The A Company is considering an investment that promises cash flows of $10,000 per year for 20 years. The cost is $48,696 (depreciation is $2,434.80 per year).

The ROI of year 1 is:

$$ROI = \frac{10,000 - 2,434.80}{48,696} = 0.155.$$

The firm requires a return of 0.16.

Should the investment be accepted?

7   The B Company has a division with the following facts:

Assets = $200,000,000 (accounting values).

Forecasted income (before interest) = $8,000,000 (a perpetuity).

Cost of money = 0.10.

Can sell assets for $50,00,000.

	Computation 1	Computation 2
Income	8,000,000	8,000,000
Interest: 200,000,000(0.10)	20,000,000	
50,000,000(0.10)		5,000,000
Economic Income	−12,000,000	3,000,000

$$ROI = \frac{8,000,000}{200,000,000} = 0.04 \quad ROI = \frac{8,000,000}{50,000,000} = 0.16$$

Should the division be divested? The company's CEO requires a 0.10 ROI.

8   The C Corporation has a 0.10 cost of money. It is considering an investment
    with the following cash flows:

Time	Cash flow
0	−3,000
1	1,450
2	1,300
3	1,150

    a.   Prepare a table showing the economic incomes. The company uses
straight-line depreciation.

    b.   Compute the NPV using cash flows.

    c.   Compute the NPV using the economic incomes.

    d.   Compute the NPV using a 0.15 discount rate.

9   a.   Management wants to maximize EPS.

    b.   Management wants to maximize future stock price.

    c.   Management wants to maximize future earnings.

    d.   Management wants to maximize future ROI.

    e.   Management wants to maximize growth.

    f.   You want to maximize _____.

    Evaluate the above and describe your recommendation.

10 Assume an annual dividend of $1, a cost of equity of 0.15 and a 0.10 growth
    rate of dividends and earnings.

    What is the value of a share of this stock?

11 (*Continue 10*) If the cost of equity falls to 0.11 and the growth stays
    constant at 0.10, what is the new value of a share?

12 (*Continue 11*) What will be the expected stock price one year later? Ten
    years later?

13 (*Continue 10*) Assume the earnings per share are $2.50 (the retention rate is
    0.6). At what *P/E* multiplier would you expect the stock to see at?

14 Assume a 0.15 cost of equity. The following cash flows are expected:

    Time

    1. $1,500

    2.   1,650

    3.   1,996.5

    4.   10,000 (terminal value)

    Compute the firm's value using the cash flows.

15 (*Continue 14*) Assume the firm's initial book value is $6,000 and depreciation
    is $1,000 per year. Compute the firm's value using economic incomes.

16 (*Continue 14 and 15*) Now assume the firm's initial book value is $9,000
    and the depreciation is $3,000 per year. Compute the firm's value using
    economic incomes.

17 (*Continue 14, 15, and 16*). Compare the present values obtained for 14, 15, and 16.

18 The XYZ Company reports operating income of $2,000,000 and a stock equity of $200,000,000. The capitalization (number of shares outstanding times stock price) is $400,000,000. The firm's cost of equity is 0.09. Is the $20,000,000 good performance?

DISCUSSION QUESTION

What are some complexities in calculation of Economic Income that you might want to solve? Why might you not want to solve them?

BIBLIOGRAPHY

Baker, G. P., M. C. Jensen, and K. J. Murphy, "Compensation and Incentives: Practice vs. Theory," *Journal of Finance*, July 1988, pp. 593–616.

Baker, G. P., R. Gibbons, and K. J. Murphy, "Subjective Performance Measures in Optimal Incentive Contracts," *Quarterly Journal of Economics*, November 1994, pp. 1125–56.

Christensen, P. O., G. A. Feltham, and M. G. H. Wu, "Cost of Capital in Residual Incomes for Performance Evaluations," *Accounting Review*, January 2002, pp. 1–23.

Ehrbar, Al, *Economic Value Added®: The Real Key to Creating Wealth*, New York, NY: John Wiley, 1998.

Ehrenberg, R. G. and G. T. Milkovich, "Compensation and Firm Performance," NBER Working Paper no. 2145, February 1987.

Ohlson, J. A., "Earnings, Book Value, and Dividends in Security Valuation," *Contemporary Accounting Research*, 11, 1995, pp. 661–87.

Pais, Abraham, *Niels Bohr's Times, In Physics, Philosophy and Policy*, New York, Clarendon Press, 1991.

Schwayder, K. "A Proposed Modification to Residual Income: Interest Adjusted Income," *Accounting Review*, April 1970, pp. 299–307.

Stern, Joel M., G. B. Stewart III, and Donald H. Chew, Jr., "The EVA® Financial System," *Journal of Applied Corporate Finance*, 8(2), 1995, pp. 32–46.

Stewart III, G. B., *The Quest for Value*, New York: Harper Collins, 1991.

——, "EVA®: Fact and Fantasy," *Journal of Applied Corporate Finance*, 7(2), 1994, pp. 71–84.

——, "EVA® Clarified," *Management Accounting*, 80(6), 1998, p. 8.

Chapter 14

Present value accounting

What you're saying, then, is that just because all the professionals in the field believe it, it must be right. If this were really true, the world is flat.

(Joel Segall, from the autumn 1969 Newsletter of the Graduate School of Business, University of Chicago)

Much of the economic analysis of evaluating prospective capital investments relies heavily on concepts such as cash flows and their net present value. The primary purpose of this chapter is to show that the discounted cash flow approach and the main accounting concepts can be reconciled, provided that the accounting concepts are appropriately defined. The estimates of value that are used for capital budgeting are necessarily forward looking and subjective which may reduce their applicability to financial reporting by corporations to the public. The concepts to be considered in this chapter provide intuition about capital budgeting procedures and a basis for managerial performance measurement systems.

A MANAGEMENT SEMINAR

The professor carefully explained the calculation of an investment's IRR and how if the benefits were increasing through time, the ROI's of the early years would be low or negative, but they would be larger in the later years. While not equal to the project's IRR, they would be of the same magnitude.

A manager in the audience pointed out that the above explanation was not adequate. His firm was a very large chemical corporation. With two or three years of below acceptable performance based on conventional accounting he would be fired. He needed a better solution. Consider present value accounting.

BASIC CONCEPTS

Assume that we are given the expected cash flow stream and an appropriate interest rate associated with an asset. $N(t)$ is the expected end of period t cash flow, positive for inflows and negative for outflows. For convenience we assume that cash flows occur only at the end of each period and that the expectation is calculated based on the information available at time 0. The periods can be as long or as short as desired. (The results in this chapter could be extended to the situation where cash flows occur continuously.) The net present value of the expected cash flows associated with the asset during all succeeding time periods is denoted as $V(t)$, where $V(t)$ is the present value of the cash flow sequence $N(t + 1)$, $N(t + 2)$, $N(t + 3)$ ... etc. Thus $V(0)$ is the present value at time 0 (end of period zero), and incorporates all of the expected cash flows in periods 1, 2, 3, and beyond. $V(1)$ is the present value at time 1, and incorporates all of the expected cash flows in periods 2, 3, 4, and beyond.

ECONOMIC DEPRECIATION, INCOME, AND RETURN ON INVESTMENT

The economic depreciation (or present value depreciation) of period t will be defined as the change in present value during a period, that is, as the present value of an asset at the beginning of the period less its present value at the end of the period. That is, $D(t)$ is defined as

$$D(t) \equiv V(t - 1) - V(t) \tag{14.1}$$

In the usual case, where the asset's present values have declined over the period, depreciation will be a positive quantity. If the present values increase during the period, depreciation will be negative, and we shall refer to the negative value of depreciation as appreciation. If $N(t)$ is the cash flow of the t period (positive for inflows and negative for outflows), the income of the period is defined as the cash flow of the period minus the depreciation of the period. That is, income denoted by $Y(t)$, is defined as

$$Y(t) \equiv N(t) - D(t) \tag{14.2}$$

Return on investment in period t, ROI(t), is defined as the ratio of the income of the period to the present value of the asset at the end of the previous period. That is,

$$\text{ROI}(t) \equiv \frac{Y(t)}{V(t - 1)} \quad \text{if } V(t - 1) \neq 0. \tag{14.3}$$

If r is the discount rate used in this analysis, each period's return on investment will be equal to r.

APPLICATION TO ASSETS WITH ZERO PRESENT VALUE

To illustrate these concepts, consider asset A whose cash flows are described in the following table. The discount rate for A is 0.10.

Cash flows of asset A	
Period	End of period cash flow
0	−$17,355
1	$10,000
2	$10,000

The calculations of the net present value of asset A at times 0 and 1 are shown in Table 14.1. Exhibit 14.1 uses data of Table 14.1 and the formulas presented previously to calculate the depreciation, income, return on investment for asset A for periods 1 and 2. Remember, economic depreciation is being used. This is consistent with equation (14.1).

As this example illustrates, if the initial outlay is equal to the present value of the subsequent cash flows, the return on investment of each year is equal to the

Table 14.1 Calculation of the net present value of asset A at times 0 and 1 ($r = 10\%$)

Period	End of period cash flow	For V(0)		For V(1)	
		Present value factor	Present value	Present value factor	Present value
1	$10,000	0.9091	$9,091		
2	$10,000	0.8264	$8,264	0.9091	$9,091
		$V(0) =$	$17,355	$V(1) =$	$9,091

Exhibit 14.1 Depreciation, income, and return on investment for asset A

For period 1
$D(1) = 17{,}355 - 9{,}091 = 8{,}264$
$Y(1) = 10{,}000 - 8{,}264 = 1{,}736$
$ROI(1) = 1{,}736/17{,}355 = 0.10$

For period 2
$D(2) = 9{,}091 - 0 = 9{,}091$
$Y(2) = 10{,}000 - 9{,}091 = 909$
$ROI(2) = 909/9{,}091 = 0.10$

discount rate used to calculate the present values, if economic depreciation is used. If there is a single Internal Rate of Return (IRR) for a zero NPV asset, if the discount rate is equal to the IRR, then the ROI of each year will be equal to this IRR. In the next section we look at an investment that has a positive NPV before the first cash flow occurs.

AN INVESTMENT WITH A POSITIVE NET PRESENT VALUE

Now consider investment B. Its initial outlay at time zero is $15,278. The subsequent cash flows are the same as for investment A. Assume that the discount rate of 10 percent is applicable to investment B, because applying that discount rate to the subsequent cash flows gives the best approximation to the asset's market value. As shown in the following tables, the net present value of investment B is $2,077 and the IRR of the asset is 20 percent.

How should we account for this investment? One solution is to recognize $2,077 of additional income and asset value at time 0, and then act as if the asset had a value and cost of $17,355 and depreciate that amount over its life. The 10 percent rate of interest would be used for discounting, and the return on investment each period after time 0 would be 10 percent. The computations for the income, depreciation and return on investment for periods one and two are illustrated in Tables 14.2 and 14.3 and Exhibit 14.1 (page 257).

Table 14.2 Computation of net present value for asset B at 10%

Period	End of period cash flow	Present value factor (10%)	Present value
0	−$15,278	1.0000	−$15,278
1	10,000	0.9091	9,091
2	10,000	0.8264	8,264
			Net present value $2,077

Table 14.3 Computation of internal rate of return for investment B (r = 20%)

Period	Cash flow	Present value factor (20%)	Present value
0	−$15,278	1.0000	−$15,278
1	10,000	0.8333	8,333
2	10,000	0.6944	6,944
			Net present value $0

258

An alternative approach would be to use the internal rate of return of the investment as the discount rate. The use of an asset's internal rate of return has the advantage of simplicity. But assets with identical cash flows except for the initial outlay would be recorded at values that are not equal to the present values that would be obtained using the same common discount factor. For example, two investments with exactly the same benefit stream would be recorded differently if they cost different amounts (their internal rates of return would differ). This would lead to two identical benefit streams being recorded at different values and leading to different returns on investments. This practice would tend to reduce the usefulness of the return-on-investment calculation as a managerial control device. Suppose that two managers are in charge of the two assets with different costs. If both do as well as expected with their assets (that is, achieve the cash flows predicted for their assets), one will have a lower return on investment, and the other, a higher return on investment. Thus, the return on investment measures not their operating ability, but the ability (or luck) of whoever originally uncovered the investment opportunities.

COMBINING INVESTMENTS

Consider two investments A and C where both investments are part of a common entity E. The appropriate rate of discount for each of the investments is 10 percent. Table 14.3 shows the computation of $V(t)$ for the joint investment E consisting of A plus C for times 0 and 1. The value of $V(2)$ is zero, since there are no cash flows after period two. Exhibit 14.2 shows the computation of depreciation, income, and return on investment for E (Table 14.4). Economic depreciation is being used.

	Time		
	0	1	2
A	−$17,355	$10,000	$10,000
C		−10,000	11,000
E = A + C	−$17,355	$0	$21,000

The returns on investment for both years are 0.10, which is also the internal rate of return of the joint investment. This illustrates that the propositions about income, return on investment and IRR apply to a collection of investments if the same discount rate is applicable to each individual investment.

There are situations in which the same discount rate is not applicable to all of the cash flows in a collection of investments. One possibility, illustrated next, is that the investments may have different risk characteristics and therefore require different discount rates. As discussed in Chapter 9 there are situations for a single

Exhibit 14.2 Depreciation, income, and return on investment for asset E

For period 1

$D(1) = 17,355 - 19,091 = -1,736$

$Y(1) = 0 - (-1,736) = 1,736$

$ROI(1) = 1,736/17,355 = 0.10$

For period 2

$D(2) = 19,091 - 0 = 19,091$

$Y(2) = 21,000 - `9,091 = 1,909$

$ROI(2) = 1,909/19,091 = 0.10$

Table 14.4 Calculation of the net present value of asset E at times 1 and 2 $(r = 10\%)$

Period	End of period cash flow	For V(0)		For V(1)	
		Present value factor	Present value	Present value factor	Present value
1	$0	0.9091	$0		
2	$21,000	0.8264	$17,355	0.9091	$19,091
			$V(0) = \$17,355$		$V(1) = \$19,091$

investment in which some cash flow components have different risks than other cash flows components. It is important to discount each cash flow stream by the discount rate that is appropriate for its risk.

TWO INVESTMENTS WITH DIFFERENT RISKS

To illustrate the correct procedure for calculating the income, economic depreciation and return on investment for an entity that contains cash flows with different risks suppose that an entity contains two investments, A and D where the appropriate discounts rates are 10 percent for the cash flows of investment A and 20 percent for the cash flows of investment D (Table 14.5). We designate as F the entity that contains both investments. We have already calculated the values, income depreciation and ROI for investment A (see Table 14.1 and Exhibit 14.1). The cash flows for investments A, D and the combined entity F are as follows:

The value of asset D at times 0 and 1 is shown in Table 14.6. It has a zero value at time 2, because there are no subsequent cash flows. The income, depreciation and ROI of investment D during periods 1 and 2 are calculated in Exhibit 14.3.

Exhibit 14.4 shows the depreciation, income return on investment for the combined entity F and its components. In constructing this exhibit, we begin by

Table 14.5 Cash flows of asset F

Period	Assets		
	A	D	F = A + D
	End of period cash flows		
0	−$17,355	−$10,000	−$27,355
1	$10,000	$8,000	$18,000
2	$10,000	$4,800	$14,800

Table 14.6 Calculation of NPV of asset D at times 0 and 1 ($r = 0.20$)

Period	End of period cash flow	For V(0)		For V(1)	
		Present value factor	Present value	Present value factor	Present value
1	$8,000	0.8333	$6,666		
2	$4,800	0.6944	$3,333	0.8333	$4,000
			V(0) = $10,000		V(1) = $4,000

Exhibit 14.3 Depreciation, income, and return on investment D

For period 1, we have

$D(1) = V(0) - V(1) = \$10,000 - 4,000 = \$6,000$

$Y(1) = N(1) - D(1) = 8,000 - 6,000 = \$2,000$

$r = \dfrac{Y(1)}{V(0)} = \dfrac{\$2,00}{\$10,000} = 0.20$

For period 2, we have

$D(2) = V(1) - V(2) = \$4,000 - 0 = \$4,000$

$Y(2) = N(2) - D(2) = 4,800 - 4,000 = \$800$

$r = \dfrac{Y(2)}{V(1)} = \dfrac{\$800}{\$4,000} = 0.20$

calculating the present values, economic depreciation income and ROI of each component using the present value accounting procedures that are illustrated earlier in this chapter. For those concepts whose units of measure are dollars, such as cash flow, income depreciation, and present value, the value for the combined entity is simply the sum of the values for the components. If the units of measure are percentages, namely ROI and IRR, the values for the combined entity must be calculated separately. For example, the ROI for the combined entity is the income of the combined entity divided by the beginning of the period value of the combined entity. The IRR of the combined entity must be calculated from the combined cash flows.

261

Exhibit 14.4 *Depreciation, income, return on investments, and IRR for the combined entity F and its components A and D*

	Assets		
	A	D	F = A + D
Period 1			
Beginning of period value	$17,355	$10,000	$27,355
Depreciation	$8,264	$6,000	$14,264
Cash flow	$10,000	$8,000	$18,000
Income	$1,736	$2,000	$3,736
End of period value	$9,091	$4,000	$13,091
Return on investment	0.100	0.200	0.137
Period 2			
Beginning of period value	$9,091	$4,000	$13,091
Depreciation	$9,091	$4,000	$13,091
Cash flow	$10,000	$4,800	$14,800
Income	$909	$800	$1,709
End of period value	$0	$0	$0
Return on investment	0.100	0.200	0.131
IRR	0.100	0.200	0.135

If there are different discount rates for the components of a combined entity, as is the case with the entity F illustrated in the example, then the ROI of the combined entity may vary from year to year. It can be shown that in each period, the ROI of the combined entity is a weighted average of the ROI's of its components, with the weights equal to the relative beginning-of-period values of the components. The analogy to a portfolio of marketable securities with different risks may be helpful. In the case of a securities portfolio, the expected rate of return on the portfolio at any time is equal to a value weighted average of the expected rates of return of the individual securities in the portfolio.

BETTER INCOME MEASURES

Consider an investment that has the following expected cash flows:

Time	Cash flow
0	−24,000
1	4,400
2	12,100
3	13,310

The project has a 0.10 cost of capital and the asset has an IRR of 0.10. With conventional accounting (straight-line depreciation) the incomes of each year are:

Year	Cash flow	Depreciation	Income	ROI
1	4,400	8,000	−3,600	NA*
2	12,100	8,000	4,100	0.256
3	13,310	8,000	5,310	0.399

*Not applicable since the income is negative.

There is a loss in year 1, reasonable operations for year 2, and superlative performance in year 3. But in all three years the actual results were merely consistent with the expected results. The calculation of economic depreciation is:

Year	Value at beginning of year	Value at end of year	Economic depreciation
1	24,000	22,000	2,000
2	22,000	12,100	9,900
3	12,100	0	12,100

Using the economic depreciation measures, the incomes and ROI's for each year are:

Year	Cash flow	Economic depreciation	Income	Investment	ROI
1	4,400	2,000	2,400	24,000	0.10
2	12,100	9,900	2,200	22,000	0.10
3	13,310	12,100	1,210	12,100	0.10

With economic depreciation the ROI's of each year are the same and equal to the assumed cost of capital for the project. For management to have superlative performance it has to exceed the expected results of the year, if economic depreciation is used. With conventional accounting, in many situations management may merely have to grow old to achieve an improved performance.

INTERNAL RATE OF RETURN AND TAXES

Let us assume a situation where an investment type of outlay may be deducted for taxes at the time the outlay is made rather than being depreciated over time. We want to show that with this assumption the internal rate of return after tax equals the internal rate of return before tax.

Assume the before-tax cash flows are

$$C_0, C_1, C_2, \ldots, C_i, \ldots, C_N$$

where C_i is the cash flow of period I, and C_0 has a negative value. We assume that the before-tax cash flow sequence is such that there exists a discount rate r that makes the present value of the entire before-tax cash flow sequence equal to zero. Then the present value of the before-tax cash flow sequence can be written as

$$\text{Before tax NPV} = C_0 + \frac{C_1}{1 + r} + \frac{C_2}{(1 + r)^2} + \cdots + \frac{C_n}{(1 + r)^n} = 0$$

Multiplying both sides by $(1 - t)$, we obtain the net present value of the after-tax cash flow sequence at the discount rate r.

$$\text{After tax NPV} = (1 - t)C_0 + \frac{(1 - t)C_1}{1 + r} + \frac{(1 - t)C_2}{(1 + r)^2} + \cdots$$

$$+ \frac{(1 - t)C_n}{(1 + r)^n} = 0$$

Thus, if the before-tax cash flows have an internal rate of return, r, then the after-tax cash flows have the same internal rate of return. The conclusion that the internal rate of return is not affected by the tax rate requires that C_0 and all subsequent cash flows be treated as taxable expenses or incomes in the years in which they occur.

Consider the following investment with an internal rate of return of 0.10.

Time	Before-tax cash flow
0	−$3,000
1	1,300
2	1,200
3	1,100

With immediate expensing of the initial outlay and a 0.40 tax rate, the after-tax cash flows and their present values using 0.10 as the discount rate would be

Time	After-tax cash flow	Present value (0.10)
0	−$1,800	−$1,800.00
1	780	709.09
2	720	595.04
3	660	495.87
		NPV = $0

The before- and after-tax internal rates of return are both 0.10. The internal rate of return is not affected by the tax rate if the initial outlay is immediately expensed for taxes.

This analysis is also applicable to types of retirement funds, known as Keogh plans or IRA's. The basic tax rules applicable to these plans are (1) the cash invested in one of these funds is tax deductible in the year in which it is invested; (2) dividends, interest, and capital gains realized by such a fund are not taxable as long as the money remains in the fund; and (3) cash withdrawn from such a fund is fully taxable in the year it is withdrawn. Suppose that the money invested in a Keogh is used to purchase assets that provide an internal rate of return of 10 percent before taxes. Then the after-tax internal rate of return to the investor is also 10 percent. This is illustrated with the following simple example, for an investor in a 40 percent tax bracket and an asset whose before-tax IRR is 10 percent.

Time	Before-tax cash flow	After-tax cash flow
0	−3,000	−$1,800
5	4,832	2,889

The after-tax cash flows will have a positive present value for any discount rate less than 10 percent. The internal rates of return of both the before- and after-tax cash flows are equal to 0.10. It is reasonable to expect the after-tax discount rate is less than 0.10 if the invested funds earn 0.10 before tax. The advantage of the Keogh plan is that after-tax funds that were invested in the asset would be subject to tax when they are earned. Without a Keogh plan they would be taxed before they were withdrawn so that the after-tax return earned on the asset would have been less than its 0.10 before tax return and the 0.10 return earned with a Keogh plan.

GLOBAL BUSINESS ASPECTS

When communism was the guiding light for the USSR, business and economic authors in that country could not use interest concepts. Interest was a capitalist notion and communistic writings did not acknowledge its existence.

Interestingly, in those countries where the interest concept has been widely accepted for centuries, there is still a reluctance to recognize the relevance of the time value of money (interest) in accounting for assets. Thus, this chapter is important for managers but it is not likely to be the basis of generally accepted accounting principles for many years.

CONCLUSIONS

It is generally accepted accounting practice to use some method of depreciation accounting that is well defined and is independent of the economic characteristics of the asset being depreciated. For tax purposes, the corporate objective in choosing among allowable methods of depreciation accounting is to write the asset off as rapidly as possible (more exactly, to maximize the present value of the write-offs). For accounting purposes, the objective is to allocate in a reasonable manner the cost of the asset over its useful life.

This chapter has suggested two alternative methods of defining depreciation. One method uses the project's IRR as the discount rate and accomplishes the important objective of equating the annual return on investment of the asset to its internal rate of return. The second method requires that the asset be recorded at its value. If we are willing to adjust the cost of the asset to its present value using the project's required rate of return, the second method leads to the return on investment being equal to the required rate of return (rate of discount defined to be appropriate) for the asset in each year of use. These procedures have the advantage of eliminating the types of distortions in the measurement of return on investment associated with the use of straight-line depreciation or accelerated depreciation when the cash flows do not decrease rapidly through time.

We know that investment decisions should be made using the available information for the entire life of the investment. The measures of performance should do likewise, or distortions will be introduced if there is a focus on the short-term measures.

If the accounting measures are converted from conventional measures to economic measures, significant improvements in the measures of performance result. They become reconciled to the economic measures of investment worth.

The severity of the distortions resulting from the use of conventional accounting was understated in the examples given in this chapter, since straight-line depreciation was used. If any of the accelerated depreciation methods had been used, the distortions would have been even larger. The performance of the early years of use would have appeared even worse than was indicated in the examples.

Management should move to a system of measuring performance where a desirable investment has desirable measures of performance as long as the actual results coincide with or exceed the forecasted results.

PROBLEMS

1   An asset costs $15,227 and will earn proceeds of $10,000 a year for two
    years. The cash is received at the end of each period. The time value of money
    is 0.20.
    a.   Compute the internal rate of return of the investment
    b.   Compute the depreciations in value of the asset, the incomes, and the
         returns on investment for the two years of life.

2 An asset costs $25,620 and will earn proceeds of $10,000 in year 1 and $20,000 in year 2. The time value of money is 0.10.
   a. Compute the internal rate of return of the investment.
   b. Compute the depreciations in value of the asset, the incomes, and the returns on investment for the two years of life.

3 An asset costs $26,446 and will earn proceeds of $20,000 in year 1 and $10,000 in year 2. The time value of money is 0.10.
   a. Compute the internal rate of return of the investment.
   b. Compute the depreciation in value of the asset, the incomes, and the returns on investment for the two years of life.

4 An asset costs $20,000 and earns proceeds of $11,000 in year 1 and $10,500 in year 2. The time value of money is 0.05.
   a. Compute the internal rate of return of the investment,.
   b. Compute the depreciation in value of the asset, the incomes, and the returns on investments for the two years of life.

5 An asset costs $20,000 and will earn proceeds of $12,000 in year 1 and $11,000 in year 2. The time value of money is 0.10.
   a. Compute the internal rate of return of the investment.
   b. Compute the depreciations in value of the asset, the incomes, and the returns on investment for the two years of life.

6 An asset costs $15,778 and will earn cash proceeds of $10,000 a year for two years, the first payment to be received two years from now. The sales will be made at the end of periods 1 and 2, and the collections at the end of periods 2 and 3. The time value of money is 0.10.
   Compute the depreciations, the incomes, and the returns on investment for the life of the investment.

7 An asset costs $8,505 at time 0 and an additional $8,000 at time 1. It will earn proceeds of $10,000 a year for two years, the first payment to be received two years from now. The time value of money is 0.10.
   Compute the depreciations, the incomes, and the returns on investment for the life of the investment.

8 (Continue 7) What is the value of the investment at time 1 (after the second investment) if the actual investment outlay was only $5,000 at time 0 and $4,000 at time 1? What is the value at time 2? Assume that the expected benefits are unchanged.

9 The XYZ Company wants to know the cost of a new building it has constructed. It paid the builder an advance of $2 million and paid the remainder when the building was completed two years later (total amount paid to the builder was $3 million).
   a. Determine the cost, assuming that the building was financed with 0.05 debentures.

b. Determine the cost, assuming that the building was financed entirely by stock.

10 An investment costs $14,059 and the expected cash flows of

Period 0	Period 1	Period 2
−$14,059	$10,000	$5,000

The time value of money of the firm is 0.05. Management wants a system for reappraising capital budgeting decisions.

a. Assume that the accounting measures of expense (except for depreciation) and revenues would be the same as the preceding. Prepare statements of income and return on investment that would be reasonable tools for reappraisal of the decisions.

b. Assume the accounting measure of net revenue in period 1 is $14,762, and the net revenue in period 2 is $0. The investment cost is $14,059. What is the ROI of years?

11 a. Find the income, depreciation, and return on investment during periods 1 and 2 using an interest rate of 25 percent (no taxes are payable).

Period	End-of-period before-tax cash flows
0	−$16,000
1	+16,000
2	−7,000
3	+15,000

b. Assume a tax rate of 40 percent on income defined in present value terms. What are the after-tax cash flows for periods 1 and 2?

12 Consider the following before-tax cash flows:

Period	0	1	2
Cash flow	−$100	$0	+$144

Suppose an investor is in the 60 percent tax bracket. Find the after-tax internal rate of return on the investment for each of the following circumstances.

a. The outlays come from after-tax funds. The taxes are paid using the present value definition of income. (Assume a before-tax discount rate of 20 percent.)

    b.   The outlays come from the after-tax funds. The proceeds are taxed using an income concept based on historical cost and straight-line depreciation.

    c.   The outlays come from before-tax funds and are tax deductible. All proceeds are taxable when realized. (This is how some pension plans work.)

13 Consider the following before-tax cash flows:

Period	0	1	2
End-of-period cash	−$8,000	+$15,000	−$5,000

    a.   Find the income and depreciation during period 1, using present value accounting. Assume no taxes and an interest rate of 6 percent in all periods.

    b.   Find the income and depreciation during period 2, using present value accounting. Assume no taxes and an interest rate of 6 percent in all periods.

14 Given the following data:

Period	End-of-period before-tax cash flows
0	−$12,000
1	+12,000
2	−6,000
3	+12,000

    a.   Find the income, depreciation, and return on investment during period 1, using an interest rate of 12 percent (no taxes are payable).

    b.   Find the income, depreciation, and return on investment during period 2, using an interest rate of 12 percent (no taxes are payable).

15 The A Company is currently earning $13,000,000 per year on $100,000,000 of stock holders' equity, or a return on investment of 13 percent. One plant with a cost base of $10,000,000 earns $800,000 per year. The chairman of the board has set a target ROI of 15 percent. The company has received a firm cash offer of $5,000,000 for the plant. The pro-forma return on investment (assuming the $5,000,000 is returned to investors) is:

$$ROI = \frac{12,200,000}{90,000,000} = 13.5 \text{ percent}$$

The chairman is pleased that the ROI will increase from 13 percent to 13.5 percent.

Should the plant be sold?

16 The AB Company has two divisions. Both divisions are earning $15,000,000 on stock equity of $50,000,000. This is an ROI of 30 percent. The firm uses a hurdle rate of 0.10. Both divisions are given the opportunity to invest $30,000,000 and earn $5,000,000 per year (a perpetuity). This is a 17 percent ROI.

What will be the ROI if the division accepts? Which division is better managed, the one that accepts or the one that rejects?

17 Consider the investment shown in the accompanying table with a 0.20 internal rate of return (there are zero taxes). Now assume a 0.34 tax rate is imposed, but all outlays are immediately expensed for taxes. The government pays if the taxable income is negative (a loss).

Time	Cash flow
0	−$3,000
1	1,600
2	1,400
3	1,200

a. What is the after-tax internal rate of return?

b. What is the after-tax internal rate of return if the tax rate is 0.68?

DISCUSSION QUESTION

The logic of present value accounting is compelling. Why might a corporation not want to use it or the FASB to require it?

BIBLIOGRAPHY

Bierman, Harold, Jr., "A Reconciliation of Present Value Capital Budgeting and Accounting." *Financial Management*, summer 1977, pp. 52–4.

Dearden, John, "A Further Study of Depreciation," *Accounting Review*, April 1966, pp. 271–4.

——, "The Case Against ROI Control," *Harvard Business Review*, May–June 1969, pp. 124–35.

Ijiri, Yuji, *Theory of Accounting Measurement*, Studies in Accounting Research, no. 10, Sarasota, FL: American Accounting Association, 1975.

——, "Cash-Flow Accounting and Its Structure," *Journal of Accounting, Auditing and Finance*, summer 1978, pp. 331–48.

——, "Recovery Rate and Cash Flow Accounting," *Financial Executive*, March 1980, pp. 54–60.

Inselbag, I. and H. Kaufold, "Two DCF Approaches for Valuing Companies Under Alternative Financing Strategies and How to Choose Between Them," *Journal of Applied Corporate Finance*, 10, 1997, pp. 114–22.

Mauriel, John J. and Robert N. Anthony, "Misevaluation of Investment Center Performance," *Harvard Business Review*, March–April 1966, pp. 98–105.

Solomon, Ezra, "Alternative Rate of Return Concepts and Their Implications for Utility Regulation," *Bell Journal of Economics and Management Science*, spring 1970, pp. 65–81.

Solomons, David, *Divisional Performance Measurement and Control*, Homewood, IL: Irwin, 1965.

Chapter 15

Performance measurement and managerial compensation

> You aren't going to win outscoring people.
>
> (Lou Holtz, Football Coach Notre Dame University,
> *New York Times*, section 8, p. 1, November 4, 1990)

Measuring managerial performance for praise or compensation determination is a difficult task. Any method used is subject to valid objections. There are four basic techniques that can be used:

1   accounting measures (e.g. income, return on investment, economic income, etc.);
2   market measures (the return earned on an investment in the company's common stock;
3   non-accounting but quantitative measures;
4   qualitative measures (a subjective evaluation of performance).

It is desirable that there be congruence between the firm's goals and the performance measures that are used. One cannot expect managers knowingly to take actions that are desirable for the firm if those actions will adversely affect their career path or compensation.

Our recommendation will be to use several measures. Since all measures will be subject to some sort of gaming by the person where performance is being measured, the use of several good measures reduces the likelihood that managers will knowingly make undesirable decisions for the firm.

PROBLEMS OF AGENCY

Problems of agency arise when a principal employs an agent to perform a task, and the interests of the principal and the agent are not identical. The corporate form is fertile soil for agency problems to take root. Consider that the relationships between shareholders (the principal) and management (the agent) are not identical. For many reasons including the increase in power, management might want the firm to grow while the shareholders would be better off with a small firm and a large cash distribution to the owners. It is necessary for the compensation method to be efficient in terms of discouraging the possibility of a wealth desiring management undertaking knowingly undesirable investments from the viewpoint of shareholders.

There can also be agency problems with different levels of employees. Consider the CEO and traders of a bank. They are all employees. They all want to increase the bank's profits. But the traders might have bonus arrangements that encourage them to take excessive risks from the CEO's perspective in order to earn a large bonus. This strategy might be good for the traders but bad for the expected profits of the bank. A trader who wins becomes rich. A trader who loses gets an identical job with the bank across the street.

Another type of agency problem arises when one group is in a position to take advantage of a second group even if the second group are not employees. Let us consider a firm financed by $9,000,000 of 0.08 debt and $500,000 of common stock. There are zero taxes. Without any new investments there is certainty of the firm earning $800,000 (before interest) and being able to pay the $720,000 interest on the debt. The stockholder would earn $80,000 per year. The firm is considering a $1,000,000 investment financed by 0.08 debt. With this new investment the two earnings outcomes for the firm are:

Probability	Earnings (before interest) with investment
0.5	$0
0.5	$2,000,000

If the outcome is $0 earnings, both the debt and stockholders receive zero earnings (the debtholders receive their initial investment.)

Subtracting the $800,000 interest on the $10,000,000 of total debt if the investment is accepted the common stockholders will earn $1,200,000 with 0.5 probability or an expected value of $600,000.

Without the incremental investment the stockholders will earn $80,000 per year. With the investment the stockholders will earn an expected income of $600,000. Many shareholders will want to undertake the investment.

273

But consider the initial $9,000,000 of initial debt. Without the investment the debtholders earn 0.08 with certainty. With the investment their return is reduced to an expected return of 0.04 since there is 0.5 probability that the debtholders will receive only their initial investment.

Obviously, debtholders will attempt to structure their indentures so that they limit the ability of the stockholders to change the nature of the business in a manner that adversely affects the position of the debtholders. This is a variation of an agency problem.

For the remainder of this chapter we will discuss performance measurement and managerial compensation. The objective will be to consider agency costs when making decisions.

Agency costs consist of two types. One is the transaction cost. Buyers of debt have to hire a lawyer that protects the debt buyers interests. Corporations hire consultants to establish systems so that the traders of derivatives cannot bankrupt the firm. These are transaction costs and agency costs. A second type of agency cost arises because of the necessity to reward the agent in a manner that makes the agent's interests more congruent with the principal's interests.

PERFORMANCE MEASUREMENT AND MANAGERIAL COMPENSATION

Measuring managerial performance for praise or compensation determination is a difficult task. Any method used is subject to valid objections.

ACCOUNTING MEASURES

The accounting measures we will consider are:

1   sales revenue;
2   operating margins, percentages, dollar amounts;
3   income;
4   ROI or ROE or ROA;
5   economic income (residual income or economic value added);
6   present value accounting (PVA);
7   earnings per share (for a period of years).

Sales revenue is an attractive measure since there are few arguments as to its magnitude. Add the share of market and growth in sales and one can become enthusiastic about the usefulness of the sales measures. But obviously something is missing, profitability.

The operating margin is a popular profitability measure. Subtract from sales revenue the direct costs of earning the revenue. For example, the operating margin of a retail store are sales minus the cost of the merchandise sold. With a manufacturer the definition of the expenses to be subtracted to compute the margin is not as exact as in retailing.

If sales are $100 and the cost of good sold are $60 the operating margin can be expressed as a dollar amount $40, or as a percentage, 40 percent. Operating margins as a control mechanism are useful. If sales are increased and operating margins are maintained, it is likely that a positive bottom line (income) will result. On the other hand many expenses (including capital costs) are omitted from the margin calculation, thus the operating margin can only be one of several performance measures that are used.

INCOME

Income is revenue minus expenses as defined by generally accepted accounting principles. Unlike the operating margin it includes the firm's fixed expenses as well as the variable expenses.

The primary area where the income measure is deficient is the expense of using capital. The cost of the equity capital used is normally not deducted in computing the income.

It is essential that the costs of all the capital used affect the performance measures. The two common measures are return on investment (ROI) in some form and economic income (EI). Economic income deserves to be used more extensively (its use is growing rapidly).

One of the underlying issues is whether performance measurement and decision-making of a firm should be on a decentralized or centralized basis. Any multidivisional firm can be turned into a completely self-contained unit by doing away with profit centers, and by considering the entire corporation as an operating entity. The arguments of this chapter are applicable to entire firms, self-contained operating components of a firm, or components that are not self-contained but in which there is a reasonable transfer pricing procedure. Although the desirability of profit centers, indeed the entire question of centralization versus decentralization, is to a large extent separate from the quantitative performance measurement, in one sense the issues merge. To compute any quantitative performance measurement of an operating unit, it is necessary to arrive at reasonable income and investment measures for the operating unit.

RETURN ON INVESTMENT (ROI)

Advocating the use of ROI implies that it is a better measure of performance than is obtained from using just the income or operating margin of the operating unit.

While this is normally the situation, not all subsidiary operating units should be judged using ROI, and ROI should always be only one of several measures. For many operating units, marketing efforts are not autonomous, and it is more appropriate to use cost minimization rather than profit maximization (or its near equivalent, maximization of ROI, subject to constraints).

Some managers tend to place excessive faith in a ROI measure, neglecting the fact that the measurement of performance (so that the measure actually reflects performance) requires more than one measure. It should be realized that ROI is not necessarily the best measure of performance, but that ROI can be a useful measure. Consider what a good ROI measure can accomplish. We have first a measure of income; but before concluding that the income level is satisfactory, we relate the income to the amount of assets used to earn the income. While $1 million of earnings may be termed to be very good, but if you are told that the operating unit used $100 million of capital to earn the $1 million, your conclusion might well shift from good to bad. To evaluate performance it is necessary to consider the amount of assets used in earning the income. Thus the use of ROI has advantages over the use of income, but it may not be the best performance measure.

Instead of ROI some firms use the return on equity (ROE). While the two measures have comparable uses and there will be times when the managers or the firm's owners will want to know the ROI, the ROE measure has several limitations.

1 It is affected by capital structure (which may not be controllable by the management being measured).
2 It adversely affects certain types of decisions (investment and divestment) because it is a percentage.
3 Equity investment create biases unless the analyst distinguishes between investments in the equity of a subsidiary and investments in real assets.

The second limitation applies equally to ROI as it does to ROE. Other terms commonly used instead of ROI are RONAE (return on net assets employed) ROFE (return on funds employed), ROCA (return on capital applied), and ROA (return on assets).

For some purposes it is useful to break ROI into two components (this is sometimes referred to as the Dupont formulation):

$$\text{ROI} = \frac{\text{Income after tax after interest}}{\text{Assets}}$$

$$\text{ROI} = \frac{\text{Income}}{\text{Sales}} \times \frac{\text{Sales}}{\text{Assets}} = \frac{\text{Income}}{\text{Assets}}$$

The term, Sales/Assets, measures the degree (intensity) of asset utilization.

The term, Income/Sales, measures profitability. The product of the two terms gives the return on investment.

The primary contribution of ROI (or ROE) is that management is held responsible for the capital used. However, it does this in a somewhat flawed manner (may adversely affect certain types of investment or asset retention decisions).

ROI AND INVESTMENT DECISION-MAKING

The use of ROI to evaluate performance can affect investment decisions because the manager knows that after accepting an investment its operations will affect the performance measurement. This leads to an incentive for the divisional (or other subcomponent manager) to reject investments that yield a lower return on investment than is being earned on the currently owned assets. Not only should top management be concerned with the return on investment of the assets being used, but also with the growth in assets and income. Growth as well as return on investment is important. A static division earning a 30 percent ROI may well be evaluated as being badly managed, whereas it may be concluded that a division that is growing and earning 15 percent is well managed.

The investment decision problem resulting from a desire to maintain a high ROI highlights the necessity of not relying on one performance measure ROI (or something else) but rather bringing in sufficient measures to restrain the impulse of persons trying to circumvent the control-evaluation system. Any defense of ROI should be based on a desire to use it as one of several methods of evaluating the performance of investments after acquisition, not so that it may be used to evaluate the desirability of undertaking investments. ROI is not an acceptable method of evaluating perspective investments.

THE CASE OF THE RESOURCE BENEFITING THE FUTURE

Measures of performance used in an incorrect manner will tend to lead to incorrect conclusions. There is a necessity to improve the measures and to use them intelligently. Consider the case of a division manager of a timber company who has the opportunity to invest in 500,000 acres of prime timberland. The catch is that the trees on the land are all seedlings and they will not mature for 30 years. It is agreed by the planning group that the land is a good investment. However, the manager's performance is measured using return on investment. The manager knows that the land will increase the denominator (investment) now, but it will be 30 years before the numerator (income) is also increased. Since the division manager only has five years to go before retirement, the investment in land is rejected.

This case has a reasonable solution. The land should be excluded from the investment base in measuring performance unless the value increment is allowed to affect the income. Unless something like this is done, there will be distortion in the investment performance analysis, and thus distortion in the investment decision-making criteria applied.

Now consider a plant being built with excess capacity to service the expected demand of year 2030. Is the normal performance measurement scheme capable of taking this situation into consideration? Probably it is not. Generally accepted accounting principles do not do a good job of assigning expenses of long-lived assets through time.

THE COMPUTATION OF INCOME AND ROI

It is widely known that straightline depreciation or accelerated depreciation, except in very well-defined and specific situations, will distort measures of ROI. Also, the ROI that results for each year will differ from the internal rate of return computed at the time of acquisition, even when the expected results are realized. The suggestion to solve this difficulty is simple to state although the implementation would require innovation. If the return at time of acquisition is correctly computed (that is, a discounted cash flow procedure is used), and if the ROI each year after acquisition is correctly computed, the two measures will be identical for each year of operation, if the events forecasted at the time of the decision actually occur. To accomplish this objective, depreciation must be defined in a theoretically correct manner, and the computation of depreciation must be consistent with this definition.

Define depreciation to be "the decrease in value of the investment during the time period." Although the definition becomes more complex if there are additional investments made during the period, it can be used to compute the income that is used in the ROI calculations if we assume that this complexity does not exist. The following example is used to show that return on investment, when properly calculated, gives useful performance measurement information.

EXAMPLE 15.1

Assume the net cash flows (and net revenues) associated with an investment costing $3,000 at time zero are:

Time	Cash flow
1	$1,300
2	1,200
3	1,100

The firm uses straight-line depreciation and the investment has a required return of 10 percent and an internal rate of return of 10 percent. There are zero taxes. Table 15.1 shows the income and investments for each of the three years of use.

Table 15.1 *Income and investments for each of the three years in use*

Year	Cash flows or net revenues	Depreciation	Income	Investment at the beginning of the period	ROI (Income divided by investment)
1	1,300	1,000	300	3,000	0.10
2	1,200	1,000	200	2,000	0.10
3	1,100	1,000	100	1,000	0.10

Table 15.2 *Present value of the investment at three moments in time*

Time	Flows	Period 1 present value factors	Time 0 present values	Period 2 present value factors	Time 1 present values	Period 3 present value factors	Time 2 present values
1	1,300	0.9091	1,182				
2	1,200	0.8264	992	0.9091	1,091		
3	1,100		826	0.8264	909	0.9091	1,000
			$V_0 = 3,000$		$V_1 = 2,000$		$V_2 = 1,000$

The fact that each year has identical returns on investment equal to the internal rate of return of the investment seems to be a coincidence. However, if we inspect Table 15.2 which shows the present value of the investment at three moments in time (V_i is the value at time i), we see that in each period the decrease in value is $1,000 (the value of V_3 is zero), and that in this very special situation the use of straightline depreciation is correct (if the cash flows are different, the depreciation schedule would be different).

The present value at time 0 is $3,000, at time 1 $2,000, and at time 2 $1,000.

Define depreciation expense to be the change in economic value. The procedure works with any set of cash flows. There need not be distortion in ROI because of the method of depreciation. In this simplified example, the internal rate of return of the investment is equal to the firm's time value of money, and the cash flows of each period equal the net revenues. Different assumptions would add to the complexity of the calculations, but these complications can be solved.

COMPARING ROI AND ECONOMIC INCOME

Economic Income offers several significant advantages over ROI as a performance measure.

First, and most importantly, the use of ROI might discourage division managers from accepting investments that offer returns that are larger than the firm's required risk adjusted returns, but that are less than the ROI the division is currently earning. If the new investment is accepted the division's ROI will be decreased.

EXAMPLE 15.2

A division is now earning $30,000,000 (a perpetuity) on an investment of $100,000,000.

$$ROI = \frac{30,000,000}{100,000,000} = 0.30$$

The division can invest an additional $50,000,000 and earn 0.15 ROI or $7,500,000 per year (a perpetuity) on this investment. The firm's required return for this investment is 0.10, thus the investment is economically desirable. Should the division accept the new investment? If it is accepted the division's ROI is reduced to:

$$ROI = \frac{37,500,000}{150,000,000} = 0.25$$

Based on the adverse effect on the division's ROI, a manager might reject this economically desirable investment. This problem does not arise if economic income is used. The economic income before the new investment is:

Initial economic income = 30,000,000 − 10,000,000 = $20,000,000

The interest cost is 0.10 of $100,000,000 or $10,000, 000. Note that the captial charge is computed on the total investment not just the portion financed by debt. After the investment the economic increases by $2,500,000:

New economic income = 37,500,000 − 15,000,000 = $22,500,000

Based on economic income there is an incentive for the division manager to accept the desirable investment.

SUMMARY OF COMPLEXITIES

The complexities of applying economic income to performance measures or compensation are:

1   the method of calculating depreciation expense;
2   the choice of the capital charge;

3   the changing value of assets (e.g. inflation or technological change);
4   risk;
5   non-controllable factors affecting the measure.

Risk

Assume a division manager concludes that an investment is desirable from the firm's perspective, but has too much risk from the viewpoint of the manager. How can the system accommodate this complexity?

Let us assume that an investment has a $100,000,000 cost. The division initiating the investment can cope with some risk and is willing to invest $20,000,000 of its funds. The firm's other divisions and the head office would be given the chance to buy the $80,000,000 of remaining equity. Assuming investors can be found then 0.8 of the gains or losses would be transferred to the entities investing the $80,000,000. Only 0.2 of the gains and losses would be charged to the division operating the asset for purposes of compensation calculation.

Another problem arises because unsystematic (firm specific) risk affects managers' decisions, but only systematic (market) risk is relevant to a well diversified investor. Assume an investment with zero systematic risk and a large amount of unsystematic risk has a 0.20 internal rate of return (the default free rate is 0.05) but has a 0.5 probability of losing $100,000,000. Investors want the investment accepted. The manager might not be willing to accept the 0.5 probability of a large loss.

One solution is to base a significant part of the manager's compensation on market performance. The market wants the investment accepted.

A second solution is to guarantee that the manager will not be adversely affected if the project is unsuccessful (this solution has flaws since it removes a significant incentive for the manager).

The third solution is for the higher levels of management (or even the board) to make the decision to accept.

Finally, we should admit that there are some situations where unsystematic risk will affect decisions. This is not all bad since some investors are not well diversified and may welcome the rejection of a high risk investment.

Non-controllable factors

An oil company executive's firm is losing $500 million. The CEO is in danger of being fired. Then oil prices double and the firm makes $800 million. It is the same manager managing in the same way but the economic environment has changed.

Obviously some attempt could be made to separate out the factors that are and are not controllable by the manager. But this is difficult, and is apt to introduce subjective measures into the evaluation.

This problem introduces the qualitative aspects of performance evaluation.

SUMMARY OF ECONOMIC INCOME ADVANTAGES

Economic income offers three primary advantages.

1   Any investment with a positive net present value or an internal rate of return larger than the firm's required return will have economic incomes with the same net present value.
2   The use of economic incomes will tend to not affect adversely investment or divestment decisions.
3   With the use of economic income management is charged for the capital it uses, thus has a direct incentive to use capital economically.

Economic income is a very sensible measure.

TIME ADJUSTED REVENUES

Instead of the cash flows and the revenue measures being identical for each period, let us assume that the timing of cash flows and revenue recognition differ (an example would be the receipt of cash advances in payment for a service not yet performed). The cash flows in period 1 are $1,300 but the revenues are $1,430 in period 2.

Continuing the initial example, assume that the following facts apply:

	Period			
	1	2	3	4
Cash flows	1,300	1,200	1,100	
Revenues		1,430	1,320	1,210

The revenue used is a sophisticated "time adjusted revenue" measure rather than a naïve measure coinciding with the amount of cash received. For example, if $1,430 were to be received at time two but the revenue is to be recognized at time one, the time adjusted revenue at time one would be $1,300. In like manner, expenses would have to be time adjusted.

Applying the present value factors for a 0.10 discount rate to the revenue measures, we obtain the following values at different points in time and the resulting economic (present value) depreciation.

Time	Value	Change in value depreciation (appreciation) for period
0	3,000	
1	3,300	−300
2	2,200	1100
3	1,100	1100
4	0	1100

The computations of accounting incomes and returns on investments for each period would be:

Period	Revenues	Depreciation	Income	Investment	Investment
1	0	−300	300	3,000	0.10
2	1,430	1,100	330	3,300	0.10
3	1,320	1,100	220	2,200	0.10
4	1,210	1,100	110	1,100	0.10

It should be noted that time adjusted revenues and cash flows are very much tied together and that they rigorously define the depreciation expense (the decrease in value) of a period.

A NON-ZERO NET PRESENT VALUE

The basic example used in this chapter sets the net present value of the investment equal to zero, that is, the internal rate of return of the investment is equal to the time value factor for the firm. Obviously this will only rarely be the case. We expect most investments to have expected returns in excess of their required return. For example, let us assume that the investment costs $2,760 instead of $3,000. The net present value of the investment at the time of acquisition is $240 using 0.10 as the discount rate, and its internal rate of return is 0.15. There are several possible paths we can take. Two methods will be described. The most straightforward solution would be to use 0.15 (the internal rate of return) as the rate of discount to compute the depreciation expenses and returns on investment.

Using 0.15 as the rate of discount we obtain:

Period	Revenue	Depreciation	Income	Investment	ROI
1	1,300	844	416	2,760	0.15
2	1,200	919	281	1,876	0.15
3	1,100	957	143	957	0.15

283

The primary difficulty with this solution is that the time value of money is defined to be 0.10 not 0.15. Thus the values of the investment at each time period using 0.10 are greater than those shown in the table. A second solution is to adjust immediately the value of the investment to $3,000, the present value of the benefits, despite the fact that the investment cost is only $2,760. This procedure would not be acceptable for conventional financial accounting purposes because of the implicit threat of manipulation, but it would be acceptable for internal managerial purposes. It is a very appealing procedure because it is relatively simple and yet is correct from the standpoint of accounts properly reflecting present values.

INCENTIVE CONSIDERATION

The use of book value based on cost to measure the investment (the denominator in the ROI calculation and the basis of the interest cost in the economic income calculation) or even the use of estimates of price level adjusted cost is subject to severe criticism. There is no reason why a system based on values estimated by management cannot be used for internal purposes instead of cost based conventional accounting. Here we have an opportunity to apply ingenuity to bypass a valid objection by managers to cost based accounting. Rather than asking an accountant or another staff person to supply the number on which the managers are to be judged, let us ask the managers to supply the value estimate. The procedure would be simple. Take a set of eligible managers and ask them to "bid" periodically for the assets they want to manage and for which a change in management is appropriate. The manager whose bid is accepted takes the asset, and the dollar amount of the bid becomes the accounting base for performance valuation. If the manager bids too high, that manager gets the asset but will find it hard to meet the return on investment requirements defined by the manager. If the manager bids too low, a competing manager will win, or alternatively the "board" may reject the bid and ask for revised bids. There is one major difficulty with this procedure. Managers can rig the time shape of projected earnings so that early targets can be easily attainable. This tendency would have to be controlled by the top managers awarding the bid. Large deferred benefits would be greatly discounted.

The procedure would have many advantages. It would establish an investment base whose measure is acceptable to both the operating manager and to the top level of management (the former sets the value, the latter must accept it). The accountant serves the very important and proper function of supplying relevant information that is used by the managers in making their respective judgments and bids. The ROI and economic income measures are improved because the investment base is appropriate to the specific investment and manager being evaluated rather than being the result of a series of historical accidents (such as the year of purchase and the method of depreciation). Most important, it requires managers to set, describe, and quantify their plans for the utilization of the assets. It would tie together planning, decision-making, and control.

EXAMPLE 15.3

Assume an investment costing $3,000 is expected to have the following benefit stream:

Period	Benefits
1	$1,100
2	1,210
3	1,331

The firm's cost of money is 0.10 and is equal to the investment's discounted cash flow internal rate of return. The results using conventional accounting and straight-line depreciation will be (assuming the actual benefits are equal to the expected):

Period	Revenues	Straight line depreciation	Income	Book investment	ROI
1	1,100	1,000	100	3,000	0.03
2	1,210	1,000	210	2,200	0.105
3	1,331	1,000	331	1,000	0.331

The first year's operations are not acceptable.

Defining economic (or present value) depreciation expense to be the decrease in value of the asset, the results would be:

Period	Revenues	Present value	Income	Book and value investment	ROI
1	1,100	800	300	3,000	0.10
2	1,210	990	220	2,200	0.10
3	1,331	1,210	121	1,210	0.10

The economic depreciation calculations are:

$V_0 = 3,000$ value at time 0 $d_1 = 3,000 - 2,200 = 800$ depreciation of period 1

$V_1 = 2,200$ value at time 1 $d_2 = 2,200 - 1,210 = 990$ depreciation of period 2

$V_2 = 1,210$ value at time 2 $d_3 = 1,210 = 1,210$ depreciation of period 3

The distortion caused by conventional depreciation accounting can be increased by assuming no (or very low) benefits until period 3. The operating results of the early years would appear to be even worse than in the example.

PVA

Present value accounting (PVA) has three important elements:

1 include a charge for all capital that is used;
2 Write off (depreciate) capital assets using economic (present value) depreciation;
3 adjust any of the accounting measures of asset value or income as needed to better reflect the measure of performance.

CASH FLOW RETURN ON INVESTMENT

Recognizing the inadequacies of conventional depreciation accounting, some managers have attempted to solve the problems by using ash flow return on investment. Since cash flows are used to evaluate the investment, why not use them to evaluate the investment's performance?

Define the cash flow return on investment to be:

$$\frac{\text{Cash flow}}{\text{Investment}}$$

Although the computation seems to be appealing because depreciation is not computed, unfortunately, the computation merely makes a bad analysis worse. Using the above example and straight line depreciation for valuing the investment, we would obtain:

Period	Cash flow	Investment	Cash flow ROI Cash flow/investment
1	1,100	3,000	0.37
2	1,210	2,000	0.61
3	1,331	1,000	1.33

Some firms have actually tried to use the historical measures as required returns for additional investments. You should note that for an investment yielding 0.10 over its life, the cash flow ROI's for the three years are 0.37, 0.61, and 1.33. The measure greatly overstates the ROI the asset is earning.

Another difficulty of the measure is that it will tend to bias management in favor of capital intensive methods of production, because capital cost is omitted from the numerator of the performance measure.

It is better to use the conventional ROI with income (after depreciation) in the numerator than to use the above cash flow ROI, which is extremely difficult to interpret and has no theoretical foundation. The use of the measure illustrated above will get management into one or more interpretive difficulties. There are alternative methods of using cash flow return on investment that are improvements over the method illustrated. Each method must be appraised based on the details of its calculations.

PLANNING IMPLICATIONS

The fact that there may be a conflict between the investment criteria used and the performance measures means that corporate planning must take into consideration the fact that all desirable investments (from the corporate standpoint) may not be submitted upward. It would be naïve to expect a division manager to recommend a plant with 60 percent excess capacity where the analysis of mutually exclusive investments indicates that this is the best alternative, if the performance measures for a period of five years will be adversely affected by the choice. Rather the division manager is likely to bury this type of alternative so the board of directors is not confused by the number of alternatives and this "undesirable" alternative specifically.

The board of directors has a similar type of conflict when it evaluates major investments that satisfy normal investment criteria, but have adverse effects on the ROI's and earnings per share of the next few years because of conventional accounting.

One alternative is to use the recommended investment criteria and hope to modify the accounting conventions that cause the distortions in measuring actual performance. Alternatively, failing that, management can attempt to explain the characteristics of the investment (and the deferred benefits) to the investing community. However, there would be the problem of excessive optimistic announcements by management, and even well-intentioned forecast may be wrong. It is not likely that management will want to report that present earnings are understated and that future earnings will justify an investment that is currently reported as being nonprofitable.

The best solution would be for the accounting profession to encourage a wide range of depreciation methods, if these methods are justified by the economic characteristics of the investment. Currently too rapid write-off (R&D, Training, Plant & Equipment) leads to:

1   bad measures of performance;
2   non-optimal decisions.

ROI is widely used as a managerial performance measure but it may lead to wrong decisions and is affected by write-off assumptions. Economic Income combined with economic depreciation is very good. It can be made as complex or simplified as you wish.

IN CONCLUSION: TO MEASURE PERFORMANCE

You *can* use ROI (never by itself) but Economic Income is strongly recommended.

To make investment decisions

You cannot use ROI as conventionally computed.

Market measures

The stockholders are the firm's residual owners and they are interested in the stock's total return. How well did the CEO perform? What was the stockholder's total return?

Unfortunately, the stock's return does not always track the CEO's performance, especially in the short run. A company may do well but the stock might go down (e.g. with an interest rate increase). Nevertheless, tying a CEO's compensation to the stock's market performance is sensible (as long as it is not the only basis of compensation calculation).

There are several comparisons that can be made. The firm's performance can be compared to a defined target return, the return earned by the market, or the returns earned by a set of comparable firms.

In addition to relating compensation to the current year's performance, it is reasonable to reward today's managers for performance for the next ten years. It is desirable to give today's managers an incentive to make decisions with a concern for the future.

Earnings per share (EPS)

EPS is frequently used to evaluate the performance of top management. There are four difficulties with its use:

1   Accounting conventions are sometimes not consistent with the change in economic well being that took place in the time period.
2   EPS as conventionally computed does not include a cost for the equity capital used.
3   EPS is a measure for this time period and does not consider the effects on future EPS of actions taken today (particularly relevant when there are mergers and acquisitions).
4   EPS may be less informative than levels of and change in cash flows from operations.

All four of the above difficulties are linked. They all imply that one has to use EPS measures (and changes) carefully and intelligently, but they do not lead a conclusion that a firm's EPS is not a relevant input into a financial analysis of a firm's well-being.

Non-accounting quantitative measures

Given the generally accepted criticisms of accounting (e.g. it is cost based) most analysts of business affairs search for other quantitative measures to complement (or replace) the accounting measures. These measures include:

1 market penetration;
2 customer satisfaction;
3 employee satisfaction and turnover;
4 units sold;
5 diversity measures (number of hired);
6 quality control measures (percentage of defectives).

If reliable useful measures can be obtained, then the non-accounting quantitative measures can take their place with the accounting measures. In many situations they will be more important than the accounting measures since they give a hint of the level of future incomes.

Qualitative measures

There are many qualitative aspects that enter into an evaluation. For example, a manager might be reliable and easy to work with. A manager might have laid the foundation for future growth by hiring talented future managers and researchers. Does the manager generate enthusiasm and creativity? There are many ways that a manager can enhance the firm's future profitability and value by actions that do not lead to current profitability. Has the manager enhanced the firm's reputation among customers and suppliers? To evaluate a manager's performance it is necessary to consider these factors.

In addition, firms can have goals other than a measurable effect on profitability. This might involve the local society or society in a broader sense (e.g. the environment beyond the legal requirements).

Intangibles are factors not subject to ready easy measurement but they can be important to the long run success of a corporation.

289

SOME GENERALIZATIONS REGARDING COMPENSATION

The basis of compensation should be both the operating results of the manager's specific unit and the results of the firm. The manager should have joint loyalties.

The basis of compensation should include quantitative objective measures, but not to the exclusion of qualitative measures. The existence of the qualitative considerations reduces the tendency of managers to game the system.

To some extent a portion of the manager's compensation should be deferred and be tied to the firm's future performance. We want managers to make decisions from a long-run perspective.

The basis of compensation should be both accounting measures and market measures. The return earned by the shareholders should affect the compensation of the managers.

REWARDING BAD PERFORMANCE

A very large company wanted to reward management if the firm did well. Since the firm could borrow at 0.08 and with a 0.35 corporate tax rate the after tax cost was 0.052, it would pay a performance bonus based on the amount that the firm's income (before interest) exceeded 0.052 of the capital (debt and equity) being used.

The hurdle for the bonus should be the firm's cost of capital times the amount of capital, not the after tax cost of debt.

GLOBAL BUSINESS ASPECTS

This chapter offers techniques for measuring performance that become the basis for determining managerial compensation.

There is one set of issues for which we do not give good answers. Why does managerial compensation (compared to other compensation) change through time? Also, why are the levels of managerial compensation different in different parts of the world?

CONCLUSIONS

Annual or quarterly accounting profits can be a poor measure of what has been accomplished by management during any relatively short period of time. Also, it is often difficult to assign responsibility for a deviation from the profit objective. Many economic events with long-run implications are not recorded by the accountant. One should not use any performance measure without considering a wide range of factors, including those factors not normally appearing in the management information system.

In many cases the ROI or economic income should not be used because it is too difficult to measure either the income or the investment. The measure of ROI can and should be improved. It can then be used to gain an impression of managerial performance, but the use of ROI should always be supplemented by the superior performance measure, economic income. This is necessary if the top management of a firm is to attempt to measure the effectiveness if the utilization of assets controlled by persons at different levels of the firm. The economic income is a very useful means of accomplishing this, if efforts are made to measure income and investment in a useful way.

Although performance measurement is a difficult task when exact reliable measures of income and investment are not feasible, it is necessary that all managers evaluate persons for whom they are responsible. As guides and indicators, ROI and economic income have their uses when the manager controls revenue, expense, and the amount of investment.

PROBLEMS

1   Equipment that costs $27,233 has an expected life of three years and an expected salvage value equal to the expected removal cost. Assume a time value of money of 0.05. It is expected that the net cash flows of each year are equal to $10,000.

Required

Compute the depreciation expense, the income, and the return on investment for each of the three years of life. Assume the cash flows are earned at the end of each year, and that we want a reasonable return on investment.

2   Equipment that costs $24,869 has an expected life of three years and an expected salvage value equal to the expected removal cost. Assume a time value of money of 0.10. It is expected that the net cash flows of each year are equal to $10,000.

Required

Compute the depreciation expense, the income, and the return on investment for each of the three years of life. Assume the cash flows are earned at the end of each year, and that we want a reasonable return on investment.

3   Equipment that costs $9,992 has an expected life of three years and an expected salvage value equal to the expected removal cost. Assume a

291 ▓

time value of money of 0.10. It is expected that the net cash flows of each year are:

1 $10,000
2 1,000
3 100

Required

Compute the depreciation, the income, and the return on investment for each of the three years of life. Assume the cash flows are earned at the end of each year, and that we want a reasonable return on investment.

4 Equipment that costs $8,430 has an expected life of three years and an expected salvage equal to the expected removal cost. Assume the time value of money is 0.10. It is expected that the net cash flows of each year are:

1     $100
2   1,000
3   10,000

Required

Compute the depreciation, the income, and the return on investment for each of the three years of life. Assume the cash flows are earned at the end of each year, and that we want a reasonable return on investment.

5 (*Continue* 4) Now assume the equipment of problem 4 costs $7,418 and the investment has an internal rate of return of 0.15.

Required

Compute the return on investment for each of the three years of life. Assume the cash flows are earned at the end of each year.

6 Assume a firm requires a 0.10 internal rate of return. An investment has the following set of cash flows (an internal rate of return of 0.10):

Time	Cash flow
0	−2,487
1	1,000
2	1,000
3	1,000

Define V_i to be the value at time i. At time 0 the value is $2,487 therefore $V_0 = 2,487$. At time 3 (after the last cash flow) the value is zero thus $V_3 = 0$. The calculation of the values of V_i using the 0.10 internal rate of return is:

1     $1,000 \times 0.9001 =$ 909
2     $1,000 \times 0.8264 =$ 827   0.9091   909
3     $1,000 \times 0.7513 =$ $\underline{751}$ 0.8264 $\underline{827}$ 0.9091   909
           $V_0 = 2,487$ $V_1 = 1,736$ $V_2 = 909$

Required

a. Compute the economic (present value) depreciation.

b. Compute the ROI for each year if the straight line depreciation method is used.

c. Compute the ROI for each year if the economic depreciation (PV) method is used.

d. Compute the cash flow ROI for each year (cash flow divided by net investment using economic depreciation).

e. Compute the ROI using the Gross Investment and depreciation expense using the straight line assumption.

f. Compute the Economic Income for each year with an interest cost of 0.10. Use present value depreciation (with a 0.10 discount rate).

7   Assume an investment with the following cash flows:

Time	Cash flow
0	−3,000
1	1,300
2	1,200
3	1,100

The firm's cost of money is 0.10.

Required

a. Compute the present value depreciation

b. Compute the ROI for each year.

8   Assume an investment with the following cash flows:

Time	Cash flow
0	−3,000
1	1,500
2	1,300
3	1,200

The firm uses straight line depreciation and has a 0.10 cost of money.

Required

a. Compute the Economic Income for each year.

b. Compute the NPV using cash flows.

c. Compute the NPV using the Economic Incomes.

d. What happens if the firm earns more than $1,500 in the first year?

293

9 Assume the following facts apply to two divisions.

	Div. A		Div. B	
Revenues	$10,000		$10,000	
Cost of goods sold	4,000		7,000	
Operating margin	6,000	0.60	3,000	0.30
Assets used	$24,000		$6,000	

The firm has 0.10 cost of money. The assets have a five-year life and straight line depreciation is used.

Is Div A or Div B doing a better job (based on the evidence)?

10 An investment costs $7,500 and will earn cash flows of $2,000 for perpetuity. This is a 0.267 IRR. For this type of investment a 0.30 equity return is required. Debt costs 0.10. There are no taxes.

What might management do if it wants the investment accepted?

11 A corporate has three decisions:

ROE

A   0.30

B   0.20

C   0.15

The Board requires a ROE of 0.16. The cost of equity is 0.10, but the Board recognizes that there are corporate costs not included in the divisional ROE.

What should management do?

12 Two divisions (A and B) are currently each earning $120 on an equity investment of $200.

$$ROE = \frac{120}{200} = 0.60$$

The management is pleased with the excellent performance. The firm has a 0.10 cost of equity.

An investment costing $500 promises to increase income by $70 to $190.

$$\frac{190}{700} = 0.271$$

A accepts the investment and lowers its ROE to 0.271.

B rejects the investment and maintains its 0.60 ROA.

Which of the division managers deserves a promotion?

13 Investment A has an initial outlay of $100 and $150 of cash flows at time one. There is an additional outlay of $150 at time one and $150 of benefits at time two (this investment is not optional).

Investment B has an initial $100 outlay and $50 of benefits at time one. There is an additional $50 outlay at time one and $150 of additional benefits at time two.

Which investment is more desirable?

14 An investment with a life of three years costing $3,000 promises the following cash flows:

Time	Cash flow
0	1,450
1	1,300
2	1,150

The firm uses a 0.10 discount rate.

a. Compute the economic incomes for each year using straight line depreciation.

b. Compute the NPV using the cash flows.

c. Compute the NPV using the economic income.

d. Compute the NPV using the cash flows and a discount rate of 0.15.

e. What is the IRR of the investment?

15 What is a reasonable goal (objective) for management to set?

16 A large manufacturing company was not happy with its ROI measures since the accounting for long-lived assets was so arbitrary. It decided that a better measure of performance would be a cash flow ROI (income before depreciation divided by the non-depreciated investment). It then compared the cash flow ROI to the firm's required return for investments.

The firm was comparing apples and oranges. One cannot compare a cash flow ROI and a cost of capital.

Consider the following investment which has a discounted cash flow IRR of 0.10

Time	Cash flow
0	−3,000
1	1,300
2	1,200
3	1,100

What are the cash flow ROI's for each year?

DISCUSSION QUESTION

ROI is a popular calculation. Evaluate its use.

BIBLIOGRAPHY

Aboody, D., M. E. Barth, and R. Kasznik, "SFAS No. 123 Stock-Based Compensation Expense and Equity Market Values," *Accounting Review*, April, 2004, pp. 251–75.

Biddle, G., R. Bowen, and J. S. Wallace, "Does EVA Beat Earnings?" *Journal of Accounting and Economics*, 24, December, 1997, pp. 301–36.

Chakraborty, A., M. Kazarosian, and E. A. Traham, "Uncertainty in Executive Compensation and Capital Investment: A Panel Study," *Financial Management*, winter, 1999, pp. 126–39.

Dodd, J. and S. Chen, "EVA: A New Panacea?" *Business and Economics Review*, 42(4), 1996, pp. 26–8.

Gaver, J. J. and K. M. Gaver, "Compensation Policy and the Investment Opportunity Set," *Financial Management*, spring, 1995, pp. 19–32.

Gibbons, R. and K. J. Murphy, 1992, "Does Executive Compensation Affect Investment," *Journal of Applied Corporate Finance*, summer, 1992, pp. 99–109.

Indjejikian, R. J., "Performance Evaluation and Compensation Research: An Agency Perspective," *Accounting Horizons*, 13(2), 1999, pp. 147–57.

Jensen, M. C. and W. H. Meckling, "Theory of the Firm: Managerial Behavior, Agency Costs, and Ownership Structure," *Journal of Financial Economics*, October, 1976, pp. 305–60.

Jensen, M. and K. Murphy, "Performance Pay and Top Management Incentives," *Journal of Political Economy*, 98, 1990, pp. 225–64.

Ryan, H. E., Jr. and R. A. Wiggins, III, "The Interactions Between R&D Investments and Compensation Policy," *Financial Management*, spring 2002, pp. 5–30.

Chapter 16

Fluctuating rates of output

If a thing cannot go on forever, it will stop.
(Herbert Stein, Nixon Adviser, quoted by Michael M. Weinstein,
New York Times, September 9, 1999)

Special investment decision-making problems occur if a firm is faced with a choice of two or more types of equipment to produce a product and if there will be fluctuations in the rate of output at which the equipment will be operated. The fluctuations in output may be the result of seasonal fluctuations in demand (which cannot be offset by storage), or the fluctuations may result because the rate of output is increasing or decreasing through time. We shall illustrate the case in which the fluctuations are due to seasonal factors. A similar, but more complicated, analysis would apply if demand were growing or falling. This analysis will assume the product cannot be inventoried. The opportunity to have inventory carried over to satisfy peak demand would make the analysis more complex; but would be preferred by the firm. The decision is to determine the type or amount of equipment that should be purchased.

When there are fluctuations in the rate of output and if the demand must be satisfied, the amount of productive capacity needed will be determined by the peak rate of output required. The seasonal pattern will determine whether the average amount produced during the year is a high or low percentage of the available capacity.

Assume there are several types of equipment available, some types having higher fixed costs, but lower variable costs, than others. For equipment that operates at a high average percentage of capacity, equipment with high fixed costs and low variable costs is likely to have lower total costs. If the seasonal fluctuations are such that the equipment operates at a low average percentage of capacity during the year, the equipment with lower fixed costs and higher variable costs is more likely to have lower total costs. The intuitive choice must be verified with calculations.

We will first determine which one of several types of equipment a firm should use if all the types of equipment can do the same task but have different costs for different levels of operations. Each type of equipment will have a fixed and variable cost component. The second problem to be solved is a situation where the production needs vary, and it is possible to buy one or more different types of equipment to service different levels of demand. Demand through time will be looked at as a pyramid where different horizontal slices of the pyramid can be serviced with different types of equipment. The objective will be to minimize the total cost for the year.

A PLANT LIMITED TO ONE TYPE OF EQUIPMENT AND TWO ALTERNATIVES

Suppose there is a choice between manual and semiautomatic equipment and that a plant is to be built in which only one type of equipment can be used. The product cannot be stored and all demand must be satisfied. (The basic cost data on the equipment are shown in Table 16.1.)

Assume the manual equipment has a capital cost of $27,244 and a life of 20 years. With a 0.10 discount rate the annual equivalent cost (AEC) is $3,200. The value of $B(20,0.10)$ is 8.5136, the present value of a 20-year annuity with a 0.10 discount rate.

$$AEC = \frac{27,244}{8.5136} = \$3,200.$$

The annual capacity of this equipment is 40,000 units.

The fixed cost per unit of capacity is $0.08.

$$\text{Fixed cost per unit} = \frac{3,200}{40,000} = 0.08.$$

Table 16.1 Basic data on equipment types

Type	Capacity per machine (units per year)	Annual equivalent fixed costs per machine ($ per year)	Annual equivalent fixed costs per unit of capacity ($ per unit of capacity)	Variable costs per unit ($ per unit)
Manual	40,000	3,200	0.08	1.00
Semiautomatic	100,000	33,000	0.33	0.50

Assume the semiautomatic equipment cost $202,771 and has a life of 10 years. The annual equivalent cost is $33,000.

$$AEC = \frac{202,771}{6.1446} = \$33,000.$$

This equipment has an annual capacity of 100,000 units.
The fixed cost per unit of capacity is $0.33.

$$\text{Fixed cost per unit} = \frac{33,000}{100,000} = \$0.33.$$

We wish to compare the total costs of a plant containing either all manual equipment or all semiautomatic equipment. The total costs consist of the fixed costs and variable costs. The semiautomatic equipment has higher fixed costs per unit of capacity than the manual, but this type of equipment has lower variable costs ($0.50 compared to $1.00). The fixed cost per unit calculation assumes that the equipment is replaced with identical equipment at the same cost.

If the equipment were to be operated at full capacity, the total costs of the semiautomatic equipment would be $0.33 + 0.50 = $0.83 per unit of output, while at full capacity the total costs of the manual equipment would be $0.08 + 1.00 = $1.08 per unit of output. Thus, at full capacity, the semiautomatic equipment has lower per unit cost. But if the equipment is not going to be operated at full capacity, the conclusion might be different.

Operating at capacity we have:

Manual $3,200 + 40,000(1) = $43,200 or $1.08 per unit
Semiautomatic $33,000 + 100,000(0.50) = $83,000 or $0.83 per unit

Table 16.2 gives the required production for each quarter. Assume the firm wants sufficient capacity to produce 4,000,000 units per year (so that the 1,000,000 units of the third quarter sales peak may be serviced). Two possibilities are:

$$\text{Number of manual units} = \frac{4,000,000}{40,000} = 100 \text{ units.}$$

$$\text{Number of semiautomatic units} = \frac{4,000,000}{100,000} = 40 \text{ units.}$$

Remember that only one type of equipment will be purchased and annual capacity of 4,000,000 units is required.

299

Table 16.2 Seasonal production pattern

Period	Required production (units per quarter)
January–March	200,000
April–June	600,000
July–September	1,000,000
October–December	600,000
Total annual production	2,400,000

Next we want to compute the firm's annual production at which there is indifference in total costs between the two types of machines. The variable cost is $1 per unit for the manual equipment and $0.50 per unit for the semiautomatic.

Let Q be the average rate of output for which there is indifference. There will be 100 units of the manual equipment or 40 units of the semiautomatic equipment acquired. To be indifferent the firm must produce Q units during the year where the total costs are equal:

$$1Q + 3,200(100) = 0.5Q + 33,000(40)$$
$$Q = 2,000,000 \text{ units}$$

With $Q = 2,000,000$ the indifference fraction of capacity utilized is 0.5 since the capacity is 4,000,000 units.

Figure 16.1 shows the total annual costs for the two alternatives.

The total annual costs for 2,000,000 units of output is:

$$TC = 1(2,000,000) + 3,200(100) = \$2,320,000 \text{ (for manual)}$$

or

$$TC = 0.5(2,000,000) + 33,000(40) = \$2,320,000 \text{ (for semiautomatic)}$$

Figure 16.1 shows that if the fraction of capacity utilized exceeds the indifferent fraction of 0.5, then semiautomatic equipment is preferred. If the fraction of capacity utilized is less than 0.5, then manual equipment is less costly. With capacity of 4,000,000 units, the fraction is 2,000,000 units.

To determine the capacity needed and the average percentage of capacity at which the plant will be operated, the seasonal pattern of production must be known. This information is contained in Table 16.2 for the example. The annual capacity is four times the maximum production of any quarter.

Since the actual fraction of capacity to be utilized is 2,400,000/4,000,000 or 0.60, the semiautomatic plant would be preferred. At that level of utilization, since the break-even amount of utilization is 0.5, the semiautomatic plant has a lower total cost.

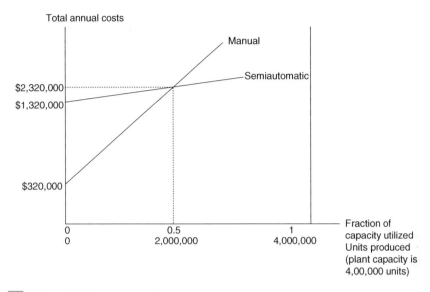

Figure 16.1 *Total costs for the two alternatives*

Assume the product cannot be inventoried. To determine the equipment capacity required, we observed the highest rate of production that is required. In the third quarter, 1,000,000 units must be produced. A plant that could produce 1,000,000 units in one quarter could produce 4,000,000 units in one year if it operated at a level rate. So the required capacity for the plant is 4,000,000 units per year. Because of seasonal fluctuations in demand, the actual output will be only 2,400,000 units per year. Therefore, the average fraction of capacity utilized will be 0.60, or 60 percent. If utilization is above 50 percent, the semiautomatic equipment has the lower cost. The above solution assumes that the units must be produced in the quarter in which they are needed (the 1,000,000 units needed in the third quarter must be produced in the third quarter), and all demand must be satisfied.

OPTIMUM EQUIPMENT MIX

So far we have assumed that only one type of equipment will be utilized. But in some circumstances several types of equipment can be used in the same plant or productive system. For example, a power-generating system may contain atomic energy generating capacity, fossil fuel capacity, and gas turbine capacity.

In designing a plant that contains several types of equipment, the objective is to have the correct amount of each type of equipment in order to minimize costs. Once a plant has been constructed, it must be operated in the most economical way possible. This requires utilizing the equipment with the lowest variable costs per unit to the maximum extent possible (that is, to its capacity) before resorting to equipment with higher variable costs per unit.

Suppose that we consider the problem of designing an optimum plant to meet the required rates of production specified in the previous example, where the required production capacity (shown in Table 16.2) can be divided between the two types of equipment – manual and semiautomatic – in whatever amounts are considered desirable. The annual capacity of 4,000,000 units is defined by the 1,000,000 units needed in the third quarter.

Note that three rates of production occur. In order of size, they are 200,000, 600,000, and 1,000,000 units per quarter. Based on these required rates of production, the required capacity of the plant can be divided into three components. The first component represents the base demand of 200,000 per quarter (equivalent to 800,000 per year). The second component represents the increment in capacity necessary to increase production from 200,000 per quarter to the next level of 600,000 per quarter. So this component requires a capacity of 400,000 per quarter (equivalent to 1.6 million per year). The final component represents the increment in capacity necessary to increase production from 600,000 per quarter to 1,000,000 per quarter. This component, therefore, also requires a capacity of 400,000 per quarter. The two types of equipment available are shown in Table 16.1.

The plant needs three different capacity increments, one of 200,000 units per quarter and two of 400,000. To select the appropriate type of equipment for each of these increments, we need to know for what fraction of the year each will be used. To determine this, we must develop a production schedule for the plant. Table 16.3 represents a format that could be used for this purpose. Each row represents one quarter of the year. The first column shows the level of production required during each quarter.

Table 16.3 Seasonal production schedule form for multiple equipment plant – analysis for first increment (thousands)

Quarter	Required production for quarter	Production increments
January–March	200	200
April–June	600	200
July–September	1,000	200
October–December	600	200
Total annual production	2,400	800
Total annual capacity	4,000	800
Average fraction of capacity used	0.6	1.0

What types of equipment should be used? The first equipment increment is determined by the need to meet the base demand. Table 16.3 shows the production plan if increment 1 is used to satisfy all of the required production in the first quarter and part of the requirements of the other quarters. Since 200,000 units can be produced by increment 1, it will operate at 100 percent of capacity in all four quarters. This is larger than the indifference amount $p = 0.50$ determined previously; thus, the optimal type of equipment for this increment is semi-automatic equipment. This equipment is less costly when operated at or above 50 percent of capacity. Since an annual capacity of 800,000 units is required for a 200,000 quarterly increment, and each semiautomatic machine has a capacity of 100,000 units per year, or 25,000 per quarter, we need eight semiautomatic machines for the increment of 800,000 units per year (200,000 per quarter).

Table 16.4 shows the status of the production plan when equipment increment 2 is assigned. It is not needed in the first quarter, but it is needed in the remaining three quarters, and it will operate at 75 percent of capacity. Semiautomatic equipment is also optimal for this component since the utilization is larger than 50 percent. Sixteen more machines are required since 400,000 units are required and each machine can produce 25,000 units in a quarter.

In Table 16.5 we note that additional output beyond increment 2 is required only in the third quarter. This output will be supplied by equipment increment 3. This increment will be used on the average at only 25 percent of its capacity (only used in one quarter). Therefore, manual equipment will be less expensive for this increment. Since an annual capacity of 1,600,000 units is required for this increment, and each manual machine has a capacity of 40,000 units per year, 40 manual

Table 16.4 Step 2: seasonal production schedule for multiple equipment plant – analysis for first two increments (thousands)

Quarter	Required production	Equipment increment	
		1	2
		Quarterly capacity per increment	
		200	400
		Production increments	
January–March	200	200	
April–June	600	200	400
July–September	1,000	200	400
October–December	600	200	400
Total annual production	2,400	800	1,200
Total annual capacity	4,000	800	1,600
Average fraction of capacity used	0.6	1.0	0.75

Table 16.5 *Final version seasonal production schedule for multiple equipment plant – analysis for all three increments (thousands)*

Quarter	Required production	Equipment increment 1	2	3	
		Quarterly capacity per increment 200	400	400	
		Production increments			Plant total
January–March	200	200			200
April–June	600	200	400		600
July–September	1,000	200	400	400	1,000
October–December	600	200	400		600
Total annual production	2,400	800	1,200	400	2,400
Total annual capacity	4,000	800	1,600	1,600	4,000
Average fraction of capacity used	0.6	1.0	0.75	0.25	0.60

machines are needed for this increment to produce 400,000 units in the third quarter. Each manual machine can produce 10,000 units in a quarter. The final production plan is summarized in Table 16.5. This plan will minimize production costs. The manual equipment is only used in the July–September quarter.

MORE PERIODS OR MORE EQUIPMENT TYPES

The procedure illustrated can be used to handle problems with any number of periods or any number of equipment types if the required conditions are satisfied.

Two conditions are important with respect to the choice of periods. First, the periods must all be of equal length. Second, although the rate of production may vary from period to period, within any given period it must be constant.

These conditions can usually be satisfied by taking the shortest period of time during which production is constant as the period length. If day-to-day variations in production are relevant, then pick a day as the period length and divide the year into 365 one-day periods. Production in some periods can be zero.

If the number of periods is large, it might be convenient to modify the production planning tables such as is exhibited in Table 16.3. As illustrated, they contain one line per period. With daily periods, this would make a very long table. A modification of Table 16.3 that is useful in this case is to design the table so that each line represents a different level of production. For example, in Table 16.5 there are two periods, the second and fourth quarters, in which the level of production is the same.

Table 16.6 is an example of a production plan in which these two quarters have been combined into one line. The line for which required production is 600 per period represents two periods, and for each increment used, the production per increment is equal to the capacity of the increment times two (the number of periods).

Table 16.6 Final version seasonal combining quarters with equal production – seasonal production schedule for multiple equipment plant (thousands)

Number of periods	Required production	Equipment increment			
		1	2	3	
		Capacity per increment			
		200	400	400	
		Production per increments			Plant total
One	200	200			200
Two	600 × 2 = 1,200	400	800		1,200
One	1,000	200	400	400	1,000
Total annual production	2,400	800	1,200	400	2,400
Total annual capacity	4,000	800	1,600	1,600	4,000
Average fraction of capacity used	0.6	1.0	0.75	0.25	0.60

CONCLUSIONS

This chapter has illustrated a method of choosing the optimal mix of equipment types when output fluctuates. If desired, algebraic solutions can be prepared that arrive at the same solutions as those illustrated. If products can be stored, the solutions become more complex, and complex mathematical solutions are necessary.

PROBLEMS

1   A new plant is to be built to produce widgets. Three types of facilities are available: fully automated, semiautomated, and manual. All three facilities have the same expected life and produce widgets that are identical in every respect. Only the cost characteristics of the three types of facilities vary. The fixed and variable costs for each type of facility are shown in Table 16.7. All costs are on an after-tax basis, and fixed costs are expressed in terms of equivalent monthly after-tax flows, after allowing for tax savings from depreciation.

Table 16.7 *Cost characteristics of alternative types of widget production facilities*

Facility type	Fixed cost per month for enough capacity to produce one widget per month	Variable cost per widget
Fully automated	$20	$25
Semiautomated	14	35
Manual	6	60

To prevent thefts, each widget is produced with the customer's name engraved on it. The name must be engraved before the widget is assembled. This makes it impractical to maintain an inventory of completed widgets. Instead, production must take place after orders are received. Since demand follows a seasonal pattern, widget production is seasonal as well. The anticipated seasonal pattern of demand (and production) is described in Table 16.8. The peak demand is 600 units per month, and a capacity sufficient to meet this peak demand is needed.

Table 16.8 *Estimated demand for widgets*

Month	Estimated demand (units)
January	100
February	100
March	300
April	400
May	600
June	500
July	400
August	400
September	300
October	200
November	200
December	100
Estimated annual demand	3,600

Average monthly demand $(\overline{Q}) = \dfrac{3,600}{12} = 300$

Suppose that the plan to be built can contain only one type of facility:

a.   Using the demand forecast in Table 16.8 which type of facility should be chosen?

b.   If Table 16.8 were modified by raising estimated demand in all months from March through August to 600 units per month, which type of facility should be chosen?

c.   If peak demand (and therefore the required capacity) remained at 600 units per month (Q_{max}), how low would average monthly demand ($\bar{Q}$) have to fall before the manual facility would be chosen?

d.   Let the total monthly cost of using the ith type of facility be

$$T_i = F_i Q_{max} + \bar{Q} V_i$$

where

T_i = total monthly cost of the ith facility

F_i = fixed cost per month for enough capacity to produce one widget per month using the ith facility

V_i = variable cost per unit for the ith facility

Q_{max} = maximum level of demand per month (equals required capacity)

($\bar{Q}$) = average level of demand (widgets per month)

Make a rough graph with T_i on the vertical axis and $\bar{Q}$ on the horizontal axis. Sketch in the first equation for each of the three facilities on this graph, using $Q_{max} = 600$ and the values of F_i and V_i from Table 16.7.

e.   What generalizations can you make about the levels of Q at which each type of facility would be used?

2   The DEF Company uses a batch-process method to produce product S. The product is very perishable, so inventories are small, and production is geared closely to current sales. There are two seasons for product S, each season lasting six months. The DEF Company has been producing and selling product S at the rate of 30 million units per month during the busy season – which lasts for six months. During the six-month slow season, production and sales are only 10 million units per month.

The company is convinced it could sell an additional 5 million units per month during the six-month busy season if additional capacity were available. There is no question that these additional sales would be profitable. There is a question of what type of production equipment should be installed.

The company has a choice between two types of equipment. The batch–process equipment is the same as the equipment currently in use. The continuous process equipment was developed a few years ago. Both types are known to be reliable and to produce equally high-quality products. Cost data are given in Table 16.9.

307

Table 16.9 Cost data

Cost item	Batch process	Continuous process
Equivalent annual fixed costs: dollars per year per unit of capacity capable of producing one unit of product per month	$2.20	$5.00
Variable costs of producing one unit of product	0.09	0.50

   a.   What action would you recommend to the DEF Company if there were no cost savings or salvage values associated with scrapping existing batch capacity?

   b.   What action would you recommend if fixed costs of $1 per year per unit of capacity could be avoided by scrapping existing batch capacity?

3   The Giant Motor Car Company is considering the size that would be most desirable for its next assembly plant. We shall assume that there are the following two alternatives (Table 16.10).

Table 16.10 Two alternative sizes

Item	Large plant	Small plant
Initial costs	$20,000,000	$4,000,000
Out-of-pocket cost savings per year, assuming the assembly of different numbers of cars per year		
100,000 cars		1,000,000
200,000 cars	0	
300,000 cars	2,000,000	
400,000 cars	4,000,000	

A forecast of car sales indicates the demand for automobiles (Table 16.11) assembled in this plant. The company has a cost of money of 10 percent. For purposes of this problem, assume an income tax rate of zero. Which one of the two plants is the more desirable?

4   Power plant design: A power system is to be constructed. Three types of generating equipment are available. Their costs are given in the following table. *Note:* There are 8,760 hours in a year. A kilowatt-hour of electricity is produced by operating a kilowatt of capacity for one hour (Table 16.12).

Table 16.11 Predicted demand for automobiles

Time	Number of cars
First year after completion of the plant	100,000
Second year after completion of the plant	200,000
Third year after completion of the plant	200,000
Fourth year after completion of the plant	300,000
Fifth year and thereafter for the expected life of the plant of 20 years	400,000

Table 16.12 Types of generating equipment and costs

Type	Fixed costs: $per year per kW of capacity	Operating costs: $per kW-hour of electricity produced
Nuclear	$200.00	$0.01
Coal	100.00	0.04
Gas	40.00	0.07

Suppose only one type of generating equipment could be used to supply an electrical need with the following characteristics:

Maximum demand, 1,000s of kilowatts:	500
Total output per year, 1,000s of kilowatts-hours	2,630,000

How much capacity should the plant have and which type of plant should be selected?

5   (*Continue 4*) Suppose more than one type of generating unit could be used to supply electrical needs with the characteristics shown in Table 16.13.

Table 16.13 Generating units and characteristics

(1) Rate of output 1,000s of kW	(2) Hours plant operates at that rate	(3) = (1) × (2) Total output 1,000s of kW-hours
500	260	130,000
400	1,200	480,000
350	2,000	700,000
300	2,300	690,000
200	3,000	600,000
Totals	8,760	2,630,000

309

An economic design for this system will include the following:

Type of equipment	Required capacity 1,000s of kWs
Nuclear	—
Coal	—
Gas	—

BIBLIOGRAPHY

Bland, Robert R., "The Cogeneration Project at Cornell University," *Facilities Manager*, spring 1987, pp. 19–24.

Childs, P. D., S. H. Ott, and A. J. Triantis, "Capital Budgeting for Interrelated Projects: A Real Options Approach," *Journal of Financial and Quantitative Analysis*, 33, September 1998, pp. 305–34.

Coleman, J. R. Jr. and R. York, "Optimum Plant Design for a Growing Market," *Industrial and Engineering Chemistry*, January 1964, pp. 28–34.

Coleman, J. R. Jr., S. Smidt, and R. York, "Optimum Plant Design for Seasonal Production," *Management Science*, July 1964, pp. 778–85.

Masse, P. and R. Gibrat, "Applications of Linear Programming to Investments in the Electric Power Industry," in J. R. Nelson (ed), *Marginal Cost Pricing in Practice*, Englewood Cliffs, NJ: Prentice-Hall, 1964, pp. 215–34.

Nguyen, D. T., "The Problem of Peak Loads and Inventories," *Bell Journal of Economics*, spring 1976, pp. 242–50.

Seshinski, Eytan and Jacques H. Dreze, "Demand Fluctuations, Capacity Utilization, and Costs," *American Economic Review*, December 1976, pp. 731–42.

Trigerorgis, L. and S. P. Mason, "Valuing Managerial Flexibility," *Midland Corporate Finance Journal*, 5, spring 1987, pp. 14–21.

Chapter 17

Investment decisions with additional information

The chances of success of a given investment (whether of capital or labour) depend on the efficiency with which all those who work in the same firm cooperate with the factor in question.

(J. R. Hicks, "The Theory of Uncertainty and Profit," *Economica*, May 1931, p. 185)

In this chapter we consider the possibility of obtaining more information before making a decision. When this possibility exists, the decision-maker needs to compare the costs and benefits of additional information in order to decide if obtaining it is worthwhile. If additional information is collected, the decision-maker must combine the new information and the previously existing information to arrive at a decision. The main topics considered in this chapter are (1) deciding if additional information is worthwhile, and (2) using additional and prior information in decision-making. This is a special form of the real option problem discussed earlier in this book.

A substantial part of the chapter considers situations in which a single type of equipment can be installed in many different locations, and the possibility exists of obtaining additional information by trying the equipment in one location before deciding what to do about the other locations. This can be thought of as a procedure for deciding whether to obtain additional information.

Let us consider a procedure that is typical of the decision-making process in many companies. At each decision-making level before the final one, three alternatives are possible: accept, reject, or send to a higher level. Sometimes rules are specified for the various levels. For example, at level 1 the accept alternative may not be available on proposals involving outlays of more than $10,000. At level 2 the accept alternative may not be available on proposals of more than $50,000. Rules such as this require that larger investments must be submitted to higher levels before an accept decision is possible. Since additional information and analysis are presumably available at each higher level, a decision (or requirement) to submit a proposal to a higher level may be interpreted as a decision to obtain additional information. Usually, a proposal can be rejected at any level. Thus, a decision at one level to submit a proposal to the next higher level implies there is not enough information to lead to a rejection decision.

THE OPPORTUNITY TO REPLICATE

Multiplant firms have an opportunity to innovate sequentially that is frequently not available to firms with single plants (unless the single plant has multiple production lines). Consider the development of a new type of equipment in a multiplant company. The analysis for a single unit of equipment indicates a negative net present value. But there is some probability that the equipment would be successful and would have a positive present value in any subsequent use. In other words, there is uncertainty about the outcome, but there is some probability that it would be a desirable investment. In such a situation, the possibility that the firm may miss out on a technological break-through may be sufficient motivation for trying the equipment as a sample investment.

If one unit of the equipment has a positive expected net present value, then some may argue that all the units should be acquired for the entire firm. On an expected value basis, this is true. Under conditions of uncertainty and risk aversion, however, trying the investment on a small scale may help to determine if the forecasted good result will actually occur. If the result is good, then the remainder of the units can be purchased. The cost of this policy is delay of the investment, however, which may be a disadvantage.

An objective of this chapter is to emphasize that an apparently poor individual investment might be good when considered in the broader context of subsequent investments. We also want to show explicitly why the greater the uncertainty, the better it is to obtain additional information, perhaps by trying an investment if the investment can be replicated (although we are not sure the investment should be undertaken until the calculations are made). Some managers will prefer to apply intuition, making the decision without the type of calculations that will be illustrated. The model, however, does incorporate the expert judgment of the decision-maker into the decision process. Most important, the model allows the decision-maker to focus on the relevant variables.

THE BASIC MODEL

The example will show an investment sampling process where the investment, although initially not desirable, may appear acceptable after considering the consequent opportunity of obtaining additional information and the possibility of sequential decisions. The requirement that there be a probability of an improvement of the initially undesirable investment follows logically.

We shall assume initially that undertaking one investment would allow perfect information about what could happen if all the identical investments were undertaken. Imperfect information complicates the analysis but does not change the basic logic of the possibility of undertaking an investment with a negative expected net present value because of the information that can be obtained. There is an "option" to replicate the investment.

Figure 17.1 shows the basic model with the net present value of the profits that could be lost by *not* undertaking the investment. V_0 is the random variable "net present value" with mean $\overline{V}_0$ for one unit of equipment, and V_b is the break-even present value. V_b is the value when V_0 is equal to zero; therefore, V_b is defined to be equal to zero.

Since the expected value of V_0, $\overline{V}_0$, is to the left of V_b, the correct decision seems to be to reject the investment. If the investment is rejected, the present value is zero. But V_0 is a random variable with a probability density function. This is a "prior betting distribution." If we are certain that the net present value of the investment is $\overline{V}_0$ (the variance of the distribution is zero), then the investment should be rejected. If there is some probability that V_0 is larger than V_b, then further analysis is required.

The line "NPV for all units" defines the relationship of the net present value potential of all the equipment for different values of the random variable. The slope depends on the number of units of equipment in which the firm can feasibly invest. The more units of equipment, the steeper the slope.

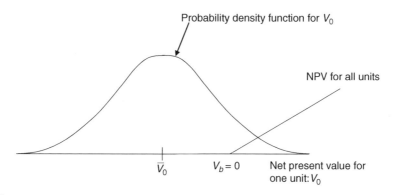

Figure 17.1 *The basic decision model*

EXAMPLE 17.1

Consider an investment that costs $1,000,000. The outcome can either be e_1 or e_2 in all future years.

Event	Probability of event	Annual outcome (a perpetuity)	Present value	Net present value	Expected present value
e_1	0.4	$150,000	$1,500,000	$500,000	$200,000
e_2	0.6	40,000	400,000	−600,000	−360,000
					−$160,000

The time-value factor (required return) is 10 percent. The expected present value of the benefits is $840,000 ($1,500,000 × 0.4 + $400,000 × 0.6). Since the investment costs $1,000,000 and the expected benefits are only $840,000, the investment has a negative net present value of $160,000. The investment should be rejected on an expected present value basis.

Assume the firm has the opportunity to undertake 11 of these investments. There is a 0.4 probability that each unit of equipment will perform to produce a net present value of $500,000, or $5,500,000 in total. There is a 0.6 probability of 11 units losing $600,000 per unit, or $6,600,000 in total. The expected value is negative ($5,500,000 × 4 − $6,600,000 × 0.6 = −$1,760,000), and investing in 11 units is not desirable. But we can modify the uncertainty by buying one item of equipment for a cost of $1,000,000 and a $160,000 negative expected value. Figure 17.2 shows the decision tree that evolves.

The firm invests in the ten additional units of equipment only if event e_1 occurs and the equipment proves to have positive value. If the process is desirable, each investment adds $500,000 of net present value. Multiplying the $500,000 by the 11 machines, we find the upper path leading to $5,500,000 of present value. With no additional information the expected value of path e_1 *for* 11 units is 0.4($5,500,000) = $2,200,000.

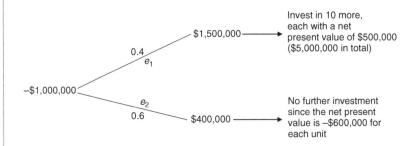

Figure 17.2 *Investment decision tree*

EXAMPLE contd.

There is 0.6 probability that the first machine will lose $600,000. This will occur if the event is e_2. This is an expected cost of $360,000. Because the expected value of the e_1 path is $2,200,000 and the expected value of the e_2 path is $-$360,000, we would advocate undertaking the single investment in the hope that we will find out that e_1 is the true state of the world. The expected net present value of trying an investment is $1,840,000.

If we changed the probabilities so that e_1 had a probability of 0.7 and e_2 a probability of 0.3 then $\bar{V}_0$ the expected NPV per unit of equipment, would be $170,000 (that is, $0.7 \times 500,000 - 0.3 \times 600,000$) per unit or $1,870,000 if all 11 units were accepted. Even though the investment is desirable, trying one unit first is still advisable if there is not a long time delay between investments. If all 11 units are undertaken, there is a 0.3 probability that all the investments will turn out to be bad. The expected loss is 11 times as large as the loss from trying one unit. The expected loss from trying one unit is $0.3 \times 600,000$ or $180,000. If all 11 of the investments are undertaken, the conditional loss can be $6,600,000 and the expected loss $1,980,000. The advantage of trying one unit is that the conditional loss is limited to $600,000. If there is no cost of delay, the sampling of investments is desirable.

DELAYING OTHER INVESTMENTS

The sampling procedure (trying one investment before proceeding with the remainder) will result in the delay of other investments, adversely affecting their present values since delay is a cost.

Should this cost be considered? Consider first investments that would otherwise be rejected. If the alternative were to make all the investments now or do nothing, the firm might do nothing. The firm wants to obtain information as cheaply as possible, which is accomplished by undertaking a minimum-sized investment that gives the necessary information. While the expected value of this investment, taken by itself, is negative, the information that can be gathered justifies undertaking the investment. Delaying the investments decreases their net present value, but it also enables the firm to avoid investing funds in undesirable investments. On balance, the sampling of one investment is a desirable strategy if the investment would otherwise be rejected and if the expected present value of all investments is positive and the cost of delay is not large.

Next consider a situation in which $\bar{V}_0$ is greater than zero. If the alternatives were to accept all the investments now or do nothing, the firm would accept all the investments now. However, if feasible, sampling may still be desirable. However, in deciding whether to accept the investments now or wait and collect additional information by sampling (or some other method), the expected decline in present value due to waiting should be considered as an additional cost.

So far we have considered situations in which it may be desirable to obtain additional information. One way of collecting additional information is to sample. This is possible when there are many similar investments, and trying one may provide information about the value of the others. If additional information were costless and could be obtained instantly, it would always be desirable whenever there was uncertainty about the investment's outcome. But in most situations, obtaining information by sampling or further study takes time and has a cost. The decision-maker needs to compare the expected value of the additional information with its expected cost to determine whether it is better to decide now or to wait while additional information is collected.

In the examples considered so far, if additional information is obtained, it is decisive. There is no question about what decision should be made. Additional information is sometimes ambiguous. With ambiguous information the computations become too complex for the objectives of this chapter.

THE WINNER'S CURSE

A very interesting investment evaluation problem arises because investment decisions are normally made based on uncertain information. The problem is most easily explained in the context of an auction, but it is more general than an auction and can occur with any investment proposal.

Assume a situation where the true (but unknown) net present value of an investment is a negative $10,000,000, and the investment should be rejected. There is less than probability one that an accurate forecast will be made. Management has to make its decision based on observations and forecasts that are not reliable. There is uncertainty. Assume that there are three outcomes (forecasts) that can occur, as follows:

Forecast of NPV	Probability of forecast
−$25,000,000	0.25
−10,000,000	0.50
+5,000,000	0.25

If the forecast is −$25,000,000 or −$10,000,000, the project will be rejected. However, if the forecast is $5,000,000, the project will be accepted because of the faulty information.

Assume an analyst comes up with the negative $25,000,000 forecast, and the management decides to reject. Later, a second analyst prepares another forecast and this time comes up with a negative $10,000,000, and again there is a reject decision. Finally, after several more analysts also conclude that the investment is not desirable, an analyst forecasts a positive $5,000,000 NPV. If top management is not informed of the first set of analyses, all recommending rejection, but is only given the final analysis recommending acceptance, there is an unacceptable bias introduced. Top management has to be told the results of all the studies, or it will be misled into making a wrong decision.

While the preceding situation is not an auction, it has consequences that are similar to an auction situation. Assume that a situation similar to the investment is put out to bid. Most of the firms invited to bid will reject the investment based on their forecasts, but if there is a large number of bidders some of the bidders will forecast a $5,000,000 NPV. They will bid somewhere between $1 and $5,000,000, and one of them will win the investment.

With a large number of bidders and an opportunity to have different opinions of the future, based on public information, it is possible that excessively optimistic firms tend to win the bid. If so, these firms will suffer a "winner's curse." After suffering losses from bidding too high, we can expect firms to scale down their bids because of a realization that this curse exists.

If a firm has special information regarding the probable outcome, the high bidder may be able to justify the magnitude of its bid. But this is a different situation than was just described.

There are two solutions to the curse associated with auctions. One is to scale down the amount you are willing to bid below the expected value. This will result in your losing some good investments, but it will also result in losing some bad investments. The second solution is to avoid auctions. A major corporation, heavily engaged in acquiring firms, will not engage in an unfriendly acquisition because of the possibility of becoming engaged in an auction (a bidding war). This "arbitrary" rule has a sound theoretical foundation.

CONCLUSIONS

The existence of uncertainty not only raises the possibility that an investment that is acceptable may turn out to be undesirable, but also that an investment that seems to be unacceptable may turn out to be desirable if additional information is obtained. The value of the additional information must be balanced against the cost of the information and the cost of delay.

PROBLEMS

1   A piece of equipment costs $10,000,000. There is 0.3 probability of it being a success with a present value of $15,000,000 (a NPV of $5,000,000).

There is 0.7 probability of it having a present value of $6,000,000 (a NPV of −$4,000,000).

Should the equipment be acquired?

2 (*Continue 1*) Assume the corporation could use six of these units if they were to be successful. Should the firm acquire one to determine if it should acquire five more?

DISCUSSION QUESTION

George Beardsley and Edwin Mansfield studied the experience of a giant multinational corporation in forecasting the profitability of new products (*Journal of Business*, January 1978). Specifically, the corporation recorded a forecast of the profitability of each new product at that time it was decided to produce the product. Each new product was post-audited nine years later, when its actual profitability was known. Beardsley and Mansfield found that "the initial forecasts tend to be relatively optimistic in cases where actual profits were small and relatively pessimistic in cases where actual profits were large. Specifically, the forecasts underestimated the profitability of ... new products where they exceeded about $1 million, and overestimated the profitability of less profitable new products" (pp. 130–1).

An interpretation of these results is listed here. Indicate whether you believe the interpretation given is necessarily wrong or is not necessarily wrong (that is, it could be correct). Give a brief explanation of your reasons.

The initial forecasts of new products whose true profitability was less than $1 million may be unbiased estimates of the true profitability of those new products.

BIBLIOGRAPHY

Berk, J. B., "A Simple Approach for Deciding When to Invest," *American Economic Review*, 89, 1999, pp. 1319–26.

Bierman, H., Jr., and V. R. Rao, "Investment Decisions with Sampling," *Financial Management*, fall 1978, pp. 19–24.

Marsh, P. R. and R. A. Brealey, "The Use of Imperfect Forecasts in Capital Investment Decisions," *Proceedings of the European Finance Association 1975*, Amsterdam: North Holland, 1975.

Merrett, A. J. and A. Sykes, *The Finance and Analysis of Capital Projects*, New York, John Wiley, 1963.

Miller, Edward M., "Uncertainty Induced Bias in Capital Budgeting," *Financial Management*, fall 1978, pp. 12–18.

——, "The Cutoff Benefit–Cost Ratio Should Exceed One," *Engineering Economist*, 46(4), 2001, pp. 312–19.

Noble, Donald J., "Using Simulation as a Tool for Making Financial Decisions in an Uncertain Environment," *Industrial Engineering*, 20, January 1988, pp. 44–8.

Pruit, Stephen W., and Lawrence Gitman, "Capital Budgeting Forecast Biases: Evidence from the Fortune 500," *Financial Management*, spring 1987, pp. 46–51.

Schlaifer, R., *Analysis of Decisions Under Uncertainty*, New York, McGraw-Hill, 1969.

Smidt, S., "A Bayesian Analysis of Project Selection and of Post-Audit Evaluations," *Journal of Finance*, June 1979, pp. 675–88.

Statman, M. and T. T. Tyebjee, "Optimistic Capital Budgeting Forecasts: An Experiment," *Financial Management*, fall 1985, pp. 27–33.

Yawitz, J. B., "Externalities and Risky Investments," *Journal of Finance*, September 1977, pp. 1143–9.

Chapter 18

Investment timing

The way some people talk about modern football [soccer], anyone would think the results of just one game [were] a matter of life and death. They don't understand. It's much more serious than that.

(Bill Shankly, manager of Liverpool's defending champions in the English Soccer League, quoted in *New York Times*, January 13, 1974, p. 7)

In this chapter the term *timing* will be used to refer to decisions about when a new investment should be undertaken and when an investment should be terminated. For certain categories of investment decisions, the question of when to start is critical. An investment may seem desirable if the only alternatives considered are to accept or reject the investment now. If the alternative undertaking the investment at a later time is possible, however, that may be preferable to accepting the investment now. In principle, the timing problem could be handled by considering a mutually exclusive set of alternatives: undertaking the investment now or undertaking it one period from now, or two periods from now, and so on. But more efficient techniques for approaching this problem are available. We shall consider some of these in this chapter.

Frequently, in making investment decisions, the useful life of the investment must be determined. This can be accomplished in at least two ways. First, the desirability of an investment may be affected by the estimate of its useful life. Thus, the estimated profits from growing trees are critically affected by assumptions about when they will be harvested. Second, the decision to undertake an investment may require terminating an existing investment. Planning a new crop of trees may require harvesting the existing stand of trees; buying a new car may require selling the old one. In these cases, the salvage value of the existing investment, the costs incurred, and the revenues that might be received if it were not scrapped now will influence the decision of when to undertake the new investment.

In timing problems, the relationships among the cost and revenue streams of the various alternatives are frequently complex. But the basic principles at work are not difficult to understand. To help focus on the basic principles, we begin with a simple example of class of situations in which timing problems are important, but no investment decision is involved.

BASIC PRINCIPLES OF WHEN TO START AND STOP A PROCESS

In Figure 18.1, the curve R represents the contribution to overhead (revenues minus variable costs) that will be generated at time t of a day if the business is operating. The line F represents the fixed costs that could be avoided if the business were not operating at time t. On the x-axis, time is measured from 0 to 24 hours.

Let us first make the assumption that the business must operate around the clock if it operates at all. For example, a private waterworks company may be obliged to operate 24 hours a day if it operates at all, although the contribution to overhead produced during certain nighttime hours does not even cover the avoidable fixed costs of the time period. In these circumstances, there is no timing problem, and it will be economically desirable to operate only if the total area under the R curve exceeds the total area under the F curve over the entire cycle of operations.

In some situations, the manager is free to decide when to operate and when to shut down. For example, the owner of a supermarket may not be obliged to operate on a 24-hour basis. In this situation, considering only explicit revenues and costs, the enterprise should operate only during the interval in which the contribution to overhead from operations exceeds the avoidable fixed costs of operating. In Figure 18.1, this interval extends from t_1 to t_2. The operations should start at t_1 and ceases at t_2, since between these points $R \geq F$; in other words, the contribution exactly equals or is larger than the avoidable fixed costs.

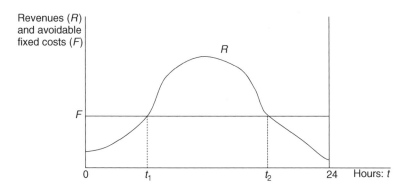

Figure 18.1 *Contribution to overhead at time t*

The conclusion from this discussion is that if there is a choice about when to start and stop an operation, it should be started when revenues equal costs and are rising; it should be stopped when revenues equal costs and are falling.

As we shall see, this simple rule is really applicable to all the situations considered in this chapter. In applying the rule, the conceptual difficulties center on identifying the relevant revenues and costs.

GROWTH-TYPE INVESTMENTS[1]

Suppose that a firm owns a tract of land and is considering planting a crop of trees. It wishes to determine the net present value of that investment. Since the net present value will depend on when the trees are harvested, an estimate of that date is required. If the firm makes the investment, it is prepared to harvest the trees when the net present value of the investment is maximized.

Let

$f(t)$ = net revenue (net of all finishing expenses) obtainable if the trees are harvested in year t

$f'(t)$ = slope of $f(t)$, that is, the rate at which the obtainable net revenue is changing with time

i = market rate of interest

C = cost of planting trees

e^{-it} = present value factor for time t (continuous discounting)

$P(t)$ = net present value of the investment

The net present value of the investment if the trees are harvested at time t is

$$P(t) = -C + f(t)e^{-it} \qquad (18.1)$$

The determination of the optimum time to harvest the trees can be seen in Figure 18.2. The curve $f(t)$ increases rapidly at first, and then more gradually. The path $a_0 a_1$ is a time-transformation curve that enables us to convert future values into present values at the assumed interest rate i. The present value of a_1 is a_0. The time transformations have a slope equal to i times their height. (The height is $a_0 e^{-it}$.) The present value of the investment is maximized if the trees are harvested at t_2, when the value of the trees is a_1 and the net present value of the investment equals $(-C + a_0)$. At t_2 the $f(t)$ curve is tangent to the time-transformation curve.

---

1 This section is based in part on Harold Bierman, Jr., "The Growth Period Decision," *Management Science*, February 1968, pp. B-302–B-309.

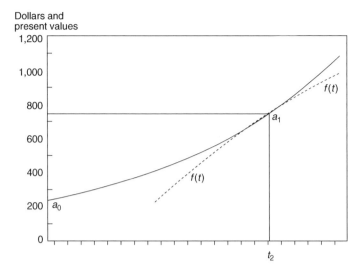

Dollars and
present values

Figure 18.2 *Determination of optimum time to harvest trees*

It follows that the slope of the $f(t)$ curve is $if(t_2)$ at t_2. Thus, the value of t at which the present value of the investment is maximized must satisfy the condition that

$$f'(t) = if(t) \qquad (18.2)$$

Recall the $f'(t)$ is the increase in the value of the trees per year. Thus, the condition for an optimum is that the increase in the value of the trees must equal the interest rate (i) times the value of the trees $f(t)$.

In terms of the criteria for stopping referred to in the previous section, the increase in the value of the trees if they are not harvested corresponds to the revenues, and the interest on the value of the trees corresponds to the fixed cost that can be avoided by harvesting.

The rule previously described for the decision when to harvest ignores the value of the land on which the trees are planted. If additional land of comparable quality is available in any desired amount at no cost, the economic value of the land is zero, and it need not be considered in deciding when to harvest trees growing on it.

Ordinarily, the value of the land must be considered. Suppose that if the trees were harvested, the cleared land would be worth an amount $V(t)$ at time t. In that case, the avoidable fixed costs incurred if the trees are allowed to grow include both the interest on the value of the standing trees and the interest on the value of the land. In these circumstances, a necessary condition that should be met when the trees are harvested is

$$f'(t) = i[\,f(t + V(t))] \qquad (18.3)$$

Of course, the value of the land depends on its best available use. For example, if the best use of the cleared land is for farming, then $V(t)$ should reflect the value of the land in that use.

Suppose, however, that the best use of the land is growing trees. Then, although equation (18.3) is still formerly correct, it is not very helpful. When the trees are harvested depends on the value of the land, but the value of the land will depend on how often trees growing on it can be harvested. In this case, the value of the land must be determined on the assumption that the trees growing on it are harvested and replanted at intervals that maximize the value of the land.

We have already shown that the present value of one crop of trees, if they are harvested at the end of t years, is

$$P(t) = -C + f(t)e^{-it} \tag{18.1}$$

Assume that the trees are replanted every T years and that we want to determine the optimum value of T. Let $V(T)$ be the present value of the land under these circumstances. Then $V(T)$ is determined as follows:

$$V(T) = P(T) + P(T)e^{-iT} + P(T)e^{i2T} + P(T)e^{-i3T} + \ldots$$

Summing this infinite series,

$$V(T) = \frac{P(T)}{1 - e^{-iT}} = \frac{-C + f(T)e^{iT}}{1 - e^{iT}} \tag{18.4}$$

We want to select the value of T that maximizes $V(T)$. It can be shown that the value of T that maximizes $V(T)$ satisfies the following relationship:

$$f'(T) = i[f(T) + V(T)] \tag{18.5}$$

In practice, the best way to determine the optimum value of T is by trial and error, using equation (18.4). Equation (18.5) is basically the same as equation (18.3), but in deriving equation (18.5) we have given an explicit method of determining the value of the land in its use for growing trees. Equation (18.5) can be interpreted as follows: A crop of trees should be allowed to grow until the annual increase in its value declines to the point where it is equal to the market interest rate times the sum of the value of the current stand of trees plus the present value of the future crops of trees that could be grown on the land if the present crop were harvested now.

EXAMPLE 18.1

Trees growing at 0.15 per year are currently worth $1,000,000. The land on which the trees are growing has alternative uses that are worth $5,000,000 (this value is not expected to change). Money is worth 0.10. Should the trees be harvested now? If harvested now, the value of harvesting now and the value of the land = $1,000,000 + $5,000,000 = $6,000,000. If harvested one year from now, the present value would be:

$$\text{Present value of harvesting on one year} = \frac{\$1,000,000(1.15) + \$5,000,000}{1.10}$$

$$= \$5,590,000$$

Harvesting now is better.

Change the alternative use value of the land to zero. Does this change the decision?

Value of harvesting now = $1,000,000

$$\text{Present value of harvesting on one year} = \frac{\$1,000,000(1.15)}{1.10} = \$1,045,000$$

Delaying a year is now better than harvesting immediately.

The fact that the land had an alternative use worth $5,000,000 caused the harvest to be accelerated. This alternative use can be thought of as being future generations of trees waiting to be planted. The sooner they are planted, the sooner they will have value.

A more complex and more accurate solution would have the alternative use value of the land be a function of the length of time the trees are allowed to grow. This is illustrated next.

EXAMPLE 18.2

THE TREE FARM

Suppose that the net realizable value of a crop of trees on a particular parcel of land as a function of their age is given by the following equation:

$$F(t) = -350 + 60t - 0.5t^2 \quad \text{for} \quad 10 \leq t \leq 30 \tag{18.6}$$

Assuming a continuously compounded rate of interest of 5 percent per year, Table 18.1 shows the net realizable value of the trees from one growth cycle at various ages, their percentage rates of growth, and their present value. If the value of the land is ignored, the trees would be allowed to grow until the rate of increase in their value declines to 4.83 percent (in year 23). This is the age at which the present value of the realizable value of the trees is maximized ($242.52).

Suppose, however, that after the trees were harvested, the land could be sold for $500 or converted to some other use whose value was $500. In that case, the amount realized when the trees were harvested would be $500 + f(t).

Table 18.1 Net realizable value from one growth cycle

Age of trees (yr) (t)	Realizable value f(t)	Annual increment in value f'(t)	Rate of increase in value f'(t)/f(t)	Present value factor e⁻ⁱᵗ	Present value f(t)e⁻ⁱᵗ
10	$200	$50	0.2500	0.6065	$121.30
11	250	49	0.1960	0.5770	144.25
12	298	48	0.1611	0.5448	162.35
13	346	47	0.1358	0.5220	180.61
14	392	46	0.1173	0.4966	194.67
15	438	45	0.1027	0.4724	206.91
16	482	44	0.0913	0.4493	216.56
17	526	43	0.0817	0.4274	224.81
18	568	42	0.0739	0.4066	230.95
19	610	41	0.0672	0.3867	235.89
20	650	40	0.0615	0.3679	239.14
21	690	39	0.0565	0.3499	241.43
22	728	38	0.0522	0.3329	242.35
23	766	37	0.0483	0.3166	242.52[a]
24	802	36	0.0449	0.3012	241.56
25	837	35	0.0418	0.2865	239.80
26	872	34	0.0390	0.2725	237.62

Note:
a Maximum present value.

Table 18.2 shows the appropriate calculations when the land value is $500. Under these circumstances, it would pay to harvest the trees when they are between the fourteenth and fifteenth year. After that time, the rate of increase in the value of the trees is less than 5 percent of the amount that could be realized by cutting the trees and putting the land to some other use. This is also the age at which the present value of the land and trees is maximized.

If the most economical use of the land is to grow trees, the value of the land in this use must be determined. But the value of the land depends on the frequency at which crops are harvested and the costs of planting a new crop. Table 18.3 shows the value of the land when crops are harvested at various ages, if the costs of planting are $50. This is an application of equation (18.4). Harvesting in year 17 maximizes the present value of the land. Table 18.4 applies equation (18.5) to this situation. Both equation (18.4) and (18.5) results in an optimum life of 17 years per crop (or slightly more if fractional years are allowed).

Table 18.2 Calculations when land value is $500

Age of trees (yr) (t)	Realizable value of land and trees $\$500 + f(t)$	Annual increment in value $f'(t)$	Rate of increase in value $\dfrac{f'(t)}{\$500 + f(t)}$	Present value factor e^{-it}	Present value $e^{-it}[\$500 + f(t)]$
10	$700	$50	0.0714	0.6065	$424.55
11	750	49	0.0653	0.5770	432.75
12	798	48	0.0602	0.5448	434.75
13	846	47	0.0556	0.5220	441.61
14	892	46	0.0516	0.4966	442.97
15	938	45	0.0480	0.4724	443.11[a]
16	982	44	0.0448	0.4493	441.21
17	1,026	43	0.0419	0.4274	438.51
18	1,068	42	0.0393	0.4066	434.25
19	1,110	41	0.0369	0.3867	429.24
20	1,150	40	0.0348	0.3679	423.09
21	1,190	39	0.0328	0.3499	416.38

Note:
a Maximum present value.

Table 18.3 Value of land when crops are harvested at various ages

Age of trees (yr) (t)	Net present value of one crop of trees growing for t years $P(t) = -50 + e^{it}f(t)$	Annuity factor $1/1 - e^{it}$	Value of land $P(t)/1 - e^{it} = V(t)$
10	$71.30	2.54	$181.10
11	94.25	2.36	222.82
12	112.35	2.20	246.81
13	130.61	2.09	273.25
14	144.67	1.99	287.39
15	156.91	1.90	297.41
16	166.56	1.82	302.46
17	174.81	1.75	305.29[a]
18	180.95	1.69	304.94
19	185.89	1.63	303.09
20	189.14	1.58	299.22

Note:
a Maximum present value.

Table 18.4 Return earned

Years (t)	V(t)	f(t)	f'(t)	f'(t)/V(t) + f(t)
10	$181.10	$200	50	0.1312
11	222.82	250	49	0.1036
12	246.81	298	48	0.0881
13	273.25	346	47	0.0759
14	287.39	392	46	0.0677
15	297.39	438	45	0.0612
16	302.46	482	44	0.0561
17	305.29	526	43	0.0517[a]
18	304.94	568	42	0.0481
19	303.09	610	41	0.0449
20	299.22	650	40	0.0421

Note:
a Closest to 0.05.

EQUIPMENT REPLACEMENT

The question of when to replace an existing piece of equipment with another machine that will perform the same function is very similar to the question of when to harvest a crop of trees. In the case of trees, we are seeking to maximize the net present value of the revenues that we can receive from the land, whereas in the equipment-replacement problem, we are seeking to minimize the net present value of the costs that will be incurred from owning and operating a sequence of machines.

In the machine problem, the costs incurred by retaining the existing machine are the costs of operating it for the current period (including any necessary repairs and maintenance), the decline in its salvage value during the current period, and the interest on the current salvage value of the existing machine. If the machine is retained for one additional period, the firm benefits by delaying for that length of time the costs of acquiring and operating all subsequent replacement machines. The magnitude of the latter cost is measured by the market interest rate times the present value of the costs of acquiring and operating all subsequent replacements. This present value will depend critically on how long each subsequent replacement equipment is retained. Thus, the decision about when to replace the current machine requires an estimate of the economic value of its anticipated replacements, just as the decision about when to harvest a crop of trees depends on the future use that will be made of the land occupied by the trees.

THE STRATEGY OF CAPACITY DECISIONS

One of the most important decisions a corporation can make is the capacity decision. How large a plant should be built and when it should be built, are two crucial decisions. An intelligent capacity strategy will greatly enhance a firm's profitability. Excess capacity and the resulting large capital costs can lead to severe drops in profit. On the other hand, a shortage of capacity gives competition an opportunity to increase its share of the market and to come more rapidly down its learning curves.

We shall consider capacity strategy from several points of view, first assuming a firm in isolation and then considering a firm in a competitive environment. Elements of game theory will be used to illustrate the complexity of the decision.

THE BASIC DECISION

The basic capacity decision presents the problem of choosing the best of a set of mutually exclusive investments. Each of the alternatives provides a different timing for adding capacity.

Consider the following two investment alternatives.

	Time 0	Time 1	Time 2
A	−$10,000		−$14,400
B	−18,000		

With alternative A, a small addition is made at time 0; then a second addition is made at time 2. With alternative B, we build the same capacity at time 0 as we obtain over the two periods with alternative A.

Which alternative is better? Assume the firm has a time-value factor of 0.20. The present value of A's outlay is $20,000, while B costs only $18,000. B is thus better than A, for in addition to costing less, B also supplies a cushion capacity over the two-year period.

With a time-value factor sufficiently higher than 0.20, the preference could shift to A. For example, if the time-value factor is 0.40, the present value of A is $17,347. This causes A to be more desirable than B. Also, A might be better if the success of the product being produced is not certain. There is less capital at risk. Also, changes in technology must enhance the choice of A.

PERFORMANCE MEASUREMENT AND THE TIMING DECISION

The timing decision for alternatives A and B was made on a straight economic basis (the maximization of the present value of the stockholders' position). It is well known that actual decisions are multidimensional, with other factors being considered beside the net present value.

Assume the firm's time-value factor is 0.20, so that B is more desirable than A. We now add the positive cash flows to the analysis.

	Time 0	Time 1	Time 2	Time 3	Time 4
A	−$10,000		−$14,400		
		+$6,000	+$7,200	+$8,000	+$10,000
B	−18,000	+$6,000	+$7,200	+$8,800	+10,080

Assume a four-year life for the product being made and the use of straight-line depreciation. We have the data shown in Table 18.5 for years 1 and 2 for the two investments (assuming a two-year life for the first unit of A and a four-year life for B).

A is superior to B in both year 1 and year 2 based on the use of return on investment (ROI). But with a 20 percent time-value factor, we know that B is better than A. The measure of performance being used is deficient. The cost of B includes the cost of excess capacity that will be used in periods after period 2. The first two periods should not be penalized for the acquisition of the excess capacity.

A shift to present value depreciation solves the problem of underperformance in year one. It is inappropriate that the entire initial investment of B be considered an investment of the first two time periods. It should not be depreciated using straight-line depreciation. One way or another, the performance measurement procedure must take these factors into consideration if the capacity decision is not to be distorted. Assume the values and depreciation expenses (Table 18.6) are computed using B's internal rate of return of 0.2512.

Table 18.5 Data for years 1 and 2 of the two investments

	Year 1		Year 2	
	A	B	A	B
Revenues	$6,000	$6,000	$7,200	$7,200
Depreciation	5,000	4,500	5,000	4,500
Income	$1,000	$1,500	$2,200	$2,700
Investment	10,000	18,000	5,000	13,500
ROI	0.10	0.083	0.44	0.20

Table 18.6 Values and depreciation expenses

Time	Investment B Value (0.2512)	Depreciation
0	$18,000	
1	16,522	$1,478
2	13,472	3,050
3	8,056	5,416
4	0	8,056

The incomes and returns on investment of B are now as shown in Table 18.7. A comparable method of income measurement for A using its IRR of 0.20 as the discount rate would lead to an ROI of 0.20 for each year. Now B is not only to be preferred on an economic basis (a higher net present value), but is also preferred using ROI for each year.

Table 18.7 Incomes and returns on investment B

Year	Revenues	Present value depreciation	Income	Investment	ROI
1	$6,000	$1,478	$4,522	$18,000	0.2512
2	7,200	3,050	4,150	16,522	0.2512
3	8,800	5,416	3,384	13,472	0.2512
4	10,080	8,056	2,024	8,056	0.2512

COMPETITORS: PREEMPTING THE MARKET

The strategy of preempting the market is very attractive for a corporation. For example, in an expanding market, a company builds before its competitors, thus making it unprofitable for others to build.

For example, assume there are 1,000,000 units of demand not being satisfied. It is expected that the cost of building capacity for 1,000,000 units per year is $10,000,000 and that the contribution margin per unit is $2. The lifecycle of the product is expected to be ten years (for simplicity, we will assume constant revenues over that period).

If 1,000,000 units per year can be sold, the net present value of the investment with a 0.10 time value factor (6.1466 is the annuity factor) is

$$2,000,000 \ (6.1446) = \$12,289,000$$
$$\text{Capacity cost} \qquad -10,000,000$$
$$\text{Net present value} \quad = \quad \$2,289,000$$

331

Assume the market is not expected to exceed 1,000,000 units per year. Therefore, if the firm builds, a competitor building additional capacity would face the expectation of selling fewer than 1,000,000 units. Also, the possibility of a smaller contribution margin than $2 exists if competitors force the price down. From a strictly present value analysis basis, the investment is not likely to be desirable if a competitor is already building a plant with a capacity of 1,000,000 units.

The plans of competitors can thus affect the desirability of capacity expansion.

It is very likely that a firm and its competitors can lapse into a form of "prisoner's dilemma." Consider a situation where the net present value of firm A will be as shown in Table 18.8.

Table 18.8 Firm A's net present value conditional on B's actions

B's actions	A does not build	A builds	Maximum profits
B does not build	$1,000,000	$2,289,000	$2,289,000
B builds	0	500,000	500,000

An analysis of Table 18.8 indicates that if B does not build, A is better off building, and if B builds, A is better off building. A has a strong incentive to build. Now consider firm B's profits, as shown in Table 18.9. The maximum profits for B occur when B builds if A builds, or if A does not build. B thus has a strong incentive to build.

Let us assume that both A and B build. If both firms build, each firm will make profits of $500,000. This sum is less than the $1,000,000 of profits that both firms will earn if both firms do not build.

While both firms acting in their own interest should build, when they do so, they will find that they have reached an inferior profit position.

A possible solution (but likely to be illegal in some countries) is for the firms to talk with each other to decide that not to build is preferable to both firms building. Still another possibility might be for the firms to merge, if that is legal.

Table 18.9 Firm B's net present value conditional on A's actions

B's actions	A does not build	A builds
B does not build	$1,000,000	$0
B builds	2,289,000	500,000
Maximum profits	$2,289,000	$500,000

If the firms cannot talk to each other, then it is likely that they will learn through time that certain actions will not be profitable.

For example, A may decide to build in the hope that B will not think that building is profitable. B will see, however, that $0 of net present value without building is less than $500,000 with building and will decide to build. Firm A will regret the construction.

Now assume that A's and B's profits are negative if both firms build. On a straight profit basis, B should not build if A builds first. However, B might choose to teach A a lesson by building the capacity even though it is not needed. If A suffers losses from building excess capacity, it might be satisfied with a more modest expansion in the next building cycle. An improved solution might be for both firms to build 500,000 units of capacity (the economics of this alternative are not given) and to share the market growth.

In some situations, the capacity expansion will also result in changes in efficiency. The firm that does not expand and improve efficiency will be at a competitive disadvantage. This will also act as an incentive for B to expand when A expands.

The strategy of constructing preemptive capacity can backfire if the competitor feels that conceding the market can have adverse long-run effects and thus reacts by building capacity, even though the market will not absorb all the capacity of the industry.

PERFECT PREDICTIONS OF INTEREST RATES

Assume the decision-maker can perfectly predict future interest rates and that interest rates can either go up or go down monotonically.

Assume a project with conventional cash flows has a negative present value. But if the firm waits and interest rates decrease the NPV will become positive. When the rates decrease, the investment should be accepted if the NPV is positive and further decreases are not expected. With further decreases expected, it might be desirable to wait longer.

If instead of the interest rates going down they are expected to go up, the investment will become even less desirable as it becomes more negative.

Now assume a project with a positive NPV and interest rates are expected to increase. If the project can be financed 100 percent with debt, the project should be financed before the rates increase. But if the project will be financed 100 percent with stock, it is possible that the increase in the interest rate (the stockholders' required return) will lead to a rejection of the project even with a positive NPV now. Assume a $100 outlay will result in $115 in one year and the stockholders want a 0.10 return. The project is acceptable. But, if the interest rate (the required stock return) were to change immediately to 0.20, the project should be rejected since it will have a negative NPV using 0.20 as the discount rate.

CONCLUSIONS

The economic analysis of capacity expansion without competitors is a straight-forward, mutually exclusive investment decision until one considers the accounting measures of performance. These measures require adjustment so that there is not a conflict between the accounting measures and the economic measures of investment desirability.

With shifts to considering strategy in a competitive situation, the possibility of a prisoner's dilemma appears. The strategy of constructing preemptive capacity is balanced by a strategy that attempts to teach the competitor that such a strategy is not profitable. Exact correct answers are lacking in a competitive situation, but we gain instead an appreciation of the degree of complexity that exists when there are competitors.

It is important to realize that the prices (and possibly costs) that exist before the capacity expansion might not be in effect after the capacity expansion. Observed prices and costs are not likely to be reliable indicators of price and costs when capacity and efficiencies are changed.

PROBLEMS

1   Trees growing in value at 0.15 per year are currently worth $1,000,000. The land itself (without the trees) is worth $5,000,000 now and one year from now. Money is worth 0.10.
    Should the trees be harvested now?

2   What is your answer to problem 1 if the trees are growing at 0.20 per year and money is worth 0.05?

3   High Voltage Electric Company has $10 million of debt outstanding, which pays 7 percent interest annually. The maturity date of the securities is fifteen years from the present. There are $100,000 of bond issues costs and $200,000 of bond discount currently on the books.

Assume that a 15-year security could be issued, which would yield 6 percent annually. The issue costs on the new issue would be $200,000, and the call premium on the old issue would be $500,000.

a. The company has a 10 percent cost of capital. Assume a zero tax rate. Should the old bonds be replaced with new securities?

b. Assume a discount rate of 7 percent. What would be your answer?

4   Referring to problem 3, how would your answer be affected by the possibility of interest rates decreasing in the future and the new bonds issued for a 30-year period?

5   Max A., the general manager of a mining company, is in need of advice. In answering, ignore uncertainty and assume the cost of money is 10 percent. All data (including the cost of money) are in real after-tax dollars.

Dry Gulch is an operating mine. Ore can be produced and sold this year for a contribution of $200 per ton. However, if production is delayed a year, a contribution of $210 per ton could be reached.

Would you recommend waiting? Explain.

6   (*Continue 5*) Wet Rock contains mineral deposits. Max plans to develop the property so that is can be mined, and then he will sell it to someone else to be mined. It will cost $1,000,000 and take about a year to get the property ready to sell. If development is started now, the property could be sold for $1,200,000 in one year. Max estimates the selling price will increase by 5 percent per year, but he anticipates no increase in development costs. Thus, the possible cash flows include the following:

Decision	Time 0	Time 1	Time 2	Time 3
Develop now	−$1,000,000	1,200,000	$0	$0
Develop in one year		−1,000,000	1,260,000	0
Develop in two years			−1,000,000	1,323,000

If Max must develop the property now or next year, what should he do? Explain.

7   (*Continue 6*) Max decides not to develop the property referred to in problem 6. However, at the beginning of year 2, he suffers a heart attack and takes a one-year's leave of absence. On returning at the end of year 2, he discovers that, in his absence, the property has been developed but not yet sold. An offer to buy the property for $1,323,000 is in hand.

Max is convinced that he can get 5 percent more by waiting another year. He feels the $1,000,000 expenditure was a sunk cost that would not affect his decision. He is inclined to wait at least another year. He wants your advice about when to sell before making up his mind.

8 Woodrow owns a plot of land in the South. The land, with no timber on it, is worth $500. The $500 value of the land is based on its potential as residential land. (It can be sold for $500.) The timber on the land is now ten years old and could be sold for $2,000 now. However, Woodrow estimates that the value of the timber will increase by $400 per year for the foreseeable future.

If Woodrow's objective is to earn a 10 percent return on his money, how many more years should he wait to harvest his timber? (For this question, assume $500 is the correct value of the land.)

9 The ABC Company has $10 million of debt outstanding, which pays 0.05 (that is, $500,000) interest annually. The maturity date of the securities is 20 years from the present.

Assume that a new 20-year security could be issued that would yield 0.04 per year. The issue costs would be $800,000, and the call premium on redemption of the old bonds is $100,000. Assume a zero tax rate for this company. The hurdle rate of the firm is 0.10.

Should the present bonds be refunded?

10 (*Continue 9*) How would your answer be modified if the maturity date of the new issue were 30 years instead of 20 years?

11 The York State Electric Corporation has $100 million of debentures outstanding, which are currently paying interest of 5.5 percent ($5.5 million) per year. The bonds mature in 24 years.

It would be possible currently to issue 30-year debentures of like characteristics that would yield 5 percent. The firm considers its cost of capital to be 8 percent. The marginal tax rate is 0.4.

The analysis in Table 18.10 has been prepared. Should the firm refund? Explain briefly.

12 The B-State Electric and Gas Corporation has $25 million of debentures outstanding, which are currently paying interest of 4.5 percent ($1.125 million) per year. The bonds mature in 24 years.

It would be possible to currently issue 30-year debentures of like characteristics that would yield 4 percent. The firm considers its hurdle rate to be 8 percent. The marginal tax rate is 0.50. An analysis has been prepared, as shown in Table 18.11.

Should the firm refund? Explain.

Table 18.10 York State Electric refunding calculations

Item	Before taxes	After taxes
Cash outlays		
Premium at $50 per $1,000	$5,000,000	$3,000,000
Duplicate interest for 30-day call period less interest received on principal at 1.4% due to temporary investment	300,000	180,000
Refunding expense (80% of $250,000, total expense of new issue based on remaining life of old issue of 24 years)	200,000	120,000
Call expense	50,000	30,000
Less tax saving due to immediate write-off of unamortized debt discount and expense		(20,000)
Total cash outlay of refunding		$3,310,000
Interest calculations		
Annual interest – old issue at 5.5%	5,500,000	3,000,000
Annual interest – new issue at 5%	5,000,000	3,000,000
		300,000
Total after-tax interest-old issue-discounted at 8% for 24 years[a] (present value factor = 10.5288)		
Total after-tax interest-new issue-discounted at 8% or 24 years (present value factor = 10.5288)	34,700,000	3,100,000
Total after-tax discounted interest savings resulting from refunding		31,600,000
Total after-tax cash outlay of refunding		3,100,000
		3,310,000
Net savings due to refunding at effective interest rate of 5%		$(210,000)

Note:
a The remaining life of the old issue.

Table 18.11 Analysis of Bi-State Electric position

Cash outlays	Before taxes	After taxes
Premium at $52 per $1,000	$1,300,000	$650,000
Duplicate interest for 30-day call period less interest received on principal at 2% due to temporary investment	54,000	27,000
Refunding expense (80% of $220,000 total expense of new issue based on remaining life of old issue of 24 years)	176,000	88,000
Call expense	25,000	12,500
Less tax saving resulting from immediate write-off of unamortized debt discount and expense		−18,000
		$759,500

DISCUSSION QUESTION

Why may a supermarket stay open during certain hours even though the store's costs are not recovered in these hours?

BIBLIOGRPHY

Alchain, A., *Economic Replacement Policy*, RAND Report No. R-224, Santa Monica, CA: RAND Corporation, 1952.

Baldwin, C. Y., "Optimal Sequential Investment When Capital Is Not Readily Reversible," *Journal of Finance*, June 1982, pp. 763–82.

Bellman, R., "Notes in the Theory of Dynamic Programming – III: Equipment Replacement Policy," RAND Report no. P-632, *Journal of Society for Industrial and Applied Mathematics*, September 1955.

Berkovitch, E. and M. P. Narayanan, "Timing of Investment and Financing Decisions in Imperfectly Competitive Financial Markets," *Journal of Business*, 66, April 1993, pp. 219–48.

Bierman, Harold, Jr., "The Growth Period Decision," *Management Science*, February 1968, pp. B-302–B-309.

Bowman, E. H., and R. B. Fetter, *Analysis for Production Management*, rev. edn. Homewood, IL: Richard D. Irwin, 1961.

Durand, D., "Comprehensiveness in Capital Budgeting," *Financial Management*, winter 1981, pp. 7–13.

Howe, K. M., "Does Inflationary Change Affect Capital Asset Life?" *Financial Management*, summer 1987, pp. 63–7.

Preinreich, G. A. D., "The Economic Life of Industrial Equipment," *Econometrica*, January 1940, pp. 12–44.

Terborgh, G., *Business Investment Policy*, Washington, DC: Machinery and Allied Products Institute, 1958.

Thakor, A. V., "Game Theory in Finance," *Financial Management*, 20(2), 1991, pp. 71–94.

Walls, M. R., "Integrating Business Strategy and Capital Allocation: An Application of Multi-Objective Decision-Making," *Engineering Economist*, 40, spring 1995, pp. 247–66.

Yoon, K. P., "Capital Investment Analysis Involving Estimate Error," *Engineering Economist*, 35, fall 1990, pp. 21–30.

Chapter 19

Buy versus lease

Always rent.

(Chuck Tanner, Manager of the Pittsburgh Pirates,
to Tony La Russa, Manager of the Chicago White Sox,
in the August 21, 1984 issue of *Sports Illustrated*)

The term *lease* in this chapter refers to a financial type of lease, that is, a lease where the firm has a legal obligation to continue making payments for a well-defined period of time. We are excluding from consideration the type of lease where an asset is acquired for a short period of time to fill a temporary need and then leasing is stopped. (A familiar example of this latter type of lease is the renting of an automobile at an airport.) We shall first deal with leases where there is a buy-or-lease option and the firm has already made the decision to acquire the asset. In this situation, the buy-or-lease decision becomes a financing decision. We shall then discuss the situation where the firm must decide whether to buy, lease, or do nothing. We shall conclude that many financial leases are very similar to debt and should be treated in essentially the same manner as debt. A lawyer would be able to point out the differences between a lease and debt (especially when there is a failure to pay the required payments), but we shall concentrate on the similarities, and the decision maker can bring the differences into the analysis in a qualitative manner.

The basic problem in analyzing a lease is that there is implicit debt financing accompanying the acquisition of the right to use an asset. Since the debt is implicit rather than explicit, conventional methods of analysis can be faulty unless they are carefully used. Normally, we exclude debt-financing flows and their tax effect from the investment analysis. With leasing, the debt flows are interwoven with the investment flows, and the extraction is more complex.

BORROW OR LEASE: THE FINANCING DECISION

We shall first assume a zero tax rate and analyze the financial aspects of the lease-versus-buy decision. Assume that a company is considering the lease or purchase of a piece of equipment. The firm has decided to acquire the equipment. The equipment will incur operating costs and will generate revenues that are unaffected by whether the equipment is leased or purchased. For any lease-or-buy decision, there will be many cash flows that are common to both decisions. There are, however, differences in the cash flows related to the method of financing the equipment. We have the cash flows associated with buying, and on the other hand, the cash flows associated with leasing. Assume that the equipment costs $100,000; we can borrow the $100,000 at a cost of 0.05 per year or we can lease the equipment at a cost of $29,000 per year. Should we lease or buy, assuming that the equipment has an expected life of four years? Because we have decided to acquire the asset, the only decision is the type of financing. The expected salvage value is zero.

There is an easy method of solving the buy-versus-lease decision with zero taxes. Since the lease payments are $29,000 per year, the decision maker can make a phone call to the firm's bank and ask what payments would be required annually for four years to repay a $100,000 loan. Assume the amount is $28,201 per year with 0.05 debt. Since the amount is less than $29,000, buy-borrow is more desirable than leasing (all other things equal and zero taxes).

We can also compute the present value of the two alternatives. The present value of the cash outlays with leasing is $29,000 times the present value of an annuity for four periods using the borrowing rate of 0.05.

$$\$29,000 \times 3.5460 = \$102,834$$

The present value of the immediate cash outlay associated with buying is $100,000, and we again prefer buying (and borrowing). The present value of the debt payment of $28,201 per year is also $100,000 if we use the borrowing rate of 0.05.

If the discount rate used in the analysis is the same as the interest rate that the firm would have to pay if it actually attempted to finance the purchase of the asset by a loan, the particular loan repayment schedule chosen will not affect the present value of the loan. Suppose that an amount C is borrowed, and interest of k is paid on the principal plus accrued interest outstanding. Using k as the discount rate, we find that the present value of the payments required to repay the loan will always be C, whatever loan repayment schedule is chosen.

By equating the present value of the four $29,000 lease payments to the $100,000 cost of the asset, we can determine the implicit interest cost of leasing.

$$\$29,000B\,(4, k) = \$100,000$$
$$B\,(4, k) = 3.443$$

By trial and error (computing present values), we find that k is approximately equal to 0.0652. The leasing is an expensive method of debt financing compared to borrowing at 0.05 from the bank. With zero taxes, the interest cost of leasing compared to the cost of buying is a sensible method of solution.

The purpose of this phase of the analysis is to determine whether the proposed lease is financially attractive. Because the lease is presumed to require a contractually predetermined set of payments compared to a bank loan, it is reasonable to compare the lease with an alternative type of financing available to the company that also requires a contractually predetermined set of payments, that is, a bank loan.

The conclusions to this point can be summarized as follows: We can buy a piece of equipment for $100,000; it has an expected life of four years. The firm could borrow the money to finance the purchase at an interest cost of 5 percent and an annual payment of $28,201. The equipment could also be acquired through a lease. If the annual lease payments were $29,000 per year for four years, there would be a financial cost disadvantage to leasing. The present value of the lease payments at 5 percent is larger than the present value of the amount that would have to be borrowed to finance the purchase through borrowing. If the lease payments required were less than $28,201, the lease would have a financial cost advantage compared to the bank loan.

A LEASE IS DEBT

Now assume the above firm normally uses a 0.10 weighted average cost of capital (debt still costs 0.05) to evaluate investments, and the asset will earn cash flow benefits of $31,000 per year. The net present value of buying using the 0.10 discount rate is:

$$\text{NPV (buying)} = \$31,000 \; B(4, 0.10) - \$100,000$$
$$= 31,000 \, (3.1699) - \$100,000 = -\$1,733$$

The present value of buying is negative, and buying is not acceptable.

A possible calculation of the present value of leasing would be

$$\text{NPV (leasing)} = (\$31,000 - \$29,000) \; B \, (4, 0.10)$$
$$= \$2,000 \, (3.1699) = \$6,340$$

The net present value of leasing is positive (using any interest rate), and leasing seems to be acceptable. But this analysis is in error, since the lease is debt and we are discounting the debt at a higher discount rate than the cost of borrowing. We just

341

concluded that if the project is acceptable, buying is better than leasing. We should not now conclude that leasing is better than buying. Leasing costs $29,000 per year, and buying with debt costs $28,201. Buying costs less than leasing. The net present value of buying if the debt repayments are included in the cash flows is

$$\text{NPV (buying)} = (\$31,000 - \$28,201)\, B\,(4, 0.10)$$
$$= \$2,799\,(3.1699) = \$8,873$$

which is better than the $6,340 of leasing.

The problem with including the debt flows in the buy analysis when the discount rate is larger than the borrowing rate is that the net present value is then affected by the timing of the debt repayment.

A reasonable solution is to compute the net present values using the cost of debt.

$$\text{NPV (buying)} = \$31,000\, B(4,0.05) - \$100,000$$
$$= \$31,000\,(3.5459) - \$100,000 = \$9,923$$
$$\text{NPV (leasing)} = (\$31,000 - \$29,000)\,(3.5459) = \$7,092$$

If we include the debt flows in the buy analysis, the net present value of the debt flows will now be zero, since all flows are being discounted using the cost of debt.

The analysis we have presented may be used to decide whether direct borrowing with an explicit debt security is more desirable or less desirable than leasing. We have not attempted to present an analysis here that proves debt is more or less attractive than other types of financing. We have kept the capital structure the same for both alternatives. Since a lease is debt, the buy alternative analysis must also use debt to make the two alternatives comparable.

The analysis we have presented cannot be used to decide whether the asset should be acquired, nor can it be used to decide whether the firm should have more or less financial leverage. If it has been decided that acquiring the use of the equipment is desirable, the analysis can be used to determine whether to buy or lease the equipment. The specific action that should be taken will depend on whether additional financial leverage and accepting the investment are desirable actions.

In addition, the preceding analysis assumes a zero tax rate. It is necessary to take income taxes into consideration to make the analysis more realistic, because income taxes will tend to influence the decision.

BUY OR LEASE WITH TAXES: USING THE AFTER-TAX BORROWING RATE (METHOD 1)

With taxes, there are three reasonably correct approaches to analyzing lease versus-buy. The easiest solution is to use the after-tax borrowing rate as the discount rate. If the firm wants to use some type of risk-adjusted rate, then arriving at a reasonable solution is much more complex.

Let us now consider the effects of a corporate income tax of 40 percent. With an income tax, we shall want to convert all cash flows to an after-tax basis, and because interest expense is deductible for tax purposes, we shall use an after-tax discount rate. If a discount rate of 5 percent (the borrowing rate) was appropriate on a before-tax basis for borrowed funds, the corresponding after-tax rate can be assumed to be $(1 - 0.4)\,0.05 = 0.03$.

Now assume the lease payments are $28,201 (equal to the debt payments). Because lease payments are a deductible expense is computing income subject to taxes, annual lease payments of $28,201 per year will become after-tax cash flows of $(1 - 0.4)\,\$28,201$, or $16,921 per year. The present value of the after-tax lease payments, using a 3 percent discount rate, will be $16,921 $\times$ 3.7171, or $62,897. This method of calculation can only be justified if the after-tax borrowing rate is being used for both the lease and buy alternatives.

The cost of the equipment is $100,000, and we shall consider borrowing that amount in order to finance the purchase of the machine. The exact pattern of after-tax cash flows will depend on the debt repayment schedule. If the lender charges 5 percent per year, equal payments of $28,201 per year for four years would be one repayment schedule sufficient to repay the interest and principal on the loan. To put these debt cash flows on after-tax basis for the borrower, we need to determine for each year how much of this amount will be considered a payment of interest and how much a repayment of principal. A different repayment schedule would lead to a different pattern of after-tax cash flows; but provided interest were computed on the remaining debt balance, the present value of the after-tax cash flows required to repay the principal and interest of the loan will always be $100,000. For example, suppose that the firm pays interest at $5,000 per year for four years and repays the principal in a lump sum at the end of the fourth year. The after-tax interest payments are $3,000 for each year. The present value of the debt using 0.03 as the discount rate is:

$$\begin{array}{rl} \$3,000 \times 3.7171 = & \$11,151 \\ \$100,000 \times 0.88849 = & \underline{88,849} \\ & \$100,000 \end{array}$$

We want to compute the cash flows of borrowing the funds to buy the equipment. If we subtract the present value of the positive cash flows associated with borrowing (plus $100,000) from the present value of the after-tax cash payments (a negative $100,000), we can find that borrowing has a zero net present value.

If we compare the $100,000 immediate cost of the asset with the $62,897 present value of the lease payments, there appears to be an advantage in favor of the lease when taxes are taken into account. However, depreciation tax deductions have not yet been considered. If the equipment is leased, the lessee cannot deduct the depreciation expense. If the equipment is purchased, the firm has the right to deduct depreciation expense. Each dollar of depreciation expense will save $0.40 of taxes. The present value of the tax savings resulting from depreciation will depend on the timing of the depreciation expense. If depreciation is charged on a straight-line basis over a four-year period, the value of the tax savings each year will be $10,000 (0.4 × $25,000), and the present value of the tax savings will be $10,000 × 3.7171 = $37,171. Subtracting this from the $100,000 cost of the investment gives a net present value of after-tax cash flows of $62,829 for the borrow-and-buy decision. This is slightly less than the present value of the $28,201 annual lease payments ($62,897).

If a more rapid method of depreciation were used, there would be a more clearly defined advantage in favor of buying. For example, if the twice-straight-line, declining-balance method of depreciations were used, the present value of the tax savings could be computed. With an interest rate of 3 percent and a life of four years, the present value of the tax deduction privilege is as follows: $100,000 × 0.4 × 0.946539 = $37,862. Subtracting this amount from $100,000 gives a net present value of $62,138 for buying and borrowing, which is $759 less than the present value for leasing.

The tax savings that result from charging depreciation if the asset is owned are not contractual. Frequently, however, there is little uncertainty associated with the amount and timing of these tax savings. Regardless of whether the particular piece of equipment performs as anticipated, the right to charge depreciation expense will generate tax savings as long as the firm as a whole has taxable income. Even if the firm does not have taxable income in any particular year, the tax-loss carry-forward and carry-back provisions of the law provide a high degree of assurance that tax savings will result, although their timing might change slightly. It should be remembered that there is also no guarantee that there will be enough revenues so that the full lease payments can be used to reduce taxes. The preceding analysis used the after-tax borrowing rate. If any other discount rate is used, the analysis is more complex.

One important difference in buying, compared to leasing, is that the firm that buys an asset owns the asset at the end of the time period of the lease. To the extent that the asset has net value at that time, this is also a net cash flow for the buy analysis. This difference will be illustrated when we discuss the buy–lease analysis for acquisition of land.

Is the equipment worth acquiring?

In the previous sections, we have shown that the present value of the cost (using twice-straight-line depreciation) of acquiring the equipment is $62,138 if it is bought and $62,897 if leased (at an annual cost of $28,201). To decide whether it is worth buying the equipment, we need to compare the present value of the benefits with the net cost of $62,138.

Suppose that the equipment has a life of four years and would lead to before tax cash savings of $31,000 per year. The after-tax cash savings are $(1 - 0.4) \times \$31,000$ or $18,600 per year. The present value of the tax savings that would result from the right to charge depreciation expense on the equipment has already been calculated and subtracted from the purchase price of the equipment, so these tax savings should not be considered again.

Using the after-tax borrowing rate of 3 percent, we find that the present value of the savings from operating the machine is $18,600 \times 3.7171 = \$69,138$. Subtracting the present value of the cost of equipment from the present value of the savings, we have a net present value of $7,000 (that is, $69,138 - $62,138), indicating that we can accept the machine on a borrow and buy basis if we are willing to accept a return equal to the after-tax borrowing rate. We can expect that the firm will want to make an adjustment for risk.

In situations such as this, we may be able to estimate the cost of acquiring the asset with a high degree of confidence, whereas the savings that would result from having the use of the asset are subject to considerable uncertainty. If the firm has not had experience with similar equipment, there may be some question as to whether the savings in cost per unit of product (or other measure of the rate of usage) will be as high as anticipated. In addition, there may be some uncertainty about the number of units of product that will be needed and about the equipment's anticipated life. For these and other reasons, a decision about whether the machine should be acquired will to a great extent depend upon management's judgments and risk preferences.

USING A RISK-ADJUSTED DISCOUNT RATE (METHOD 2)

If some rate other than the after-tax borrowing rate is used, then we cannot merely find the after tax present value of leasing by computing the present value of the after-tax leasing flows since this creates a bias for leasing.

Assume the lease payments are $29,000 per year. The first step using a risk-adjusted rate (say 0.10) is to compute the debt equivalent of the lease payments using the 0.05 borrowing rate: $29,000 B (4,0.05) = \$102,834$. The second step is to complete a debt amortization schedule for the debt equivalent of the lease.

Time	Amount owned	Interest (0.05)	Principal[a]
0	$102,834	$5,142	$23,858
1	78,996	3,949	25,051
2	53,925	2,696	26,304
3	27,621	1,381	27,619
4			

Note:
a Principal = $29,000 minus interest.

The "Principal" column gives us the basic lease tax deduction component that is the equivalent to the depreciation tax deduction of buying. Using the 0.10 risk adjusted discount rate, the present value of these tax deductions converted into tax savings is:

$$\text{Present value} = 0.4\left[\frac{\$23,858}{1.10} + \frac{\$25,051}{(1.10)^2} + \frac{\$26,304}{(1.10)^3} + \frac{\$27,619}{(1.10)^4}\right]$$

$$= 0.41(\$81,0192) = \$32,408$$

The net present value of leasing is

$$\text{NPV (leasing)} = \$102,834 - \$32,408 = \$70,426$$

The net cost of buying using straight-line depreciation for taxes and a 0.10 discount rate is

$$\begin{aligned}
\text{NPV (buy)} &= \$100,000 - \$25,000\ (0.4)\ B\ (4, 0.10) \\
&= \$100,000 - \$10,000(3.1699) \\
&= \$100,000 - \$31,699 \\
&= \$68,301
\end{aligned}$$

Buying costs less than leasing in this example.

COMPUTING THE IMPLIED INTEREST RATE ON THE LEASE (METHOD 3)

The third method is to compute the internal rate of return (IRR) of leasing compared to buying. This calculation gives the interest cost (after-tax) of leasing. The calculations for the above example are given below. The annual outlay of leasing is again $29,000 per year. The implied interest rate on the lease is 0.0377 which is slightly higher than the 0.03 after-tax cost of borrowing (Table 19.1). Buying is preferred to leasing.

Table 19.1 *Cash flows*

	Leasing	Buying	Leasing minus buying
0	$-17,400^a$	$-100,000$	$+100,000$
1	$-17,400$	$+10,000^b$	$-27,400$
2	$-17,400$	$+10,000$	$-27,400$
3	$-17,400$	$+10,000$	$-27,400$
4	$-17,400$	$+10,000$	$-27,400$
			IRR = 0.0377

Notes:
a $29,000 (1 - 0.4) = 17,400$. The after-tax cost of leasing.
b $25,000 \times 0.40 = 10,000$. The value of $25,000 of annual depreciation tax deductions.

RISK CONSIDERATIONS IN LEASE-VERSUS-BORROW DECISIONS

We began this chapter by suggesting that many leases are essentially financing instruments, comparable to debt contracts. It is desirable to consider the risks associated with the financial decisions (borrow or lease) that we have been evaluating.

For practical purposes, it may be reasonable, in some circumstances, to treat the financial cash flows as being free of any uncertainty. This assumption will not always be valid, as we shall see. If the likelihood of any substantial deviation from our predictions is very small, the time and cost involved in any detailed analysis of the uncertainties may not be worth the effort.

Given a specific set of contracts, it might be possible to analyze the cash flows under various foreseeable alternatives. What would happen if the firm could not meet the legal requirements? Would it be declared bankrupt? Could the lease be terminated earlier? Could the loan be extended or renewed, or is it callable?

Possible changes in the corporate income tax rates are worth considering. If a decrease in the corporate income tax is anticipated, it will tend to raise the after-tax cash flows (benefits net of costs) for any of the alternatives considered. The effect of this increase on the net present value of any alternatives considered.

The effects of these sources of uncertainty could be analyzed in detail if such an analysis were considered worthwhile. The following section illustrates such an analysis when there is uncertainty about how long the asset will be needed.

THE RATE OF DISCOUNT

Some analysts of the buy-versus-lease decision do not want to use the after-tax borrowing rate as the rate of discount. They argue that the residual value of the asset and the tax savings from depreciation deductions are different from other cash flows associated with buy decisions, and it is appropriate to test the sensitivity of the buy–lease decision to a change in the rate of discount.

Leasing combines the elements of investment and financing. If we use a discount rate other than after the after-tax cost of borrowing, the buy-versus-lease analysis becomes much more complex. The complexity arises because the debt flows are excluded from the buy analysis and included with the lease analysis. We want the two analyses to be comparable relative to the treatment of the debt flows and the deductions arising from the non-debt flows.

Since depreciation is deductible if we buy, we want to isolate a deduction with leasing that is comparable to depreciation. With leasing, the noninterest component of the lease payment is deductible but there is no depreciation (whereas with buying, depreciation is deductible).

Let us consider the following cash flows of buying:

Investment flows

- investment outlay;
- depreciation tax savings;
- positive after-tax cash flows (benefits) and residual value.

Debt flows

- cash proceeds from debt
- principal payments;
- interest flows;
- interest tax-shield savings.

We have listed six different cash streams, but the list can be reduced by combining the two debt flows (principal and interest) and the two tax shields (depreciation and interest). The debt flows are contractual, thus relatively risk-free. The riskiness of the tax deductions (savings) depends on the firm's total taxable income and possible changes in tax laws. The after-tax benefits and residual value are likely to be high-risk, but the benefits from the project are common to both the buy and lease alternative; thus, their affect is neutral. Time discounting is not likely to affect significantly the present value of the investment outlay, since the outlays are close to time 0. We can define a different discount rate for each cash flow with a different riskiness.

The cash flows of the lease alternative divided into its components for purposes of this analysis are:

- lease outlay – interest equivalent;
- lease outlay – principal equivalent;
- lease tax deduction – interest equivalent;
- lease tax deduction – principal (depreciation) equivalent.

It is important that each of the lease cash-flow components be discounted at the same magnitude of interest rates as the equivalent component of the buy alternative.

RECOMMENDATIONS

The primary recommendation

The recommended solution is to use the after-tax borrowing rate to evaluate the alternatives. It is reliable and easy to apply.

One recommendation if a risk adjusted discount rate is used

For lease: Discount the interest and principal components at a before-tax discount rate to determine the debt equivalent of leasing. Subtract the present value of the lease tax savings from the principal (depreciation) equivalent component of the lease.

For buy-borrow: Only use the investment flows: Subtract the present value of the depreciation tax savings from the cost of investment.

A second recommendation if a risk adjusted discount rate is used

If all the lease flows are discounted, this is equivalent to including the debt flows in the buy analysis. Now many alternatives are possible. One important consideration is to have the debt included in the buy analysis be comparable to the debt included in the lease analysis. This is a second best solution.

LEASES AND PURCHASE OPTIONS

In making investment decisions, we generally separate the cash outlay (the investment) from the financing (the source of the cash). In leasing decisions involving land, it may not always be possible to separate an investment from its financing, as they frequently become interwoven. Suppose land is being leased, but the company leasing the land can acquire the land for a nominal price at the end of twenty years. Are the lease payments for the use of the land, or are they for the use of money during the twenty-year period plus payments for the land? A bargain purchase may convert a lease into a purchase contract for tax purposes.

Consider the following situations: Company A owns land and has offered to lease it to Company B at a cost of $80,242.65 per year for twenty years. After the twenty years, A retains ownership of the land.

B is a very large, stable company, and A considers a lease with B to be the equivalent of a certain cash flow. Using the current long-term debt rate of 0.05, A has offered to sell the land to B for $1 million. (A would not be taxed on this transaction.) Should B buy? B can obtain long-term funds at a cost of 0.05. These funds would have to be repaid at the end of twenty years. B's tax rate is 0.40, and B has taxable income. B's analysis follows. B finds the before-tax present value of the $80,242.65 per year to be $1,000,000.

Present value of lease

The after tax present value of leasing is obtained by multiplying the dollar amount of the lease by the tax factor $(1 - t)$ and multiplying this amount by the present value factor using the after-tax borrowing rate (with a 0.4 tax rate). The present value of annuity for twenty periods using 0.03 is 14.8775.

$$\text{After-tax cost of leasing} = (\$80,242.65) \times 0.60 \times 14.8775$$
$$= \$716,000$$

IMPORTANCE OF TERMINAL VALUE

The cost of buying the land is the immediate outlay of $1 million. The after-tax cost of leasing seems to be less than the cost of buying. In considering the buy decision, however, we ignored the value of land at the end of the twenty years. The residual value cash flow of the twentieth year may affect the decision.

We will compare the $716,000 after-tax cost of leasing with the $1 million after-tax cost of buying and compute the break-even value of land (at the end of twenty years). Let X be the value of the land after twenty years.

$$\$716,000 = \$1,000.000 - X(1 + 0.03)^{-20}$$
$$\$284,000 = 0.5537X$$
$$X = \$513,000$$

Based on the after-tax computation, if the land is expected to have a value of less than $513,000, we should lease; otherwise, we should buy. A change in the rate of discount from 0.03 would change the necessary residual value of the land.

We can compare the two alternatives year by year. Assume that the land will be worth its present purchase price of $1,000,000 at the end of twenty years. The lease plan does not have a buy option. With a balloon payment debt (constant interest payments), the after-tax cash flows (in dollars) are as given in Table 19.2.

The $18,146 is the extra cost (per year) of leasing compared to buying. Assuming that the land does not depreciate in value through time, the advantage is clearly with buying. If the $80,242.65 of lease payments were $50,000 per year before tax and $30,000 after tax, there would be indifference between buying and leasing.

Lease and then buy

There is an additional complication. Suppose that Company B can lease and then buy the land for $300,000 at the end of twenty years. A lease decision is preferable, based on the after-tax economic analysis. The Internal Revenue Service will probably object to the deduction of the lease payment for tax computations, however, and will consider a large part of the cash outlay as being a payment for the land (which it is).

Leasing of land is a possible method of financing the use of land. If Company A thinks the value of the land will be increasing, it may lease to B at a price that seems low to B, if B thinks the value of the land will decrease. To the extent that the Internal Revenue Service allows lease payments to be deductible when there is an option to buy at a reduced price (that is, a price less than the expected market price) at the termination of the lease, there may be a tax advantage to leasing land. But this tax advantage cannot be automatically assumed, as it is possible that the lease payments will be interpreted by the tax authorities to be a purchase payment and thus not deductible for tax purposes.

Table 19.2 Balloon payment debt and after-tax cash flows

	Year				
	1	2	3–19	20	
Lease	−$48,146	−$48,146	−$48,146	−$48,146	
Buy	−30,000	−30,000	−30,000	−30,000	Interest
				−1,000,000	Repayment of debt
				+1,000,000	Value of land
Difference (lease–buy)	−$18,146	−$18,146	−$18,146	−$18,146	

LEVERAGED LEASES

There are three major financial parties to a leveraged lease. One is the lessee; the second is the long-term creditor, who furnishes the major portion of the financing; and the third is the lessor, who is the equity participant. The lessor furnishes a relatively small percentage of the capital but is considered by the tax authorities to be the owner and thus is able to take the tax deductions associated with the asset (any investment tax credit that is available and accelerated depreciation deductions). Congress periodically defines the conditions necessary for the lessor to be considered the owner for tax purposes. These conditions include

1   lessor's equity as a percentage of cost;
2   the value of the asset at the end of the lease;
3   the remaining life at the end of the lease;
4   the option price to buy at the end of the lease;
5   lessor must expect to make a profit.

A leveraged lease is characterized by the lessor using a large proportion of debt to finance the asset. Frequently, there will be a party organizing the lease financing, and one of the groups will be the equity participants (the lessor).

Leveraged leases may give rise to multiple IRR equity investments. The lessor will supply equity capital and will make an initial investment outlay to acquire the asset that will be leased (this is a negative cash flow). There will then be periods of positive cash flows caused by the investment tax credit (if any) and tax-reducing depreciation deductions. These positive cash periods will be followed by periods of negative cash flows associated with cash outlays (debt repayments) as well as increased tax payments arising from the related tax shield (the reduced depreciation deductions resulting from the use of accelerated depreciation.) Finally there is a positive cash flow if the asset has residual value.

It is important to remember that these are cash flows to the equity investors, not basic investments flows.

An investment may have more than one internal rate of return if there is more than one sign change in the cash flow sequence. A conventional investment has one or more periods of outlays followed by one or more periods of benefits (the cash flows have one sign change). A multiple IRR investment has additional outlays after the benefits have started, so that there is more than one sign change in cash flows.

EXAMPLE 19.1

Assume that a piece of equipment having a life of six years and costing $210,000 can be financed with $150,000 debt, costing 10 percent (the debt payments are $34,441 per year). The equipment can be leased to a firm at $40,000 per year. The tax rate is 0.4, and there is no investment tax credit. We assume zero salvage value to simplify the example. The tax depreciation method used is the sum of the years' digits.

The cash flows are shown in Table 19.3. Table 19.4 shows the debt amortization. This table is used to determine the interest expense. The tax saving of time 1 is computed as follows:

Revenue		$40,000
Tax depreciation	$60,000	
Interest	15,000	−75,000
Loss		−$35,000
Tax rate		×0.40
Tax saving		−$14,000

Table 19.3 Cash flows

Time	Outlay	Revenue	Depreciation	Interest	Tax	Cash flow
0	−$60,000					−60,000
1		$40,000	$60,000	$15,000	−$14,000	19,559[a]
2		40,000	50,000	13,056	−9,222	14,781[b]
3		40,000	40,000	10,917	−4,367	9,926
4		40,000	30,000	8,565	574	4,985
5		40,000	20,000	5,977	5,609	−50
6		40,000	10,000	3,131	10,748	−5,189

Notes:
a $40,000 − $34,4412 − tax = $5,559 + $14,000 = $19,559 where the $34,441 is the annual debt payment.
b 5,559 − Tax = 5,559 − (−9,222) = 14,781.

Table 19.4 Debt amortization

Time	Amount owed	Interest	Debt amortization principal payment
1	$150,000	$15,000	$19,441
2	130,559	13,056	21,385
3	109,174	10,917	23,524
4	85,650	8,565	25,876
5	59,774	5,977	28,464
6	31,310	3,131	31,310

EXAMPLE Contd.

The depreciation method used is the sum of the years' digits. The sum of the years is $6(1 + 6) = 21$, and the first year's depreciation is $6/21 \times \$210,000 = \$60,000$. The depreciation of each year is $10,000 less than that of the previous year.

The cash flows shown in Table 19.3 have an interesting pattern. There is an immediate outlay, followed by four periods of benefits, followed by two periods of outlays. This is potentially a multiple-yield investment (this investment can have as many as two internal rates of return).

The positive cash flow of periods 1 to 4 reflects the rental payments received that are tax shielded by the accelerated depreciation taken for tax purposes. The cash flows go negative as the tax-depreciation expense shield becomes small and the debt payments continue. The owner would like to abandon the asset at the end of the period 4 (the last year of positive cash flows) but would have to be careful of depreciation expense recapture provisions as well as the loan provisions, since the obligation to pay continues. If the loan is a nonrecourse loan, there would be an incentive to abandon (or donate) the equipment if there is no depreciation recapture.

CANCELABLE LEASES

The examples of this chapter have assumed that the leases are financial leases that are the equivalent of debt. Now assume that the lease is cancelable at the option of the lessee. The present value of the lease (the present liability) is reduced because there is not a firm debt.

The preferred solution is to consider the lease outlays to be the equivalent of any other outlay associated with the investment. This implies that the same discount rate would be used to discount labor costs, material, utilities, etc. The use of a higher discount rate will result in a lower present value of the lease.

EXAMPLE 19.2

The cost of the equipment is $100,000. Funds can be borrowed at 0.05 per year but the firm's weighted average cost of capital is 0.10. The lease payments are $29,000 per year. There is zero residual value and zero taxes. The life of the asset and the lease are both four years. Previously, we determined that buying was more desirable since the debt outlay would only be $28,201. But, if the lease payment is the equivalent of any other annual outlay, the present value is:

$$PV = 29,000 \; B(4, 0.10) = \$91,926.$$

Now leasing costs less than buying. Leasing is not the equivalent to buy–borrow since the lease can be canceled. If the asset is purchased the firm must pay the $100,000 of debt. If the asset has not increased in value the proceeds from the sale of the asset might not be sufficient to pay the remaining debt.

One way to view a lease that can be canceled is to value a lease that cannot be canceled and then subtract from this value the estimated value of an option to cancel the lease. Unfortunately, the value of the option to cancel is not directly observable and will be difficult to estimate.

THE ALTERNATIVE MINIMUM TAX

The 1986 Tax Reform Act introduced the Alternative Minimum Tax (AMT), and the 1989 Revenue Reconciliation Act modified it drastically. The AMT is very complex so the explanation to follow is considerably simplified. The objective of the AMT is to prevent corporations from exploiting certain tax provisions to reduce their income tax to zero if they are profitable based on other definitions of profit. The tentative minimum tax (TMT) is equal to the alternative minimum tax income (AMTI) times 0.20, or TMT $= 0.20$ AMTI. The AMT is the amount the TMT exceeds the 0.35 regular tax. If a firm is paying AMT the marginal tax rate can be 0.20, but there are other possibilities (a mixture of 0, 0.20, and 0.35).

The AMT provisions define several tax preferences, but the only one we will focus on is the tax preference arising from the use of the modified accelerated cost recover system (MACRS). The amount that MACRS exceeds 150 percent of the declining balance depreciation is a tax preference.

Thus, the TMT consists of three components: (1) earnings and profits; (2) tax preference; (3) tax adjustments, and each is multiplied by a constant and added to obtain the AMTI, which is then multiplied by 0.20 to obtain the TMT.

While the AMT affects all investments (both the cash flows and the discount rate) if the firm is in the AMT range, it is particularly relevant to the buy-versus-lease decision. The buy alternative might trigger the AMT provisions, but a tax-qualified lease alternative does not affect tax preferences or tax adjustments.

GLOBAL BUSINESS ASPECTS

What is a lease for tax purposes? The answer to this question will differ based on local tax laws. The answer will affect the preferred structure for a lease and the economic analysis of buy versus lease.

A lease may be treated differently than debt for interest allocation rules (affecting the amount of allowed foreign tax credit), thus the tax law affecting interest allocation for the foreign tax credit calculation may affect the buy versus lease decision.

CONCLUSIONS

Leasing is an important financial device. For smaller firms without access to debt money, it may be the only way of acquiring equipment. But for many potential leases the option to buy is available and, with ready access to the debt-capital market, the relevant decision is to compare buy–borrow and lease, since firm lease commitments are, in effect, debt type obligations. Furthermore, in focusing on the incremental cash flows of buy–borrow and lease, the use of the after-tax borrowing rate enables us to choose the form of the debt. The use of a conventional investment hurdle rate or WACC to discount the lease flows is likely to be in error.

Many firms have made the wrong financing decision by not following these principles. Comparing buy (without including debt flows) with lease flows using a high discount rate creates an inherent bias toward the leasing alternative, and we suspect that the phenomenal growth rate in leasing is, in part, the result of faulty analysis.

PROBLEMS

1 Assume zero taxes. Equipment can be leased at $10,000 per year (first payment one year hence) for ten years or purchased at a cost of $64,177. The company has a weighted average cost of capital of 15 percent. A bank has indicated that it would be willing to make the loan of $64,177 at a cost of 10 percent.
Should the company buy or lease? There are no uncertainties. The equipment will be used for ten years. There is zero salvage value.

2 If the bank in problem 1 was willing to lend funds at 9 percent, should the company buy or lease?

3 If the company in problem 2 pays $64,177 for the equipment, it will save the $10,000 a year lease payments for ten years.
What internal rate of return will it earn on its "investment"?

4 (Continue 1) Now assume a marginal tax rate of 0.4. Assume that the funds can be obtained for 0.10 at a bank. The company uses sum-of-the-years' digits depreciation for taxes.
Should the firm buy or lease? (Assume that the present value of the depreciation deductions is 0.79997 per dollar of depreciable assets using 0.06 as the discount rate.)

5 (Continue 1) Now assume a marginal tax rate of 0.4 and that a loan can be obtained from the bank at a cost of 9 percent.
Should the firm buy or lease? Using 0.054, the present value of depreciation is 0.811. Use 0.054 as the discount rate.

6 (Continue 5) Assume that the lease payments of $10,000 start immediately and that they are paid at the end of each year. There are ten payments.
Compute the present value of leasing; compare the present value with that obtained for problem 5.

7 Assume that there is a 0.4 marginal tax rate. An asset with a life of three years can be bought for $25,313 or leased for $10,000 per year. Funds can be borrowed at a cost of 0.09 (payments of $10,000 per year).

a. What is the present value of the debt (the liability) if the funds are borrowed at a cost of 9 percent? Assume that the payments to the bank are $10,000 per year.

b. What is the present value of the lease payments of $10,000 (the liability).

8 (*Continue 5*)

a. Include the borrowing cash flows in the buy analysis. Assume equal payments of debt. How does this change the net cost?

b. Assume that the net cost of buying was computed using the cost of capital of 15 percent. Now include the borrowing cash flows. How will this change the net cost of buying (you do not have to compute the present value)?

9 What factors might make a lessor's expected cost of acquired and disposing of equipment less than the lessee's expected cost?

10 Why are leasing companies (lessors) so highly levered?

11 Consider the following investment:

Cash flows at time			Internal rate of return
0	1	2	
−$1,000	$576	$576	10%

If debt can be obtained at a cost of 5 percent, determine the net present value of the equity cash flows discounted at 15 percent if

a. no debt is used to finance the investment.

b. $500 of debt is used to finance the investment.

c. $900 of debt is used to finance the investment.

Repeat the calculations using 5 percent as the discount rate.

12 Suppose that $100,000 is borrowed at 8 percent and is to be repaid in three equal annual instalments. Prepare a debt amortization table and show that the net present value of the after-tax cash flows of the debt is zero using the after-tax cost of debt as the discount rate. The tax rate is 40 percent.

13 Suppose a firm has taxable income and a small amount of depreciable assets. The tax credit reduces taxes by $80,000 at time 0.

a. What are the after-tax equity cash flows if it buys a machine for $800,000, takes a 10 percent investment tax credit, and leases the machine to a user for $120,000 per year for eight years payable at the beginning of each year? Further, suppose that the firm borrows $700,000 at 10 percent to help finance the purchase of the machine and that the bank is to be repaid in three equal instalments. Assume a 40 percent tax rate. It is expected that the machine will be worth $160,000 (after tax) at the end of eight years. The entire $800,000 of cost can be depreciated using straight-line depreciation for tax purposes over a five-year life.

357

b. If the next best alternative is to earn 15 percent after tax, is this a good investment?

14 a. MBI has offered to sell or lease computing equipment that has an expected life of three years to Cornell University. If the equipment is purchased, the initial cost would be $2 million. If it is leased, the annual lease payments would be $800,000 per year. Cornell can borrow money at about 7 percent on its endowment and pays no taxes. Ignoring salvage value, what should Cornell do?

b. MBI has offered the same deal to EXNOX Corporation. If EXNON can borrow money at 10 percent, has a weighted average cost of capital of 11 percent, and has a 40 percent marginal tax rate, what should EXNOX do? Assume straight-line depreciation with a life of six years, a 7 percent investment tax credit, and no salvage value.

15 The ABC Company can purchase a new data processing machine for $35,460 or rent it for four years at a cost of $10,000 per year. The estimated life is four years. The machine will result in a saving in clerical help of $11,000, compared with the present manual procedure. The corporation has a cost of capital of 0.10 and a cost of available short term debt of 0.05. The incremental tax rate is 0.52. Assume that the investment tax credit does not apply. The analysis in Tables 19.5 and 19.6 was prepared for the two alternatives.

The net present value is −$3,255, using 0.10 as the discount rate. They buy alternative was rejected, since the net present value was −$3,225. The lease alternative was accepted, since the present value of the savings is positive for any positive rate of discount.

Comment on the decision to lease.

Table 19.5 Lease analysis (1)

Item	0	1	2	3	4
Outlay	−$35,460				
Savings before tax		$11,000	$11,000	$11,000	$11,000
Depreciation[a]		17,730	8,865	4,432	4,432
Taxable income		$14,500	$2,135	$6,568	$6,568
Tax on savings (0.52 of income)		(3,500)	1,110	3,415	3,415
Net cash flow		$14,500	$9,890	$7,585	$7,585
Present value factor (using 0.10)		0.9091	0.8264	0.7513	0.6830
Present values	−$35,460	$13,182	$8,173	$5,699	$5,181

Note:
a Assume that the depreciation of each year for tax purposes is computed using the twice-straight-line method of depreciation with a life of four years.

Table 19.6 Lease analysis (2)

Item	Year			
	1	2	3	4
Gross savings	$11,000	$11,000	$11,000	$11,000
Lease payments	−10,000	−10,000	−10,000	−10,000
Savings before taxes	$11,999	$1,000	$1,000	$1,000
Income tax	520	520	520	520
Net savings	$480	$480	$480	$480

16   The assistant treasurer of the ABC Company has argued that the firm should use the after-tax borrowing rate to compare the lease alternative to the buy–borrow alternative for an asset when the firm has already decided to proceed with the asset.

The treasurer is unimpressed with the position, stating that "Just this past summer we issued preferred stock, common stock, and long-term debt. Why should we use the after-tax debt rate to discount for time when we know that capital has a higher cost than that to the firm? We will have to enter the market again this winter. The debt rate does not measure the average cost of obtaining capital."

Evaluate the position of the treasurer.

17   *Empire State and Prudential*

In 1991 the Prudential Insurance Company offered for sale the Empire State Building at a price (approximately) of $50,000,000. The current lease contracts pay $3,400,000 per year and will run to 2076 (85 years).

a.   If the investor uses a 0.09 discount rate, how large does the building's value have to be in 2076 to paying $50,000,000 now? Assume zero taxes.

b.   If the Empire State Building has a value, without the lease, of $800,000,000 as of 1991, what rate of value increase is necessary to justify the $50,000,000 price (if the leases exist)?

DISCUSSION QUESTION

Inspect the footnotes of any annual report of a major corporation and you will find a large amount of leases. Why do you think this is the situation?

BIBLIOGRAPHY

Ang, J. and Pamela P. Peterson, "The Leasing Puzzle," *Journal of Finance*, September 1984, pp. 1055–65.

Bierman, H., Jr., "Analysis of the Buy–Lease Decision: Comment," *Journal of Finance*, September 1973, pp. 1019–21.

Brealey, R. A. and C. M. Young, "Debt, Taxes, and Leasing-A Note," *Journal of Finance*, December 1980, pp. 1245–50.

Copeland, T. E. and J. Fred Weston. "A Note on the Evaluation of Cancellable Operating Leases," *Financial Management*," Summer 1982, pp. 60–6.

Crawford, P. J., C. P. Harper, and J. J. McConnell, "Further Evidence on the Terms of Financial Leases," *Financial Management*, Fall 1981, pp. 7–14.

McConnell, J. and J. S. Schallheim, "Valuation of Asset Leasing Contracts," *Journal of Financial Economics*, August 1983, pp. 237–62.

Mehran, H., R. A. Taggart, and D. Yermack, "CEO Ownership, Leasing, and Debt Financing," *Financial Management*, 28(2), 1999, pp. 5–14.

Mukherjee, T. K., "A Survey of Corporate Leasing Analysis," *Financial Management*, fall 1991, pp. 96–107.

Myers, S. C., D. A. Dill, and A. J. Bautista, "Valuation of Financial Lease Contracts," *Journal of Finance*, June 1976, pp. 799–820.

O'Brien, J. J. and B. H. Nunnally, Jr., "A 1982 Survey of Corporate Leasing Analysis," *Financial Management*, summer 1983, pp. 30–35.

Sharpe, S. A. and H. H. Nguyen, "Capital Market Imperfections and the Incentive to Lease," *Journal of Financial Economics*, 39, December 1995, pp. 271–94.

Name index

Antikarov, V. 191

Bankhead, Tallulah 187
Bautista, Alberto J. 150
Bethe, Hans 1
Bierman, Harold Jr. 5–6, 322
Black, F. 191, 195
Bohr, Niels 243
Borison, A. 189

Copeland, T. 191
Corman, Avery 228
Cox, J. C. 191

Dean, Joel 5
Dill, David A. 150

Einstein, Albert 221, 243

Forrester, John R. 5–6
Franklin, Benjamin 3

Gates, Anita 41
Gitman, Lawrence J. 5–6
Goldwym, Samuel 41
Gorbachev, Mikhail 21
Graham, J. 6–7, 189
Greenspan, Alan 145

Harvey, C. 6–7, 189
Herbert, Bob 1
Hicks, J. R. 311
Holtz, Lou 272

Kissinger, Henry A. 21

Litsky, Frank 219
Lutz, F. 5
Lutz, V. 5

Miller, Arthur 1
Mumford, Lewis 43
Myers, Stewart C. 150

Rhodes, Richard 243
Ross, S. A. 191
Ruback, R. S. 22,
   29, 31

St John, Allen 189
Scholes, M. 191, 195
Segall, Joel 255
Shankly, Bill 320
Sharpe, William 191
Smidt, S. 5
Solow, Robert M. 95
Stein, Herbert 297
Stigler, George J. 79
Sundem, G. 6

Tanner, Chuck 339
Thatcher, Margaret 162
Tierney, Bill 219
Tobin, James 129
Triantis, A. 189

Wright, Frank Lloyd 43

Subject index

abandonment options 206–8
acquisitions of firms 238–41
adjusted present value (APV) 21–2, 25, 28–9, 34, 37, 157
agency problems 273–4
Alternative Minimum Tax (AMT) 355
American options 192–3, 206–7
Anheuser-Busch (company) 58
appreciation 256
arbitrage 195
asset values 21, 25; by node 101–3
auction-like situations 317
automation 151

bad performance by managers, rewarding of 290
bank loans 340–1
bankruptcy 37, 52, 174–5, 347
"bidding" by managers for use of assets 284
binomial option pricing procedure 195–6
Boeing (company) 52
bonds, present value of 12–13
bonus arrangements 273, 290
book values 233, 237–8, 245–8, 284
borrowing, definition of 222
borrowing rates 57; after-tax 342–5, 349, 356
"buy *versus* lease" decisions *see* leasing

call options 192; on common stock 193–5; multi-period 199–202; valuation formulas 195–6
capacity decisions 329–33
capital asset pricing model (CAPM) 69, 73–4, 79, 127–31, 134, 191
capital budgeting: conclusions on 17–18; conventional approach to 145, 158, 210, 243, 263, 266; elements to be considered in decision-making 62; evolution of practice 5;

objectives of 112; state preference approach to 79–91, 97, 163; surveys of practice 5–7; with uncertainty 162–84
capital cash flow (CCF) 21–2, 24–5, 26–9, 37
capitalization of the firm 176
capital market 16–17
capital market line (CML) 128–9
capital market perspective 73
capital rationing: external 221–2, 225; internal 222–5; programming solutions for 224
capital structure: changes in 22, 37; constant 23, 37; effect on weighted average cost of capital 173–4; optimal 166, 174–5
cash flow: after-tax 22; components of 8; incremental 17; riskiness of 136, 179; summaries of 46; *see also* capital cash flow; component cash flow procedure; expected cash flow; free cash flow; project cash flow procedure
cash flow return on investment 243, 286–7
centralized and decentralized decision-making 275
certainty equivalents (CEs) 52–3, 58, 62–3, 67–9, 75, 83, 178, 202; formulas for option valuation 198–9; and two-period options 201–2
chief executives, compensation of 288
collateralized debt 195
combination of investments 259–62
communism 265
comparable firms, operating results of 231–2, 238
compensation of managers 273–4, 280–2, 288, 290
component cash flow procedure (CCFP) 145–54, 157

363

conflicts of interest 168
correlated investments 124–6
correlation: imperfect 122; perfect 120–2
correlation coefficient 118
cost-based accounting 284
cost of capital 29–31, 135, 181;
   after-tax 172; *see also* weighted average
   cost of capital
costs and benefits of information for
   investment decision-making 311
countercyclical assets 84
co-variance 117–20, 126
currencies other than the US dollar,
   use of 36–7
cutoff rates for investment 222

debt capital: advantages and disadvantages
   of 174–5; implicit 339; substituted
   for equity (as a means of valuation)
   236–7
debtholders, interests of 274
decision-making processes 275, 311–12
decision rules 59
decision trees 206, 314
deferred compensation 290
delaying of investments 315–16
depreciation 155, 265–6, 278–9, 282–3, 287;
   accelerated 246, 266, 278, 352; definition
   of 278–9; straight-line type 278; *see also*
   present value depreciation
derivatives 58
discounted cash flow (DCF) 5, 7, 135, 163,
   255; accepted by financial theorists 244;
   dividend model 69; used to value a
   firm 238
discounting of stock equity flows 179–81
discount rates 7–8, 17, 21–6, 35–6, 63–75,
   96–7, 145–8, 164, 223, 259–60; assumption
   about 69; calculation of 8; composite
   152–4; definition of 166; determination of
   53–6, 157; differences between 262; for
   leasing arrangements 347–9; and taxation
   156–7, 160–1, 349; *see also* interest rates:
   default-free; risk-adjusted discount rates
disruption of business activity 174
distributed earnings 167
diversification: of financial risk 13–14,
   112–15, 122–7, 132–4, 239; of a firm's
   products 57–8
dividends 167–8; present value of
   229–30, 244
divisibility of investments 133
dollar risk adjustment 165, 179, 184
Dupont formulation 276

earnings before interest and taxes
   (EBIT) 23, 29
earnings per share (EPS) 174–5, 287–8
economic depreciation *see* present value
   depreciation
economic income 243–50, 275, 284, 287–8,
   291; advantages from use of 282; compared
   with return on investment 249–50, 280;
   present value of 237–8, 244; used for
   valuation 246–8
economic value 329
efficient frontier of investment alternatives
   120, 122, 129
employees as investors 133
equilibrium expected rate of return 96, 135
equipment: acquisition of 344–5, 355; choice
   of 298–301; optimum mix of 301–4;
   replacement of 328–9
equity capital, cost of 169–71, 181
European options 192–3
evaluation of securities 131
excess returns 132
exchange rates 56
exercise prices 192
expansion options 209–10
expected cash flow 62, 71, 75, 133, 163–5;
   conversion of 68–9; net present
   value of 164–5
expected monetary values 51–2
expected rates of return 103–7, 130–1; by
   asset and node 103–5; differentials in 132;
   equilibrium values 96, 135
expected risk adjustment 84

factors of production, scarcity of 223
finance theory 244
financial distress, costs of 29, 57, 174
financial leases 154, 339
finite-life assets 36
finite-life projects 152–4
firms, valuation of 219, 228–41
flexibility: present value *with* and *without*
   190–1; of a project 164
fluctuating output 297
foreign investment 58, 133–4, 158
foreign tax credits 172
forward rates 12
free cash flow 21–9, 32, 37, 166; used for
   valuation 232–3, 248
funding sources for investment 166–7, 171–2

government securities 56, 178–9
growth opportunities 277; present value of 230
growth-type investments 322–8

hedge portfolios 193–5
historical betas 133
homogeneous expectations 127
hurdle rates 36, 59, 135, 147–9, 223, 356

income measures 262–3, 275–6
income tax status of stock-holders 167
independent investments 122–4
indifference curves 128
insurance policies 82
intangibles 289
interest payments, tax deductibility
    of 156–7, 171
interest rates: default-free 53–7, 62, 67, 75,
    83–4, 96, 127, 184, 162, 178–9, 195; for
    lending and for borrowing 222, 225; perfect
    predictions of 333–4; term structure of
    11–13, 145, 178–9; on US government
    bonds 56; see also borrowing rates;
    discount rates
internal rate of return (IRR) 5–7, 54, 147–9,
    153–4, 225, 258–66, 278–9, 283, 331; before
    tax and after tax 263–5; for leasing
    arrangements 346–7
investment: definition of 5; information for
    decision-making on 311–17; mix of 14;
    process of 63–6; tactical and strategic
    decisions on 15; tax implications of 17;
    uncertainty of 43–4, 50–1
investor preferences 16, 18

joint ventures 179
The Journal of Business 5

Keogh plans 265

land: buying of 350–1; leasing of 349–50;
    value of 323–7, 350
language differences 224
"lease then buy" decisions 351
"lease versus borrow" decisions 347
leasing 154–6, 219, 339–56; cancellation of
    arrangements 354; as debt 341–2, 355;
    of equipment 355; interest-rate cost of
    346–7; of land 349–50; with leverage
    352–4; and taxation 342–4
life-span of an investment 320
liquidity price premium 56

managerial compensation 273–4, 280–2
managerial talent, scarcity of 223
market capitalization 236
market portfolio 129–33
market research 57

market risk see systematic and unsystematic risk
maturity dates of contracts 192
mergers of firms 240–1, 322
Merrill Lynch (company) 133
Modified Accelerated Cost Recovery
    System 355
money, time value of 10, 62, 172, 184, 265
Monte Carlo simulation 48–50, 86, 91, 162,
    181–2
multiperiod investments 86–8
multipliers, use of 231–2, 248–9

net operating profit after tax (NOPAT) 233
net present value (NPV) 1–7, 15, 52, 57–8,
    135, 147–50, 157, 190, 221, 257–9, 333;
    and evaluation of investments 176; of
    expected cash flows 164–5; of lease
    payments 340–5
new assets, acquisition of 176
new products 146–7

objectives, corporate 3–4, 18, 53, 135, 164,
    166, 272, 289
operating leverage 153–4
operating margins 275
opportunity costs 222–3
optimal capital structure 166, 174–5
optimum mix of equipment 301–4
options 187–217; to abandon 206–8;
    exercising of 192–4; to expand 209–10;
    on a firm's assets (for purposes of valuation)
    237; several associated with the same asset
    210, 215–17; theory of 79, 191; valuation
    of 191–2, 195–203, 210; see also
    real options
overheads, contributions to 321
ownership rights of stock-holders 4, 18

payback periods 5, 162, 164
performance measurement for managers 219,
    272–82, 288–91
period-by-period summaries 46–7
portfolio analysis 114–16
"portfolio problem" 114–17, 133
portfolio valuation 199
preempting the market 331–3
present value: addition rule 11; of bonds
    12–13; calculation techniques 157; of
    dividends 229–30, 244; of earnings minus
    new investment 230; of economic income
    237–8, 244; of growth opportunities 230;
    multiplication rule 11; problems with
    determination of 10; of underlying assets 203;
    with flexibility and without flexibility 190–1;

present value (*Continued*)
  see also adjusted present value; net
  present value
present value accounting (PVA) 219,
  255–66, 286
present value depreciation 248, 250, 256–63,
  276, 285, 330
present value factor 10; *see also* risk-adjusted
  present value
present value profile 162–3
price-earnings multipliers 232
price levels 178
price takers 127
prices: with certainty 79–80; with
  uncertainty 80–2
principal-agent problems 273–4
prior betting distributions 313
"prisoner's dilemma" 322
production scheduling 302–5
profit centers 275
profits: maximization of 4, 135; as a measure
  of managerial performance 290
project analysis 15
project cash flow procedure (PCFP) 145–51
projected earnings 248–9
psychological impact of losses and gains 183
pure play method of calculating the cost of
  capital 177–8
put options 192–3; American 206–7

qualitative element in decision-making 18
qualitative measures of performance 290
qualitative valuations 210
quantitative measures of performance 289–90

ranking of investments 223–5
real estate investments 179
real option analysis (ROA) 210
real options 9–10, 190; valuation of 202–3
reinvestment of investment proceeds 108
replacement of equipment 328–9
replicating portfolios 193–202; composition of
  196–8; and two-period options 199–200
required rates of return 54–5, 79, 85–6, 130,
  147, 171, 173, 176, 179, 266, 333–4
residual income *see* economic income
resolution of uncertainty 96–7, 106–9
retained earnings, costs of 167–9
retirement funds 265
return on equity (ROE) 276–7
return on investment (ROI) 5–6, 249–50,
  256–63, 275–9, 283–4, 287–8, 291, 330–1;
  compared with economic income 280;
  components of 276–7; and investment

decision-making 277; *see also* cash flow
  return on investment
Revenue Reconciliation Act (1989) 355
risk: differing between two investments
  260–2; evaluation of 10, 17; investor
  attitudes to 16, 18, 43, 50–2, 58; from the
  manager's viewpoint 281; seeking of 18;
  and time 8–9, 53–4; trade-off against return
  14; two elements of 13; *see also* systematic
  and unsystematic risk
risk-adjusted discount rates (RADRs) 53–5,
  58–9, 64–75, 163–6, 176, 178, 184,
  345–6, 349
risk-adjusted present value (RAPV) 82–91,
  101, 165
risk adjustment: of assets 165; expected 84
risk analysis 48–9, 58; steps involved in 182
risk aversion 50, 62, 67, 71, 73, 75, 113–14,
  127–9; constant 69–71
risk-free assets 127, 129, 132
risk-free interest rates *see* interest rates:
  default-free
risk neutral probability (RNP) 199–202, 205
risk preferences 13, 16, 50–2, 58–9, 127,
  130, 135, 184, 345
risk premium 126, 130–1, 165, 178
risky assets, definition of 95–6
rollback procedure 199–200

sample investments 312–16
scarcity of factors of production 223
scenarios 44, 46, 52
seasonal variations 297–304
securities, definition of 172
security market line 130
sensitivity analysis 47, 162–4, 181–2
separation theorem 129
short periods, option valuation making
  use of 213–15
short sales 127
simulation 48–50, 181–2
sinking funds 175
skill shortages 223
state of nature 44
state preference approach to capital budgeting
  79–91, 97, 163
stochastic processes 182
stock equity flows, discounting of 179–81
stock market performance 288
stock options 192–3
stockholders: conflicts of interest between
  168; income tax status of 167;
  interests and preferences of 3–4,
  127, 166

strategic planning and decision-making
14–15, 53
strike prices 192
stripping of interest payments 13
subjective evaluation of man-agerial
performance 282
synergy 133, 239
systematic and unsystematic risk 8, 95–6,
113–14, 125, 130–3, 281

taxation 263–4; and depreciaton 155, 343–4,
348; and discount rates 156–7; domestic
and foreign 172; and interest payments
156–7, 171; and investment decisions 17; of
investors 167–71; and leasing 342–8, 351
tax credits, foreign 172
tax deductibilily 21–2, 32, 343–4, 348, 351
Tax Reform Act (1986) 355
technological breakthroughs 312
Tentative Minimum Tax (TMT) 355
terminal value model of the firm 231
time-adjusted revenues 282–3
time discounting principle 10
time-risk interaction 8–9, 63
timing: of information releases 95–6; of
investment 320–34; of the start and finish of
a process 321–2
trade-off between risk and return 14
transaction costs 133, 168, 274
treasury bills 179
tree diagrams 43–6, 80, 86–9, 98, 102, 104
trees, investment in 322–8

uncertainty: of investment 43–4, 50–1, 316;
reduction of 57–8; resolution of 96–7,
106–9
underlying assets 192; present value of 203;
without flexibility 203–6
United States government securities 56, 179
utility functions 51–3, 84

valuation: of a *firm* and of a *project* 228;
using managers' estimates 284;
using models 164
value-at-risk (VAR) techniques 183
Value Line investor service 133
variance of a portfolio 124–5

waiting options 9–10
weighted average cost of capital (WACC) 6–7,
22–3, 31–6, 53–5, 59, 63, 135, 147, 156–7,
164–7, 172–80, 356; and capital structure
173–4; computation of 172–3; and debt
31–2; and investments 175–7; for a project
177–8
Wells Fargo Bank 133
"winner's curse" 317
write-off assumptions 287
writers of options 192

yield curve 11–12

zero-coupon bonds 11
zero-debt valuation of a firm 233–6
zero-valued assets 257–8

Made in the USA
Columbia, SC
27 May 2020